Ancient Warfare

Ancient Warfare:

Introducing Current Research, Volume I

Edited by

Geoff Lee, Helene Whittaker and Graham Wrightson

Cambridge
Scholars
Publishing

Ancient Warfare: Introducing Current Research, Volume I

Edited by Geoff Lee, Helene Whittaker and Graham Wrightson

This book first published 2015

Cambridge Scholars Publishing

Lady Stephenson Library, Newcastle upon Tyne, NE6 2PA, UK

British Library Cataloguing in Publication Data
A catalogue record for this book is available from the British Library

Copyright © 2015 by Geoff Lee, Helene Whittaker, Graham Wrightson and contributors

All rights for this book reserved. No part of this book may be reproduced, stored in a retrieval system, or transmitted, in any form or by any means, electronic, mechanical, photocopying, recording or otherwise, without the prior permission of the copyright owner.

ISBN (10): 1-4438-7694-1
ISBN (13): 978-1-4438-7694-0

CONTENTS

Preface viii

Introduction ix

Chapter One 1
Symbolic Aspects of Warfare in Minoan Crete
Professor Helène Whittaker

Chapter Two 14
Death of a Swordsman, Death of a Sword: The Killing of Swords
in the Early Iron Age Aegean (ca. 1050 to ca.690 B.C.E)
Dr. Matthew Lloyd

Chapter Three 32
Filling the Gaps: Catapults and Philon of Byzantium
Dr. Aimee Schofield

Chapter Four 43
Aeneas Tacticus and Small Units in Greek Warfare
Dr. Nick Barley

Chapter Five 65
To Use or not to Use: The Practical and Historical Reliability
of Asclepiodotus's 'Philosophical' Tactical Manual
Dr. Graham Wrightson

Chapter Six 94
Furious Wrath: Alexander's Siege of Thebes and Perdiccas' False Retreat
Dr. Borja Antela-Bernárdez

Chapter Seven 107
Civil War and Counterinsurgency in Greece: Rival Systems of Hegemony
during the Fourth Century BC
Konstantinos Lentakis

Chapter Eight 124
The Problem of the Four Hundred Wagons: The Provisioning of the Ten
Thousand on the March to Cunaxa
Dr. Stephen O'Connor

Chapter Nine 147
War as Training, War as Spectacle: The *Hippika Gymnasia*
from Xenophon to Arrian
Dr. Anna Busetto

Chapter Ten 172
Trouble Comes in Threes: From Chariot to Cavalry in the 'Celtic' World
Alberto Pérez-Rubio

Chapter Eleven 191
The Late Bronze–Early Iron Age Transition: Changes in Warriors
and Warfare and the Earliest Recorded Naval Battles
Dr. Jeffrey P. Emanuel

Chapter Twelve 210
Thucydides' Narrative on Naval Warfare: *Epibatai*, Military Theory,
Ideology
Dr. Matteo Zaccarini

Chapter Thirteen 229
Commemorating War Dead and Inventing Battle Heroes: Heroic
Paradigms and Discursive Strategies in Ancient Athens and Phocis
Dr. Elena Franchi and Dr. Giorgia Proietti

Chapter Fourteen 252
Ajax, Cassandra and Athena: Retaliatory Warfare and Gender Violence
at the Sack of Troy
Dr. Susan Deacy and Dr. Fiona McHardy

Chapter Fifteen 273
Treating Hemorrhage in Greek and Roman Militaries
Dr. Julie Laskaris

Chapter Sixteen 291
Are You (Ro)man Enough? Non-Roman *Virtus* in the Roman Army
Dr. Adam Anders

Chapter Seventeen 309
To the Victor the Spoils? Post-Battle Looting in the Roman World
Joanne Ball

Chapter Eighteen 331
The Role of the Peace-Makers (*Caduceatores*) in Roman Attitudes
to War and Peace
Dr. Hannah Cornwell

Contributors 349

Indices 353
    Index of Places
    Index of Units
    Index of Armaments
    General Index

Preface

The chapters in this volume are based on some of the research papers presented at the International Ancient Warfare Conference 2013 (IAWC13). The conference theme was deliberately inclusive and academics from any discipline were invited to present papers on any aspect of ancient warfare. Presenters ranged from postgraduates to more experienced academics. The apparent eclecticism of the volume is due to this rationale, and far from seeing this as a lack of coherence, this is a vindication of the conference and editorial strategy.

As lead editor, I have been very fortunate in having the support of two experienced academics as co-editors: Professor Hélène Whittaker and Dr. Graham Wrightson. Each chapter benefitted from the feedback of a blind peer review from at least one of three reviewers: Dr. Jason Crowley, Dr. Erin Garvin, and Dr. James Thorne. In addition, the entire volume was blind peer reviewed by an external reviewer. The manuscript was proofread by Theodora Wrightson.

Financial support for the conference and this volume was gratefully received from the Institute of Classical Studies. Professors Bjorn Weiler and Robert Ireland, of Aberystwyth University, and Professor Mike Edwards of the University of Wales: Trinity Saint David offered guidance, and Sian Davies, the Classics Faculty administrator, handled the finances for the conference and this volume. Florence Melley, Ben Lee, and Jade Evans helped as conference assistants. The staff at the National Library of Wales in Aberystwyth gave personal support to me as conference organiser and to all of the conference delegates. The feedback from delegates on the conference and the facilities was very positive. Wales can be very proud of such a fantastic resource in terms of both the infrastructure of the National Library, and its people.

Diolch yn fawr- Thank you very much.

Geoff Lee
Aberystwyth University.

INTRODUCTION

This volume on ancient warfare presents eighteen chapters dealing with a variety of areas of current research. Ranging from archaeology and social history to more traditional tactics and strategy, it represents a range of different aspects of military history. Most of these chapters developed from papers which were presented at a conference on "Ancient Warfare," held at the National Library of Wales in Aberystwyth, Wales, from the 18th to the 20th of September, 2013, organized by Geoff Lee.

The chapters in this volume can be viewed in thematic sections. The first two chapters (by Professor Helène Whittaker, and Dr. Matthew Lloyd), deal primarily with archaeological evidence from the Greek Bronze and Iron Ages. The next three chapters (by Dr. Aimee Schofield, Dr. Nick Barley, and Dr. Graham Wrightson) are concerned with using tactical manuals to inform history, and the first and last also make use of experimental archaeology. This is a comparatively under-researched area of ancient military history but one that is becoming particularly prominent, especially with the use of experimental archaeology. The next three chapters (by Dr. Borja Antela-Bernárdez, Konstantinos Lentakis, and Dr. Stephen O'Connor) deal with more traditional areas of research into military history, in this case Greek warfare, namely tactics, strategy and logistics. These chapters show that despite generations of study in these areas there are still new ideas and interpretations that are important to consider. Following this are two chapters (by Dr. Anna Busetto, and Alberto Pérez-Rubio) that deal with the use of cavalry in warfare. This is another traditional avenue of military scholarship, but in these two cases dealing with aspects that could be considered the edge of traditional analysis, namely literary *topoi* and Celtic armies. Continuing the variation of traditional themes are two chapters (by Dr. Jeffrey P. Emanuel, and Dr. Matteo Zaccarini) on naval warfare but again each deals with new aspects of the field: very early depictions in the Mediterranean and using modern military terminology to interpret ancient Greek warfare. Next are four chapters (by Dr. Elena Franchi and Dr. Giorgia Proietti, Dr. Susan Deacy and Dr. Fiona McHardy, Dr. Julie Laskaris, and Dr Adam Anders), dealing with more social or cultural aspects of warfare: commemorating the war dead, the treatment of women, army medicine, and courage. All these aspects of military history are crucial and yet until recently under-researched. Finally, there are two chapters (by Joanne Ball and Dr. Hannah Cornwell) that deal with what happens after battle or war. This is very much a new area of research blurring the lines between traditional definitions of historical areas such as military, social, and political history. These papers serve as a suitable closing point for a volume that seeks to break down any perceived barriers between different aspects of warfare.

CHAPTER SUMMARIES

Chapter 1: *Symbolic Aspects of Warfare in Minoan Crete*, by Professor Hélène Whittaker, provides an overview of the various symbolic or ritual contexts in which objects and representations pertaining to warfare have been found and argues that the practice of warfare as well as its ideological aspects were closely intertwined with religious meaning in the Aegean during the Bronze Age. The focus is primarily on Crete in the second half of the second millennium BC.

Chapter 2: *Death of a Swordsman, Death of a Sword: the Killing of Swords in the Early Iron Age Aegean (ca. 1050 to ca. 690 BCE)*, by Dr. Matthew Lloyd, looks at the chronological and geographical context of "killed" weapons, their relationships to the types of burial in which they appear, and the other grave goods which accompany these burials. It suggests that the swords "killed" in the period *ca.* 950-825 are the result of societal conditions relating to the value of iron, the exclusivity of warfare, and conscious acts of destruction in burials at this time. On the other hand, the later burials in Eretria relate to changing factors in the deposition of weapons, new ideas about exclusivity and value, and reflecting the way in which warfare changed in the late eighth century. It also suggests that arguments so far have ignored important metallurgical observations about "killed" swords, and what they reveal about sword use and ownership in the EIA Aegean

Chapter 3: *Filling the Gaps: Catapults and Philon of Byzantium*, by Dr. Aimee Schofield, investigates the historical and literary contexts of Philon and his work. It explains how experimental reconstructed catapults can give a different perspective on what would otherwise be considered abstract and esoteric texts. The conclusion is that by applying a practical element to research on military history, it is possible to gain a fresh and new understanding of the military technology of the ancient world.

Chapter 4: *Aeneas Tacticus and Small Units in Greek Warfare,* by Dr. Nick Barley, presents research into the role and influence of officers from the lower ranks of command in Greek armies. Secondary levels of command are rarely discussed in the sources but can be inferred from a number of incidents which can best be explained by the ability of individuals to react rapidly, and in an organized fashion, to changing events. These events suggest that individuals other than generals were able, and indeed expected, to exercise leadership and give commands during battle. This chapter also considers the use of small, semi-independent units in pitched battles and less conventional engagements, with particular emphasis on the frequent use of units of 300 men to achieve specific objectives.

Chapter 5: *To Use or not to Use: The Practical and Historical Reliability of Asclepiodotus's 'Philosophical' Tactical Manual,* by Dr. Graham Wrightson, argues that Asclepiodotus was a philosopher writing practical works just as much as theoretical ones. The terminology that Asclepiodotus uses to describe the command hierarchy largely is confirmed by historically attested officer ranks and he occasionally describes other names for officers that were used in the past. Supported by practical archaeology, this chapter shows that the military information provided by Asclepiodotus is both reliable and historical and should be integrated fully into any history of the Macedonian army.

Chapter 6: *Furious Wrath: Alexander's Siege of Thebes and Perdiccas' False Retreat,* by Dr. Borja Antela-Bernárdez, analyses the destruction of Thebes by Alexander the Great. Although the sources suggest a siege it is perhaps more of a campaign as the extant sources suggest that there was at least one pitched battle and a siege. It is, in fact, during the siege of Thebes and the related campaign that we can note some deceptive tactics used by Alexander and Perdiccas in order to gain access to the besieged city. The sack and destruction of Thebes is used as a case study to analyse the deep impact of Alexander's military leadership against the civil population. It is where he used an iron fist to shock the Greek cities and other peoples in the ancient world.

Chapter 7: *Civil War and Counterinsurgency: Rival Hegemonic Systems in Fourth Century Greece,* by Konstantinos Lentakis, examines the four hegemonic systems that were established in mainland Greece during the fourth century BC by the powers of Athens, Macedon, Sparta, and Thebes. The variables of hegemony that are assessed are the systems of government and alliance that were imposed by the great powers, the varying use of force of each of them, and the causes that led each power to intervene in smaller states' domestic disputes. After examining these systems this chapter will then proceed to evaluate which policies of empire were successful in the Greek theatre of war, and which were less successful and why. Conclusions on hegemony will be reviewed to see how they can lead us to a better understanding of which policies and strategies are useful for peacekeeping and maintaining stability and providing security in the conflict zones of the 21st century.

Chapter 8: *The Problem of the Four Hundred Wagons: The Provisioning of the Ten Thousand on the March to Cunaxa*, by Dr. Stephen O'Connor, combines a detailed reading of the first book of Xenophon's *Anabasis* with a narratological analysis of the *Anabasis* as a whole to show that the Ten Thousand provisioned themselves on their march to Cunaxa in the settlements they passed along their route, i.e. by purchase from markets provided by the cities through which they marched, and by requisitioning in the villages where they stopped. Cyrus's army did not, as often thought, usually acquire their supplies from imperial stores or from the Lydian *agora* located in the non-Greek part of the army. The four hundred wagons full of wheat-flour and wine reported by Xenophon (at *Anab.* 1.10.18) to have been provided by Cyrus did not, contra the scholarly consensus on this issue, accompany the army during the whole of their march, but only from Pylae, and then as a provisioning 'safety net' designed to increase the tactical flexibility of Cyrus's army in its manoeuvres before the imminent battle with the King.

Chapter 9: *War As Training, War As Spectacle: The Hippika Gymnasia From Xenophon To Arrian,* by Dr. Anna Busetto, investigates the *loci paralleli* in the descriptions of *hippika gymnasia* in Xenophon's *Hipparchicus* and Arrian's *Tactica*. The Xenophonian echoes appearing in the *Tactica* show not only a generic literary influence by an admired model, but also the vitality – across centuries and cultures – of specific aspects of military training. In Arrian's treatise, their re-enactment is mediated by the *Adlocutio Hadriani*, an epigraphic record of a speech by the Emperor Hadrian at Lambaesis, where he witnessed a spectacular performance by the auxiliary troops stationed there. Certain precise lexical correspondences suggest that the *Tactica* might be – in its "Roman part" (chap. 32, 3-44, 3) at least – a sort of literary re-working of the earlier *Adlocutio*.

Chapter 10: *Trouble Comes in Threes. From Chariot to Cavalry in the 'Celtic' World,* by Alberto Pérez-Rubio, analyses how the 'Celtic' cavalry practice known as *trimarkisia* gives us insight into the evolution from chariotry to cavalry in Iron Age temperate Europe. A close look at the etymology and symbolism of the word *trimarkisia* reveals both the importance of the triad in the 'Celtic' mindset and the later development of cavalry in regard to chariotry. Chariot warfare is then examined, taking into account literary sources and iconography to show how three men probably made up the chariot fighting team. Finally, a model which explains the transition from the chariot to the *trimarkisia* is advanced, tackling its tactical and symbolical dimensions in regard to knowledge networks in the 'Celtic' world.

Chapter 11: *The Late Bronze–Early Iron Age Transition: Changes in Warriors and Warfare and the Earliest Recorded Naval Battles,* by Dr. Jeffrey P. Emanuel, argues that the transition from the Late Bronze to the Early Iron Age in the Eastern Mediterranean and Aegean worlds is marked in part by a change in the representation and iconography of warriors and warfare. This change includes the first depictions and written accounts of true sea battles in recorded history, which are represented in Egyptian relief and text, on Mycenaean and East Aegean-West Anatolian pictorial pottery, and in Hittite documents, all of which date to the late 13th or 12th centuries BCE. This is also the time when the Helladic oared galley, a revolutionary new vessel type well-suited for raids, piracy, and ship-borne combat, makes its first appearance. This chapter investigates the earliest representations and descriptions of naval combat, with a special emphasis on the appearance and employment of new maritime technology and its effect on maritime operations and naval warfare. Also considered are the changes in fighting that had to be made in order to adapt to this early form of ship-based combat.

Chapter 12: *Thucydides' Narrative on Naval Warfare: Epibatai, Military Theory, Ideology,* by Dr. Matteo Zaccarini, proposes that our perception of ancient Greek naval warfare is heavily biased by the classical Athenian concept of *naumachia*. Following the Athenian adoption of the 'fast' style of sea combat Thucydides scornfully disdained the 'old way' of fighting over the sea, regarding the Peloponnesians, whose ships were often overloaded with soldiers, as clumsy amateurs lacking *techne*. An analysis of surviving sources leads to the questioning of this 'Athenian myth' of fast triremes, and this chapter argues that embarked soldiers, *epibatai*, often had an important role requiring skills and training. The peculiar status of the *epibatai* occasionally puts them as being similar to hoplites, however, this chapter argues that there are several major differences which need to be understood to fully appreciate the role they played.

Chapter 13: *Commemorating War Dead and Inventing Battle Heroes. Heroic Paradigms and Discursive Strategies in Ancient Athens and Phocis,* by Dr. Elena Franchi and Dr. Giorgia Proietti, argues that commemoration of the war dead must be considered in the light of the fluidity and malleability which are intrinsic to the social practices of memory. It uses two historical examples, each different in space and time. One example focuses on the commemoration of the war dead in Classical Athens, and disputes the common assumption that they were honoured with a *strictu sensu* heroic cult and argues instead that they were the recipients of a canonical cult of the dead, though extended in a civic dimension. It does, however, recognize that they were at the core of a complex web of discursive strategies, which, through time, actually represented them as 'founding heroes'. Using the second example, this chapter advances a new interpretation of the base of a Phocian monument dedicated at Delphi in the 4th or 3rd century BCE, and argues that this monument shows both the Classical and Hellenistic-Roman attitude to reshaping the collective memory of an archaic event and the permeability between different means of commemoration.

Chapter 14: *Ajax, Cassandra and Athena: Retaliatory Warfare and Gender Violence at the Sack of Troy,* by Dr. Susan Deacy and Dr. Fiona McHardy, builds on recent work arguing for the centrality of violence against women to ancient warfare. It uses Gaca's model of retaliatory warfare to frame a discussion of how, in representations of the sack of Troy, the actions of the Greeks fit ancient patterns of violent behaviour and may reflect evolutionary dispositions too. The authors argue that this is even – perhaps especially – true of the actions of Locrian Ajax, whose behaviour has previously been interpreted as flying in the face of acceptable behaviour but whose ill-treatment of Cassandra displays expected, even required, warrior behaviour towards enemy females. The chapter comes out of the research that the authors are currently undertaking for a book on ancient Greek gender violence in various contexts including 'domestic', 'street', and 'battlefield'.

Chapter 15: *Treating Hemorrhage in Greek and Roman Militaries,* by Dr. Julie Laskaris, considers that military medicine is a largely neglected field in the studies of ancient warfare and of ancient medicine. Christine

Salazar's excellent work, *The Treatment of War Wounds in Graeco-Roman Antiquity* (Brill 2000), is the sole recent book-length treatment. She does not, however, devote much time to the aspect of trauma care that was, and is still today, of the greatest initial concern: the ability to stop blood loss. This chapter traces the methods for treating hemorrhage that were available to the doctors who travelled with Greek and Roman militaries, and argues that doctors' skills were honed through their regular practice of venesection and their frequent treatment of obstetric hemorrhage.

Chapter 16: *Are You (Ro)man enough? Non-Roman Virtus in the Roman Army,* by Dr. Adam Anders, argues that scholarly discussions of the function of Roman armies have often overlooked the significance of troops commonly classified as light infantry and the possibility that 'light' infantry tactics may have been the most common form of combat in Roman warfare. Investigation into 'light' methods of combat in Roman warfare reveals that 'light' infantry, particularly the *velites* of the Roman republic, were the most tactically versatile troops available to Roman commanders. Their replacements, the auxiliaries, although varied in equipment, organization and role from their predecessors, were no less tactically versatile. It further argues that not only were these non-Roman troops more frequently deployed than Roman legionaries, but also that they displayed a noticeably greater zealousness (*audacia* and *virtus*) in combat than their legionary counterparts. This, in turn, may have been a cause of their aforementioned frequent deployment.

Chapter 17: *To the Victor the Spoils? Post-Battle Looting in the Roman World,* by Joanne Ball, argues that looting in the Roman world did not strip the battlefield of all significant archaeological evidence. Although some archaeologists and historians consider that no archaeological evidence was left, as battlefield archaeology develops as a discipline, it becomes possible to test these preconceptions of field-stripping against the archaeological record. It is evident that Roman battlefields can survive in the archaeological record, and they have been identified in Germany and Spain with assemblages numbering in the thousands for metal artefacts, particularly small finds. This chapter suggests that current ideas of Roman battlefield looting and its impact on the archaeological survival of these sites need to be reassessed as Roman battlefield assemblages were often not entirely looted, and may manifest with characteristic assemblages which are distinctively non-martial in nature.

Chapter 18: *The Role of the Peace-Makers (Caduceatores) in Roman Attitudes to War and Peace*, by Dr. Hannah Cornwell, examines the ways in which the roles and possible relationships between the *fetiales* and *caduceatores* can be used to understand some aspects of how the Romans conceptualised the making and breaking of war and peace, and aims to locate the *caduceatores* within a picture of Roman diplomatic practices and war-mongering. The *caduceatores*, it will be argued, should not be understood primarily as Roman officials, unlike the *fetiales* and *legati*, but rather as a Roman conceptualisation of non-Roman diplomacy. Indeed, the uses of the term *caduceatores* in Latin Literature present us with an insight into how Romans conceptualised peace, as not something they themselves sought, but rather imposed.

Geoff Lee, Graham Wrightson and Helène Whittaker

CHAPTER ONE

SYMBOLIC ASPECTS OF WARFARE IN MINOAN CRETE

PROFESSOR HELÈNE WHITTAKER

Questions concerning the prevalence and role of warfare in European societies during the Bronze Age have been at the focus of much recent research.[1] The widespread occurrence of fortifications, burials with weapons, and weapon hoards would seem to indicate that this was a period that was in many places characterised by organised forms of inter-personal violence, and perhaps on a fairly large scale. That social organisation and institutions may have been in some way defined by warfare is suggested by a perceptible interest in representations of combat in imagery in various parts of Europe and by the aesthetic elaboration of weapons and armour that were probably used solely in military display, since they are sometimes non-functional. The ideological aspects of warfare as they relate to the social persona of the warrior have also been amply explored with regard to Scandinavia, Britain, continental Europe, and the Aegean.[2] Possible religious aspects have been given rather less attention.[3] This is particularly the case in research on the Aegean.

The purpose of this paper is to investigate connections between warfare and religious beliefs and ritual on Crete during the second millennium BC, during the Middle and Late Bronze Ages.[4] My focus is on the evidence

---

[1] See for example, Bradley 1990; Kristiansen 1998, 2002; Driessen 1999; Harding 2000, 271-307; Otto et al. 2006; Whittaker 2008; Molloy 2010; 2012.
[2] Treherne 1995; Peatfield 1999.
[3] See for example, Whittaker 2008.
[4] The Cretan Bronze Age, which commences some time before the beginning of the third Millennium BC, is often referred to as the Minoan period. The beginning of the second millennium BC coincides more or less with the beginning of the Middle Bronze Age or Middle Minoan period. The beginning of the Late Minoan

from so-called nature sanctuaries. The first part of this paper consists of a general presentation of these sanctuaries, their location, the finds, and the rituals associated with them, with an emphasis on the ways in which they reflect the symbolic importance of warfare. The cave sanctuary at Psychro and the peak sanctuary on Mount Juktas are discussed in particular detail because the material recovered from these sites indicates that they were associated with the religious activities of the palatial elites. In the second part, I attempt to provide an interpretation of the military aspects of Minoan religion, both in general terms and in relation to the political circumstances of the Neopalatial period. My argument is in part based on parallels with the Near East and with later Greek religion.

Minoan civilisation has long been regarded as uniquely non-militaristic in comparison with its neighbours. The absence of defensive walls around palaces, other important buildings, and settlements gave the impression that the Cretans lived in peace with little or no internal strife and had no reason to fear enemy attacks from outside the island. This last may have been either because Crete, not being rich in natural resources, was of little interest to the great powers of the eastern Mediterranean or because the palatial elites invested in sea power in order to keep potential attackers at bay. This is an interpretation that was suggested by Thucydides' review of Greek history at the beginning of the *Peloponnesian War*, in which he claimed that the Cretans under their legendary king Minos ruled the seas.[5] Also in contrast with Egypt and the Near East, Minoan representational art is seemingly characterised by a lack of interest in depicting scenes of combat.[6] This view of Bronze Age Crete as a place of love and peace, where people lived their lives in tune with nature, devoting their time and energies to the performance of elaborate rituals, represents an idealisation of an ancient civilisation which has great emotional appeal.

Unfortunately, it has the force of evidence against it. It is now increasingly being recognised that the warlike aspects of Minoan

---

period is dated to around 1600 BC. The political and social landscape during most of this time was characterised by the presence of monumental structures, usually referred to as palaces, which were in all probability centres of political and economic power. In an alternative chronology the period of the Middle and Late Bronze Ages is divided into the Protopalatial, Neopalatial, and Postpalatial periods. The transition between the Protopalatial and Neopalatial periods is dated to the latter part of the Middle Bronze Age, around 1700 BC.

[5] Thuc. 1.4.
[6] Higgins 1981, 94-98; Immerwahr 1990.

civilisation have been seriously underrated, ignored, shoved under the carpet, or explained away. Although scenes of interpersonal violence that can be taken to reflect warfare are not common, they do occur. Depictions of fully armed warriors can be seen on seals, as can images, the purpose of which would seem to be to glorify martial violence.[7] And not least, it is noteworthy that the first appearance of the sword in the Aegean is on Crete, where it may have been invented independently of its more or less contemporaneous occurrence in central Europe.[8] Because the sword is the first weapon which was not in the first instance a tool or a hunting weapon but was developed expressly for the wounding, maiming, and killing of other human beings in close combat, its invention must reflect a real interest in doing just that. The presence of guard posts in connection with routes of communication is further evidence that conditions on Crete may not always have been peaceful.[9]

Artefacts and imagery that pertain to warfare are not uncommonly found in cultic contexts on Crete during the Bronze Age. They are particularly well represented in so-called peak sanctuaries, cult places located in the open air in a mountainous location, and in cave sanctuaries. Both cave sanctuaries and peak sanctuaries usually lie at some distance from the nearest settlements and are therefore often referred to collectively as nature sanctuaries or extra-urban sanctuaries.[10] That they received large numbers of visitors is evident from the quantities of votive material recovered from those that have been excavated. Many of the finds, such as rudimentary animal figurines or human body parts made of terracotta, indicate that they seem to have served the general population of farmers and herders in the surrounding areas. Objects made of valuable material and characterised by high quality of workmanship indicating elite involvement, such as seals made of semi-precious stones and inscribed stone offering tables, have been found in some sanctuaries. This mixture of different types of objects of varying quality and elaboration suggests that both cave sanctuaries and peak sanctuaries were the location for communal rituals, which reflected the beliefs and values of all levels of the population.[11]

---

[7] See, for example, CMS II.3.32, II.6.15, II.8.276, II.3.16.
[8] Harding 2000, 277.
[9] Tzedakis et al. 1989.
[10] Kyriakidis 2005, 19.
[11] See Peatfield 1990, 2009; Watrous 1996; Jones 1996; Rutkowski & Nowicki 1996; Zeimbeki 2004; and Kyriakidis 2005 for the locations and characteristics of sacred caves and peak sanctuaries. The importance of peak sanctuaries and cave

One of the most spectacular cave sanctuaries is the Psychro Cave, which lies high in the mountains overlooking the Lasithi plateau in central Crete.[12] It was used for habitation in the Neolithic and the first part of the Early Bronze Age and for burial in the Early Bronze Age. After a period of abandonment, it became the location for cult activities from sometime in the Middle Bronze Age to the Roman and Byzantine periods. The Psychro cave, also known as the Dictaean Cave because it was thought to have been identified in Antiquity with the mythological birthplace of Zeus on Mount Dicte, is a very impressive cave with large upper and lower chambers that go deep into the mountain.[13] At the bottom of the cave, in the lower chamber, there is a deep pool of water surrounded by stalagmites, which also rise above its surface, while stalactites descend from the ceiling. The votive material found in the cave was exceptionally rich and has also a decidedly military character. It includes daggers and spearheads, which are actual weapons, and numerous replicas of sword or dagger blades and double axes, which had most probably been made specifically for ritual deposition.[14] The replicas of weapons are either miniatures made of cast bronze or full-size blades made of thin bronze foil. The majority of the replicas of blades and double axes were found inserted into the stalagmites and stalactites of the lower chamber.

The peak sanctuary on Mount Juktas in north-central Crete seems to have been one of the richest and most spectacular open air cult places on Crete.[15] In contrast with most other peak sanctuaries there are extensive traces of architectural elaboration. The remains of an enclosure wall and a multi-roomed building have been identified, in front of which two stepped terraces had been constructed in order to provide the area with a level surface. A number of valuable items, including a number of seal stones and an engraved cup with a Linear A inscription, were found in this building. A stepped altar, constructed on the edge of a deep chasm in the bedrock, was identified to the west of the terraces. Large and small double axes and daggers were found close to the altar.

---

sanctuaries as sites of religious ritual is generally recognised in Minoan archaeology. However, many remain unexcavated and many of those that have been investigated have not been published in any great detail.
[12] Boardman 1961; Watrous 1996; Rutkowski & Nowicki 1996. The cave lies 200 metres above the plateau at an altitude of 1025 metres.
[13] Watrous 1996, 18-19.
[14] See Haysom 2010 on the double axe as a weapon.
[15] Karetsou 1981.

Although the material from the Psychro Cave and the peak sanctuary on Mount Juktas can be considered exceptional from an archaeological perspective, other nature sanctuaries were also characterised by rich finds pertaining to warfare.[16] One of the most spectacular weapon finds from this period is a deposit found at Arkalochori in central Crete. It included swords, replicas as well as actual weapons, and double axes, functional ones as well as replicas made of thin bronze or gold foil.[17] The Archalochori deposit, which was found under a rock shelter, is not a primary context. The material had in all likelihood, for some unknown reason, been removed from a cave sanctuary or a peak sanctuary.

In Aegean archaeology religion and warfare are usually discussed from the standpoint that they are two very different things, even if it has been noted that military and religious symbolism would seem in some cases to be interchangeable.[18] Although finds of weapons and artefacts with martial imagery in cultic contexts have sometimes been interpreted as evidence for deities associated with warfare or with the production of weapons, most often they have been interpreted as valuable offerings that were intended to show off the power, wealth, social status, and personal prestige of the dedicants, possibly identifying them as warriors.[19] This is in line with a tendency in Aegean archaeology to see votives as representations of the concerns of the dedicants rather than as expressions of religious beliefs or cosmological realities. The swords and other weapons that were left as votive offerings in sanctuaries in Minoan Crete represent a deliberate choice on the part of the dedicants, which must be meaningful in some way. Rather than interpreting them solely in terms of social expression, I would argue that they reflect a world view in which the practice of warfare was enmeshed with religious beliefs.

The existence of an inseparable association between warfare and religious beliefs is attested at other times and places in the ancient Mediterranean world. Warfare lay at the heart of ancient Greek cosmology. As related by Hesiod in the *Theogony*, it is through warfare that the world of the gods moves forward from one generation to the next and Zeus achieves supremacy, a supremacy which he must always be prepared to defend with violence. Strife among humans was believed to reflect the

---

[16] See Jones 1999; Kyriakidis 2005, 128-168 for and overview of comparable material from other nature sanctuaries.
[17] Marinatos 1935; Rutkowski & Nowicki 1996, 24-26.
[18] Molloy 2012, 115.
[19] Kilian-Dirlmeier 1993, 13; Molloy 2012, 115.

struggles of the gods and beliefs of this kind were materialised in the popularity of scenes of the gods at war in Greek imagery in religious contexts and of weapons, pieces of armour, and representations of warriors as votive offerings in sanctuaries.[20] The story of the siege and destruction of Troy illustrates, as do several other myths, how warfare was also believed to regulate the relationship between humans and gods. When the Trojan prince Paris flouts the laws of hospitality by running away with or abducting the wife of his host, the Greek king Menelaus, this was not just a breach of good manners, but also an offence against Zeus, and as such, a violation of the bond between humans and gods. Moreover, the Trojans have form and Paris' behaviour is just the latest in a long line of transgressions against divine law. As a consequence, warfare was inflicted upon them as the means through which the gods could restore cosmic order. The suffering and dying of the Greeks, who no more than the Trojans want the war, can be said to represent collateral damage in this regard. Given the choice, the Greeks would have much preferred to have said good riddance to the silly woman for whom the war was being fought and to have got on with their lives. Beliefs similar to those found in early Greek literature, that warfare was essentially a manifestation of the will of the gods rather than of wilful human action, have a long history in the ancient Near East and Egypt.[21] The existence of close ties between religious beliefs and warfare in Minoan Crete may therefore reflect a communality of beliefs in this regard over a larger area in the eastern Mediterranean during the Bronze and Iron Ages, although this is difficult to prove in the present state of the evidence. However, Crete was in close contact with the Near East and Egypt throughout the Bronze Age and it has recently been argued that as regards religion Crete was an integral part of the wider Near Eastern world.[22]

The weapons and other artefacts that pertain to warfare that have been found in sanctuary contexts on Crete were often valuable artefacts in terms of material, quality of workmanship, or both, indicating that they had been made for those possessing wealth, status, and power. Even a blade made of thin bronze would probably not have come cheap. This suggests that members of the elite found it in their interests to invest ostentatiously in the materialisation of the religious and cosmological significance of warfare, which would indicate that the ritual aspects of military display played an important ideological role. The fine ware pottery found in the

---

[20] For example, at Olympia.
[21] Hamblin 2006.
[22] Marinatos 2010.

Psychro cave was made in the workshops of the palace at Malia, suggesting that ritual activities in the cave were directly associated with the expression of palatial power.[23] The pottery and votive material found at the peak sanctuary on Mount Juktas show that it was associated with the palace of Knossos.[24]

Both the Psychro Cave and the Peak Sanctuary at Juktas lie at some distance from the centres of power with which they were associated. The distance from Malia on the northern coastal plain up to the cave is around twenty kilometres and a difference in height above sea level of more than a thousand metres. Mount Juktas is located c. thirteen kilometres to the southwest of Knossos and its highest peak, on which the sanctuary is located, lies at 811 metres above sea level. Ritual ceremonies would therefore have been initiated by processions over considerable distances and sometimes difficult terrain. Journeys from palace to sanctuary may have lasted several days and involved many people, either as participants, who would have joined the procession at different points along the way, or as spectators. Both at Juktas and at Psychro many people could have gathered in the area of the sanctuary. The presence of a large constructed terrace outside the entrance to the cave at Psychro is further confirmation that ritual activities seem regularly to have involved many people. The types of pottery that have commonly been found in cave sanctuaries and peak sanctuaries indicate eating and drinking, as does the presence of animal bones.[25]

The thick layers of ash that were found at Juktas have been interpreted as the remains of bonfires, indicating that ritual activities probably took place at night. At Psychro a number of lamps found in the upper chamber of the cave are possibly an indication that ceremonies in cave sanctuaries also took place at night, although they would in any case have been necessary for moving deeper into the cave. It is also possible that a dramatic contrast between the dark chill of the cave and the bright light of the day was an integral part of the ritual experience.[26] For those who made their way down into the lower chamber with their offerings, the visual effect of the reflections from the pool and the gleam and flash of the bronze axes, spearheads, and blades that others before them had placed in the stalagmites and stalactites must have been tremendous. We can therefore imagine elaborate and costly rituals centred on the celebration of

---

[23] Watrous 1996, 31-40, 51.
[24] Karetsou 1981, 145.
[25] Tyree 2001, 45; Kyriakidis 2005, 78-79.
[26] Watrous 1996, 20; cf. Tyree 2001, 44.

warfare and warrior values taking place at the sanctuaries patronised by the palatial elites.

I conclude this paper by attempting to put the discussion of the religious aspects of warfare in Minoan Crete into some sort of historical narrative. Although daggers and knives are found in burial contexts from the Early Bronze Age, and some of the daggers and double axes found as votives in sanctuaries may date to the Middle Bronze Age, a focus on the dedication of weapons and, by extension, a particular interest in the religious aspects of warfare would seem to be a later phenomenon, which may not antedate the Neopalatial period. This corresponds temporally with what seems to be an unprecedented interest in the depiction of weapons and combat in representational art, most clearly evident on seals.

Also relevant in this connection are a type of stone vessels with figurative scenes carved in low relief which date to this period. Several whole vessels and a number of fragments are known. As a category, these vessels are characterised by exceptional quality of craftsmanship and must have been high status artefacts. This is corroborated by traces of gold leaf which have been identified on some fragments. Several fragments from vessels of this kind show young men performing ritual actions at what may be peak sanctuaries. A large conical cup shows two young warriors facing one another. Only male figures are represented on these vases, which is noteworthy because female figures generally have a prominent place in Minoan iconography. The context in which these vessels were used is uncertain but it has been speculated that they had been made for elite banquets at which male values were celebrated.[27] While the majority of the scenes depicted on these vases do not have any overt references to warfare, the intention seems in many cases to have been to glorify the display of physical strength and agility, which may reflect the role that athletic performance played in palatial culture, the purpose of which can also be seen as part of a process of militarisation in that it reflects the training undergone by warriors.[28]

This is also the same general timeframe within which the sword was either adopted or invented by the Minoans. As has recently been emphasised, the sword is not merely a new weapon but also involves technological innovations and the adoption of a new and far more complex

---

[27] Logue 2004, 169.
[28] Cf. Logue 2004, 169-170.

fighting technique which requires sustained training.[29] Its appearance on Crete in the latter part of the Protopalatial period can therefore be said to represent a very definite interest in investing substantially in weapons and warriors. Arguably, the new emphasis on the materialisation of warfare in a religious context and the appearance of the sword are not unconnected, but represent two sides of the same coin, namely the increasing prevalence of organised violence between different groups among the inhabitants of the island.

It is generally accepted that central and eastern Crete was divided into an unknown number of states from the early part of the second millennium BC. The construction of the first palaces at the beginning of the Middle Bronze Age may, accordingly, represent the consolidation of territorial claims by regional elites. The palaces at Knossos, Phaestos, and Malia are broadly comparable architecturally in that they are monumental court-centred structures with public areas, shrines, and storage rooms. Differences between them can be seen in material culture, such as the styles of pottery or the workings of the administrative system. Towards the end of the Middle Minoan period all the palaces suffered extensive destruction, but were rebuilt on a larger and more magnificent scale. It is possible that the palatial rulers were simply taking advantage of the destructions in order to build better and bigger but it could also be that the splendour of the new palaces reflects competitiveness between the palatial states, which was ultimately to spiral out of control.

Around 1450 BC all the palaces with the exception of Knossos were destroyed and not rebuilt. Many settlements were also abandoned or deliberately destroyed by fire. It seems that administrative centres were particularly targeted, indicating a desire to destroy the political infrastructure.[30] Because it is clear that the destructions took place within a longer period of time their attribution to human action is irrefutable. That these were unsettled times is also evident from the fact that in some places steps were taken to protect food storage and water supplies by building enclosures and restricting access. Finds in different parts of Crete of hoards of bronze objects that had been placed under the floor in buildings that had been destroyed or abandoned at this time reinforce the picture.[31] Although we know very little about the relations between the palace states

---

[29] Molloy 2010, 413-414.
[30] Driessen & McDonald 1997, 35-41.
[31] Ayia Triada, Mitropolis, Gournia, Mochlos, Malia, Palaikastro, Kato Zakros, Knossos (Driessen & MacDonald 1997, 65-70).

in the Middle and Late Bronze Ages, it is possible that they were from the beginning defined in part by military might, as has often been the case in other times and places. In the early part of the Late Bronze Age, the balance of power may have become disturbed and episodes of strife that may not previously have been entirely uncommon could have started to become more frequent and ever more serious and destructive. Knossos is the only palace that was not destroyed at this time and there is evidence indicating that the end result of this period of unrest was the domination of Knossos over much of Crete.

To sum up, my contention in this paper has been that, as was the case in the contemporary Near East and the later Greek period, there may have been a general conceptual connection between warfare and religion in the Aegean during the Bronze Age. However, the unprecedented material elaboration of the military life in ritual contexts that we see on Crete in the Neopalatial period should be seen as a matter of contingency, constituting a response to particular historical circumstances and events. The emphasis on military display in a ritual context, which indicates that the palatial elites had become particularly interested in the material amplification of religious beliefs that equated political instability with cosmic disorder, can be seen in relation to a need or desire to strengthen their military capabilities, which was motivated by fear of enemy attacks, territorial aspirations of their own, or both at the same time. In order to promote the idea that participation in warfare meant complying with the will of the gods and inspire enthusiasm for combat, the status of the warrior was enhanced and ritualised and the symbolic aspects of warfare were celebrated in spectacular rituals within the palaces and at important nature sanctuaries, materialised in the ceremonial elaboration of weapons, and variously represented in elite iconography.[32]

BIBLIOGRAPHY

Boardman, J. (1961) *The Cretan Collection in Oxford: The Dictaean Cave and Iron Age Crete.* Oxford.
Bradley, R. (1990) *The Passage of Arms. An Archaeological Analysis of Prehistoric Hoards and Votive Deposits.* Cambridge.
Brumfiel, E. M. (2004) "Materiality, Feasts, and Figured Worlds in Aztec

---

[32] My argument here is similar to that put forward by Brumfiel (2004) with regard to the Aztec state. I disagree, however, with the implications of her account that elites are unfailingly cynical, clever, and devious and the general population naive, a bit thick, and easily duped.

Mexico. Rethinking Materiality", in E. DeMarrais, C. Gosden and C. Renfrew (eds.) *The Engagement of Mind with the Material World*, 225-237, Cambridge.

CMS (*Corpus der minoischen und mykenischen Siegel* Available at: <http://www.arachne.uni-koeln.de/browser/index.php?view[layout]=siegel>) [Accessed: 01/06/14].

Driessen, J. (1999) "The Archaeology of Aegean Warfare", in R. Lafineur (ed.) *Polemos. Le contexte guerrier en Égée à l' âge du Bronze. Actes de la 7e rencontre égéenne internationale, Université de Liège, 14-17 avril 1998*, 11-20, Liège.

Driessen, J. and C. McDonald (1997) *The Troubled Island: Minoan Crete before and after the Santorini Eruption*. Liège.

Hamblin, W. J. (2006) *Warfare in the Ancient Near East to 1600 BC: Holy Warriors at the Dawn of History*. London.

Harding, A. (2000) *European Societies in the Bronze Age*. Cambridge.

Harrison, R. (2004) *Symbols and Warriors: Images of the European Bronze Age*. Bristol.

Haysom, M. (2010) "The Double-Axe: A Contextual Approach to the Understanding of a Cretan Symbol in the Neopalatial Period", *Oxford Journal of Archaeology* 29(1), 35-55.

Higgins, R. (1081) *Minoan and Mycenaean Art*. London.

Immerwahr, S. (1990) *Aegean Painting in the Bronze Age*. University Park, Pennsylvania.

Jones, D. W. (1999) *Peak Sanctuaries and Sacred Caves in Minoan Crete. A Comparison of Artifacts*. Jonsered.

Karetsou, A. (1981) "The Peak Sanctuary of Mt. Juktas", in R. Hägg and N. Marinatos (eds.) *Sanctuaries and Cults in the Aegean Bronze Age. Proceedings of the First International Symposium at the Swedish Institute in Athens, 12-13 May, 1980*, 137-153, Stockholm.

Kilian-Dirlmeier, I (1993) *Die Schwerter in Griechenland (ausserhalb der Peloponnes), Bulgarien und Albanien*. Stuttgart.

Kristiansen, K (1998) *Europe before History*. Cambridge.

—. (2002) "The Tale of the Sword —Swords and Swordfighters in Bronze Age Europe", *Oxford Journal of Archaeology* 21, 319-332.

Kyriakidis, E. (2005) *Ritual in the Bronze Age Aegean. The Minoan Peak Sanctuaries*. London.

Logue, W. (2004) "Set in Stone: The Role of Relief-Carved Stone Vessels in Neoplatial Minoan Elite Propaganda", *Annual of the British School at Athens* 99, 149-172.

Marinatos, N. (2012) *Minoan Kingship and the Solar Goddess*, Urbana, Chicago and Sprinfield.

Marinatos, S. (1935) "Ἀνασκαφαὶ ἐν Κρήτῃ", *Praktika tes en Athenais Archaiologikes Hetaireias*, 196-220.
Molloy, B. (2010) "Swords and Swordsmanship in the Aegean Bronze Age", *American Journal of Archaeology* 114(3), 403-428.
—. (2012) "Martial Minoans? War as Social Process, Practice and Event in Bronze Age Crete", *The Annual of the British School at Athens* 107, 87-142.
Otto, T., H. Thrane, and H. Vandkille, (Eds.) (2006) *Warfare and Society. Archaeologcal and Social Anthropological Perspectives*. Aarhus.
Peatfield A. (1990) "Minoan Peak Sanctuaries: History and Society", *Opuscula Atheniensia* 18, 117-132.
—. (1999) "The Paradox of Violence: Weaponry and Martial Art in Minoan Crete. Polemos", in R. Laffineur (ed.) *Le contexte guerrier en Égée à l' âge du Bronze. Actes de la 7e Rencontre égéenne internationale, Université de Liège*, 67-74, Liège.
—. (2009) "The Topography of Minoan Peak Sanctuaries Revisited", in A. L. D'Agata and A. Van de Moortel (eds.) *Archaeologies of Cult: Essays on Ritual and Cult in Crete in Honor of Geraldine C. Gesell*, 251-259 Princeton.
Rutkowski, B. and K. Nowicki (1996) *The Psychro Cave and Other Sacred Grottoes in Crete*. Warsaw.
Treherne, P. (1995) "The Warrior's Beauty: The Masculine Body and Self-Identity in Bronze-Age Europe", *European Journal of Archaeology* 3(1), 105-144.
Tyree, E. L. (2001) "Diachronic Changes in Minoan Cave Cult", in R. Laffineur and R. Hägg (eds.) *Potnia. Deities and Religion in the Aegean Bronze Age. Proceedings of the 8th International Aegean Conference/ 8e Rencontre égéenne international Göteborg, Göteborg University, 12-15 April 2000*, 39-50, 39-50, Liège.
Tzedakis, Y., S. Chryssoulaki, S. Voutsaki and Y. Veniéri (1989) "Les routes minoennes: rapport préliminaire. Défense de la circulation ou circulation de défense?" *Bulletin de correspondance hellénique* 113, 43-75.
Watrous, L. V. (1996) *The Cave Sanctuary of Zeus at Psychro. A Study of Extra-Urban Sanctuaries in Minoan and Early Iron Age Crete*. Liège.
Whittaker, H. (2008) "Warfare and Religion in the Bronze Age. The Aegean in the European Context. The Aegean Bronze Age in Relation to the Wider European Context", in H. Whittaker (ed.) *Papers from a Session at the Eleventh Annual Meeting of the European Association of Archaeologists, Cork, 5-11 September 2005*, 73-93, Oxford.

Zeimbeki, M. (2004) "The Organisation of Votive Production and Distribution in the Peak Sanctuaries of State Society Crete: A Perspective Offered by the Juktas Clay Animal Figurines" in G. Cadogan, E. Hatzaki and A. Vasilakis (eds.) *Knossos: Palace, City, State. Proceedings of the Conference in Herakleion Organised by the British School at Athens and the 23rd Ephoreia of Prehistoric and Classical Antiquities of Herakleion, in November 2000, for the Centenary of Sir Arthur Evans's Excavations at Knossos*, 351-361, London.

Chapter Two

Death of a Swordsman, Death of a Sword: The Killing of Swords in the Early Iron Age Aegean (*ca.* 1050 to *ca.* 690 B.C.E)

Dr. Matthew Lloyd

Introduction

After decades of research, Early Iron Age Greece is still best understood through its burials. One of the defining characteristics of these burials is the inclusion of weapons. It is, in fact, the development of iron weapons which led many scholars to define this period as a true "Iron Age", although others disagree.[1] But burials are complex, intentional deposits which require careful interpretation. The question which this paper addresses is part of the overall complexity of the relationship between the dead and their grave goods, specifically a man and his sword, and how this changes throughout the Early Iron Age. The phenomenon I will discuss is the act of "killing" swords. While this phenomenon is widespread in Crete and the northern Aegean, the main focus of this paper will be on Athens, Attica, and central Euboea.

The term "burials with weapons" has been adopted by scholars to replace the more subjective "warrior burial".[2] "Burial with weapons" is an all-inclusive term, essentially incorporating any burial which includes a weapon or combination of weapons. "Warrior burial" identifies the deceased as a warrior, which can be defined as *one who makes* (or rather, made) *war*.[3] The difficulty with this definition is that we may then proceed

---

[1] Haarer 2001.
[2] E.g. Whitley 2002, 218-220; D'Onofrio 2011.
[3] Molloy 2012, 88.

to assume that the deceased was a warrior, implying biographical information onto an individual when in reality what we have is an identity based on social roles and constructed in burial.

The difficulty with "burial with weapons" or "weapon burial ritual" is that these are descriptive terms, not analytical meanings. The former incorporates any burial with weapons, such as the eleventh-century Grave 147 from the south bank of the Kerameikos in Athens, where an arrowhead was embedded in the shoulder of the deceased, an eight- to eleven-year old child. It is clearly not the case that this arrowhead was one of the grave goods in this burial; it is more likely that the weapon was the cause of death of the child, which was not or could not be removed and thus was unintentionally buried.[4] On the other hand, it is unclear how the emphasis on "weapons" should lead us to approach the eighth century Tomb 45 in Argos, which contained armour, a breastplate and a helmet, but no obvious offensive weapons. Furthermore, burials such as the ninth century Tomb 79 in the Toumba Cemetery at Lefkandi have so many valuable and impressive objects that it seems narrow minded to focus simply on the weapons deposited in them.[5]

Parker Pearson compares the necessity of a warrior, "or individual of warrior status", carrying a sword to a modern executive requiring a mobile phone as a means to show that it is possible to lie through grave goods;[6] however, the metaphor is faulty: the mobile phone of a modern executive is not only a status symbol but a functional object which has changed the way in which business operates. While the relationship between grave goods and the individual with whom they are buried might not be a simple one, if these symbols are to have any power they must have some kind of presence beyond the funerary sphere. A non-functional object has no symbolic power unless it signifies something which is functional. Weapons may have symbolic value, but they are essentially used for violence.[7]

Throughout this paper the term "burials with weapons" will be employed, despite its flaws. While in some respect most of the individuals buried with weapons probably deserve identification as "warriors", this is not the place to argue this point. Rather, the attention of this paper is

---

[4] Ruppenstein 2007, 277, 279.
[5] Popham and Lemos 1995.
[6] Parker Pearson 2003, 9.
[7] Keeley 1996, 90.

focussed particularly on the *weapons*, and so it is fair to emphasise their place in the burial. The relationship between the "killing" of these weapons and the "warrior" identity of the deceased will be discussed further in the conclusions.

THE GEOGRAPHICAL AND CHRONOLOGICAL SPREAD OF BURIALS WITH WEAPONS

Burials with weapons are a common feature of the Late Bronze Age in Greece, although they decline somewhat in the Late Helladic III A-B period, the fourteenth and thirteenth centuries.[8] The situation in the post-palatial twelfth century is seen as something of a revival in burials with weapons, with a geographical spread incorporating Achaia in the west Peloponnese to Thessaly in the north, across to Rhodes and as far south as eastern Crete.[9] But despite this apparent popularity, in reality the majority of known burials with weapons are in Achaia, with moderate occurrences in eastern Crete. A prime example of the overemphasis on the burials with weapons is the case at Perati, where only three burials were associated with weapons out of approximately two-hundred tombs containing six-hundred burials, and yet these three instances have encouraged scholars to insist that "this type of burial was common in post-palatial Mycenaean Greece."[10] However, most cemeteries do not include significant burials with weapons and in much of Greece burials with weapons are not a core element of post-palatial society.

In the Early Iron Age the situation is much the same, with certain areas showing a strong tendency towards burial with weapons, whereas in others the rite is completely absent. During the eleventh and tenth centuries in Athens and Crete, men are regularly buried with weapons; but it is not until the middle of the tenth century that they become popular at sites such as Lefkandi on Euboea, and throughout northern Greece from Epirus to Macedonia. In most of these places there is a significant absence of burials with weapons in the immediately preceding period, with the exception of east Crete.

Burials with weapons are most common in the Aegean in the eighth century. Although received wisdom understands that Athenian burials with

---

[8] Cavanagh and Mee 1998, 125-127.
[9] Deger-Jalkotzy 2006.
[10] Deger-Jalkotzy 2006, 167.

weapons decline in the Late Geometric period,[11] which they certainly do proportionally, they persist until at least the third quarter of that century. It is also in this century that burials with weapons become particularly popular in Argos. Few burials with weapons have been discovered in other Peloponnesian sites such as Corinth, Sparta, and Nichoria, but it seems clear that they first appear in the ninth and eighth centuries. In some cases it could be argued that exploration of the Early Iron Age remains at these sites have been minimal, and further excavations may change this picture; for example, there are two tenth century burials with weapons in Tiryns and one or two in Argos. However, the number of Argive burials known from this period indicates that these are exceptions to the general trend of burial without weapons.

Cremation is the most common burial rite at Athens and Knossos in the Early Iron Age. Cremation was an irregular rite in the Late Bronze Age but in the eleventh century it becomes a particularly important rite at Athens and Knossos.[12] Until the eighth century in Athens, and the late seventh in Knossos, cremation is the prevailing rite for adults, with very few exceptions. It is also the most common rite associated with burials with weapons; in Athens there are several Sub-Mycenaean (mid-eleventh century) and Middle Geometric (late ninth to early eighth centuries) inhumations with weapons at transitional points between the popularity of inhumation and cremation, but these are rare. At Lefkandi cremation and inhumation are contemporary practices; weapons are associated with both, although more commonly with cremation, which appears to be the more exclusive burial rite. Regions where burials with weapons are a late phenomenon, such as the Argolid and Corinthia, favour inhumation throughout the Early Iron Age.

In all of the regions where the ritual "killing" of swords is practiced they are associated with cremations. But the situation is more complicated than this suggests.

RITUALLY "KILLED" SWORDS

Grave goods, including swords, are known to have been intentionally destroyed throughout the Late Bronze Age in the Aegean.[13] There is little evidence for this practice in the twelfth century but it has been noted that

---

[11] Van Wees 1998, 336.
[12] On the introduction of cremation in Early Iron Age Greece see Ruppenstein 2013.
[13] Åström 1987.

the destruction of fragile objects is often obscured by the fact that much is found broken with or without human agency, and it may be difficult to distinguish between the two.[14] In the specific case of swords it is usually much more obvious what damage has been caused intentionally and what could be accidental.

The typical description of a "killed" sword focuses on those which have been bent out of shape, in half or into a U-shape or a circle. One exceptional Athenian grave includes a sword which has been bent into an S-shape. But the definition can encompass a number of different kinds of intentional destruction. In his study of burials with weapons, Whitley incorporates those swords which have been broken into pieces as well as those which have been bent out of shape, including the sword in the burial of the so-called "hero" of Lefkandi.[15] In cases of broken swords it is questionable whether this represents intentional destruction of the weapon as a part of the funeral ritual, as Whitley asserts, or if the breaking of the sword is the result of post-depositional factors. Even swords from inhumations can be found broken, such as the one in Middle Geometric Athens "Holy Street" Grave 109.

In other cases the weapons of the deceased are placed with him on the funeral pyre. The most obvious examples of this are primary cremation pyres which include weapons, where the deceased was buried at the site where he had been cremated, such as those at Lefkandi and at Halos in Thessaly. In Athens primary cremation is rare, although the weapons also seem to have been placed on the pyre in a number of secondary cremation burials. These are known as "trench-and-hole" cremations, where the ashes are interred in an urn, which is placed in a hole, while most of the rest of the finds are swept into the trench. In some cases of secondary cremation, however, it is unclear whether or not the sword was even placed on the pyre. The sword of the "hero" at Lefkandi, for example, retained traces of its wooden scabbard, which seems unlikely if it had been burned on the pyre.

The difficulty with classifying the cremated sword with other kinds of "killed" weapons is that they place no special emphasis on one particular object. In the primary cremations it is not only the sword but many or even all of the grave goods which are placed on the pyre. The act of cremation itself should be considered an intentional destruction of the body and any

---

[14] Cavanagh and Mee 1998, 112.
[15] Whitley 2002, 224-225.

other goods placed upon it.[16] In Knossos attention has been drawn to the destruction of the antique Cypriot tripod stand found in Tomb 201 of the North Cemetery, probably destroyed during the cremation rite.[17] In Athenian graves that include so-called "shield bosses", it has been observed that these must have been detached from their wooden or leather backing in order to fit in the grave;[18] similarly the metal heads of spears must have been detached from their wooden shafts,[19] or these shafts must have been destroyed in the cremation pyre. But in this study the attention will remain firmly on the sword, considering the intrinsic meaning of these weapons in particular.[20] Justification of this emphasis is necessary as it becomes increasingly obvious that other grave goods were also intentionally destroyed in this period, including other weapons.

The example of Lefkandi-Toumba Tomb 79, the so-called "warrior-trader", can be used to show how this act placed extra emphasis on the killed sword.[21] This grave is a secondary urn cremation in a bronze cauldron in which every grave good, from the weapons to the cheese grater, had been placed on the funerary pyre, with the exception of the urn itself, the cloth in which the ashes were wrapped, and two oinochoai which may have been used to douse the pyre or to pour libations during the ceremony.[22] Even these oinochoai were smashed when they were thrown in the grave.

But the smashing of these vases, along with the other pottery from the grave which included two monumental kraters, does not compare with the bending out of shape of the sword. These vases would smash as they were thrown into the shaft of the grave; this could be achieved on the spot. Similarly, while the placing of grave goods on the pyre signals the intent to destroy these objects, this requires no additional effort above and beyond the destruction of the corpse already taking place. The sword is bent into a circle, an act which required not only additional effort and skills but also the incorporation of a professional to perform the bending. This clearly indicates that the emphasis in these graves was on the swords.

---

[16] Rebay-Salisbury 2010.
[17] Coldstream and Catling 1996, 194; Whitley 2002, 223.
[18] Lemos 2002, 124.
[19] Tsountas observed this for the Bronze Age, 1897, 147.
[20] D'Onofrio suggests this approach, although she does not justify it, 2011, 651.
[21] Popham and Lemos 1995.
[22] Crielaard 1996, 65.

An exception to this is the cemetery of Prinias in central Crete. Several burials from this cemetery have revealed spearheads on which the blades have been folded up and the sockets bent. These spearheads are considerably longer than those found in graves at Athens and Lefkandi, as well as many of the daggers found in Cretan burials. In this case it is apparent that the emphasis is not on the sword, but on the spear; a practice which does not appear elsewhere before the end of the eighth century, when damaged spearheads occur as dedications at the sanctuary of Apollo at Abai (Kalapodi).

How to Kill a Sword

Iron was of great symbolic value to the Early Iron Age élite.[23] Specialists were still required to manipulate and control the metal. Furthermore, many of these swords have been so perfectly bent that it is impossible to imagine that this was carried out by anyone other than a professional. As D'Onofrio phrased it, the "desired warping" would require a smith, "heating and hammering, contributing to the lavishness of the funerary ceremony."[24] The blades of the sword and dagger from Kerameikos Geometric Grave 28, for example, are curved into loops; other examples have simply been bent at angles until they form a loop, such as the sword in Lefkandi-Toumba Tomb 50. Differences in bending may indicate different levels of proficiency, but the manipulation of iron was not a widespread skill in tenth-to-ninth century Greece. This act goes beyond other forms of deliberate destruction.

Indications suggest that while this was a difficult process the iron swords themselves may not have been the most effective weapons. The more ductile an iron sword is the less efficient it will be as a weapon, which could have caused difficulties on the battlefield.[25] In order for an iron object to be manipulated in this way the iron must be soft; harder iron swords could not have been bent in this way because they would have snapped, which may explain why some swords were broken instead. The original value as weapons of the swords which are found bent in burial contexts may have been secondary to their value as impressive and large iron objects. However, it is important to emphasise that these ideas are theoretical and would require proper metallurgical analysis to show how far they are correct.

---

[23] Morris 2000, 208-218.
[24] D'Onofrio 2011, 651.
[25] Haarer 2000, 221.

Other physical properties of the swords are important as well. Leaving aside the dagger in Kerameikos Geometric Grave 28, all of the other "killed" swords in Athens, Lefkandi, and Eretria are amongst the longest in their respective regions and across Greece in the periods in which they were "killed". The Athenian and Eretrian examples are between eighty and ninety centimetres long; those from Lefkandi are around seventy-five. It is possible that in creating a visually impressive weapon of such a length, longer than the Bronze Age swords of the same type, metal quality was sacrificed.

It is unlikely that these burials, which include some of the most impressive in the Early Iron Age Aegean, were emphasising the impracticality of their weapons through bending them out of shape. It is much more likely that there is significance to this ritual, and especially to the inconsistency of its use. Part of the explanation may be the variable quality of iron. Some may have identified the fact that weapons in their possession were made of poorer quality iron, and have chosen to deposit these items into the grave of a recently deceased associate.

While the metal might have been soft, bending a sword in this way will still almost certainly have required an ironsmith. It is unclear how obvious this act of destruction would be – D'Onofrio suggests that it would have been part of the lavishness of the funerary ceremony, but we cannot show that this act of destruction was visible. It may have been performed out of sight, the perfectly bent weapon only revealed during the ceremony to add to the mysticism of the destruction. The killed sword itself was visible; in the cases where the sword is bent into a circle it is often around the neck of the urn, and unlike spear- and arrowheads it was never inside the urn. At the very basic level, this is an act of conspicuous consumption in which a prestigious, valuable, and rare object is taken out of commission visually by an individual or group: an élite and restricted social practice whereby the destruction of grave goods adds additional status to the deceased.

KILLED SWORDS 950-825 BCE

The terminology used to describe these destroyed swords is particularly loaded. "Ritual killing" is the favourite, but carries with it the presumption that these swords were considered to be *alive* that they might be killed. Quotation marks are generally used around the word "killed", as if to stress that it is not really what the scholar means, but there is no attribution or explanation. The origin of the term "killed" sword is an analogy with prehistoric Germanic warriors whose "faithful companion", their sword, was killed to join them in the afterlife.[26] On this interpretation the sword has a life of its own and in order to join its owner in the afterlife it must be destroyed.[27]

It is difficult to corroborate this interpretation with our only evidence for belief in the afterlife in Early Iron Age Greece: the Homeric epics. The bleak, unconscious underworld presented in the *Odyssey* does not encourage the suggestion that these weapons were faithful companions (*Od.* 11.34-50). On the other hand, the burial rites requested by and performed for Elpenor are the most similar examples in epic to the rites described here, and should not be disconnected from them (*Od.* 11.71-78,12.8-15). With no promise of a happy afterlife, the warrior must transcend death through action in life which allows him to be commemorated in epic.[28] The pinnacle of this is a beautiful death, going out in a "blaze of glory", and results in the destruction of the body and the weapons in cremation.[29] Elpenor's inglorious end, falling off the roof where he had fallen asleep when drunk, and the explicit description of him as a poor fighter, should indicate that it was not necessary to actually achieve this glory (*Od.* 10.552-561); however, the only other example from the epics of a man cremated with his arms is Andromache's father Eëtion, who was killed in battle with Achilles, and it is a mark of great respect that he was cremated with his arms (*Il.* 6.414-420).

The epic accounts accord well with the general evidence for both burials with weapons and those weapons "killed" through cremation with their owner. But there is no particular mention of bending the swords out of shape. If we connect the burials with weapons in the epics to those in the archaeological record questions remain, and we certainly cannot attribute their "killing" to a belief in the afterlife. Furthermore, this interpretation is difficult to sustain because of the inconsistency in the application of the rite, which is not applied to all swords consistently. If there is a "spiritual" element it is much more likely to relate to an unobservable phenomenon: perhaps these are the swords of men who lost duels, retired from combat, or killed unlawfully or sacrilegiously, and thus needed cleansing or taking out of use. However, these explanations remain speculation.

---

[26] Desborough 1972, 142, n.11.
[27] Desborough 1972, 312.
[28] Treherne 1995, 122-123.
[29] Whitley 2002, 227.

A somewhat prosaic explanation, favoured by excavators, is that swords were bent so that they might fit in the grave.[30] There are immediate difficulties with this interpretation. To begin with, it fails to explain variations in the evidence from the bending in half of the swords in Athens-Kerameikos Geometric Grave 38 and Lefkandi-Toumba Tomb 14, to the S-shape of the sword in the Athens Metropolitan Street burial. More importantly there is the "killed" dagger of 27 cm in Athens-Kerameikos Protogeometric Grave 28, wrapped around the neck of the urn with a sword 90 cm in length. Furthermore, the contrasting examples of the Late Protogeometric (950-900) Athens-Agora Grave 46 (N 16:4), which included an unbent sword 70.5 cm long, and the Early Geometric I (900-875) Athens-Agora Grave 27 (D 16:4), where the 88.3 cm long sword was bent into a circle around the neck of the urn. It is unclear if the trench of Grave 27 was large enough to contain this sword, but it seems unlikely that the effort required for expanding the grave less than 15 cm was greater than destroying the sword. Ultimately the argument is teleological; it explains the destruction of these weapons as if the size of the graves was predetermined, rather than understanding that the graves are that size because they did not need to be any bigger.

The burials with weapons in the Agora are a good example illustrating how restricted a practice bending swords out of shape really is. Both are near-contemporary examples of the Athenian "trench-and-hole" cremation. The Athenian "killed" swords where the sword is bent out of shape all appear in graves of the Late Protogeometric or Early Geometric period (*ca.* 950-825). Grave 46 is one example of a burial with a sword which has not been bent in this period; other examples also come from the Agora, such as Grave 32 (R 20:1) and AR II, the latter of which is a primary cremation. There are several more Middle and Late Geometric burials with weapons in which the swords have not been bent.

At Lefkandi the "killing" of weapons lasts for about the same amount of time. In the earliest burial with weapons, the tomb of the Middle Protogeometric "hero" (*ca.* 1000-950), the sword may have been broken but it was not bent. Several burials included swords which had been bent out of shape, from Toumba Tomb 14 in Late Protogeometric to Toumba Tomb 79 in Sub-Protogeometric II (*ca.* 850), while in others the sword was intact, such as Late Protogeometric Toumba Tomb 26 and Sub-Protogeometric I/II Palia Perivolia Tomb 47 (*ca.* 900-850). However, the cemeteries at Lefkandi are abandoned at about 825. Throughout this

---

[30] Snodgrass 1999, 37; Coldstream and Catling 1996, 518; Smithson 1974, 341.

period both "killed" and undamaged swords are deposited in different graves, again suggesting the exclusivity of the rite. But the rite cannot be said to have declined, as we do not have burial evidence from Lefkandi after 825.

The decline in the bending of swords in Athens coincides with other changes in the burial practices of Athens. In the course of the Middle Geometric period inhumation resumes and becomes the predominant rite in Athens. At the same time, the absolute number of burials excavated increases through a number of processes – increase in population, a change in burial practices which makes burials more archaeologically visible, and the inclusion of children in burial plots with adults.[31] In the later eighth century burial with weapons comes to an end, as weapons begin to be dedicated in sanctuaries.[32] But before this they appear to become restricted to the Dipylon cemetery, amongst the most prestigious burials in Athens at this time. The social system of Athens was being shaken up, and within this structure there was no place for killing swords.

Around the same time as these changes were taking place in Athens it is likely that the similar events were taking place at Lefkandi. The formation of the new cemeteries at Toumba and Palia Perivolia are explained as the result of socio-political upheavals and it is likely that their abandonment is the result of the same factors.[33] The nature of these changes is a separate question which cannot be fully addressed in this paper. It is likely to relate to the weakening hold of the élite, and perhaps broadening of the political classes. Within this structure we have the removal of the practice which encouraged the destruction of swords, but not their burial. If the destruction of swords is tied to the value of the iron it may relate to the wider availability of this metal; if it is tied into a specific practice such as duels, then it may be the result of restrictions on the practice and a limited number of élites dying in a way which resulted in the necessity of the destruction of their sword.

It is vital to understand that technological developments as well as social developments are essential to our understanding of warfare. In the Early Iron Age, it is often proposed that the technology to produce metal armour had been lost with the destruction of the Mycenaean palaces *ca.*

---

[31] Morris 1987.
[32] Snodgrass 2000, 281.
[33] Lemos 2006, 521-523.

1200.[34] There is room for debate over this, as it is possible that armour existed, but that it was just not deposited in graves;[35] this comes up against the descriptions in the epics, which suggest that men would have been cremated in their armour, and the likelihood is that armour in the Early Iron Age was made of perishable materials which would not survive cremation. Furthermore, the most prestigious close-quarter weapons, swords, may not have been as useful as we suppose, if they could regularly be bent out of shape in this way. In amongst the social changes, it is possible that there was an adoption or development of better iron production technology which prevented the swords from being bent.

KILLED SWORDS AFTER 800

At the end of the eighth century a series of especially wealthy burials begins in the area of the later West Gate at Eretria. There are seven adults cremated and buried in bronze cauldrons, and nine children who were inhumed. These burials span about a generation (*ca.* 715-690) and probably represent a powerful family.[36] Five of these burials have been identified as adult males with weapons, and are extraordinary for a number of reasons. While superficially similar to previous Euboean burials with weapons, such as the "hero" and Tomb 79 in the Toumba cemetery, the objects in these burials are much more prestigious – almost entirely metal, including gold and bronze, in significant quantities.

The most important of these burials for the present study are Tombs 6 and 9. Tomb 6, usually interpreted as the earliest of the burials, contained four iron swords, five iron spearheads, and a bronze spearhead. While this bronze spearhead was originally interpreted as a Mycenaean heirloom, a much more convincing proposition is that it is a contemporary spearhead from Europe, probably Switzerland.[37] Tomb 9 contained two iron swords and four iron spearheads. These are extraordinary numbers of weapons; there are no figures on Late Geometric pottery with more than three spears or two swords, and those are usually a sword and a dagger. The excavator suggested that Tomb 6, at least, was a double burial,[38] but this is not confirmed from the skeletal examination of the remains.[39] Like the killed

---

[34] Snodgrass 1999, 41-42.
[35] Van Wees 1998, 339-340.
[36] Hall 2013, 134.
[37] Bettelli 2001.
[38] Bérard 1970, 32.
[39] Blandin 2007, 43-45.

swords before them, the Eretria weapons are amongst the longest iron swords of this period.

While burials with weapons continue in eighth-century Athenian inhumations, after the abandonment of the Lefkandi cemeteries the record of Euboean burials with weapons becomes scarce. Two burials from Eretria contained damaged swords, one of which is contemporary with the last burials at Lefkandi and the other slightly later. In both of these cases the blade is bent, although not as much as to form a U-shape, S-shape, or a circle. These burials were both primary cremations and it is likely that at least some of the damage was the result of post-depositional corrosion. In the eighth century several cremations in the Harbour Cemetery at Eretria contained spearheads, but the excavations have never been fully published. These do not appear to contain swords, and so it is unlikely that any of these weapons were "killed". It is possible that the undiscovered Late Geometric cemeteries of Lefkandi, or earlier ones at Eretria, contain evidence which would bridge the gap between the "killed" swords of the late ninth century and those at Eretria at the end of the eighth. However, from the evidence as it stands the burials at Eretria could reflect re-emergence as easily as continuity. Eighth-century burials with weapons in which the swords have not been destroyed have been excavated throughout Greece. For example, among the burials with weapons at Argos there are no examples of swords which are bent out of shape.

Another extraordinary factor about the Eretria burials is that they are amongst the last of their kind in central Greece. While it is not until the eighth century that burials with weapons are found throughout much of Greece, by the end of the century they have stopped in Athens and Argos, although they continue in northern Greece and Crete.[40] The main arena for the deliberate deposition of weapons at this time is the sanctuary. While the sanctuaries of Zeus at Olympia and of Apollo at Abai receive the majority of these dedications, they are also present at the Athena sanctuaries at Sounion and Delphi, the sanctuary of Poseidon at Isthmia, and other sanctuaries in smaller numbers. At Olympia and Isthmia, these dedications are primarily armour. Some of these weapons are intentionally damaged, although this becomes more common in the seventh and sixth centuries.

The correlation between the decline in the appearance of weapons in burials and the rise in their dedication at sanctuaries is surely not a

---

[40] Whitley 2001, 188.

coincidence. The interpretation of both depositional acts as a form of competitive destruction of wealth performed as a means of ranking aristocratic households stresses the similarities between deposition in burials and sanctuaries; the difference being that dedication in a sanctuary can be used by the élite to show that their actions have social worth as a means of interaction with the gods.[41] It is also worth emphasising that weapons are only one part of this process, which incorporates most metal objects previously deposited in graves. While there is much of worth in Morris' interpretation, focusing on the similarities between dedication in sanctuaries and burials with weapons ignores the considerable differences between the dedications, which are primarily armour, and the burials, which are more likely to contain weapons.

Armour is valuable – this assumption is the basis of the concept of its dedication as competitive destruction of wealth. Morris argues from the perspective of gift exchange as a means by which objects of value are moved around.[42] But warfare is another way in which valuable objects can be obtained, especially armour. Armour stripped from the bodies of the dead – *skyla* – is frequent amongst dedications of armour when they are identified by inscriptions.[43] The earliest probable attestation of stripped armour comes from late seventh-century Aphrati on Crete,[44] but the absence of earlier epigraphic evidence should not deter the interpretation of earlier dedications of armour as *skyla*. If we return to the *Iliad*, Andromache states that Achilles chose not to strip her father, Eëtion, of his armour out of respect; it was unusual for a warrior killed on the battlefield to retain his arms, and Hector strips Patroklos of his (*Il.* 18.125-131). Men buried with their armour were those who managed to hold on to their arms, such as Eëtion, Elpenor, and the man in Argos Tomb 45, the "panoply tomb". On the other hand, some of the armour being dedicated in sanctuaries is likely to have been *skyla*, stripped from battlefield dead so that it could not be buried with the original owner. Stripping a defeated enemy of his armour is another way in which valuable objects could be obtained. It is possible that the dedication of armour in sanctuaries corresponds to the beginning of the practice of taking an enemy's arms in earnest as a way of making public the achievements of the dedicant in combat, especially at a time when armour has become more impressive and thus more valuable.

---

[41] Morris 1986, 13.
[42] Morris 1986, 8.
[43] Pritchett 1979, 277.
[44] Hoffmann 1972, 15-16.

The practice of stripping the defeated is not restricted to armour. The "Lambros oinochoe", a Late Geometric vase in the Louvre, has been interpreted as a scene of disarming captured warriors by their victorious enemies.[45] These arms primarily include spears and swords, although the captured enemies also have helmets and shields. As with the armour above, the weapons would have added value as a result of being won on the battlefield. While these weapons could have been reused more easily than armour, which might be ill-fitting, it is also probable that they were dedicated. However, at the time of the Eretria burials, it does not appear to have become the norm that they are dedicated in a sanctuary. It is possible that the captured arms were bent out of shape, explaining both the condition of the weapons in the Eretria burials and those in sanctuaries which have been intentionally damaged.

The bronze spearhead in Tomb 6 from the West Gate cemetery at Eretria can be further understood in this context. Bettelli highlights the similar treatment of this weapon and the other weapons in the grave in that it is destroyed completely; he suggests that it was conveyed to Eretria from central Europe via north Italian intermediaries. But if we place these weapons in the context of eighth-century warfare, with the emerging emphasis on captured arms and armour, it is possible to suggest that the means by which this spearhead reached Eretria was as a spoil of war, captured in Italy. In these graves we may have the deposition of war spoils, destroyed and deposited alongside those who had captured them, to emphasise the skills and achievements of the deceased. The exclusivity and added value of these objects of dedication was that they could not be bought or made; they could only be won on the battlefield.

CONCLUSIONS

"Killed" swords offer a perspective on various aspects of warfare and society in Early Iron Age Greece. On the social level, these are prestigious objects which are both conspicuously and competitively destroyed through their removal from circulation in graves and sanctuaries; the ability to destroy them was both impressive and restricted. On the other hand, they are also likely to have been particularly unimpressive weapons. They must be understood in the different contexts of warfare in the tenth and ninth centuries, which is likely to have been on a much smaller, personal scale than in the eighth century, when men went to war in part with the hope of gathering precious arms and armour from their enemies. These were

---

[45] Ahlberg 1971, 23-25.

sometimes dedicated to the gods; this practice was just as much about enforcing the status of those who had taken these weapons from the defeated as it was for the prestige of the community.

BIBLIOGRAPHY

Ahlberg, G. (1971) *Fighting on Land and Sea in Greek Geometric Art.* Stockholm.

Åström, P. (1987) "Intentional Destruction of Grave Goods", in R. Laffineur (ed.) *Thanatos: Les coutûmes funéraires en Égée à l'âge du bronze [Aegaeum 1].* Liège, 213-217.

Bérard, C. (1970) *Eretria Fouilles et Recherches III. L'Hérôon à la Porte de L'Ouest.* Bern.

Bettelli, M. (2001) "A supposed Mycenaean Spearhead from Eretria", in *Studi Micenei Ed Egeo-Anatolici,* 189-193.

Blandin, B. (2007) *Eretria XVII: Les Pratiques Funéraires D'Époque Géométrique à Érétrie Volume II - Catalogue, tableaux et planches.* Renens.

Cavanagh, W. and C. Mee (1998) *A Private Place: Death in Prehistoric Greece.* Jonsered.

Coldstream, J. N. and H. Catling (eds.) (1996) *Knossos North Cemetery: Early Greek Tombs.* 4 vols. London.

Crielaard, J-P. (1996) *The Euboeans Overseas: Long-distance Contacts and Colonization as Status Activities in Early Iron Age Greece.* Amsterdam (unpublished PhD thesis).

Deger-Jalkotzy, S. (2006) "Late Mycenaean Warrior Tombs", in S. Deger-Jalkotzy and I. Lemos, (eds.) *Ancient Greece. From the Mycenaean Palaces to the Age of Homer.* Edinburgh. 151-179.

Desborough, V. R. d'A. (1972) *The Greek Dark Ages.* London.

D'Onofrio, A. M. (2011) "Athenian burials with weapons: The Athenian warrior graves revisited", in A. Mazarakis Ainian (ed.) *The "Dark Ages" Revisited.* Volos. 645-673.

Haarer, P. (2000) *Obeloi and Iron in Archaic Greece.* Oxford (unpublished DPhil thesis).

—. (2001) "Problematising the Transition from Bronze to Iron", in A. J. Shortland (ed.) *The Social Context of Technological Change. Egypt and the Near East, 1650-1550 BC.* Oxford. 255-273.

Hall, J. M. (2013) *A History of the Archaic Greek World ca. 1200-479 BCE.* Oxford (1st ed. 2007).

Hoffmann, H. (1972) *Early Cretan Armorers.* Mainz.

Keeley L. H. (1996) *War Before Civilization.* Oxford.

Lemos, I. (2002) *The Protogeometric Aegean. The Archaeology of the Late Eleventh and Tenth Centuries BC.* Oxford.

—. (2006) "Athens and Lefkandi: A Tale of Two Sites", in S. Deger-Jalkotzy and I. Lemos, (eds.) *Ancient Greece. From the Mycenaean Palaces to the Age of Homer.* Edinburgh. 505-530.

Molloy, B. (2012) "Martial Minoans? War as social process, practice and event in Bronze Age Crete", in *Annual of the British School at Athens* 107, 87-142.

Morris, I. (1986) "Gift and commodity in Archaic Greece", in *Man* 21, 1-17.

—. (1987) *Burial and ancient society: The rise of the Greek city-state.* Cambridge.

—. (2000) *Archaeology as Cultural History: Words and Things in Iron Age Greece.* Oxford.

Parker Pearson, M. (2003) *The Archaeology of Death and Burial.* Stroud (1st ed. 1999).

Popham, M. and I. Lemos (1995) "A Euboean Warrior Trader", in *Oxford Journal of Archaeology* 14.2, 151-157.

Pritchett, W. K. (1979) *The Greek State at War. Part III: Religion.* Berkeley.

Rebay-Salisbury, K. (2010) "Cremations: fragmented bodies in the Bronze and Iron Ages", in K. Rebay-Salisbury, M. L. Sørensen, and J. Hughes (eds.) *Body Parts and Bodies Whole: changing relations and meanings.* Oxford. 64-71.

Ruppenstein, F. (ed.) (2007) *Kerameikos XVIII: Die Submykenische Nekropole. Neufunde und Neubewertung.* Munich.

Ruppenstein, F. (2013) "Cremation burials in Greece from the Late Bronze Age to the Early Iron Age: continuity or change?", in M. Lochner and F. Ruppenstein (eds.) *Cremation burials in the region between the Middle Danube and the Aegean, 1300-750 BC.* Vienna. 185-196.

Smithson, E. L. (1974) "A Geometric Cemetery on the Areopagus: 1897, 1932, 1947", *Hesperia* 43, 325-390.

Snodgrass, A. M. (1999) *Arms and Armor of the Greeks.* Baltimore and London (1st ed. 1967).

—. (2000) *The Dark Age of Greece. An Archaeological Survey of the Eleventh to Eighth Centuries BC.* Edinburgh (1st ed. 1971).

Treherne, P. (1995) "The Warrior's Beauty: The Masculine Body and Self-Identity in Bronze-Age Europe", *Journal of European Archaeology* 3.1, 105-144.

Tsountas, C. (1897) *The Mycenaean Age: A Study of the Monuments and Culture of Pre-Homeric Greece.* Chicago.

Van Wees, H. (1998) "Greeks bearing arms: the state, the leisure class, and the display of weapons in archaic Greece", in N. Fisher and H. van Wees (eds.) *Archaic Greece: New Approaches and New Evidence.* London. 333-378.

Whitley, J. (2001) *The Archaeology of Ancient Greece.* Cambridge.

—. (2002) "Objects with Attitude: Biographical Facts and Fallacies in the Study of Late Bronze Age and Early Iron Age Warrior Graves", in *Cambridge Archaeological Journal* 12.2, 217-232.

Chapter Three

Filling the Gaps: Catapults and Philon of Byzantium

Dr. Aimee Schofield

Philon of Byzantium was a technical author who probably wrote around 200 BC.[1] His works originally covered a wide range of topics, including *On Levers*; *The Making of Harbours*; *Artillery*; *Pneumatics*; *Automatic Machines*; *Siege Preparations*; *Siegecraft*; and *Stratagems*, of which only four survive (*Siege Preparations*; *Siegecraft*; and *Artillery* survive in Greek; *Pneumatics* survives in Arabic).[2] Together with three other authors – Heron, Biton, and Vitruvius – Philon provides us with details of how to build the catapults used in the ancient world. This paper will set out how the reconstruction of ancient catapults, by using experimental archaeology, can fill the gaps left in the text of Philon's artillery treatise, the *Belopoeica*. By using as a case study the design and interpretation of one particular component in the stone-shooting torsion catapult (the ὑπόθεμα or "counter-plate"), this paper will show that a practical approach can considerably improve our understanding of how catapults were constructed in the Hellenistic period.

Experimental Archaeology

The methodologies used in experimental archaeology can generally be divided into three main categories: the replication of objects, the replication of behaviours, and the replication of processes.[3] This paper relies on the first of these methodologies in combination with a close reading of the ancient artillery treatises. However, object replication can also be subdivided into three categories: visual replicas (i.e. recreated

---

[1] Marsden 1971, 8, and Rihll 2007, 148.
[2] Marsden 1971, 156 n. 2.
[3] Mathieu 2002, 2-6.

artefacts which have the same appearance and form as the original object, but may not be created from "authentic materials"), functional replicas (which operate in the same way as the original artefact, but are not necessarily "authentic in every respect"), and full replicas (which are made to "a high degree of accuracy" and are as authentic as possible).[4] In the project discussed in this paper, the functionality of the replica catapult was considered especially important, since the engine was built to be tested against historical sources. However, each component also needed to be built to a high degree of accuracy, since without a high level of authenticity it would have been impossible to compare like with like.[5] Therefore, this approach resulted in questions being raised around the parts of Philon's treatise which gave limited or reduced details about particular components (in particular the ὑπόθεμα) and how it could be possible to work around these omissions or gaps in the text.

Catapults have been built for the purposes of experimentation before. However, the Hellenistic stone-shooting catapult has been left largely untouched by researchers. Nevertheless, Schramm, who reconstructed catapults in the early twentieth century, built a replica of Philon's stone-shooting catapult,[6] which unfortunately did not survive the Second World War. As will be discussed in more detail below, the information which does survive on his catapults lacks some of the detail needed in order to understand his interpretation of Philon's treatise. Marsden, who built replica catapults in the 1960s and 1970s, does not include the Hellenistic stone-shooting catapult in his discussion of his own reconstructions,[7] so it seems unlikely that he built one himself. This means that there is a gap in our understanding of how these catapults were constructed, as well as of their role on the battlefield. With this in mind, this paper follows in the footsteps of scholars such as Schramm and Marsden, using the principles of functional replication to show how the problem of the gaps in Philon's text can be overcome using experimental archaeology.

---

[4] Mathieu 2002, 2-3.
[5] N.b. the ὑπόθεμα illustrated in this paper is made of plywood. This material was chosen to test the theories advanced in this paper because of its cheapness, versatility, and strength. Ash, the main building material of the catapult, is much more authentic.
[6] Schramm 1980, 8.
[7] Marsden 1971, 232-233, 254-265, and Pl. 4, 6-8.

Philon of Byzantium

Philon was writing in approximately 200 BC according to information given within his text. He appears to have travelled to the centres of learning around the Mediterranean, and particularly to Alexandria where he interviewed the students of an earlier engineer, Ctesibius (Ph. *Bel.* 72.24-26).[8] This places him approximately one generation later than Ctesibius, the dating of whose working life has been disputed, but for which scholarly consensus now points to between 270 and 230 BC, meaning that Philon was probably writing twenty-five to thirty years later.[9] In addition to his research in Alexandria, he also seems to have visited Rhodes (Ph. *Bel.* 73.21-23), another city noted for its connection with the development of artillery.[10] His own home town, Byzantium, took up the catapult early in its development, lending at least part of its arsenal to Perinthus when it was besieged by Philip II of Macedon in 340 BC (Diod. Sic. 16.74.4); this may have given Philon a background in and an enthusiasm for catapult design.[11] Philon appears to have been an engineer in his own right as well as a researcher, as sections in his work discuss his own catapult designs (Ph. *Bel.* 56.16-73.20), along with explanations of designs made by other people (Ph. *Bel.* 73.21-78.22).

The Technical Treatise

Philon's *Belopoeica* is the longest of the extant artillery treatises. It takes the reader through what Philon tells us are the standard artillery pieces of the day (Ph. *Bel.* 51.8-56.15), and then goes on to explain and describe innovations made by Philon himself, which he suggests will result in a more efficient catapult known as the "wedge-engine"[12] (Ph. *Bel.* 56.16-67.27). Philon goes on to describe catapults designed by other engineers: he tells his reader about the bronze-spring engine of Ctesibus, and gives his own version of the catapult (Ph. *Bel.* 67.28-73.20); he describes the construction, use of, and problems with the repeating catapult built by Dionysius of Alexandria (Ph. *Bel.* 73.21-77.6); and he explains the pneumatic catapult which was also built by Ctesibius (Ph. *Bel.* 77.9-78.22). All of the catapults described in the treatise are torsion powered, with skeins of twisted ropes providing the energy which allows

---

[8] Marsden 1971, 6, and Rihll 2007, 148-9.
[9] Marsden 1971, 8, and Rihll 2007 148.
[10] Rihll 2007, 149.
[11] Rihll 2007, 148.
[12] *"τὸ διὰ τοῦ σφηνὸς ἐντεινόμενον"*.

the engine to shoot missiles. Vitruvius' catapults, too, are all torsion powered (Vitr. *De arch.* 10.10-12), but are significantly improved and updated in comparison to Philon's engines.[13] Biton's treatise focuses on non-torsion catapults, which operate in much the same way as a crossbow, and describes two stone-shooting and two bolt-shooting engines (Biton, *Construction of War Machines* 44.7-51.4 and 61.2-68.1 respectively). Heron's treatise considers both types of catapult, beginning with a description of the earliest catapult, the *gastraphetes*, which is non-torsion (Heron, *Bel.* 75.10-81.2), then moving on to early torsion catapults (Heron, *Bel.* 81.3-90.5), later torsion catapults (Heron, *Bel.* 91.1-114.7), and finally considering methods by which catapults may be scaled up and down using the theorem of the two mean proportionals (Heron, *Bel.* 114.8-119.2).[14] Of the three authors whose texts date from the Hellenistic period (Philon, Heron, and Biton), Philon is the most detailed and the most technical; moreover, his is the only Hellenistic text to provide figures by which the dimensions of any given torsion catapult may be determined.

Philon's treatise uses a system of proportional measurements to describe the components needed to build a catapult (Ph. *Bel.* 53.8), a system also used by Vitruvius much later. This means that the final dimensions of the pieces of the catapult are not given. Instead, so that the engineer can adjust the size of the catapult to suit his own circumstances, all of the dimensions are calculated by multiplying or dividing the size of one basic component: the diameter of the spring-hole. To keep the rope skeins which power the catapult tight and in position, the rope is looped through holes in the frame of the catapult, and then through washers which sit above and below the frame. The size of the holes dictates how much rope can be used in the catapult, and thus how much power can be generated. This dimension, therefore, is the ideal base measurement from which the dimensions of the other components may be calculated, since the size of the spring-hole determines the calibre of the weapon.

---

[13] Marsden 1969, 43.
[14] This is a theorem which allows an engineer to work out the diameter of a spring-hole for a given stone-shooting catapult based on one of a different size which has already been calculated. Because the initial calculation for any one spring-hole involves working out cube roots, which would take a considerable amount of trouble without modern logarithmic tables or calculators, this method simplifies the process. As a result only one spring-hole diameter needs to be calculated from scratch even if a number of machines of different sizes need to be built – the theorem of the two mean proportionals allows the engineer to scale the sizes up or down according to need. See Marsden 1971, 59.

It is worth asking the question of why there are gaps in the text in the first place. The text itself seems to be remarkably complete, and the gaps do not exist as a result of lacunae. It seems unlikely, given the level of detail which Philon provides elsewhere in the text, that he deliberately omitted information to prevent his reader from being able to use the text to construct catapults – there are, after all, ways for a catapult builder to work around the gaps or to fill them in, as this paper will show. Neither is it likely that Philon was ignorant of the information needed at the points in his text where the gaps appear, as shown by the level of detail he gives and the nature of his own research shows (e.g. Ph. *Bel.* 72.24-26, where he describes interviewing other engineers about their work and that of their predecessors). However, the text survives without the illustrations which appear to have been part of the original documents, though medieval interpretations of some of the illustrations do survive in the manuscripts.[15] As will be discussed in more detail below, sections of Philon's treatise use letters to describe line drawings (e.g. Ph. *Bel.* 52.20-53.7). He also refers directly to illustrations, guiding the reader through an image which is no longer present, with figures referred to by given letters (Ph. *Bel.* 63.18-66.4).[16] It may well be that these illustrations provided a much better way of presenting Philon's ideas and instructions, and so he simply did not bother to put full descriptions in the text. It may also be that Philon assumed a certain level of knowledge from his reader and felt no need to state what he considered to be obvious, but that knowledge has not been transmitted to the modern reader.

The ὑπόθεμα

For the majority of the components in Philon's treatise, we are given the three dimensions needed for their construction.[17] For those where Philon only gives us two dimensions, very often the third can be estimated based on the component's location in the catapult and the pieces of the machine which surround it.[18] However, for one crucial component, only one dimension (the thickness) is given. This component, the ὑπόθεμα (counter-plate), is designed, according to Philon, to rest under the

---

[15] Diels and Schramm 1970, 26 Bild 11 and 27 Bild 12.
[16] Of particular note is the opening portion of this section of the treatise: ἔστω δὲ ὑπὸ τὴν ὄψιν κείμενος ὁ παραστάτης τῷ σχήματι ὑπάρχων ὁ ὑπογεγραμμένος, ἐφ' οὗ τὸ Α ("let the visible part of the side-stanchion be in form as already sketched out as at A").
[17] i.e. any three of the following: length, thickness, height, and width.
[18] Marsden 1971, 266-269.

περίτρητον (hole-carrier);[19] he also tells us that, using the proportional system of dimensions, the thickness of the ὑπόθεμα should be equal to one quarter of the spring-hole's diameter (Ph. *Bel.* 53.16). No further details are given.

This particular component is especially worthy of discussion because it has been almost entirely ignored in scholarship to date. Schramm fails to include the component in his diagrams of Philon's stone-shooting catapult, though he includes at least an interpretation of every other piece.[20] Diels and Schramm also ignore the ὑπόθεμα in their commentary on the text.[21] Marsden, too, leaves the ὑπόθεμα out from his diagrams,[22] and in his commentary notes only that its function in Philon's stone-shooting catapult is substantially different from the component of the same name in Heron's equivalent engine.[23] The fact that there is so little discussion around the problems posed by this component suggests that it has not previously been noted as a difficulty within the text. Indeed, it seems likely that this problem could only be noticed as a result of an attempt to build a catapult by following Philon's instructions. As a result, the previous research in this field has left a significant gap in our understanding of the shape, positioning, and function of this component of the Hellenistic stone-shooting catapult.

How, then, should we approach the construction of this component? One method is to use the other technical authors as a base for comparison. Biton's treatise is not useful here, since his work deals only with non-torsion catapults. Nor can Vitruvius provide us with any more detail, since his design of a stone-shooting catapult is radically different from Philon's and does not include a counter-plate at all. We also cannot use Heron directly, since, as noted above, the ὑπόθεμα in his stone-shooting catapult plays a completely different role.[24] This means that we can only make use of information held within the treatise itself to determine the component's design.

---

[19] The part of the catapult's frame through which the spring-holes (which hold the rope skeins) are cut. The hole-carriers are fastened to two stanchions and form the main body of the half-spring.
[20] Diels and Schramm 1970, Tafel 1, and Schramm 1980, Tafel 4.
[21] Diels and Schramm 1970, 14-15.
[22] Marsden 1969, 35 fig. 17.
[23] Marsden 1971, 160 n. 20.
[24] See above, n. 21.

Where Heron's treatise can be useful, however, is in the shaping of this component. Despite the fact that the ὑπόθεμα plays a distinctly different part in Heron's engine, its shaping to some degree relies on the shaping of the hole-carrier which sits above it. Philon's description of how to sketch out the shape of this component lacks some of the details necessary to construct the rhomboidal shape needed (Ph. *Bel.* 52.20-53.7). He offers two methods, the first of which fails to explain how the measurements he gives should be applied to the design and does not explain that curvature needed to be applied to the design, nor the radius required for the curve (Ph. *Bel.* 52.20-29). The second method also fails to explain what radius of curvature is needed and neglects to explain how the dimensions should be applied to the drawing (Ph. *Bel.* 52.30-53.7). It seems likely, from the way these descriptions are set out and from the use of letters to indicate the placement of lines within the sketches outlined that this is one place in the treatise where illustrations, now lost, would have originally accompanied the text. Heron's description of the shape of the hole-carrier is much more detailed, but his lacks the dimensions which Philon gives (Heron, *Bel.* 94.1-96.2).

This means that it is possible to combine the techniques proposed by Philon and Heron – using Philon's dimensions and Heron's drawing method – so that the overall design is of an appropriate shape and size for the catapult which is being built. The rhomboid with curved sides can then be used as a template both for the hole-carrier and the ὑπόθεμα.[25] As proof that this method is sound, when Heron's method is used to construct the rhombus, the acute angle in the shape is the same as that specified by Philon in the first method he suggests.[26]

We now have the basic shape of the ὑπόθεμα. However, the way in which it fits into the structure of the catapult's frame still needs to be established. Philon gives us full dimensions for the remaining components in the upright parts of the frame (two half-springs joined by horizontal beams). The hole-carriers (of which there are four in total, two in each half of the frame) are each one diameter high. The two washers, which sit above the upper hole-carrier and below the lower hole-carrier, are each one and a half diameters tall. The side-stanchions are five and a half diameters tall (but we need only count them once, since they are set parallel to each other). As noted above, the ὑπόθεμα is a quarter of a diameter tall, and two ὑποθέματα are needed for each half-spring (Ph. *Bel.*

---

[25] Fig. 3.1.
[26] The angle discovered by Philon's method is 65.46° – Marsden 1971, 159-160.

53.8-17). In total, then, we have a half-spring which is nine and a half diameters high. This leaves the catapult builder with a problem because Philon tells us that the overall height of the half-spring should only be nine diameters (Ph. *Bel.* 53.16-17). Since we also know that the ὑποθέματα sit below the hole-carriers, this tells us that they must be positioned inside the half-spring, between the stanchions rather than resting above them.[27]

In order for the ὑποθέματα to be supported without losing any of the stanchions' height, the only way in which they can be held in place must be by means of tenons which pass through the stanchions. Moreover, since they support the hole-carriers, the ὑποθέματα must slot into the half-spring at the very ends of the stanchions. The ὑποθέματα must also be narrower than the hole-carriers by the thickness of the stanchion at each end, since otherwise they would be too wide to fit between the stanchions. The rhomboidal shape must therefore be narrowed and tenons added at the point where they slot through the stanchions. The stanchions must also have slots cut into them to allow the ὑποθέματα to be held in position.[28] In this example, the tenons and slots were positioned on either side of the central tenon which connects the stanchion to the hole-carrier, but theoretically they could be placed at any point on the stanchion and ὑπόθεμα, so long as enough wood is left on either side to support the tenons coming from the ὑπόθεμα. This particular positioning was chosen to give the ὑποθέματα as much support as possible.

KILLING TWO BIRDS WITH ONE STONE: THE OUTER FRAMEWORK

A side effect of having tenons coming from the ὑπόθεμα and through the side stanchion is that it allows a second problem to be solved. Philon gives measurements for the framework beams which hold the two half-springs together but does not explain how they are attached either to the half-springs or to each other. Marsden seems to imply that the best way to fit the framework to the half-springs is to simply fasten them tightly around the uprights.[29] Marsden and Schramm's diagrams demonstrate that their interpretations of how the framework is attached to the half-springs involve some kind of pegging arrangement at each end of the longer framework beams, but not enough detail is shown for it to be possible to

---

[27] Fig. 3.1.
[28] Fig. 3.2.
[29] Marsden 1969, 32.

Fig. 3.1

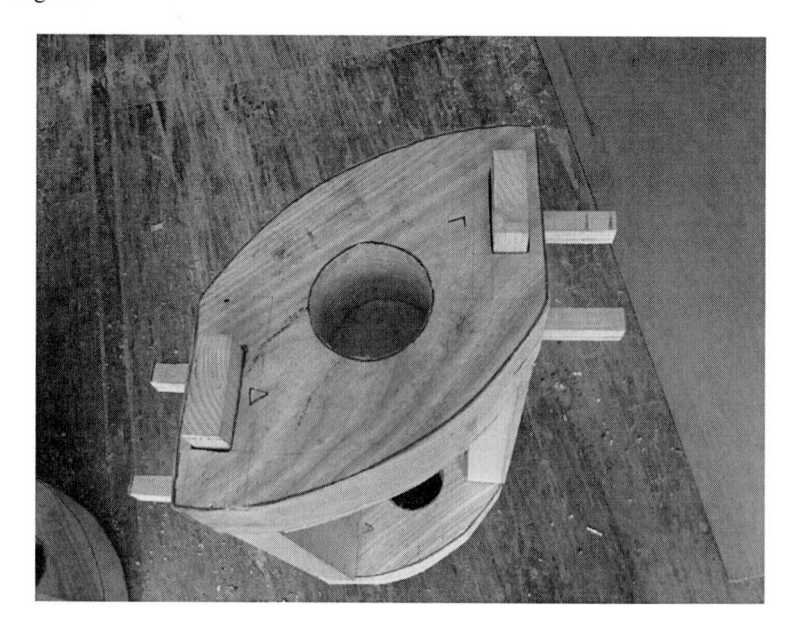

Fig. 3.2

determine exactly how they thought the framework construction worked.[30] However, if we accept the interpretation of the ὑπόθεμα as outlined above, it is possible to fix the outer framework to the half-springs very easily.

Since the tenons on the ὑπόθεμα extend through the side-stanchions, their ends are in the same position as the shorter eight of the twelve framework beams.[31] This means that if the tenons are extended it is possible to use them a second time to hold the short framework beams in place, by including mortices in their design, through which the tenons can be fitted. The ends of the shorter beams can be turned into tenons to connect with the longer beams in the same way. This technique creates a sturdy frame for the catapult which is able to hold the two half-springs securely and with relative ease of use.

CONCLUSION

Without any examples of the wooden components of the Hellenistic stone-shooting catapult appearing in the archaeological record, it is impossible to tell if the ὑπόθεμα existed in the form in which it appears in this paper. However, this paper shows that by taking a practical approach to Philon's artillery treatise and by looking at the problems posed in this text from the engineer's perspective, it is possible to find solutions to the gaps left by Philon that are also consistent with the limited information with which he supplies us. The solution proposed in this paper resolves the two issues of how the ὑπόθεμα works in practice and how the outer framework may be attached to the half-springs.

Moreover, this paper highlights a greater problem with the scholarship of ancient technology, both military and civilian: that without paying close attention to the practicality and functionality, we risk overlooking problems which exist in the texts, or writing off potentially significant details without giving them due consideration. A practical approach to the texts forces the researcher to confront every small detail, since a component which may at first glance appear to be of little interest or usefulness can turn out to be crucial to the functioning of the machine. A practical approach also increases our understanding of both the texts and

---

[30] See above, n. 18 and n. 20.
[31] There should be one on each side of the top and bottom of each stanchion in order to keep the frame stable – without short beams in the centre, the half-springs are at risk of twisting when the whole frame is put together, and without short beams on the outside, the inner beams are too weak to hold the frame together.

the technology itself. In addition, it demonstrates that experimental archaeology is an important and useful methodology by which our knowledge and understanding of ancient military technology may be expanded significantly.

BIBLIOGRAPHY

Bradford Welles, C. (trans.) (2003) (reprint) *Diodorus Siculus: Library of History Books XVI.66-XVII*. Cambridge, Massachusetts.
Diels, H. A., and Schramm, E. (1970) *Herons Belopoiika, Philons Belopoiika*. Leipzig.
Rihll, T. (2007) *The Catapult: A History*. Yardley.
Marsden, E. W. (1969) *Greek and Roman Artillery: Historical Development*. Oxford.
—. (1971) *Greek and Roman Artillery: Technical Treatises*. Oxford.
Mathieu, J. R. (2002) "Introduction – Experimental Archaeology: Replicating Past Objects, Behaviours, and Processes", in J. R. Mathieu (ed.) *Experimental Archaeology: Replicating Past Objects, Behaviours, and Processes*, 1-11, Oxford.
Schramm, E. (1980) (2nd Edition). *Die antiken Geschtüze der Saalberg*. Bad Homburg vor der Höhe.

CHAPTER FOUR

AENEAS TACTICUS AND SMALL UNITS IN GREEK WARFARE

DR. NICK BARLEY

In recent years, a great deal of thought has been devoted to the mechanics and structure of hoplite battle; arguments about the meaning of *ôthismos* (the 'push' of hoplite combat described, *inter alia*, as a literal massed physical shove or a combination of individuals and a psychological push of effort) and just *how* hoplites and the phalanx formation worked have been batted back and forth across the Atlantic for the last fifty years, with little sign of a consensus being reached.[1] A result of these interesting and illuminating arguments has been the development of an image of warfare in which the hoplite and the phalanx reigned supreme, and where the 'hoplite ethos' pervaded both warfare and society as a whole;[2] some scholars have even praised the way the Greeks made war upon each other, seeing in it a form of honour and glory sorely missing from the sometimes faceless and detached warfare of the industrial age. Thus Hanson commented on the "...wonderful, absurd conspiracy..." of hoplite battle, a system of warfare which he viewed as operating not to end lives, but, paradoxically, to save them.[3] Hanson's contributions to the field have been of great importance, but his

---

[1] In support of a massed shove see Woodhouse 1933, 78-9; Gomme 1937, 135 Grundy 1948, 267; Adcock 1957, 4; Anderson 1970, 175-6; Cartledge 1977, 16; Holladay 1982, 95-7; Pritchett 1985, 65; Hanson 1991, 7; 2000, 28-9, 246; Schwartz 2002, 44-9; 2009, 183-200. Against this position see Fraser 1942; Cawkwell 1978, 152-3; 1989, 375, 389; Krentz 1985, 55-7; 1994, 45; 2010, 53-59; Goldsworthy 1997, 5-6, 24; van Wees 2004, 184-191. See Crowley 2012, 54-7 for a useful summary and analysis of the arguments.
[2] On the importance of war and struggle to Greek thought and literature see Vernant 1990, 29, 47; Hanson 2000, 22, 219; van Wees 2001, 38-9; Hornblower 2007, 22-3, 28.
[3] Hanson 1991, 6.

interpretation of, and focus on, particular aspects of fighting has resulted in a model of warfare which raises as many questions as it answers.

Over the last fifteen years, a contrasting school of thought has appeared, one which seeks to analyse Greek warfare and hoplite battle as a form of warfare that was grounded in practicality and only limited by the inventiveness of those who fought within it. Thus, in 2000, van Wees contributed a chapter to his own edited volume, *War & Violence in Ancient Greece*, in which he questioned many of the most influential theories at that time; this argument was greatly expanded in his *Greek Warfare: Myths and Realities*, published four years later.[4] Meanwhile, in 2002, Peter Krentz suggested that Josiah Ober's 'Rules of war' could not stand as a pseudo-legal, or even pseudo-moral, framework with which to analyse and understand Classical Greek warfare.[5] There were, according to Krentz, no formal rules regarding the conduct of battles and no expectation of a 'fair' fight, indeed a successful general was one who did his utmost to ensure the fight was as unfair as possible – Aeneas Tacticus' advice to only attack an enemy force when it was drunk and in unfamiliar terrain seems to fit this bill.

While this work has generally been well received and has had enough of an impact to allow a recent study to attempt to 'reinstate' the importance of the hoplite and the *othismos* to Greek warfare,[6] it has not fundamentally changed what is regarded as the 'orthodox', and accepted, image of Classical Greek battle, and discussions of pitched battles involving thousands of hoplites from several states still dominate the scholarship.[7] This has resulted in a fascination with the hoplite and a sharp focus on the pitched battle, the result of which has been a relative lack of detailed attention to what we could call 'everyday' warfare between small neighbouring states.

Fortunately, perhaps I should say surprisingly, we have an author who gives us a glimpse of how the 1,500 or so 'average' sized *poleis* of the late-Classical period approached warfare and the defence of their territory: Aeneas Tacticus. We know relatively little about Aeneas' life. A fourth-

---

[4] van Wees 2000, 125-66; 2004.
[5] Ober 1996, 53-72; Krentz 2002.
[6] Schwartz 2009.
[7] As most recently seen in Kagan and Viggiano 2013. The book is a fine piece of scholarship but focuses on defining and re-defining the arguments, rather than offering any new solutions.

century author who is tentatively linked with the Peloponnesian state of Stymphalos,[8] his sole surviving work, the *Porliocetica*, is a manual offering advice on how to survive under siege.[9] This description is accurate and to the point: Aeneas relates many ways in which a general could defend his city from external and internal attack, and offers examples and analysis as to how this has been attempted, successfully or otherwise, in the past.[10] However, the manual is rather more than this, and a significant amount of the advice Aeneas offers is to do with taking the battle to the enemy; indeed, Aeneas would probably agree with the statement that the best defence is a good offense. For Aeneas Tacticus the advantages offered by familiar terrain, coupled with the risk of betrayal or panic if an enemy army managed to march up to the city walls, meant that an organised resistance should initially be offered as far away from the city as possible (E.g. 8.1; 16.16).[11] As a result of this, his work is not just a guide on how to survive while the town itself is under siege, but also a significant source of information and advice on how to engage enemies in the field, with the most important theme, for my purposes here, being that of the link between general and subordinate commanders in charge of small units. This link lies at the very core of Aeneas Tacticus' conception of warfare, and he directly explains its importance several times, while we can also impute the link at various other points in his narrative.

This paper is not going to examine the internal conditions of a city when besieged or under threat, suffice it to say that Aeneas recognised the danger that a surprise invasion represented to the state and described various ways by which internal stability could be maintained. Aeneas does not regard organising Greek citizen troops as something that could be achieved on the fly, as it were, and he advises his readership to take steps to ensure that various systems of communication and organisation were in place, including organised places of muster, pre-determined patrol and command positions, and the ability for messages to be sent throughout its territory by fire-signal and runner.[12] We get our first glimpse into the

---

[8] Whitehead 1990 for discussion of how far we can take the evidence regarding the Stymphalos connection.
[9] Whitehead 2002, 4-13.
[10] See, e.g. 2.1-6; 24.3-14; 28.5-7.
[11] By doing so it would also be possible to use naturally occurring boundaries, such as rivers and mountain passes, as defensive features: e.g. Xenophon *Anab* 2.3.10-14.
[12] Aen. Tact. 1-2, 22.2-3, 26. Also 7.4 where he says he has outlined how best to use fire signals in his *Paraskeuastike biblos*, which has not survived to us, although some details of Polybius 10.44 may originate there.

organisation (or lack thereof) of Greek citizen forces in one of Aeneas' first remarks regarding how to deal with panic and terror: the first reaction of the citizenry will, apparently, be to rush into the countryside to gather or protect their own property.[13] Aeneas advises that while such panic is natural, a sensible general will have plans in place to prevent it getting out of hand and will, indeed, use it as an opportunity to order his forces. As individuals and groups respond to the emergency signal and filter from the hills and the city to the rallying point, they are to be held until a critical mass is reached, assigned a 'sensible' leader, and then sent off as a group (15.2).

Throughout Aeneas' text we are told that an effective general will have taken command down to the street level, with the citizens knowing who to look to in times of danger. These subordinates form the backbone of Aeneas' overall conception of how to protect the state from physical attack, and through them, and his concentration on the importance of reliable communication, we can detect glimpses of his concern for order. Aeneas adds further detail to the initial response to enemy attack described above - his concern is to get as many citizens organised and into the field in as short a time as possible. However, it just would not do to risk them getting lost or wandering off should the fancy take them, so he advises to "...place signs at the turning-points, bottoms of hills and road junctions – anywhere where routes diverge – to prevent the stragglers from mistaking their way and becoming detached from their comrades" (Aen. Tact. 15.6). Aeneas advises that multiple small units of troops, both light infantry and hoplite, should be sent into the outer territory in order to hunt down the invaders. Chapters 15 and 16 give detailed instructions of the order of battle and when best to strike; the enemy should never be met in the open or when there is no 'home' advantage. Indeed, they should be left alone for the most part, free to ravage the countryside, steal food and possessions from houses and storage buildings, and allowed to fall into a false sense of security. The final attack should only be launched once the invaders have found and consumed a large quantity of looted wine, at which point, Aeneas helpfully remarks, they will be less able to offer effective defence, not just by dint of their inability to co-ordinate their own movements, but, significantly, because they would be more belligerent and less willing to respond to the commands of their own officers (16.5-7). Organisation, again, is stressed, although this time as something that, if lacking, could be a fatal weakness. This attack is designed to be final and complete - Aeneas' advice, if followed, is ruthless, and the home state's triumph final

---

[13] C.f. Thuc. 2.20-2.

and unexpected by the enemy, coming as it does when they are enjoying the fruits of their labour.

The importance of subordinate commanders to hoplite forces can be seen in the structure of Classical Spartan and Athenian armies, both of which had various formal levels of command below the general. The Spartan system was rather more complicated than the Athenian, and allowed Spartan phalanxes to exercise an impressive degree of battlefield adaptability and survivability in the face of concerted attack, or in the event of their general being targeted and killed. This system evolved during the fifth and fourth centuries,[14] and we are fortunate that a number of excellent sources contain information regarding the levels of command and organisation within the Spartan army at that time. The oath of the Greeks apparently sworn before the battle of Plataea, and preserved in a mid-fourth century inscription from Acharnae, contains a sentence which is vital to our understanding of both Spartan and Athenian approaches to command at all levels:

> I shall not desert my *taxiarchos* or my *enômotarchês*, whether he is alive or dead, and I shall not leave unless the *hêgemones* lead us away, and I shall do whatever the *stratêgoi* command...[15]

The oath may refer to a mixture of Spartan and Athenian military officers:[16] the position of *enômotarchês* was solely Spartan;[17] the Athenians elected their *stratêgoi* each year but the word is not used to describe Spartan officers; the Spartans referred to their Kings as *hêgemones*;[18] both states had a subordinate officer known as a *taxiarchos*.[19] Or it may refer to a purely Spartan system of command, in which the *hêgemones* refers to their position as leaders of the alliance against Persia,[20] and the *stratêgoi* refers to a 'council of the allies' generals', presumably dominated by Spartans, and not the Athenian

---

[14] See, most recently, van Wees 2006.
[15] Tod II.204, 21-29. The oath is partially reproduced in various literary sources: Lycurgus *Against Leocrates* 81; Diod. Sic. 11.29.3l; FGrHist 115 F 153. van Wees 2006, 125 for a summary of the arguments regarding the inscription's authenticity; he regards it as an "...exact copy of the real thing" 153.
[16] Suggested by van Wees 2004, 244. Lazenby 1993, 220 n.15 is sceptical.
[17] Hdt. 1.65. van Wees 2006, 127.
[18] Hdt. 9.53.
[19] Hdt. 9.53; Aristot *Ath Pol* 61.1-3; Aristoph *Acharnians* 575. van Wees 2006, 127-8, n.10, 11.
[20] As at, e.g., Hdt. 7.149, 159, 204, 208, 8.2-3.

office.[21] Thus the oath possibly reflects a joint effort by Spartan and Athenian individuals to create an oath suitable for all the states present at the battle, or is an indication that Spartan command and control of the allied army was stronger than previously thought, with the allies swearing not to abandon the battlefield before the Spartans, or to disobey any orders which the 'council of generals' issued. The latter suggestion has the benefit of avoiding the need to imagine Spartans and Athenians swearing loyalty to each other's officers and leaders,[22] while highlighting the importance of the basic tactical unit used by the Spartans, the *enômotia*. The 'Oath of Plataea' can be compared with the 'Oath of the Ephebes', found on the same inscription, to highlight the primary difference between Spartan and Athenian forces. The Ephebic oath stresses loyalty to one's neighbour in line and the obligation to defend and strengthen the state: obedience to officers does not feature, although obedience and loyalty to *all* loyal soldiers does.[23] The generic tone of the oath, and its function in the 'coming of age' of Athenian youths, reduces its impact as a reflection of Athenian military practice, and it does not indicate that a chain of command, or subordinate officers, were not important to Athenian military thought and practice.

Despite uncertainty regarding its specific details the oath remains useful as it still sheds light on, at least, the levels of Spartan command present at the battle of Plataea, and also because it suggests that the 36 states present at the battle would have understood and appreciated the position of *taxiarchos* – if it was shared by the Spartan and Athenian military systems then it is fair to assume that others also used it, or were at least familiar with the concept. Also the oath makes it clear that the Spartan command system was more integrated than other states, with another level of command existing between the general's immediate subordinate and the rest of the men.[24] This level, the *enômotarchês*, was the commander of the 'sworn band' to which he belonged; a unit which, by Xenophon's time, also had six file leaders, adding a further level to the Spartan system.[25]

---

[21] As at, e.g. Hdt. 8.49, 56-9, 78, 9.21. Siewert 1972, 60-61, 95-6, now followed by van Wees 2006, 131.
[22] van Wees 2006, 131. 127 for the point that an Athenian *taxiarchos* commanded large units, while an *enômotarchês* commanded the smallest unit possible in the Spartan system: the two are not comparable, and the most plausible explanation is that the oath refers to two Spartan positions, rather than an Athenian and a Spartan.
[23] Lines 5-20.
[24] Van Wees 2004, 100.
[25] Hdt. 1.65; Xen. *Lac Pol* 11.4-8. van Wees 2006, 125.

Within each *enômotia* of about 40 men there were thus seven officers, a level of organisation increased by the ability of Spartan generals to direct 'year-classes' to undertake specific actions.[26] The flexibility of this final element of the Spartan system was demonstrated by its use at times when Spartan phalanxes found themselves under attack by light infantry; these were dangerous situations which required an immediate response from the general, and having the ability to direct specific groups of men, all of whom had gone through the *agoge* together, was a significant advantage.[27] These additional levels of command created an environment in which each individual Spartan was aware of his, and his immediate neighbours', position in the chain of command, and was thus able to take, or give, orders as and when required. It is important to note that this not only gave Spartan forces the ability to respond to changing tactical circumstances quickly, but may also have been the foundation for their effectiveness as *fighters* as well: having such a system of command would allow those involved in the actual fighting to direct their efforts more effectively as part of a group. Thus the strength of the Spartan 'cutting edge' was in its organisation and its capacity for teamwork, not just any physical superiority the Spartans enjoyed, a point emphasised by Plutarch:

> And yet the Spartans, who were of all men past masters in the art of war, trained and accustomed themselves to nothing so much as not to struggle or get into confusion upon a change of formation, but to take anyone without exception as neighbour in rank or in file, and wheresoever danger actually threatened, to seize that point and form in close array and fight as well as ever.[28]

The importance of teamwork and the 'onion layer' system of subordinate command to the continued effectiveness of Spartan forces is further demonstrated by Thucydides' description of the Spartan response to the appearance of an Argive-led army on the day of the battle of Mantinea:

> When the king is in the field he is in complete command. He personally determines the requisite orders and gives them to the polemarchs; they pass them on to the divisional commanders, and then in sequence the orders are transmitted from divisional commander (*lochagos*) to company commander (*penteconter*) to unit commander (*enômotarchês*) to unit. Any subsequent instructions needed follow the same route and arrive quickly.

---

[26] Thuc. 5.68; Xen. *Hell* 6.4.12, 17. van Wees 2004, 98, 277.
[27] E.g. Thuc. 4.125-7; Xen. *Hell* 4.5.14-16.
[28] Plut. *Vit.Pel.* 23 (trans Perrin.). Lazenby 1985, 160; Wheeler 2007, 215.

Virtually the whole of the Spartan army is a system of command within command, and responsibility for action is widely shared.[29]

Thucydides most likely gave this description of the Spartan officer system as an introduction to, or pre-emptive explanation of, the refusal of Agis' orders by two subordinate commanders which occurred later in the battle, and it reinforces the point made above about the complexity of the Spartan command structure.[30] Thucydides does not explain the purpose behind this structure, or directly compare it to that of any other state, but the implication is relatively clear: other states used their own systems of subordinate command, but the Spartan system was quicker, more effective, and more professional.[31] Indeed such was the importance of the subordinate command structure to Spartan armies that each of the seven divisional commanders present at the battle of Mantinea decided upon the depth of his own formation.[32]

Thus each division of the Spartan army was able to arrange its ranks according to the nature and size of the enemy force directly opposing it while also adhering to the overall formation structure and battle plan, decided upon by Agis. However, at Manintea this battle plan was changed by Agis at the last minute when he attempted to shift two divisions to the left in order to match the enemy line; Agis' orders were refused by the polemarchs of the divisions, and a hole was left in the Spartan phalanx as a result.[33] The polemarchs were later exiled for cowardice, but their decision, indeed their *ability*, to refuse a direct battlefield order indicates the importance of subordinate commanders to the Spartan army, the close connection between the polemarch and his division, and the difference in experience and ability between the polemarchs present and Agis, in overall command. Indeed, Agis does not seem to have been a particularly gifted commander: his order would have resulted in the two divisions presenting their unshielded side to an advancing enemy in close proximity, a potentially disastrous situation that the two polemarchs flatly refused to be drawn into.[34] This tactical mistake can be added to the one he nearly made

---

[29] Thuc. 5.66 (trans Hammond.) Anderson 1970, 71-2; Cawkwell 1989, 382.
[30] Hornblower 2008, 174.
[31] Lazenby 2004, 121.
[32] Thuc. 5.68.
[33] Thuc. 5.71.
[34] Thuc. 5.71-2. 5.10 for the danger of marching with the unshielded side to the enemy. Tritle 2010, 124, who also comments that this has factor has, hitherto, been unrecognized by modern scholars. Lazenby 2010, 123-5.

the day before the battle, which was only avoided by the shouted advice of a 'veteran',[35] and his earlier decision to agree to a peace treaty with Argos when he could have crushed their army in the field; a decision he took without consultation and for which he was heavily criticised.[36] On each occasion Thucydides directly or indirectly implies that Agis' authority was challenged or defied by subordinates – men who were narrowly able to prevent the King from leading them into dangerous situations thanks to their official authority within the Spartan system and, presumably, their influence over, and loyalty with, the men in their division.

Throughout his work, Aeneas Tacticus emphasises the need for the state's general to remain in overall command of the defence of the city and to engage in a proactive defence of the borders and external territories of the state.[37] However, he does not expect the general to act alone, and offers a significant piece of advice to his audience which would increase their ability to command the defence and control their forces: the creation of street level sub-ordinate commanders. The discussion of these commanders comes in the second half of an analysis of how best to post guards; Aeneas first advises that in the event of a panic or an unexpected attack the tribes of the city should be assigned by lot a section of wall to guard (3.4-6). It is unlikely that this initial organisation would be by street, unless the citizens of the street in question were actually working together during the time the threat was detected. However, the existence of these street commanders would allow a recognised system of command to exert itself until the initial ad-hoc units could be re-organised into the units within which the citizens were used to fighting. Aeneas Tacticus advises that this system be adopted as it provides an immediate and effective response should anything occur during the night, a time when street-level command is an obvious choice. However, it is clear that it would be effective at other times, and also carries with it several other distinct advantages which fit well with Aeneas Tacticus' view of how to resist enemy aggression.

By taking command down to the street level the general could organise armed forces, undertake military action, maximise the advantage to be gained from local geographical knowledge, and could gain a simpler and more accurate count of his military forces. Street-commanders also

---

[35] Thuc. 5.65.
[36] Thuc. 5.61-3. Hornblower 2008, 167-8: Agis was fined and could no longer withdraw an army from enemy land unless he had the support of ten appointed Spartiates; however, his ability to otherwise command the army was not reduced.
[37] See, e.g. 1.7; 15-16; 22.2-5; 26.11.

highlight the level of preparedness, caution, and attention to details which Aeneas Tacticus recommends; the general should do his utmost to keep the enemy away from the walls of the city, but should also be realistic and have procedures in place in case the walls are breached, a situation where the ability to organise and command a 'rolling' system of street fighting would be vital (1.4-9). The response of the Plataeans to the Theban incursion into their city in 431 is a fine example of how effective such a system could be:

> They gathered together by digging through the party walls between their houses, to avoid being seen on the move in the streets; they dragged carts without their draught-animals into the streets to act as a barricade; and they made all other arrangements which seemed suitable in the circumstances. (Thuc. 2.3)[38]

This was a complex, but effective, response to the Theban attack; Thucydides gives no clue as to how it was organised, but the principles behind it are the same as those that Aeneas Tacticus advocates: local knowledge of terrain and geography was combined with a surprise attack, resulting in the Thebans being surrounded and unable to escape.[39]

Although the break out was successful, it caused a minimum of damage to the Peloponnesian force, so perhaps something similar to Brasidas' ambush of Cleon at Amphipolis is a more appropriate example: constant observation of the enemy, combined with Brasidas' desire to engage an army that was, according to Thucydides, light on discipline and effective leadership, resulted in a comprehensive Peloponnesian victory.[40] Before the engagement, Thucydides has Brasidas deliver a speech, of which Aeneas Tacticus would undoubtedly approve, in which he praises the use of unorthodox methods and distances himself from any set 'form' of engagement, stating that:

> These are the tricks of war, and win great acclaim when the enemy is

---

[38] Trans. Hammond.

[39] Thuc. 2.3-5, 75-8; 3.21-4. Aeneas clearly knew of Thucydides' account of the siege of Plataea, and comments on the effectiveness of the Plataean response in 2.2-6, however his detail regarding the Plataean authorities delaying and distracting the Theban incursion force is not found in Thucydides. Hornblower 1991, 240-3; Whitehead 2002, 102-3.

[40] Thuc. 5.8-11. See Anderson 1965, 1-4 and Best 1969, 29-35. Aeneas would probably prefer the general to survive such actions, however.

completely fooled to the maximum benefit of one's own side.[41] (Thuc. 5.9)[42]

Later in the speech Brasidas points out that reinforcements are more formidable to the enemy than those soldiers already fighting, a point reproduced, in very similar language, by Aeneas Tacticus (38.2). Hornblower recognises the importance of this, however he does not comment on the military significance;[43] clearly Aeneas Tacticus knew his Thucydides, and Thucydides, like Aeneas Tacticus, recognised the importance of communication, ruse, subordinate commanders, and mixed forces to effective generalship.[44] Indeed, the sentiments expressed by Brasidas, and the attack that followed, are so close to Aeneas Tacticus' overall conception of warfare that we must credit Thucydides as being, if not a significant influence, then at least a significant source of information for him.[45]

A vital element of Aeneas Tacticus' advice is the use of small units, and an important point regarding the effectiveness and importance of subordinate commanders, and the flexibility of hoplites themselves, can be made by examining the evidence for small phalanxes and elite units in the contemporary historians of Classical Greece.[46] These units can be found in the pages of all the major contemporary historians, where they operate independently and in conjunction with other phalanxes, and also appear to

---

[41] Thucydides specifically refuses to refer to this engagement as a *parataxis*. See 4.126 where Brasidas suggests the skirmishers his army faces are cowardly and undisciplined; his speech appears more motivational than rhetorical as he closes with the warning that the enemy still pose a significant threat if they are underestimated.

[42] Trans. Hammond.

[43] Hornblower 1995, 53; 1996, 444. Whitehead 2002, 201.

[44] Thucydides also has Lamachus make a variation on this point at 6.49, where he advises that the Athenians must attack Syracuse sooner rather than later, as the longer an army remains on enemy soil without attacking the less fearful it is to the enemy.

[45] Hornblower 1996, 444 describes the similarity of Aen. Tact. 38.3 and Thuc. 5.9 thus: "This shows that one not very famous or obvious bit of Th. was known to one not specially intellectual reader, and this has implications for our view of the reception of Th." However, it also has great implications for our understanding of the development of warfare, and surely indicates that Aeneas Tacticus cannot be fairly described as 'not specially intellectual'! Amphipolis is discussed below.

[46] Discussions of such units can be found in Van Wees 2004, 57-60. See also Pritchett 1974, 221-5; Lazenby 1985, 54-6; 55-6; Hutchinson 2000, 100-1; Hunt 2007, 144-5; Wheeler 2007, 220-1.

have been highly flexible. Some are examples of infantry undertaking specific 'missions' in, usually, highly dangerous situations which required the ability to react to changing circumstances, while others appear to show the importance of a fine 'cutting edge' to a phalanx of hoplites; they are vital to any discussion of infantry battle in Classical Greece, and their implications have not been fully realised.

The most famous example of a small unit of hoplites is, of course, that of the 300 Spartans who fought to the death at Thermopylae, however, I believe less exceptional examples can be more fruitfully examined, so I will pass over 'The' 300 here and move on to other units of 300 used during the Persian invasions. Units of this size were used by both the Thebans and Athenians during the battle of Plataea and, although little information regarding the Theban unit survives, beyond their fighting to the death, we are better informed about the Athenian unit (Hdt. 9.67).[47] According to Herodotus, the Megarian contingent of the allied Greek army was under heavy cavalry attack and sent a message threatening to abandon their position if help was not forthcoming; a contingent of 'picked' Athenian hoplites and archers, under the command of the previously unmentioned Olympiodorus, volunteered to help.[48] The description of the men as 'picked' (λογάδες) raises the question 'picked by whom?' No elite body of Athenian hoplites existed at this time, and Diodorus' assertion that they were the bodyguard of Aristides is difficult to accept, as no other source supports a tradition that Athenian generals were assigned a bodyguard as a matter of course.[49] Indeed, the assignation of such a bodyguard seems very unlikely for Athenians in this period given the tradition concerning Peisistratos' bodyguard and the imposition of tyranny.[50] The unit of 300 in question may have been picked on the spot by Olympiodorus himself, or may have been pre-selected as a 'rapid-reaction force.' The latter seems more likely given the need for a quick and

---

[47] The 300 Thebans are described as πρῶτοι καὶ ἄριστοι (foremost/best and bravest) and, given the existence of Theban units of 300 in Thucydides and Xenophon, it is reasonable to assume they were a distinct group: Van Wees 2004, 59. Herodotus also reports that 300 Spartans, commanded by one Arimnestus, fought to the death when they took on the entire Messenian army at the battle of Stenyclerus: 9.64.
[48] Hdt. 9.21-3. How & Wells 1912, 295; Lazenby 1993, 222-3; van Wees 2004, 181.
[49] Diod. Sic. 11.30.3. Diodorus may have confused the Spartan institution of *hippeis* with the force that Herodotus describes. Lazenby 1993, 222; Hunt 2007, 144.
[50] Hdt. 1.59; Aristotle *Const. Ath* 14.1.

effective response, which may not have been possible had an *ad hoc* unit been assembled.[51] Regardless of why and how the unit was formed, the principle remains the same: the Athenian response to an urgent request for help was to send a unit of 300, led by a subordinate commander, *not* to march with a large force under the command of a general.

Herodotus reports that the new Athenian deployment was effective; the Persian cavalry commander Masistius' horse was hit by an arrow, and Masistius himself was immediately set upon and killed (Hdt. 9.22; Plut. *Vit. Arist* 14.5).[52] The account of this incident suggests the Athenian force was flexible and under effective command; in order to take out Masistius, hoplites would, presumably, have had to leave the formation and engage him in combat or finish him off, while the order to do so must have come quickly if Masistius was dead by the time the Persian cavalry came around for another pass (Hdt. 9.20-4).[53] The conspicuous glory of the Athenian force could suggest a potential difficulty with the account, however, the Athenians seem to have been the only contingent to have brought an organised force of archers to the battle, and therefore their deployment against cavalry would have made a great deal of sense.[54]

The first notable battle descriptions of the Peloponnesian War were not hoplite engagements, but rather city-fighting, siege breaking, and clashes between hoplite forces and light infantry. The initial response of the Plataeans to the Theban incursion into their city is discussed above, but the break *out* of the city by Plataean forces after nearly two years of siege has not yet been analysed. This break out was innovative and effective and was designed to limit the impact that a patrolling unit of 300 Peloponnesians could have on the escape; clearly the Plataeans regarded the speed and flexibility of this small unit as a significant threat (Thuc.

---

[51] E.g. while the mercenaries of the 10,000 formed a unit of slingers to counter the range of Persian archers, they did so *after* they had escaped the ambush – if professionals could not form such a unit on the spot it seems unlikely that amateur Athenians could. Xenophon *Anab* 3.3.6-20.
[52] How & Wells 1912, 295.
[53] Burn 1984, 517-8; Lazenby 1993, 222.
[54] Burn 1984, 424 for the suggestion that this force was a "… 'task force' specially adapted for advanced guard action…" The suggestion is sensible, especially given the later Spartan request for their deployment to a different section of the line: Hdt. 9.60. Green 1996, 246 refers to them as "…a special Athenian commando force…which had been posted well ahead of the main line, perhaps as shock troops" which seems a bit much. See also Lazenby 1993, 222.

3.23).[55] Thucydides does not record any details regarding who was in command of the breakout, although he does give good details about the action itself: the force made use of scouting and intelligence by observing that the Peloponnesian guards withdrew to the towers of the circumvallation wall during inclement weather and the Plataeans exploited this by making their breakout during a stormy and moonless night.[56] Stealth and surprise were vital if the force was to be successful, so each man was only lightly equipped, while the force as a whole was spread out in order to prevent weapons from clashing and alerting the guards (Thuc. 3.21-2).[57] The advantages that scouting, stealth, and surprise offered the Plataeans were increased by the effective use of ruse: as the breakout force approached the Peloponnesian wall, the remainder of the Plataeans launched an overt attack on the section of wall directly opposite, and lit a number of beacon fires in response to a Peloponnesian fire signal to Thebes indicating enemy action:

> Beacons were lit to send the signal of enemy action to Thebes, but the Plataeans in the city countered by lighting several beacons on their own walls (they had prepared them in advance for this very purpose) to confuse the beacon-signals received by the enemy, in the hope that they would misinterpret what was happening and not arrive in support until their own escapees had got clear and reached safety. (Thuc. 3.22)[58]

So the Plataean breakout was supported by intelligence regarding the probable Theban response, and a method to counter this was devised. Finally, the breakout force carried a mixture of weapons, with archers and javelin throwers proving their worth by engaging the enemy at a distance (Thuc. 3.23-4). The initial Plataean resistance, discussed above, and this breakout, could not have been achieved without several subordinate commanders being in place to offer advice or take control of confusing and dangerous situations that occurred in darkness, while the Peloponnesian unit of 300 represents a concern on their part for the ability to respond to any aggression from the city rapidly and effectively.

Thucydides' account of the battle of Sphacteria in 425 contains a great deal of useful information regarding the power and flexibility of small

---

[55] See also 7.43 where the Syracusans form a unit of 600 hoplites to guard Epipolae.
[56] Although he does mention that it was originally suggested by Theaenetus, a seer, and Eupompides, a general: Thuc. 3.20.
[57] Lazenby 2004, 52.
[58] Trans. Hammond.

units, and the willingness of Greek commanders to focus on results, rather than methods. He states that the Athenian forces included 800 archers, a similar number of peltasts, and the crews of 70 ships, variously equipped. These men were organised into units of around 200, occupied the high ground, and constantly harassed the Spartan hoplites; their missiles were highly effective, and they appear to have remained under command and control by their own commanders throughout the engagement (Thuc. 4.31-2).[59] Local knowledge was also important: the commander of the Messenian contingent requested that he be given a unit in order to find a path behind the Spartan position, while the Spartans themselves were unaware of the vulnerability of their position until it was too late.[60]

> With no end in sight, the commander of the Messenians came up to Cleon and Demosthenes and told them that they were wasting their efforts: if they were prepared to let him have a section of the archers and the light infantry he would go round behind the Spartans by any route he could find, and he thought he could force the approach. (Thuc. 4.36)[61]

The allusion to chance or luck ("...any route he could find...") here is suspect. Indeed, Thucydides credits the Athenian general Demosthenes with so much luck during the Pylos/Sphacteria campaign that his account has been doubted in this regard: Messenian reinforcements just happen to arrive before the engagement (Thuc. 4.9), and the Athenians accidentally burn down the woodland on Sphacteria, thus revealing the Spartan positions (Thuc. 4.29-30).[62] It would be fair to state that the Messenian commander knew of, or had been told about, a path behind the Spartan position, and suggested to the Athenian commanders that an attack be launched to exploit it (Thuc. 4.36).[63] The engagement epitomises the combination of qualities and techniques which Aeneas Tacticus advises are

---

[59] Hornblower 1996, 189.
[60] Thucydides compares the Spartan situation to that of Thermopylae; however, it is likely that this is as a result of the encirclement which ended the engagement, rather than the significant role of any path. Hornblower 1996, 32-4, 191-2. Connor 1984, 118 for the comment that Thucydides' comparison is designed to enhance the shock of the Athenian victory, as the Spartans would have been expected to fight to the death.
[61] Trans. Hammond.
[62] I find it entirely unlikely that the fire was accidental: Thucydides himself points out the importance of fire to Demosthenes' defeat in Aetolia only the year before. See also Woodcock 1928, 101; Best 1969, 21-4; Wilson 1979, 103; Roisman 1993, 33-41. Also Miller 1998.
[63] On this see Roisman 1993, 33-41.

most important: the Athenians scouted the terrain, removed obstacles, occupied high ground, attacked with multiple small units, and used ruse and surprise to their advantage. The Athenian general, Demosthenes, does not appear to have joined in the fighting. Instead, he appears to have taken on the role of director, as Aeneas Tacticus advises: the fact that the Messenian commander sought out Demosthenes and Cleon to request forces for his flanking attack indicates that both were distant from the front line; most likely they remained with the hoplites on an elevated position and let subordinates carry out the attack as previously planned – Thucydides does not say.[64] The Athenian attack relied upon several units of light infantry attacking simultaneously. These units were under the command of subordinate officers who appear to have been aware of an overall strategy, but who had to request permission from Demosthenes to deviate from this strategy. The victory on Sphacteria was not lucky, or based solely on a mis-match between light infantry and hoplites fighting on difficult terrain; rather it was based on intelligent generalship and the effective use of multiple subordinate commands.

The use of small units by the Spartan general Brasidas in engagements in 423 and 422 differed significantly from that of Demosthenes. At Lyncus in 423, Brasidas commanded a phalanx of 300 hoplites as a 'flying rearguard' and left the command of his main phalanx to a subordinate (Thuc. 5.9-10). This battle was not a pitched battle, but it is of central importance to this discussion as a Spartan subordinate commander, Clearidas, is directly mentioned by Thucydides, and the presence of such commanders in the Athenian army can also be inferred. The engagement is also interesting as it demonstrates that armies could survive the death of their general, and could continue the engagement with little interruption if a clear chain of command existed.[65] Indeed, the Peloponnesian force was able to make a significant tactical shift during this final phase of battle; a shift which

---

[64] That a hoplite general would remain with his hoplites, probably in the front ranks, is argued by Hanson 2000 108-116. Wheeler 1991, reacting to the first edition (1989) of *The Western Way of War* attempted to demonstrate that generals did not *always* stand in the front ranks, but nonetheless based his theory on leadership by example and the emotional link between general and army. Anderson 1970 70-1. Schwartz 2009, 180-183 follows Hanson closely, stating that "The best way a general could exert himself was…by being among his men and setting a good example in order to boost morale and fighting spirit." See also Paul 1987, 307-8, and Crowley 2012, 114-7. While the sources indicate that generals usually fought in the front ranks, I do not see any tactical or doctrinal reason why they could not be elsewhere.

[65] *contra* Hanson 2000.

resulted in a comprehensive victory and which is all the more significant when it is remembered that Brasidas' mortal wounding occurred early in the battle (Thuc. 5.10).[66] The existence of an authoritative and immediate source of orders and authority appears to have been more important than the continued existence of the ultimate source of orders and authority as vested in Brasidas.[67]

Brasidas was aware that Cleon was advancing on Amphipolis, but decided to withdraw rather than risk a pitched battle; Thucydides reports that Brasidas regarded the Athenians as being superior troops, although given Brasidas' previous experience it is more likely that the expertise of his troops lay in methods of engagement other than pitched battle, such as ambush, ruse, and shock attacks (Thuc. 5.8).[68] This expertise was to be demonstrated with a planned assault from two city gates, although Cleon was able to deduce such an attack was imminent and passed orders to begin an immediate withdrawal to the nearby port of Eion.[69] This order resulted in the Athenian right flank marching parallel to the city, thus presenting their shield-less side to attack, an opportunity that Brasidas seized immediately, leading 150 hoplites directly against the Athenian centre. This advance was supported by the rest of his forces, led by Clearidas, who led the main phalanx from a different gate. This was successful, and Brasidas' force suffered only seven casualties, although

---

[66] Brasidas was carried from the fighting back to the city, apparently expiring shortly after being told his attack had been successful.

[67] See also Xen. *Hell* 3.5.17-20 where a Spartan force was able to rally and counter attack, despite having lost their commander – a subordinate or other influential individual must have played an important role.

[68] Gomme 1962, 116 describes Brasidas' admission as a "…notable tribute to the Athenian hoplite…" Hornblower 1996, 440 agrees, describing the "…reference to Peloponnesian inferiority in quality (as) remarkable…" However, Brasidas' remark is less a tribute to the quality of the Athenian troops than a realisation that his own troops were unaccustomed to fighting pitched battles versus hoplites. Lazenby 2004, 102 makes the valid point that if Brasidas felt his troops to be inferior in every respect then one has to wonder why he attacked at all.

[69] Anderson 1965, 1-4 suggests the signal was given by trumpet but was not immediately obeyed by the whole army; Krentz 1991, 116-7 suggests a trumpet signal in such a scenario is insufficient given the complicated nature of the command. Cleon would have had to make several manoeuvres if he was to withdraw without presenting his phalanx's shield-less side to the city. Lazenby 2004, 103 suggests the order could have meant 'retreat in good order', given that Thucydides has Nicias believe he had plenty of time to make his reconnaissance and withdraw. See also Kagan 1974, 327-9; Hornblower 1996, 446-7.

Brasidas himself was one of these (Thuc. 5.10).

The Athenian force was pursued and harried for some distance, although the right wing offered some resistance and was able to retreat to a nearby hill. Thucydides does not comment on how this retreat was organised, but given that Cleon had been killed it is reasonable to assume that subordinate commanders, or experienced individuals, were able to rally the wing and establish some sort of order. From this hill, the Athenians were able to repulse two or three attacks from the main body of Peloponnesian hoplites before being surrounded by cavalry and peltasts and broken by a hail of javelins. The marshalling and effective use of cavalry and peltasts by the Peloponnesian force suggests that Clearidas, realising the strength of the Athenian position and the danger of continuing to attack with his hoplites, issued orders which resulted in the cavalry and light infantry surrounding and attacking the Athenians from range (Thuc. 5.10).[70]

Thus far we have seen units of 300 forming 'flying reserves' and rapid reaction forces, as well as a unit of 150 forming a 'shock' phalanx used in an ambush which, although led by a general, not a subordinate, was based on the same principle: a small, manoeuvrable and flexible force with which to disrupt and distract the enemy. We have space here for one more example. In 414 a unit of 300 Athenian hoplites was created in order to secure a section of the Syracusan wall, which they captured with the aid of an unspecified number of light infantry (Thuc. 6.100-101). Thucydides describes the light force as 'picked' (λογάς) and explains that the rest of the army was divided into two, each half commanded by a general, which suggests the picked force was under the command of at least one subordinate.[71] A comparison to the picked force of hoplites and archers

---

[70] Trans. Hammond.
[71] The Athenian force had been reduced to two generals after the arrest of Alcibiades: Thuc. 6.62. Nicias and Lamachus had, after this, split the army between them by lot, and so were presumably familiar with the men under their direct control. One of the Athenian responses to Nicias' letter in book 7 was to promote two officers, Menandrus and Euthydemus, to act as co-commanders. It is possible one, or both, of these individuals was in charge of the unit of 300 – Develin 1989 suggests, plausibly, that they had been *taxiarchs* (regimental commanders) up to the point they were promoted. They appear to have been promoted to 'full' command (στρατηγοί) but do not feature in the discussion between Nicias and Demosthenes after the failed attack on Epipolae (7.47), hence they may only have acted as generals when Nicias required assistance and before the reinforcements arrived. Dover 1988, 392; Hamel 1998, 196-200; Hornblower

which the Athenians deployed at the battle of Plataea can be made: both were used to solve particular problems, both involved the combined use of hoplites and light infantry, and both operated under the command of a subordinate. Some 66 years separates the engagements, and as such I am reluctant to describe this as a specialist 'Athenian tactic', however, the similarity is so striking that the possibility that Olympiodorus' command survived in the collective Athenian military memory, or was an ingrained or 'default' response to emergencies, cannot be dismissed.[72]

Small, and elite, units are also found in the pages of Xenophon's *Hellenica* where they engage in skirmishing and baiting tactics (Xen. *Hell* 2.4.5-8, 31-35), ambush enemy troops (Xen. *Hell* 4.5.13-18; 4.8.34-8), and serve as the bodyguard of a King in a large phalanx (Xen. *Hell* 6.4.13-14).[73] In the *Anabasis*, small units are formed to deal with specific threats (Xen. *Anab* 3.3.6-20), and to act as a rear-guard (e.g.4.3.20), while the 10,000 as a whole was structured in such a way that the creation and dissolving of units with specific tasks was relatively simple.[74] There is not space to examine and incorporate these examples here, suffice it to say that they continue the trend identified above.

Subordinate commanders leading small units were vital to the ability of the Greeks to resist the Persian invasions; that they were used during moments of crisis by both Athens and Sparta suggests they were not a new or innovative response, while their ability to move rapidly, to resist both infantry and cavalry attack, and to operate with archer support indicates they were flexible and under effective command. These qualities remained central to Greek military thought throughout the fifth century, and a number of small units, some 300 strong, some smaller, played important, illuminating, and generally underappreciated roles in the Peloponnesian War. The deployment and success of these units has interesting implications for the on-going discussions regarding the mechanics and theories behind warfare in the Classical Greek world, and further study of

---

2008, 569-70.
[72] Yaginuma 1990, 281-5 for the observation that this sentence contains 137 words, compared to an average in Thucydides of 25.3, because of the scale of Athenian action in the build-up to the capturing of the wall. The situation was certainly complex, involving numerous units and phalanxes all working to one goal, but semi-independently of each other, another reason to compare this engagement with that of Plataea.
[73] Lazenby 1985, 156-7, although see Figuera 2006, 73-4.
[74] See, e.g, *Anab* 3.4.19-23.

the social and military issues raised by their presence in the source material will greatly aid our understanding of how, and why, the Greeks engaged in warfare.

Modern scholarship is slowly, reluctantly, giving Aeneas the recognition he deserves: in his *Western Way of War*, published in 1991, Hanson referred to him as presenting an "...especially idiosyncratic viewpoint..." and I note with pleasure that in his contribution to the *Cambridge History of Greek and Roman warfare* Hanson has upgraded Aeneas to a "...pragmatic guide...." Perhaps in ten years' time we will see Aeneas installed in his rightful place, as a man who used his practical and theoretical knowledge to codify what seemed to him to be the most effective way of keeping a state, broadly defined, safe. Significant parts of his work can be read as a guide to engaging the enemy in the field, and it is noteworthy that at no point does he discuss the need, or desire, to engage in a pitched battle. His advice relies heavily on the use of small units, communication, and the predictability of human nature; the enemy must not be underestimated, he tells us, and it should be assumed that they will be as well prepared, and as ruthless, as the defenders.

The importance of small units and subordinate commanders in Aeneas' text can also be found in the pages of the three great historians of the Classical age, where they operate in a similar fashion; undertaking specific actions with regard to an overall plan, whether it be to support weak sections of a massive and static army, to launch a diversionary attack, or to cover the retreat of a larger body of men. These units, beyond the Theban Sacred Band, do not really feature in the writings of the orthodox school, and it is perhaps easy to see why. They represent everything that *the Western Way of War* sought to play down: they indicate that the Greeks, from the time of the Persian Wars, were not bound to a system of warfare which concentrated on 'getting it over and done with' in a single, somehow fair, engagement; that tactical concerns beyond depth of rank and width of file existed and were considered; and, with Aeneas Tacticus' work, that the 'everyday' form of warfare that the vast majority of states engaged in was focused on one thing - the destruction of the enemy by any means necessary and possible.

BIBLIOGRAPHY

Adcock, F. E. (1957) *The Greek and Macedonian Art of War*. Los Angeles.
Anderson, J. K. (1965) "Cleon's Orders at Amphipolis," *Journal of Hellenic Studies* 85, 1-4.
—. (1970) *Military Theory and Practice in the Age of Xenophon*. Berkeley.
Best, J. (1969) *Thracian Peltasts and their Influence on Greek Warfare*. Groningen.
Burn, A. (1984) *Persia and the Greeks: The Defence of the West*. London.
Cartledge, P. (1977) "Hoplites and Heroes: Sparta's Contribution to the Technique of Ancient Warfare," *Journal of Hellenic Studies* 97, 11-27.
Cawkwell, G. (1978) *Philip of Macedon*. London.
—. (1989) "Orthodoxy and Hoplites," *Classical Quarterly* 39, 375-89.
Crowley, J. (2012) *The Psychology of the Athenian Hoplite*. Cambridge.
Figuera (2006) "The Spartan Hippeis," in S. Hodkinson & A. Powell *Sparta and War*. Swansea, 57-85.
Fraser, A. (1942) "The Myth of the Phalanx Scrimmage," *Classical Weekly* 36: 15-16.
Green, P. (1996) *The Greco-Persian Wars*. Berkeley.
Goldsworthy, A. (1997) "The *Othismos*, Myths and Heresies: the Nature of Hoplite Battle," *War in History* 4, 1-26.
Gomme, A. (1937) *Essays in Greek History and Literature*. Oxford.
—. (1962) *More Essays in Greek History and Culture*. Oxford.
Grundy, G. (1948) *Thucydides and the History of his Age*. Oxford.
Holladay, A. (1982) "Hoplites and Heresies," *Journal of Hellenic Studies* 102, 94-103.
Hanson, V.D. (ed.) (1991) *Hoplites: the Classical Greek Battle Experience*. London.
—. (2000) *The Western Way of War*. Berkeley.
Hutchinson (2000) *Xenophon and the Art of Command*. London.
Hunt, P. (2007) "Military Forces," in Sabin, van Wees & Whitby, 108-146.
Hornblower, S. (1991 – 96 - 08) *A Commentary on Thucydides,* 3 vols. Oxford.
—. "Warfare in Ancient Literature: The Paradox of War," in Sabin, van Wees & Whitby, 22-53.
How, W. and Wells, J. A. (1912) *A Commentary on Herodotus*. Oxford.
Kagan, D. (1974) *The Archidamian War*. Ithaca.
Krentz, P. (1985) "The Nature of Hoplite Battle," *Classical Antiquity* 4, 50-61.
—. (1991) "The Salpinx in Greek Battle," in Hanson, 110-20.

—. (1994) "Continuing the *Othismos* on *Othismos*," *Ancient History Bulletin* 8: 45-9.
—. (2002) "Fighting by the Rules: the Invention of the Hoplite Agon," *Hesperia* 71, 23-39.
—. (2010) *The Battle of Marathon*. Yale.
Lazenby, J. (1985) *The Spartan Army*. Warminster.
—. (1993) *The Defence of Greece*. Warminster.
—. (2004) *The Peloponnesian War: A Military Study*. London.
Luther, A; Meier, M; Thommen, L. (eds.) *Das Fruhe Sparta*. Stuttgart.
Miller, A. (1998) "Thoukydides 4.30.4: Kleon, Demosthenes and Collusion of the Pylian Campaign?," *Mnemosyne* 51, 443-446.
Ober, J. (1996) *The Athenian Revolution: Essays on Ancient Greek Democracy and Political Theory*. Princeton.
Pritchett, W. (1974) *The Greek State at War*, vol 2. Berkeley
—. (1985) *The Greek State at War*, vol 4. Berkeley.
Rawlings, L. (2007) *The Ancient Greeks at War*. Manchester.
Roisman, J. (1993) *The General Demosthenes and His Use of Military Surprise*. Stuttgart.
Sabin, P, van Wees H & Whitby, M (eds.) (2007) *The Cambridge History of Ancient Warfare vol.1*. Cambridge.
Schwartz, A. (2002) "The Early Hoplite Phalanx: Close Order or Disarray?" *Classica et Mediaevalia* 53, 31-63.
—. (2009) *Reinstating the Hoplite*. Stuttgart.
van Wees, H. (ed.) (2000a) *War and Violence in Ancient Greece*. London.
—. (2004) *Greek Warfare: Myths and Realities*. London.
—. (2006) "The Oath of the Sworn Bands. The Acharnae Stela, the Oath of Plataea and Archaic Spartan Warfare," in Luther, Meier & Thommen (eds), 125-165.
Vernant, J-P. (ed) (1990) *Myth and Society in Ancient Greece*. New York.
Wheeler, E. (2007) "Land Battles," in Sabin, van Wees & Whitby, 186-222.,
Whitehead, D. (1990) *Aeneas the Tactician: How to Survive Under Siege*. Bristol.
Wilson, J. (1979) *Pylos 425 B.C: A Historical and Topographical study of Thucydides' Account of the Campaign*. Warminster.
Woodcock, C. (1928) "Demosthenes, Son of Alcisthenes," *Harvard Studies in Classical Philology* 39, 93-108.
Woodhouse, W. (1933) *King Agis of Sparta and his Campaign in Arkadia in 418B.C.* Oxford.
Yaginuma (1990) "Thucydides 6.100," in E. M. Craik (ed) *Essays On Classical Subjects for Sir Kenneth Dover*, 281-285, Oxford.

Chapter Five

To Use or Not to Use: The Practical and Historical Reliability of Asclepiodotus's 'Philosophical' Tactical Manual

Dr. Graham Wrightson

1 Introduction

Hellenistic and Roman tactical manuals dealing with the Macedonian style army were often, though not always, written by philosophers as theoretical exercises, but they were probably based on historical trends or examples.[1] They were designed to explain to readers the organisation and tactics of the armies with which they were familiar, both contemporary and historical.[2] The earlier manuals, such as those of Xenophon and Aeneas Tacticus, were explanatory pieces without being too theoretical and there is little conclusive evidence to show that the later manuals did

---

[1] The following paper will examine only extant tactical manuals that deal with Macedonian style armies, and only that of the earliest, Asclepiodotus, in detail. The phrase 'Macedonian style army' refers to the use of the sarissa phalanx (a phalanx is a closely packed formation of infantry) rather than the traditional Greek hoplite phalanx. The sarissa is the long pike first employed by Philip I of Macedon and subsequently used in all Macedonian style armies.

[2] Since manuals that discussed Macedonian style armies were written, according to Aelian's and Arrian's list of previous writers (see below), from the fourth century through to the second century CE they must have developed from discussing contemporary armies to inform readers about earlier historical armies. Aelian, in his *prooimion*, suggests that Frontinus, the well-known Roman politician, scholar and soldier, regarded Greek (meaning Macedonian style) warfare to be just as important to study as Roman (Aelian. *Tact.* Pr.3). On the use of military (and other technical) handbooks by the Romans see Campbell 1987.

not continue this educational aim.[3] Although the extant manuals of Asclepiodotus, Aelian and Arrian were primarily written by philosophers,[4] they are still sources of invaluable historical information about the organization and tactics of ancient Macedonian style armies. We cannot exclude everything that is evident in the tactical handbooks simply because they are theoretical creations. Although we cannot accept the reconstruction of an army in any manual as being a true historical account of the actual military structure in its entirety, some parts of it must be historical.[5] Consequently where there is supporting evidence from histories, inscriptions or other less philosophical sources we must conclude that that aspect of the tactical manual is historical. To what extent then can we find history in tactical manuals?

The first part of this paper will discuss the (philosophical) genre of tactical manuals concerning Macedonian style armies. The second part will examine in detail Asclepiodotus' manual, as the earliest of the extant manuals, to determine what parts may be considered historical. There is

---

[3] Xenophon wrote both *On the Cavalry Commander* and *On Horsemanship* as practical handbooks, and it is possible that the semi-fictional *Cyropaedia* was also meant to be educational. However, though his works on the cavalry are perhaps intended to be somewhat instructive, each one is "still far from being a military treatise from a literary point of view ..., and the purpose of the work is above all a didactic essay." Vela Tejada 2004, 141. Xenophon is not mentioned in Aelian's list (*Tact.* 1.2) of earlier tactical writers. Aeneas Tacticus is listed by Aelian as the first writer of tactics after Homer (*Tact.* 1.2), and he is also said, by Aeneas himself (7.4; 8.5; 11.2; 14.2; 21.1; 21.2; 38.5; 40.8) and again by Aelian (*Tact.* 1.2), to have written numerous works other than the one extant text *On the defence of fortified positions*. He is not of concern here as he wrote before the rise of the sarissa phalanx. On Aeneas' life and works see in particular: Whitehead 1990; Vela Tejada 1993. On the development of military writing up to and including the fourth century see Vela Tejada 2004.

[4] The first two were well known for their philosophical studies. Arrian alone of the three it seems was viewed as a philosopher as well as being a politician and military commander. See below (section 2.1) for more on Arrian.

[5] As Oldfather rightly states in his introduction to the Loeb text of Asclepiodotus, "It would be a mistake, however, to think too lightly of the value of even these late theoretical works upon phalanx tactics. They must consist in large part of quotations from early military handbooks, and these quotations are of the utmost historical value, even though they may be sometimes misunderstood, improperly elaborated, and occasionally treated in too theoretical a fashion. The materials for a reconstruction of Macedonian tactics are after all in a large measure preserved here, and it is the proper task of criticism to understand and interpret them." Oldfather 1923, 232-233.

not space to similarly examine Aelian's and Arrian's works. Six times Asclepiodotus, in discussing terms or unit divisions of the phalanx, states what used to be the case and what actually occurs now suggesting that he is indeed attempting to represent historical trends in the structure of the Macedonian style phalanx.[6]

2 MACEDONIAN TACTICAL MANUALS

The introductions to the manuals of Aelian and Arrian provide a list of earlier tactical writers (Arr. *Tact.* 1.1; Aelian. *Tact.* 1.1-4).[7] Aelian's is the most detailed.[8] After a discussion of Homer, Aelian mentions Aeneas Tacticus first, who he says wrote numerous works on tactics and was abridged by Cineas the Thessalian. Next, he mentions Pyrrhus the Epirote and his son Alexander (Aelian. *Tact.* 1.2). These, it seems, are Pyrrhus, who invaded Italy, and his son Alexander.[9] Following them he lists Clearchus, Pausanias, Euangelus, Polybius the Megalopolitan, Eupolemus, and Iphicrates. He concludes his list noting that "The Stoic Poseidonius also wrote a tactical theory" (Aelian. *Tact.* 1.2).[10] He goes on to say that many others have written about tactics either as introductions or in large volumes on tactics but are "too commonplace to be worthy of particular mention." (Aelian. *Tact.* 1.2). He complains further that "all these writers address those who are already acquainted with these matters." (Aelian. *Tact.* 1.3).

2.1 AELIAN AND ARRIAN

The manuals of Aelian and Arrian have been analysed in detail previously.[11] Aelian claims to want to write a manual that overcomes

---

[6] The numbers in the base unit; the name of the base unit and the names of its constituent parts and commanders; the position that the supernumeraries were attached; the name for the commander of a *taxis*; the name for wing commander; the name for the general. See below (Section 3.1) for a full discussion.

[7] The first part of Arrian's list is regrettably lost, but the rest closely parallels Aelian's. Polybius is described by Aelian as "much learned" and Poseidonius as "the Stoic." See Kochly and Rustow 1885, 1-209, 311-355.

[8] Of the three extant treatises Aelian's is the longest and Arrian's the shortest (if the section dealing exclusively with the Roman cavalry is excluded). See Devine 1994, 316-319,

[9] Pyrrhus' writings are mentioned by Cicero (*Ad. Fam.* 9.25.1) and Plutarch (*Vit. Pyrr.* 8.2). There is no other reference to Pyrrhus' son Alexander writing a work on tactics.

[10] All references to Aelian's work are from the Devine 1989 translation.

[11] Aelian: Devine 1989; Matthew 2012. Arrian: Stadter 1978; Bosworth 1993;

deficiencies in using technical language and can serve as an introduction to new students of warfare (Aelian. *Tact.* 1.4-6). However, in his preface Aelian admits that he has no experience of warfare but aims his work "as a Greek theoretical work and a polished dissertation," but that "the book will afford you [Trajan] an evocation of the dead, since in it you will observe Alexander the Macedonian's endeavours in marshalling his forces." (Aelian. *Tact.* Pref.6). Aelian, then, believed that the material in his work adequately described the historical army of Alexander. Aelian's work was read extensively in the sixteenth and seventeenth centuries as a model for the European armies that utilised the pike alongside the musket.[12] However, Bosworth dismisses Aelian's work as "wholly derivative, devoid of reference or relevance to the contemporary world."[13]

Arrian of Nicomedia was a Roman citizen of Greek ancestry in Bithynia and is best known now as a historian.[14] He studied at Nicopolis under Epictetus, and is the source for Epictetus' *Diatribae*.[15] He held numerous political posts under Rome at the time of Hadrian and was legate of Cappadocia.[16] However, in his own time Arrian was best known as a distinguished philosopher.[17] Arrian's work on tactics is later than Aelian's but is very similar in content, except that on occasion he includes other material and both are assumed to have shared a common source.[18]

Devine 1994; Devine 1995.

[12] For a full discussion of the reception of Aelian from Byzantium onwards see now Matthew 2012, xiii-xvii.

[13] Bosworth 1994, 257.

[14] See Wheeler 1977; Stadter 1980. Arrian is best known as the author of a key history of Alexander the Great, the *Anabasis*. On the *Anabasis* see Bosworth 1980, and 1988.

[15] See Stadter 1980, 4-5, 19-31; Brunt 1977. On Arrian's minor works see in particular Bosworth 1993. On Arrian's literary work see Bosworth 1972.

[16] On Arrian's life and position in Rome see Wheeler 1978; Stadter 1980; Bosworth 1993, 226-233; Devine 1994, 312-315. On his role as governor of Cappadocia see Bosworth 1977; Wheeler 1978; Devine 1994.

[17] Two inscriptions record Arrian as a philosopher (AE 1971.437 (Athens); AE 1968.473 (Corinth); cf. Bowersock 1967) and the *Suda* records that Cassius Dio wrote a history of Arrian the Philosopher. "To have earned his reputation as a philosopher Arrian presumably wrote widely in that genre; yet apart from his transcription of Epictetus' lectures and the miserable fragments of his pamphlet on comets our ignorance is absolute." Bosworth 1993, 233.

[18] For detailed comparison of the works of Aelian and Arrian side by side see: Stadter 1978. The early German edition of Aelian and Arrian by Kochly and Rustow 1855 2.1, 218-471 prints each text side by side. For other similarities and

Arrian's manual is distinctly separated into two sections. The first deals with the Macedonian style infantry phalanx and is the section that closely parallels Aelian and Asclepiodotus (Arr. *Tact.* 1-32). The second section deals with the maneuvers of the Roman cavalry and is much more detailed (Arr. *Tact.* 33-44). He also states that this section is meant to accompany an earlier work written on the Roman infantry that is now lost (Arr. *Tact.* 32.3). Stadter argues for Arrian's didactic intention for the *Tactica* in view of the clear similar intention for the *Expedition against the Alans*.[19] Arrian at least made an occasional attempt to keep his account of the Macedonian army relevant.[20]

Wheeler 1979 argues that Arrian actually describes the Roman army adopting a phalanx formation in battle, though Bosworth notes there are key differences between adopting a closely packed phalanx formation and fielding a Macedonian style phalanx armed with the sarissa.[21] Arrian, however, is clear himself that the phalanx structure and manoeuvres he presents are those used in the past but that no one would choose to be ignorant of them (Arr. *Tact.* 32.2).

2.2 POLYBIUS

Having discussed briefly the extant manuals of Aelian and Arrian, I shall now turn to the notable earlier manuals mentioned on the list of Aelian that were the forerunners of the extant texts. After Aeneas Tacticus (discussed above n. 3), Polybius, the famous historian of the late Republic, is the first notable name mentioned on the list about whose tactical manual we know something. He states in the *Histories* that he wrote a tactical work entitled *Notes on Tactics* (Polyb. 9.20.4).[22] He gives a brief account

---

differences alongside Asclepiodotus see also Devine 1995. On Aelian's and Arrian's work being based on an earlier original see in particular: Stadter 1978; Devine 1989; Devine 1994; Devine 1995.
[19] Stadter 1978, 119. For Arrian's manual being dedicated to Hadrian see in particular: Wheeler 1978.
[20] Arrian has received much attention from scholars in view of his position as the author of one of the key histories of Alexander the Great, the *Anabasis*. As stated above, he was a military commander himself, unlike Aelian, and so is deemed to be more militarily knowledgeable. On the history in Arrian's text see: Bosworth 1977; Bosworth 1993, 253-263; Devine 1994, 316-332. On Arrian's writing career see in particular Bosworth 1972.
[21] Bosworth 1994, 257. See also Wheeler 1978; Campbell 1987, 17-18 (concerning Aelian and Arrian), 24-27 (concerning the phalanx).
[22] See also: Ziegler 1953; Pedech 1969; Walbank 1972; Poznanski 1980. For the

of what he propounds in this work when trying to justify to his audience why a commander must learn astronomy and geometry before mastering the art of generalship in terms of organizing the layout of the camp. A discussion of geometrical and astronomical organization must then have figured as part of his tactical treatise, as well as the necessary discussion of strategy, training, and tactics.[23]

In his introduction to the *Histories* Polybius states that his goal in writing history is twofold: To provide useful training and experience for the actual politician and to show how to bear changes in Fortune by understanding those that overcame others (Polyb. 1.1.2). Polybius even criticizes earlier historians for confusing their aims in writing history and therefore blurring any benefits they can bring to their readers. He emphasizes that a successful historian should write about things with which he has had personal experience or at the very least a personal inquiry (Polyb. 12.25.4-12.28.5).[24] Truth is the goal of a historian,[25] and preferably unbiased or absolute truth.[26] Polybius also states that the first task for someone who wants to acquire the art of generalship is to study histories and the lessons in them (Polyb. 11.8.1-2)[27] and elsewhere that generalship is learned by normal experience, inquiry or specific experience (Polyb. 9.14.1). Polybius intended his history as an educational work,[28] and, considering his emphasis on truth and practical experience, his work on tactics probably had the same purpose.[29]

---

newest discussion of this topic see Sekunda 2006, 128-129.
[23] Aelian (Aelian. *Tact.* 3.4) states that Polybius defines tactics as: where a man takes a group of men, orders them into ranks and units and trains them sufficiently in all military matters.
[24] See Walbank 1970, vol. 1, 10.
[25] Polyb. 1.14.5-6, 2.56.2, 2.56.12, 3.47.6, 8.8.5-9, 10.21.8, 12.7.3-6, 12.2.8, 12.12.3, 12.27-28, 34.4.
[26] Polyb. 38.4.5. On Polybius' determination for truth in history see in particular Walbank 1970, vol. 1, 10-16.
[27] The term is used by Polybius to refer more specifically to military treatises (e.g. 10.44.1 to refer to Aeneas Tacticus' work), and some translations use this, but Walbank 1967, vol. 2, 279 states that there is no need to restrict the meaning from histories in this instance. Either translation suggests the same, that Polybius viewed histories to have an educational aim.
[28] "The didactic view of history which appears here [1.1.2] is common to the earlier Greek historians," and the view "...persists of course into Roman times;" Walbank 1970, 39.
[29] Pompey was marked out as having gained his knowledge of warfare through experience rather than reading (Cic. *De Imp. Cn. Pomp.* 27-8.), and Cicero

Devine argues that Polybius' manual was the archetype for all the later manuals including Poseidonius' as well as the three extant works of Asclepiodotus, Aelian and Arrian.[30] His argument resides solely on "the striking resemblance"[31] between parts of the three extant manuals and one section of Polybius' *Histories* where he describes the Macedonian phalanx.[32] It seems too much of a stretch in view of such a small sample size of evidence to conclude, as Devine does,[33] that this resemblance "argues very strongly for Polybius as the ultimate source of the entire tradition." He is perhaps right that Polybius' manual was the basis for Poseidonius' treatise,[34] but since neither of them is extant in significant fragments, let alone entire sections, this is surely conjecture that verges on an *argumentum ex silentio*. All we can say for certain is that Poseidonius wrote a work of history that was an acknowledged continuation of Polybius' *Histories* and that Poseidonius' work on tactics was written after Polybius' manual.[35] Poseidonius (and Asclepiodotus, Aelian and Arrian) may well have made use of Polybius' manual but there is nothing to suggest how much so.

2.3 POSEIDONIUS

The last person mentioned by name on Arrian's and Aelian's list of earlier writers, Poseidonius, was one of the most famous philosophers of his day. He was born in the late second century in Syrian Apamea on the Orontes in the Seleucid Empire.[36] He may have been a soldier[37] and went

---

(*Lucullus* 1.1-2) praises Lucullus, though he was leaving for command without military knowledge, for becoming a general through study. These statements suggest that it was possible to use manuals to become a general, as Polybius states. On the educational aims of manuals in Rome see: Campbell 1987.

[30] Devine 1995. Cf. Devine 1989, 33.
[31] Devine 1995, 41; Devine 1989, 33.
[32] Polyb. 18.29.1-18.30.4; Asclep. *Tact.* 5.1-2; Aelian. *Tact.* 14.1-6; Arr. *Tact.* 12.6-10.
[33] Devine 1995, 41; cf. Devine 1989, 33.
[34] Devine 1995, 41.
[35] Arrian's and Aelian's list of works confirms this obvious order of publication (Arr. *Tact.* 1.1; Aelian. *Tact.* 1.1-4). For more on Poseidonius see below section 2.4.
[36] *Suda*. Kristeller 1993, 124.
[37] Sekunda (1994, 5) argues that he was probably from a military family in Apamea and "would have had ample opportunity to see military service." According to Plutarch a certain Poseidonius was present on the Greek side at the battle of Pydna and wrote a life of Perseus in a number of books (Plu. *Vit. Aem.*

Chapter Five

to Athens for his education under Panaetius,[38] whose position as the most renowned philosopher he inherited,[39] spending most of his life teaching philosophy at Rhodes.[40] Existing fragments of his work, especially his *Histories*, show a deep-rooted interest in military affairs from tactics through to weapons.[41]

In view of Poseidonius' rhetorical training, it is generally believed that his work on tactics was purely theoretical, that it was a philosophical undertaking to create a logically structured army that was perfect in its formation. However, Sekunda points out that Poseidonius' theoretical army was probably based, however loosely, on the Seleucid army with which he was familiar and in which he may have served.[42] Galen twice calls Poseidonius the most scientific of all the Stoic philosophers.[43] Nock, after reviewing all the evidence for Poseidonius' philosophical writing and influence, concludes that "we can call him both a philosopher of science and a scientist."[44] This scientific approach suggests that Poseidonius was

---

19.4-5). However, this must be a different Poseidonius since the Stoic philosopher lived over 100 years later. Another Poseidonius is sent as one of three soldiers to negotiate with Judas Maccabeus in 161 (*2 Mac.* 14.19).
[38] *Suda*. Nock (1959, 4) suggests that Posidonius was introduced to Polybius' works through Panaetius.
[39] Strabo 16.2.10 describes Posidonius as "a man of the most extensive learning among the philosophers of our times" (tr. H.C. Hamilton). Posidonius was so revered by Pompey Magnus that on visiting his house he "forbade the lictor to knock at the door, as was the usual custom; and he, to whom both the eastern and the western world had yielded submission, ordered the fasces to be lowered before the door of a learned man." (Plin. *Nat.* 7.31, tr. J. Bostock).
[40] *Suda*. According to Strabo (7.5.8) Poseidonius became *prytanis* at Rhodes and Plutarch (*Vit. Mar.* 45.4) records him visiting Marius at Rome as part of a Rhodian embassy. He was a renowned philosopher there, as Pompey, after hearing one of his lectures, asked Poseidonius for advice (Strabo 11.1.6; cf. Cic. *Tusc.* 2.61). Cicero (Cic. *Tusc.* 5.107) includes him as someone who never returned to his birthplace. For general works on Poseidonius see: Bake 1810; Van Straaten 1946; Reinhardt 1953; Laffranque 1964; Kidd 1988.
[41] See Malitz, 1983, 8-10; Kidd 1988, 861-982; Muller 1896, vol. 3 245-96; Jacoby 1920, 87 & vol. 2 154-220. Rawson (1985, 109), in her review of Malitz 1983, states that "he [Posidonius] is surprisingly interested in warfare".
[42] Sekunda 1994, 5-6; and 2006, 128.
[43] Galen *De Placitis* 4.390, 8.652. Cf. Kidd 1988, 71 (T83, T84). "Thus, from very numerous quotations in Strabo and others, we gather that he was at any rate a scientist of very considerable repute." (Dobson 1918, 190).
[44] Nock 1954, 3.

concerned with fact not theory.[45] Arrian in his introduction to his tactical manual (Arr. *Tact.* 1.1-2) seems to suggest that Poseidonius was the only previous writer to produce a *techne taktike* as opposed to a *syggrammata*.[46] He goes on to criticize his predecessors for writing for experts and for not explaining their terminology, therefore, making their works useless to laymen. Perhaps, then, Poseidonius wrote a very scientific work infused with historical examples and terms that were not easily understood out of their historical context.[47]

Poseidonius is known to have written a history covering the Roman Republic from the point that Polybius finished through to the dictatorship of Sulla, suggesting that he was not averse to using historical evidence.[48] He also wrote a historical work on Pompey Magnus (Strabo 11.1.6). In fact, Galen comments that Poseidonius was wont to use historical examples in philosophical works (*PHP.* 4.397-403). Kidd in his commentary on the passage states that: "this is also clear evidence that history was used by him [Poseidonius] as an ethical tool".[49] Kristeller states that Poseidonius "distinguished himself in the field of historiography" and that "he shows a great interest for historical particulars".[50] A rhetorician described history as being philosophy with examples.[51] Strabo was of the view that his own work of history was useful as philosophy.[52] But Poseidonius was a

---

[45] Seneca (*Ep.* 90) records a level of practicality even in a rather fanciful description of the Golden Age of philosopher rulers. Nock (1954, 2-3) suggests that Poseidonius was Aristotelian in his tendency to search for explanations and facts. In his view it was this dedication to factual explanations that lifted Posidonius' writing on military tactics above other earlier Stoic philosophers: "He wrote, again, about the science of war, whereas most earlier Stoics would have been interested only in the theoretical assertion that the Wise Man would be the perfect general…"

[46] A tactical treatise rather than a simpler book.

[47] This is very similar to what we find in Asclepiodotus of a mixture of mathematically perfect formations given historically attested names. From Arrian's introduction we can perhaps infer that this technical style we see in Asclepiodotus was the common way of presenting a tactical manual and was used by *all* the previous authors of the genre, including Polybius and Poseidonius, and is not simply evidence of Asclepiodotus abbreviating Poseidonius' work in his own style.

[48] See: Kidd 1988, 861-982; Malitz 1983, 8-10.

[49] Kidd 1988, 594.

[50] Kristeller 1993, 124-5.

[51] [D. Hal.] *Ars rhet.* 11.2.

[52] 1.1.23 "Having already compiled our Historical Memoirs, which, as we conceive, are a valuable addition both to political and moral philosophy,…" (tr. H.C. Hamilton).

philosopher who was interested in history and not vice versa. "Posidonius would hardly have written so extensive a historical work had he not deemed it a task appropriate for a philosopher."[53] His purpose, perhaps, was to ensure that philosophy was better understood through the use of historical examples. Although it is possible that Posidonius constructed his ideal army purely for the philosophical exercise without a foundation in any real army, in view of his preference for fact, science and historical examples, the likelihood is that he was influenced to some degree by military practices with which he was familiar or that were historically attested.

Posidonius believed that a study of technical arts and sciences was different from philosophy, but often necessary for the philosopher in a study of the human condition (Sen. *Ep.* 88.21-8). Polybius is clear in his discussion of his own tactical work that it was intended as an actual guide for generalship, as discussed above. So Posidonius' tactical treatise, assuming that he wrote a work of tactics to match Polybius after continuing his history, may also have been intended for practical purposes. His choice of the Seleucid army as his model may have been designed to reveal to his Roman audience the merits and mysteries of a neighbouring empire's military system. As Sekunda states, "it would be logical to assume that the theoretical army whose organization was described by Posidonius was based, even if only loosely and in part, upon the Seleucid army in the last decades of the second century BC."[54] If Posidonius' work was based on a real army, then the subsequent authors, who may have used his treatise as the basis for their own, must also have some string of truth to their discussions.[55]

2.4 ASCLEPIODOTUS

Asclepiodotus is the author of the first fully extant military manual after Aeneas Tacticus. It is not clear precisely who Asclepiodotus was. He may have been a pupil of Posidonius, or may have simply listened to his lectures after they both graduated from the school of Panaetius at Athens before 109 BCE. An Asclepiodotus, son of Asclepiodotus of Nicaea, is

---

[53] Nock 1959, 4.
[54] Sekunda 1994, 6.
[55] Sekunda concludes the same thing concerning Asclepiodotus' manual: "...it would be reasonable to suppose that the military organization described by Asclepiodotus should, at least in part, reflect the organization of the Seleucid Army in the final decades of the second century," (Sekunda 1994, 6).

mentioned in a papyrus from Herculaneum which states that he was a pupil of Panaitius and that he probably also visited Rome.[56] Seneca (*Q Nat.* 2.26.6) describes a certain Asclepiodotus as an "*auditor Posidonii*" (lit. a listener of Posidonius) and references this Asclepiodotus repeatedly and separately from Poseidonius, clearly viewing him as an independently trustworthy scientific source.[57] He was certainly philosophically trained, whether by Poseidonius or Panaetius.[58] Other than that we can conclude very little about him. His only extant work is his tactical manual. It is generally agreed that his manual is an abbreviation or précis of Poseidonius' work.[59]

In view of the lack of evidence for the work of Poseidonius itself, it is perhaps rather presumptive to conclude that Asclepiodotus' manual is a summary of that of his contemporary, and here we should review the evidence for this argument.

1. Neither Aelian nor Arrian mention Asclepiodotus on their list of earlier writers.

2. Asclepiodotus' text seems to be rather cursory and somewhat elementary, and so is assumed to be a summary of an earlier, fuller account.

3. The manuals of Aelian and Arrian seem to be based on some earlier manual almost in entirety, because of their many mutual similarities, and there are differences from the manual of Asclepiodotus, so it cannot have been his. Poseidonius is the direct forerunner of all three authors, and the last name mentioned on Arrian's and Aelian's list of earlier writers, and so the differences between Asclepiodotus and the other two writers must be because his work is an all too brief summary of Poseidonius.

---

[56] Traversa 1952, 73, 3.
[57] Sen. *Q Nat.* 2.26.6; 2.30.1; 5.15.1; 6.17.3; 6.22.2.
[58] See below for a discussion of the evidence and the effect of Asclepiodotus' identity as a philosopher on the nature of his tactical work.
[59] See for example Sekunda 1994, 6: "Whoever 'Asclepiodotus the philosopher' was, and whatever his precise relationship to Poseidonius may have been, it is generally agreed that his tactical treatise must be very closely related to that of Poseidonius." See among others Muller 1896; Pedech 1969; Stadter 1978; Devine 1995.

Let us review these points. Firstly, 1 and 2: - Arrian and Aelian did not think that Asclepiodotus' work was worthy of a specific mention once they had listed Poseidonius. Perhaps to them the works of Poseidonius' successors were too similar to the earlier work to be worth categorizing. Aelian could be referring to Asclepiodotus when he mentions later works that were inferior and so not worthy of his list. Aelian mentions in his preface that tactical theory was "written about by many whose standing in scholarship was not reputed equal to mine," (Aelian. *Tact.* Pref.1), and perhaps this is intended as a slur on other Stoic philosophers such as Asclepiodotus. Aelian also states that his own ignorance of contemporary Roman military theory and practice prevented him "from handing down a science forgotten and moreover long out of use since the introduction of the other system by your [Trajan's] predecessors." (Aelian. *Tact.* Pref.2). This may imply that after the final Roman victory over Macedon, the Seleucids and Hellenistic Egypt, the number of tactical works written on Macedonian style armies lessened. Asclepiodotus, of course, wrote before the final Roman victory and so his manual would still reflect contemporary reality, at least in the Seleucid and Egyptian armies.

Arrian, as noted above, criticizes all the previous treatises for being too technical. Perhaps he omitted Asclepiodotus from the list because his work was not similarly technical. The cursory nature of Asclepiodotus' work lends weight to this argument. So Asclepiodotus' omission from the two lists may be not because his work was well known to later authors simply as an abbreviation of Poseidonius, but rather because his work was not detailed enough to be worthy of consideration. Omission from the list proves nothing. It is likely that other tactical treatises were written between Poseidonius and Aelian which were probably classified in his list as "too commonplace to be worthy of particular mention" (Aelian. *Tact.* 1.2), and unfortunately these other works have not survived in part or as references elsewhere.

Secondly, 3: - If Poseidonius' treatise was the basis for both Arrian's and Aelian's later works, and Asclepiodotus' text is simply a précis of Poseidonius' work, then these differences from Asclepiodotus have to be explained. The simplest explanation, and one that we cannot discount, is that Arrian, Aelian, and Asclepiodotus used some degree of originality in creating their manuals but followed the parameters set down by their most illustrious predecessor, Poseidonius. There is no evidence that Arrian and Aelian used Asclepiodotus' text as a basis for their own other than their many similarities to it in content and language.[60] If all three authors used a previous text as their main source, similarities would exist in each of their works without them actually having copied one another directly.[61] Since Poseidonius was possibly Asclepiodotus' lecturer and is the last author mentioned on the list of Arrian and Aelian, then his work was probably that mutual source. The similarities in the three authors exist because they all used Poseidonius' work as their main source, but each one added their own individual interpretations of the details creating noticeable differences.[62]

There is some debate amongst scholars concerning whether the work of Poseidonius that is assumed to be the archetype for the extant manuals of Asclepiodotus, Aelian and Arrian, was in fact Polybius' treatise.[63] However, the fact that Aelian ended with Poseidonius shows that he viewed this work as an important addition to the number of tactical manuals that preceded his. For him then to ignore it in writing his work and go back to Polybius' text would be rather strange. That is not to say that Poseidonius did not base his manual on Polybius'. Poseidonius' *History* was certainly a continuation of Polybius' work and so Poseidonius may have similarly intended to echo his predecessor's earlier work. If Asclepiodotus did produce a summary of Poseidonius' work without any innovations on his part, then Polybius' work cannot be the primary basis for Asclepiodotus' tactical treatise unless it was also the only source of Poseidonius' treatise. This is highly unlikely since this would undermine Poseidonius' status as the greatest original philosopher since Aristotle, as his large volume of work implies.[64] Sekunda rightly states that, "there is no reason to doubt that the work of Poseidonius was an entirely original work, based on his own knowledge and experience."[65]

---

[60] See Stadter 1978, 117-118.
[61] Kochly 1851 argued that Aelian's and Arrian's manuals were in fact different versions of the same manual. Dain 1946, 26-40 showed that this, and the view that Arrian copied Aelian, was false.
[62] See in particular Stadter 1978; Devine 1989; Devine 1994; Devine 1995.
[63] For a detailed discussion see: Sekunda 2006, 125-135. Sekunda is correct that when Aelian refers to Polybius' details in his tactical treatise he uses him as a point of contrast showing that Polybius' work differs from Aelian's source. Also see section 2.3 above on Polybius.
[64] Pedech 1969, xiii is indeed correct that Asclepiodotus could not be based on Polybius.
[65] Sekunda 2006, 128.

We can see that there is no definite reason for concluding that Asclepiodotus simply wrote an epitome of his professor. In fact we have more evidence for the contrary view. It is as follows: Seneca's references to Asclepiodotus show that he wrote independent and valuable philosophical works, but with similar themes to his more distinguished contemporary, specifically concerning meteorology.[66] If Asclepiodotus is correctly identified as the pupil of Panaetius and auditor of Poseidonius, then he and Poseidonius were direct contemporaries at school in Athens. This relationship is often used as evidence for Poseidonius' tactical manual being one of his early works so that Asclepiodotus could copy it. Sekunda states this when concluding that Asclepiodotus' manual was an epitome of Poseidonius'. But in the very next sentence he states that: "The precise relationship between the *Art of Tactics* of Poseidonius and Asclepiodotus is unknown. It could be held that Asclepiodotus simply copied Poseidonius, but there would be no evidence whatsoever for such a view. It seems more likely that we have a paraphrase or epitome of Poseidonius' earlier work."[67] Sekunda is correct that there is no evidence for Asclepiodotus having copied Poseidonius, but there is no definite evidence for him having epitomized his work either.

It seems very likely that Asclepiodotus and Poseidonius both wrote tactical manuals because that was one of the topics which a distinguished Greek philosopher was expected to consider. Vela Tejada notes that the genre of writing technical manuals, *Technai*, "whose subject deals with practical knowledge," developed from Ionian "practical catalogues" around 440 BCE "and finally became general in scientific-technical learning."[68] He goes on to discuss the influence of Sophists in teaching military science;[69] "the surest witnesses attest that Sophists were the first to teach *hoplomachia*, tactics and strategy."[70] Xenophon and Aeneas Tacticus, the earliest writers of military handbooks, were probably

---

[66] Asclepiodotus is referenced five times by Seneca. On each occasion he is used as an independent source for facts or interpretations on natural phenomena. Q Nat. 2.26.6; 2.30.1; 5.15.1; 6.17.3; 6.22.2-4. Although the Latin is corrupt, Seneca provides the title of Asclepiodotus' work, *aitiai phusikai* (causes of nature). See Kidd 1988, 30-33; 810-2; 819.
[67] Sekunda 2006, 130.
[68] Vela Tejada 2004, 144.
[69] Vela Tejada 2004, 145. Thesleff (1966, 106) notes that the Sophists did not begin the creation of technical manuals but rather popularized their use. On the Sophists' use of books see in particular O'Sullivan 1996, 116.
[70] A *hoplomachia* is the skill of fighting as a hoplite in the phalanx.

influenced greatly by the Sophists and Socrates.[71] Aelian notes that others before him believed that military science was the most useful of the sciences and quotes Plato (*Laws*. 626a) as evidence.[72] Xenophon (*Mem.* 3.1) notes that a famed philosopher, Dionysodorus, came to Athens to teach tactics. It is certainly possible that Asclepiodotus may have written his work after reading the text of his contemporary, but for Asclepiodotus to simply copy or summarise the work of his colleague, while having aspirations to be a distinguished philosopher himself, would have been foolish.

Kidd, in his commentary on the fragments of Poseidonius, states that "the Senecan evidence strongly suggests that he [Asclepiodotus] wrote his own book(s) on the subject [meteorology], and did not merely summarise or abridge his master's work."[73] However, Kidd goes on to state that Asclepiodotus' tactical manual was simply an abridgement of Poseidonius' work and that Aelian and Arrian only knew of Poseidonius' work through Asclepiodotus' epitome of it. He continues that, "that is no argument for thinking that the same situation held good with respect to Seneca, Poseidonius and Asclepiodotus on meteorology."[74] If that is a valid argument for proving that Asclepiodotus did not simply summarise Poseidonius' work on meteorology, surely the reverse logic can be used to show that he did not summarize his tactical treatise either.[75] Why would someone write independent works in an attempt to be a renowned philosopher in his own right and then undermine his reputation with a basic summary of his more famous contemporary?[76]

---

[71] See Vela Tejada 2004, 145; Thesleff 1966, 107; Oldfather 1923, 6.
[72] Cf. Plat, Lach, 18le-184c.
[73] Kidd 1988, 31. Kidd later states, "we certainly cannot assume that Asclepiodotus merely reproduced Poseidonius in his *aitiai phusikai*" 1988, 819.
[74] Kidd 1988, 33.
[75] Arrian also wrote a work on Meteorology, therefore showing a similar body of work to Asclepiodotus. That all the works of both authors were simply summaries of those of Poseidonius is highly unlikely.
[76] We know of another of Poseidonius' pupils who did write epitomes of his teacher and his own works, namely Geminus. However, we only know of one individual work ascribed to him, an elementary introduction to Astronomy, which is more similar to a basic textbook than a serious work of science or philosophy. Moreover, if the date of Geminus is correctly calculated to be the early first century CE then he cannot have been Poseidonius' pupil and so his epitome of the great philosopher is perhaps simply a summary for use by later students alongside his own astronomical textbook. For a discussion see Kidd 1988, 33-5.

Asclepiodotus' tactical treatise must at least in parts be his own work, albeit inspired by his mentor's earlier text. Kidd arrives at the same conclusion stating that, "the language and composition…is so stark that it must be Asclepiodotus' own notes, and not abstracts taken from Posidonius (contrast Geminus in F18)".[77] Kidd cites the fragment of Geminus' summary of Poseidonius' work on meteorology as sufficient evidence to show the difference between an account using Poseidonius' own words and an entirely new one. If Kidd can prove that Asclepiodotus' work is almost entirely written in his own voice, or at least not in the voice of Poseidonius, then what evidence remains to claim Asclepiodotus simply abbreviated his mentor's account? In my view there is no secure evidence for any claim that Asclepiodotus simply edited and reissued Poseidonius' work in its entirety or as a précis, since we have no concrete version or details of the original.

3 THE HISTORICITY OF ASCLEPIODOTUS' MANUAL[78]

Now we can proceed to a more detailed analysis of the historicity of Asclepiodotus' work, in part using the evidence of experimental archaeology. I have argued elsewhere that Asclepiodotus' description of supernumeraries (the signallers and other staff that accompany a military unit as separate from the fighting troops) uses attested historical terms and as a result is useful for analysing the command positions and structure of the Macedonian army.[79]

3.1 HISTORICAL USE OF TERMS FOR UNITS OR RANKS

Aside from supernumeraries, the one term that Asclepiodotus definitely does use historically for Macedonian style armies is *dimoirites*. In Arrian's *Anabasis of Alexander* this denotes a low ranking soldier. A certain Abreas ascended the wall at the siege of the Malli and died defending Alexander (Arr. *Anab.* 6.9.3; 6.10.1-2). He is described repeatedly as a *dimoirites,* but other than that we know little of him. Here we have Asclepiodotus using a historically attested word for a type of

---

[77] Kidd 1988, 334.
[78] What follows is an analysis of only those sections of Asclepiodotus' manual that concern the sarissa phalanx. There is neither space nor time to analyse in similar detail the sections on light infantry and cavalry. For a brief, but detailed, review of these sections see Sekunda 1994, 10-11 (light infantry), 20-28, and esp. 31 Diagram 4 (cavalry).
[79] Wrightson 2010.

soldier in Alexander's army. *Dimoirites* is rarely used elsewhere so the fact that two instances of identical usage of the term exist, despite its rarity, suggests that this was its meaning and confirms its existence in the Macedonian army.[80]

Asclepiodotus' description of the base unit of his army and its junior commanders closely parallels Arrian's account of Alexander's army when he attempted to create a mixed phalanx of Macedonians and Persians (Arr. *Anab.* 7.23.3-4).[81] Whether this phalanx composition was ever implemented is uncertain, but it must have been formed along the same lines as a standard Macedonian phalanx. This is the only occurrence of any of these low ranks in Arrian's *Anabasis*.[82] Aclepiodotus' version of the unit is only

---

[80] The concern here is with the instances of the term *dimoirites* appearing in the context of a Macedonian style army. As a general military term, it does appear in Classical authors, but these cannot refer to the later Macedonian style army as described by Asclepiodotus. *Dimoirtites* appears only 20 times in the TLG and 12 of those are in the tactical manuals. In the other eight instances, the person referred to is clearly a low ranking soldier, thus confirming Asclepiodotus' use of the term as a junior rank.

[81] The unit is called a *dekas*, originally consisting of ten men but increased to sixteen later. It is commanded by a *dekadarch* who fights in the front rank. Behind him is a man on double pay, called a *dimoirites*, and behind him is a ten-stater man, who gets paid more than the average soldier but less than the *dimoirites*. In the mixed phalanx there then follow twelve Persian troops, and another ten-stater man at the back. Bosworth 1989 accepts the view that the Persians were missile troops. Arrian *Anab.* 7.23.4 says the Persians were archers and those who carried thonged javelins. That would, however, nullify the effectiveness of a pike phalanx and the open order and consequent mobility of missile troops. This is not the scope of this paper but is an interesting problem.

[82] None of these lower ranks (e.g. *dimoirites* or *dekadarch*) is mentioned by the Alexander historians in the meetings that Alexander had with his senior officers and so we can conclude that these were not officers; they were probably more like modern Non-Commissioned Officers (N.C.O.s) (cf. Arr. *Anab.* 2.10.2, 3.16.11, 3.9.6). On Alexander's meetings with officers see Wrightson 2010, 88-89. The *dekadarch* was probably the equivalent of a modern sergeant and the *dimoirites* and ten-stater man similar to a corporal and lance-corporal respectively. The term *dekadarch* is mentioned frequently in our sources. For example, it is used three times by Josephus and twice describing the same person Aiboutius (*Vit.* 115 & *BJ.* 3.144. The other instance is *BJ.* 2.578). Xenophon uses it 18 times either in the *Cyropaedia* (*Cyrop.* 2.1.22-23 (x3); 2.1.26; 2.1.30; 2.3.21; 3.3.11; 4.2.27 (x3); 8.1.14 (x2)) or *On Horsemanship* (*Horse.* 2.2; 2.4; 2.6;2.7; 4.9 (x2)). Plutarch uses it twice in his *Life of Lysander* showing that the term was at least used for an officer in the Spartan army also (*Vit. Lys.* 5.3 & 14.1), though Classical Greek armies are out of the scope of this paper. Dionysius of Halicarnassus uses it no less

slightly different. He mentions some of the same terms as Arrian in the same role (*dimoirites*) but he also mentions others (*lochagos* (commander of the *lochos*) for Asclepiodotus is the equivalent to *dekadarch* (commander of the dekas) in the *Anabasis*).

Many of the other terms that Asclepiodotus uses for commanders and units also are attested elsewhere in Macedonian style armies, most notably in the sources for the army of Alexander the Great.[83] *Lochagoi* are mentioned in the Alexander historians,[84] for example, and so are *taxiarchs*.[85] *Chiliarchs* and *pentakosiarchs* (commanders of a thousand and five hundred respectively) are also attested in the Alexander historians, albeit sparingly.[86] I have discussed the position of the *lochagos*, as well as *taxiarch*, *chiliarch* and *pentakosiarch*, in the command structure of Alexander's phalanx battalions at length elsewhere.[87] There is not space here to discuss the other terms in the command structure in detail, except to state that Sekunda argues that the rank of *pentekontarchos* (commander of fifty) mentioned by Asclepiodotus in copying Poseidonius, "drew upon

---

than 25 times in the *Roman Antiquities* (Dion. Hal. 2.14.4; 2.57.3; 10.57.3; 10.57.4; 10.58.1 (x2); 10.58.3; 10.58.5; 10.60.2; 10.60.4; 10.61.1; 11.1.6; 11.4.3; 11.5.4; 11.9.2; 11.15.4; 11.19.4; 11.22.3).

[83] Note that Aelian (*Tact.* Pref.6) makes a specific claim in the preface to his manual that reading his work will make it easier to understand the army of Alexander. Clearly this was supposed to be the army on which his manual was based, however loosely. However, Pedech (1961, 113-4) notes that Polybius did not understand the differences between the sarissa phalanx of Alexander and the later Macedonian style phalanxes. If this is true, then it is unlikely that the authors of the later tactical manuals that followed Polybius and Poseidonius did either.

[84] This term appears in Arrian's *Anabasis* only three times suggesting the low status of a *lochagos* in Alexander's army (Arr. *Anab.* 2.10.2; 3.9.6; 3.16.11)..

[85] *Taxiarch*, like *lochagos*, is also used a number of times in our sources – 269 times in the *TLG*. Arrian only uses it three times in the *Anabasis* and all in connection with *lochagos*. In fact most uses of *taxiarch* are in conjunction with lochagos, strongly suggesting a connection between the two terms that is closer than the *taxiarch* being the eponymous commander of the whole phalanx, as is often stated. In most cases the *taxiarch* seems to be a more important officer than the *lochagos* but not the most important, exactly as Asclepiodotus states; see Wrightson 2010, 91-92, esp. 91 n. 67. Sekunda (1994, 6-7; 2006, 35) equates the Asclepiodotean *taxiarch* with the Roman centurion citing Polybius 6.24 as evidence. He is probably right, and, if so, this adds another level of historicity to the army described by Asclepiodotus.

[86] *Chiliarch* and *pentakosiarch* references in the Alexander historians: Arr. *Anab.* 1.22.7, 3.29.7, 4.30.6, 5.23.7, 7.25.6; Plut. *Vit. Alex.* 76.3; Curt. 5.2.3.

[87] Wrightson 2010, 88-92.

contemporary late Hellenistic Ptolemaic or Seleucid practice for the title of *pentekontarchia*."[88]

The term *syntagma* is also attested, though Sekunda states that it was not used in the Macedonian, Antigonid or Ptolemaic armies.[89] Asclepiodotus uses it to describe a unit of 256 men (16x16), which he states is the base tactical unit of the phalanx.[90] Its usage elsewhere makes it hard to definitely state that it was the historical term for this unit of the phalanx particularly, as it usually merely defines an amalgamated unit or the combination of two armies.[91]

The one passage that may help us confirm Asclepiodotus' use of the term is Polybius *Histories* 18.32.13. When describing the Macedonian defeat by the Romans, Polybius enters a discussion of the drawbacks of the Macedonian phalanx compared with the Roman military system. There he says that people should not continue to wonder how and why the Macedonian "*syntagma* of the phalanx" is defeated by troops armed in the Roman style. He could have simply said phalanx here but used the term *syntagma* instead. He is likely referring to the main tactical unit of the Macedonian phalanx, which is exactly what the *syntagma* is in Asclepiodotus' theoretical army.[92] The fragmentary nature of Polybius'

---

[88] Sexunda 2006, 34. For a fuller discussion of Hellenistic reform and Asclepiodotus see also: Sekunda 2006, 35-36, 41, 50-51, 62-65, 100-104, and Appendix B 125-135.

[89] Sekunda 2006, 100.

[90] Sekunda (1994, 7) is confused by Asclepiodotus using the term *syntagma* instead of *semeia*. The latter is clearly used to describe the same unit strength in the Ptolemaic maniple by Polybius and so Sekunda expects Asclepiodotus to use the same term. Yet, as discussed below, Polybius does actually use the term syntagma to describe the main tactical unit of a Hellenistic phalanx. Clearly *syntagma* and *semeia* were both interchangeable terms used to describe the unit of 256, what Sekunda terms the Ptolemaic maniple. Sekunda actually concludes that Asclepiodotus used *syntagma* because *semeia* was in use in the Seleucid cavalry and he wanted to differentiate the infantry. Yet other terms such as *lochagos* exist in both the cavalry and the infantry elsewhere (see Wrightson 2010, 88-92) so that would not be such a problem for Asclepiodotus or his audience.

[91] For example Xenophon uses the term for units sent by allies *Hell.* 3.4.2 & 5.2.20. Diod. Sic.17.60.3.5 uses the term to mean the battalion of Darius.

[92] Sekunda (1994, 8; 2006) argues that the army described by Asclepiodotus mirrors a Hellenistic army after an adaptation to employ Roman structures, namely the maniple (cf. Wrightson 2010, 76-77, notes 18, 19, 20). However, he uses Ptolemaic evidence to show that the Ptolemaic maniple usually numbered closer to 128 not the 256 of the *syntagma* described by Asclepiodotus (Sekunda 2006, 36).

Histories has probably denied us other examples of similar uses of the term,[93] but this instance alone suggests that the way Asclepiodotus uses *syntagma* is historically correct for a Macedonian style army of Polybius' time. Sekunda suggests that Asclepiodotus uses *Syntagma* instead of *Semeia* as the term for the maniple, since "the normal Greek term already in use to designate the infantry maniple may not have been adopted by the Seleucid army because the word *semaia* was already in use for a cavalry formation."[94]

So a number of the terms for officers and units that Asclepiodotus uses exist elsewhere, albeit some apparently describing different levels on the hierarchy. The fact that he uses the terms differently is problematic. If he is basing his hierarchy on the real army then the real terms he uses should have the same function. However, since we do not know exactly which Hellenistic army Asclepiodotus' is using as his model, it is difficult to say for certain that his use of the terms is incorrect.

Asclepiodotus repeatedly states that there had been a change in nomenclature from previous armies. The first instance is when he notes that different people use different numbers (8, 10, 12, or 16) for the base unit of the phalanx (Asclep. *Tact.* 2.1). Asclepiodotus also notes a change when describing the nomenclature of the base unit (Asclep. *Tact.* 2.2). He states that the name of the file, as well as the names of its constituent parts

---

Polybius 11.23.1 actually uses *syntagma* (and *speira* another term for *semeia*) to refer to the Roman cohort. Sekunda concludes that in Asclepiodotus' army "the transference of the supernumeraries from the *taxis* to the *syntagma* implies the replacement of the century by the maniple as the principle sub-unit of the army." Perhaps, however, Asclepiodotus is describing the army replacing the maniple with the cohort; though there is little other evidence for this since a Roman cohort was made up of three maniples, one each of *triarii*, *principes* and *hastate*, meaning that light and heavy infantry were combined, something that clearly does not happen in the phalanx described by Asclepiodotus. On the implications of this passage of Polybius see Walbank 1967, 302.

[93] According to the *TLG* there are nine instances of the term *syntagma* in Polybius and 257 in total throughout the corpus. Clearly, then, the term was a common one, even discounting the number of times it is used in the tactical manuals. The linguistic origin of the word *syntagma*—a joining together—does suggest that it originally referred to two parts of a force combined on the next level on the hierarchy. This linguistic usage may account for the many instances of the term in Greek literature rather than proving the military use of Asclepiodotus and Polybius.

[94] Sekunda 2006, 100, though he is clear this is a very speculative possibility.

and commanders, was changed when it was reorganized. When he states that the commander of a *taxis* is the *hekatontarch,* he comments that it used to be the *taxiarch* (Asclep. *Tact.* 2.8). At the level that the supernumeraries are attached, Asclepiodotus mentions a change when the size of the phalanx was doubled (Asclep. *Tact.* 2.9). He also notes the previous name of the wing (*telos*), and that the general is now called the *phalangarch* (Asclep. *Tact.* 2.10).[95] Even a slight reference to previous usage strongly suggests that his creation of a theoretical army is not all of his own devising. But since he mentions six such occasions where something was different before, he must at least be acknowledging the historical reality, even if not using it as the foundation for the whole of his work.

If he is simply creating an imaginary theoretical army with no historical basis whatsoever why would he include such a statement? If, rather, he is summarizing the actual hierarchy of a Hellenistic army, then he would be forced to mention the change as something required for his readers, who may have known about it and been confused.[96] It seems that he is trying to present a summary of all the terms that have been used up until his time. This is why he states that there were these changes in the organization of the phalanx. If this is true, then he cannot be creating a purely theoretical army, either his own or based on Poseidonius' earlier work. As Sekunda concludes, "it would be reasonable to suppose that the military organization described by Asclepiodotus should, at least in part, reflect the organization of the Seleucid Army in the final decades of the second century," (Sekunda 1994, 6). Any attempt at mentioning historical trends means that he is giving a historical summary of the organization of the army. There must then be an underlying historicity to Asclepiodotus' "theoretical" army.

3.2 MANEUVERS

His description of the various maneuvers of the phalanx that were possible, and suggested, is also rooted in fact (Asclep. *Tact.* 10.1-21; 12.1-11). All of the drills that Alexander had his army carry out in front of the Illyrians, which scared the enemy away, are described by Asclepiodotus (Arr. *Anab.* 1.6.1-4). This is not entirely surprising since the basic drills of

---

[95] On Asclepiodotus' description of the *telos,* see Sekunda 1994, 9-10; 2006 103-104.
[96] For an excellent reconstruction of the hierarchy of Asclepiodotus' army see Sekunda 1994, 29-31.

any phalanx would be the same. The ability to change the front is still standard drill in modern armies, and swift parade ground movements are an indispensible part of a professional military.[97] Even if his army is entirely theoretical, Asclepiodotus would have had to list the same drills that were used in reality. Although this does not add to the factual aspect of his manual, it does not take anything away from it either. This shows that by Asclepiodotus' time, the drills, maneuvers, and tactics of the Macedonian phalanx were probably set and well established.

As part of a research project in Calgary we had a set of 32 replica sarissas built. The main research agenda for this process was to examine the likelihood of Alexander the Great's phalanx separating for chariots at the battle of Gaugamela.[98] To do this I trained a group of volunteers of all shapes and sizes to use a sarissa in formation. Few of these individuals had any military training or experience, and as a result even basic drill was a problem. In a certain case the height difference was such that one individual had to always be in the front rank. However, I later had an opportunity to train a group of men, all of similar sizes, and such problems were significantly reduced.

The process of training a group of people in a phalanx was enlightening as to the problems that may have occurred historically. The main difficulty of our sarissa phalanx was to move at the right time so as not to hit each other with the long weapon. I used a number of the commands and turns as described by Asclepiodotus demonstrating that they are valid and achievable. What was clear is that the details concerning drill provided by Asclepiodotus' tactical manual transfer perfectly to reality. Not only that, but Asclepiodotus' information corresponds well with what we know, or are able to reconstruct, about the phalanx of Alexander and the Successors. In fact, no other source preserves the specific commands given for the basic drill maneuvers of the Macedonian style phalanx.[99]

---

[97] In the Greek and Macedonian armies relying on a compact phalanx, the drills and maneuvers would have been crucial in battle, especially in the professional Macedonian armies of the fourth century where the adoption of the oblique battle line, the tactical withdrawal, and the use of the unwieldy sarissa required extra precision.

[98] Heckel, Willekes and Wrightson 2010.

[99] For comparative details and modern diagrams of the very similar commands given in Aelian's manual see Matthew 2012, 198-224.

Asclepiodotus also provides diagrams for the different formations of the phalanx (Asclep. *Tact.* 11.1-8). The most interesting is his description of how each *syntagma* drawn up in loose formation is arranged "by parallelograms" with only the corners touching (Asclep. *Tact.* 11.7). This is possibly a description of the Greek version of the Roman "chequer" formation.[100] This may be Asclepiodotus instigating this Roman tactic for his theoretical Macedonian army, but it would not be surprising if the late Hellenistic armies did adopt this practice, since they certainly adopted Roman armament for some of their heavy infantry.[101] So Asclepiodotus here may provide proof of a tactical innovation in late Hellenistic armies that is otherwise unattested.[102]

3.3 UNIT TOTALS

The one aspect of Asclepiodotus' manual that causes the most problems for historians is how neatly the numbers that he gives for each unit divide to one. Mathematics and the beauty of numbers was one of the principal concerns of philosophers.[103] Even though there are many historical instances of the file in a phalanx numbering eight or sixteen,[104] not least the example from Arrian discussed above, many scholars still believe this is the number used by Asclepiodotus only because it is

---

[100] See Wheeler 1979, 306.

[101] See Polyb. 30.25.3 for the Seleucid army at Daphne containing a Roman armed unit. Also see 1*Macc.* 6.35 for a similar unit at the battle of Beth-Zacharia.

[102] This would match well with the manipular reform in the Ptolemaic infantry sought by Sekunda 2006. It would make sense for a phalanx to adopt manipular tactics of the chequer formation if also adopting a manipular hierarchical organization. It may also reflect, as Wheeler 1979 argues, that the Romans found Greek tactical manuals relevant when using the legion as a phalanx (discussed above section 2.2). However, Asclepiodotus, unlike Aelian and Arrian, is writing before the Hellenistic phalanx became obsolete and so his need to relate to Roman tactics is less important.

[103] Sekunda (2006, 130) suggests that "Poseidonius was interested in numbers, and hence his desire to demonstrate that the best way to organize an army, under ideal conditions, would be to divide it down to unity." He believes that Poseidonius is creating an ideal army with ideal numbers but then in the very next paragraph argues that "In fact most Greek armies, at least at unit and sub-unit level in the infantry, were divisible to unity." (2006, 131) If that is the case then there is no evidence to confirm the numbers preserved in Asclepiodotus are fabricated and not actually based on reality. Sekunda (2006, 132) actually presents evidence that strongly suggests the easily divisible numbers is a system that "is documented in reality".

[104] See in particular Polyb. 18.30.1.

mathematically perfect. Where the problem should lie is when his numbers for the phalanx differ from what we know elsewhere.

Asclepiodotus has units of 500 and 1000, commanded by a *pentakosiarch* and a *chiliarch* respectively (Asclep. *Tact.* 2.10). This matches well with evidence of other Hellenistic armies. The Antigonid battalion may have been 2000 strong.[105] Bar-Kochva, in his invaluable summary of the Seleucid Army, spends little time on the hierarchy and organization of the phalanx because of a lack of evidence.[106] He states that the Seleucid phalanx may have been divided into *strategiai* of 4000 and *chiliarchies* of 1000, as the Antigonid and Ptolemaic phalanxes were, but that there is little evidence for them. There is some possible evidence for Seleucid *chiliarchies* in the phalanx. Athenaeus (Ath. 4.153b), quoting Poseidonius' *Histories*, tells us that Herakleon, the Seleucid general and a contemporary of Poseidonius, had his army eat their dinner separated into units of a thousand. Furthermore at the battle of Beth-Zacharia the Seleucid army had to march through a defile and so was split into 32 separate divisions (*I Maccabees* 6.35; Jos. *AJ* 12.371). Each division grouped around one of the 32 elephants and comprised 1000 infantry and 500 cavalry. Although these instances do not mention the *chiliarch,* and are not necessarily referring to phalanx infantry, they do prove the existence of units of 1000 in a Hellenistic army of Asclepiodotus' time, once more adding support to Asclepiodotus' hierarchy.[107] So in fact, where we may expect history to prove Asclepiodotus wrong, he is actually proved right.

What of Asclepiodotus' higher numbers? Following his mathematical doubling of the army from one man upwards he stops at an army of 16,384 (Asclep. *Tact.* 2.7). There must be a reason he ends with this number and does not continue.[108] Hellenistic phalanxes of the second century did in

---

[105] See: Lesquier 1911, 62; Welles 1938, 248-9; Walbank 1940, 293 & 1967, 286.
[106] Bar-Kochva 1976, 66-67.
[107] Polybius often uses the term *chiliarch* to refer to Roman military tribunes. In the post-Marian Roman army, tribunes were often given command of a number of cohorts and so can be seen as the equivalent of commanders of 1000 men. There were six tribunes to every legion, though the first one was an observer more than a commander. This left five to command the ten cohorts. A cohort of roughly 400 men would give a command of approximately 1000 the same as the *chiliarch*.
[108] Sekunda (1994, 6; 2006, 62-65) argues the same thing, that 16,384 represents "an ideal establishment strength", the Hellenistic reality citing the same examples as are below.

fact number 16,000 men.[109] At the battle of Magnesia the Seleucid phalanx was 16,000 (Livy 37.40.1; App. *Syr.* 32) and at the battle of Pydna, Livy states that the Macedonian phalanx was the same size also (Livy 33.4.4). So we have a historical basis for why Asclepiodotus stopped doubling at 16,384; because that was possibly the real total of the Macedonian-style phalanx.

We also have examples of a Hellenistic phalanx being split into two equal wings, as Asclepiodotus says that tactically it would be (Asclep. *Tact.* 2.10). Polybius states that during the Fourth Syrian War the Ptolemaic phalanx was trained and commanded by two different people (Polyb. 5.65.4), and at the battle of Raphia the Seleucid phalanx was commanded by two generals (Polyb. 5.79.5). So in the same conflict the two Macedonian style Hellenistic phalanxes were both able to be divided into two. Moreover, at the battle of Cynoscephalae, Philip V advanced to attack the Romans with the peltasts and the right of the phalanx while Nikanor followed behind with the rest of the army (Polyb. 18.24.2. cf. Livy 33.8.8). Thus we can see that another of the tactical divisions in Asclepiodotus' army is in fact historically attested in each of the three principal Macedonian style Hellenistic armies, the Antigonid, the Ptolemaic and the Seleucid.[110]

So even in the area that is the most philosophical of those with which Asclepiodotus is concerned, namely mathematics, never does he take liberties with what is historically attested elsewhere. In fact, much of what he says colours our understanding of the historical evidence. Completing his army at 16,384 proves that that was the standard phalanx size in Hellenistic armies. The army splitting into two wings was a common practice and was part of the training and organization of the phalanx. Undoubtedly the exactly symmetrical numbers he uses are ideal, but they

---

[109] Clearly there is a significant difference between army, or unit, totals on paper (paper strength) and in actual battle. However, since Asclepiodotus' army is entirely a paper army this is not so troublesome. The evidence of historically attested phalanxes of 16,000 may suffer from historians using round numbers, but the approximations are close enough to Asclepiodotus' numbers to be useful as comparative evidence.

[110] Sekunda (1994, 10; 2006, 104), as well as the Seleucid army at Raphia, also discusses the example of one wing of the Seleucid army being sent against Judas Maccabeus (*1 Mac.* 9.1), and the Seleucid army being split into half-wings (Polyb. 5.53.6). He concludes that, "the formal division of the phalanx into a right and left wing may represent late Hellenistic reality rather than mere Poseidonian or Asclepiodotan caprice."

cannot be discounted since he builds everything from the smallest unit of 16 men, which was the actual subdivision in many Hellenistic armies.[111]

4 CONCLUSIONS

So what can we say about the tactical manual of Asclepiodotus? If he was concerned with creating a theoretical army for a philosophical exercise, then many of the terms he uses seem unnecessary. Six times he states what used to be the case and what actually occurs now. Clearly he is concerned to show his readers what the historical reality was in these instances. There is no significant place in the hierarchy described by Asclepiodotus that is not attested historically. The terms for the positions may be rarely mentioned elsewhere and the unit divisions may seem far too precise and mathematically perfect, but that alone is not enough to discount his text as purely theoretical.

Without a tactical manual contemporary with Alexander or his Successors we can never be sure that the descriptions that survive in Asclepiodotus are historical. We can, however, be certain that these manuals were based however loosely on what the authors believed to be historical fact. Their descriptions seem very mathematical but the numbers they use for unit sizes are historically attested as are the majority of the terms we see. If Asclepiodotus believed firmly that his treatise on the Hellenistic army was instructive to his audience then the descriptions must be historically accurate. These manuals of a Macedonian style army should be given more attention by scholars, especially in view of the lack of other evidence elsewhere.

BIBLIOGRAPHY

Bake, J. (1810) *Posidonii Rhodii Reliquiae doctrinae.* Leiden.
Bar Kochva, B. (1976) *The Seleucid Army.* Cambridge.
Bosworth, A. B. (1972) "Arrian's Literary Development," *CQ* 22, 163-185.
—. (1977) "Arrian and the Alani," *Harvard Studies in Classical Philology*, 81, 217-255.
—. (1980) *A Historical commentary on Arrian's History of Alexander.* Vol. 1. Oxford.

---

[111] As Sekunda (2006, 134) rightly concludes, "there was certainly nothing outlandish in describing an army which was divisible down to unity, as for most of the Hellenistic period this was practically universally the case."

—. (1988) *From Arrian to Alexander: Studies in historical interpretation* Oxford.
—. (1989) *Conquest and Empire. The Reign of Alexander the Great.* Cambridge.
—. (1993) "Arrian and Rome: the Minor Works," *ANRW* 2.34.1, 226-275.
Bowersock, G. W. (1967) "A new inscription of Arrian," *GRBS* 8, 279-280.
Brunt, P. A. (1977) "From Epictetus to Arrian," *Athenaeum* 55, 19-48.
Campbell, B. (1987) "Teach Yourself How to Be a General," *The Journal of Roman Studies*, 77, 13-29.
Dain, A. (1946) *Histoire du texte d'Aelien le tacticien* Paris.
(1989) "Aelian's Manual of Hellenistic military tactics: A new translation from the Greek with an introduction," *AncW* 19: 31–64.
Devine, A. M. (1994) "Arrian's Tactica," *ANRW* 34.1, 312-337.
—. (1995) "Polybius' lost Tactica: the ultimate source for the tactical manuals of Asclepiodotus, Aelian, and Arrian?" *Ancient History Bulletin* 9.1, 40-44.
Dobson, J. F. (1918) "The Posidonius Myth," *The Classical Quarterly*, 12.3/4, 179-195.
Heckel, W., C. Willekes and G. Wrightson (2010) "Scythed Chariots at Gaugamela," in E. Carney and D. Ogden (eds.) *Philip II and Alexander the Great: Father and Son, Lives and Afterlives,* 103-113, Oxford.
Jacoby, F. (1920) *Die Fragmente der griechischen Historiker*. Berlin.
Kidd, I. G. (1988) *Posidonius the Commentary.* 3 vols. Cambridge.
Kochly, H. (1851) *De libris tacticis, qui Arriani et Aeliani feruntur*, dissertatio, Index lectionum Zurich, reprinted in *Opuscula academica*, vol. 1 (Leipzig, 1853).
Kochly, H. and W. Rustow (eds.) (1885) *de Re Strategica*. in *Griechische Kriegsschriftsteller* 2. Leipzig.
Kristeller, P. (1993) *Greek Philosophers of the Hellenistic Age.* New York.
Laffranque, M. (1964) *Poseidonios d'Apamee.* Paris.
Lesquier, J. (1911) *Les Institutions militaires de l'Egypte sous les Lagides.* Paris.
Malitz, J. (1983) *Die Historien des Poseidonios.* Munich.
Matthew, C. (2012) *The Tactics of Aelian: A new translation of the manual that influenced warfare for fifteen centuries* Barnsley.
Muller, K. (1896) *Fragmenta Historicorum Graecorum*. Paris.
Nock, A. D. (1959) "Posidonius," *The Journal of Roman Studies*, 49, Parts 1 and 2, 1-15.
Oldfather, W. A. (1923) *Aeneas Tacticus, Asclepiodotus, Onasander, Asclepidotous.* London and New York.

O'Sullivan, N. (1996) "Written and Spoken in the First Sophistic," in I. Worthington (ed.) *Voice into Text: Orality and Literacy in Ancient Greece*, 115-127, Leiden.
Pedech, P. (1961) *Polybe*: "Histoires," *Livre XII*. Edited and translated by Paul Pedech. Paris.
Pedech, P. (1969) *La methode historique de Polybe*. Paris.
Poznanski, L. (1980) "A Propos du "Traité de tactique" de Polybe," *Athenaeum* 58, 340-352.
Reinhardt, K. (1953) "Poseidonios," *RE* 22, 558-826.
Rawson, E. (1985) "Posidonius' *Histories*," Review of *Die Historien des Poseidonius* by Jürgen Malitz 1983, *The Classical Review*, New Series, 35. 1, 107-109.
Sekunda, N. (1994) *Seleucid and Ptolemaic Reformed Armies 168-145 BC. Volume 1: The Seleucid army.* Stockport.
—. (2006) *Hellenistic Infantry Reform in the 160's BC*. Gdansk.
Stadter, P. A. (1978) "The *Ars Tactica* of Arrian: Tradition and Originality," *Classical Philology*, 73, 2, 117-128.
—. (1980) *Arrian of Nicomedia*, Chapel Hill.
Thesleff, H. (1966) "Scientific and Technical Style in Early Greek Prose," *Arctos* 4, 89-113.
Traversa, A. (1952) *Index Stoicorum Herculanensis*. Genoa.
Van Straaten, M. (1946) *Panetius, sa vie, ses ecrits et sa doctrine avec une edition des fragments*. Amsterdam.
Vela Tejada, J. (1993) "Tradicion y originalidad en la obra de Eneas el Táctico: la génesis de la historiografía militar," *Minerva* 7, 79-92.
—. (2004) "Warfare, History and Literature in the Archaic and Classical Periods: The Development of Greek Military Treatises," *Historia: Zeitschrift für Alte Geschichte*, Bd. 53, H. 2, 129-146.
Walbank, F. W. (1940) *Philip V of Macedon.* Cambridge.
—. (1970, vol. 1, 1967, vol. 2, 1979, vol. 3) *A Historical Commentary on Polybius*. Oxford.
—. (1972) *Polybius*. Berkeley.
Welles, C. B. (1938) "New Texts from the Chancery of Philip V of Macedonia and the Problem of the "Diagrama"," *American Journal of Archaeology* 42, 245-60.
Wheeler, E. L. (1977) "Flavius Arrianus: a political and military biography," Diss. Duke University.
—. (1978) "The Occasion of Arrian's "Tactica"," *Greek, Roman and Byzantine Studies*, 19:4, 351-365.
—. (1979) "The Legion as Phalanx," *Chiron* 9: 303-318.

Whitehead, D. (1990) *Aineias the Tactician: How to survive under siege*, Oxford.

Wrightson, G. (2010) "The nature of command in the Macedonian sarissa phalanx," *Ancient History Bulletin 24,* 71-92.

Ziegler, K. (1953) "Polybios," in *Pauly-Wissowa* 21, 2, 1440-578.

CHAPTER SIX

FURIOUS WRATH: ALEXANDER'S SIEGE OF THEBES AND PERDICCAS' FALSE RETREAT

DR. BORJA ANTELA-BERNÁRDEZ

In some way, the path that led to the siege and destruction of Thebes in 336 B.C. began, in fact, as a result of the battle of Chaeroneia in 338 B.C.[1] When the Greeks found out that Philip of Macedon had been assassinated,[2] the Thebans threatened to expel the Macedonian garrison quartered at the Cadmea fortress that kept watch over the city's loyalty to Macedonian hegemony. Alexander's fast answer to this first Theban uprising was decisive. By moving personally to central Greece with his army, he extinguished the rebellion and silenced political instability among the *poleis*. Once the zone had been secured by the renewal of the diplomatic structures that ensured Macedonian hegemony,[3] Alexander drove his soldiers to the northern frontier, where the warlike neighbours of the Macedonians, Illyrians and Thracians, had decided to profit from the death of Philip and the absence of Alexander to start a rebellion. During the management of this northern campaign, a new Theban revolt began as a result of some rumours concerning the death of Alexander during the campaign against the Illyrians.[4] Our purpose in the following lines is to reconstruct the way the siege and destruction of Thebes took place, to show the kind of Macedonian tactics used in order to gain access to the city. Especial attention will be paid to Perdiccas' withdrawal, apparently accidental, but actually with a clear intention to mislead the Theban

---

[1] Lane Fox 1973, 86-89; Hammond 1992, 59-63; Bosworth 1997, 42-45, 281-283; Cartledge 2004, 80-83; Antela 2007a; Worthington 2007; Antela 2011.
[2] Antela 2012.
[3] Antela 2007a, 2011.
[4] Arr. *Anab.* 1.7.2; 1.7.6.

defenders, as far as the use of a similar tactic in Halicarnassus's siege seems to show. Finally, after Thebes' defeat, the Macedonian treatment of the defeated, especially of the non-combatant population, will also be observed.

As our sources explain,[5] the Theban insurrection was caused by some exiles, who had fled from the city or had been expelled from it by the time of the victory of Philip over the city's forces in the battlefield of Chaeroneia. Arriving during the night, these anti-Macedonian exiles tried to take the Macedonian garrison in the Cadmea fortress by surprise. However, they only managed to kill a few of the Macedonian soldiers, those who were on guard outside the Cadmea, but did place the Cadmea and the Macedonian garrison under siege.[6] At the same time, the exiles began some political activities in order to make contact with the anti-Macedonian forces in other Greek cities, while the Theban assembly abolished the oligarchic constitution established by Philip.[7]

The Macedonian response was decisively swift. Alexander himself directed his forces without delay to Boeotia, covering a distance of around 400 km in thirteen days.[8] The Thebans were entirely surprised by the arrival of an army led by Alexander in person and were placed under siege.[9] In fact, Alexander's unexpected promptness in moving his forces towards the enemy in order to strike fear into the rebels was a brilliant strategy, but this time the result was not the same as the year before. However, at least the other Greeks that were considering supporting the Theban rebellion now retreated and determined to wait out the course of events.

Outside the Theban walls, Alexander called for the instigators to be delivered to him and for the unconditional surrender of the city. The Thebans bravely resisted Alexander. They asked all of the Greeks that wanted to fight for freedom to join them in resisting the Macedonian

---

[5] Diod. Sic. 17.8.2 – 9.5; Plut. *Vit. Alex.* 11.7-9; Arr. *Anab.* 1.7.2-3.
[6] Aesch. 3, 240 states that Demosthenes was involved in bribing some unidentified mercenaries to betray the fortress for the price of 5 talents. Nevertheless, the treasonous negotiation seems to have failed, since the gold was never paid. Din. 1.18-22 discusses this event in a similar way.
[7] Diod. Sic. 17.8.3; 9.1; Arr. *Anab.* 1.7.1-2; Plut. *Vit. Alex.* 11.8.
[8] Arr. *Anab.* 1.7.5.
[9] But not immediately: Plut. *Vit. Alex.* 11.7-9; Arr. *Anab.* 1.7.7.

king.[10] Both sides were eager and ready to start hostilities. As regards chronology, it is very difficult to determine the exact number of days the siege lasted because our sources do not provide any precise information. However, a careful analysis of the relevant sources suggests that it was no more than a few days, during which time Alexander remained outside the city waiting for an improbable Theban surrender. After both sides had demanded each other's surrender,[11] Alexander camped in a place near the walls, traditionally dedicated to Iolaus,[12] waiting for a change in the hostile position of the Thebans.[13]

As Bosworth has observed,[14] after the fast march by the Macedonian army to reach Boeotia as soon as possible, a good rest was necessary if they were to have the strength to fight a decisive battle in the following days. Surely, Alexander expected that the deployment of his army in front of the city, in plain view of any Theban resident, would make a deep impression and present surrender as the only option for survival to the Theban population. As siege equipment is heavy, hard to manage and very slow to move, the fast movement of Alexander's troops to Thebes did not allow the siege engines to arrive. According to Diodorus, the Macedonians built siege machines after their arrival at Thebes, though he does not say what kind, they could not have been very complex.[15] Other sources do not mention any siege engines, so the question of whether any were built is disputed, but the Macedonians would probably have had time to build ladders of some kind, or even wooden towers.[16] So, the Macedonians

---

[10] Diod. Sic. 17.9.5. Vid. Brosius 2003; Antela 2007b.
[11] Diod. Sic. 17.9.1
[12] Arr. *Anab.* 1.7.1. The location has been discussed in the light of the information provided by Plut. *Vit. Pel.* 18, who says that Iolaus' Tomb was inside the walls of Thebes. It seems probable that Arrian was actually referring to the site of Iolaus' Gymnasium, which is described by Paus. 9.23.1. The fact that the tomb of Pindar was located in the vicinity and the relationship with the famous mention of it in Plut. *Vit. Alex.* 11.12, seems to validate this itinerary.
[13] Plut. *Vit. Alex.* 9.2; Diod. 17.9.2-4; Just. 11.3.6.
[14] Bosworth 1981, 78.
[15] Diod. Sic. 17.11.1.
[16] If they could be finished in three days: Diod. Sic. 17.9.6. We must bear in mind the serious difficulties to transport heavy siege engines from Macedonia to Thebes. Likewise, this can also be an argument in favour of the short length of the siege, in that no machines were needed to be sent to Thebes. On the other hand, although the invention of assembled components to build siege machines was one of the better known successful inventions of Alexander's engineer Diades, it seems to have taken place after the beginning of the Asian campaign: Antela 2012, 93 n.95;

followed the usual tactic of surrounding the city in order to isolate it from any external help.[17] This Macedonian strategy had a fast answer from the Thebans, who sent a cavalry force with a great number of light infantry to break the encirclement and harass the Macedonian forces. This surprise attack probably led to some loss of life among the Macedonians. The Theban aim does not seem to have been to start a battle but to take profit from the moment to put pressure on the enemy, who were probably busy in camp activities. Although the Theban attack had some success, the Macedonian response was quick. Alexander sent his light armed infantry accompanied with some archers to repel the attack and secure his defensive lines.[18]

The next day, as Arrian records,[19] the Macedonian army began to move around the city. This was probably the moment when the siege was definitively established. At the same time, as other examples show, these Macedonian movements along the walls probably had the aim of getting to know the site and searching for the best places from which to launch the attack on the city. Also, some Macedonian interest seems to have been focused on the gate called Electra,[20] which faced towards Attica.[21] So we can be certain that the camp was near this gate, probably in a place as close to the Cadmea fortress as it was possible to be on the outside of the walls. Both locations, the Cadmea and the Electra Gate, were in the south quadrant of the city,[22] and the Macedonian camp can therefore be understood to have been situated close to these locations. We also know

---

98 n. 129; 111 and n. 223, with bibliography.
[17] Antela 2012, 128.
[18] Arr. *Anab.* 1.7.8-9. See Bosworth 1980, 78.
[19] Arr. *Anab.* 1.7, 9.
[20] Paus. 9.8.4; 11.1. In the vicinity of this Gate lay the ruins of the House of Amphytrion, where in the time of Pausanias the visitor could still contemplate the room of Alcmena, mother of Heracles, and also the tombs of the Heraclids killed by Heracles during his madness. It seems probable, then, that Alexander's choice of this place for his camp was not by chance, but by a premeditated will by virtue of the close links between the Macedonian royal family of the Argeads and Heraclids as descendants of Heracles. Concerning Argeads as Heraclids, see Hdt. 8.137-138; Thuc. 2.99.3. Also see Greenwalt 1986; Borza 1982; Hammond 1989, 16-19.
[21] Cloché 1952, 199; Fuller 1958, 86. Bosworth 1980, 78 claims that the aim of this measure was to control the communications between the Thebans and Athens.
[22] Bosworth 1980, 78, "three of the sides of the Cadmeia were enclosed by the circuit of the walls, and only the south side was vulnerable to penetration from the outside".

that the Thebans had made a fence, trenches and other kinds of defences in the area of the Cadmea Gate,[23] trying to isolate the Macedonian garrison from the enemy forces outside the walls.[24] This can be considered as a further indication that the Macedonian camp was located near this point. However, we do not know whether the fence and other obstacles were put in place before Alexander's arrival or after it. Moreover, the Thebans blockading the Cadmea fortress inside Thebes would probably have wished to avoid any possibility that the Macedonian soldiers of the garrison could leave the fortress and help Alexander's besieging army, which would catch the Thebans between two fronts. It is therefore possible that all these defensive constructions are to be interpreted as a preventive action to isolate the garrison.

After talking about a probable new attempt to negotiate the surrender of the Thebans,[25] Arrian stresses one more time that Alexander wished to avoid the confrontation and made serious efforts to obtain a diplomatic solution.[26] Nevertheless, peace dialogues failed again, and strictly speaking it was this failure that marks the start of the siege. Our best source for the details of the assault is, surprisingly, Diodorus, who explains that, as an answer to the Thebans' arrogance in refusing the proposals for peace, Alexander ordered his men to prepare to assault the city. Concerning the plan of attack, again Diodorus provides useful information when he describes how Alexander divided the Macedonian forces for the attack into three groups: one occupied the fences outside the city, while a second group faced the Theban battle line. The third one stayed as a reserve. The Thebans also divided their forces, and while the cavalry

---

[23] Cloché 1952, 199 explains that it was the official at the head of the Macedonian garrison in the Cadmea who decided to begin to make some trenches and defensive barricades at the same time as he ordered the soldiers to get the supplies of arms from the warehouses.
[24] Diod. Sic. 17.8.3.
[25] Plut. *Vit. Alex.* 11.8; Diod. Sic. 17.9.5-6.
[26] Arr. *Anab.* 1.7.9-10. Nevertheless, the apparent responsibility of Perdiccas for the risky attack that, according to the sources, led to the beginning of the Macedonian offensive against the city walls noticeably contrasts with the marked absence of responsibility of Alexander in the later destruction of the city. The decision to sack the city, according to the surviving accounts, was made by the Boeotian allies of Macedon that took part in the siege, and not Alexander. See Bosworth 1980, 79. Of course, Ptolemy's account of the events at Thebes probably was very hostile to Perdiccas, as he was very interested in defaming Perdiccas and his decisions under Alexander's command, in order to justify the conflict between them after Alexander's death.

defended the inside of the city in order to secure the fences, other groups of defenders, formed heterogeneously of freed slaves[27] and foreigners, occupied and defended the walls. Women and children sought shelter in the temples and prayed for help from the gods.[28] Surprisingly, no mention of the Theban light armed infantry is recorded in our sources, although we know from preceding actions that there were some light infantry in the city. It is possible that they had been sent to confront the Macedonian infantry in the plain before the city walls.

The fighting started with the sound of the trumpets. The battle was bloody and very violent, judging by the accounts given by our sources and the impact that this clash between Alexander and Thebes made in the memories of the Greeks.[29] The harsh combat is recorded in our sources as very bitter, without a clear winner during a good part of the battle. This must surely mean that the Thebans were able to resist furiously the well-trained Macedonian forces.[30] Nevertheless, at the peak of the battle, Alexander made a masterly tactical movement, calling to fight the soldiers in reserve, which gave the Macedonians the upper hand and led to them winning the battle.

Although we have many descriptions of the bravery of the Thebans in our sources, it seems very probable that Alexander's decision to bring in his reserve troops[31] provoked the withdrawal of the Thebans to the city. This would explain an episode described by both Diodorus and Arrian concerning Perdiccas and his forces being involved in a military action that cannot have been a casual, unplanned, attack. According to Arrian, who here uses the account of the direct witness Ptolemy,[32] we know that

---

[27] Aen. *Tact.* 10.6.
[28] Diod. Sic. 17.11.2-3. Especially, the temple of Melqart: Bonnet 1988, 53.
[29] Diod. Sic. 17.11.3-5; 12.1-2.
[30] The action taken by the Thebans recalls intensely the advice of Aen. *Tact.* 16.7.
[31] This seems to be one of the usual tactics of Alexander's army: Sinclair 1966. Taking into account that in other episodes we know of, for example the siege of Halicarnassus, where the third section consisted of veteran soldiers, it seems possible that also here, in Thebes, the veterans could have been held in reserve by Alexander to lead the definitive attack. This would actually be a logical action, if we consider it as a way to preserve his better soldiers, keeping them away from the first clash against the Boeotian forces.
[32] Concerning what this implies in an episode focused on Perdiccas, Bosworth 1980, 80-81 has explained Arrian's account here as a reflection of the later conflict between Perdiccas and Ptolemy, the direct source of Arrian. Ptolemy's hostility towards Perdiccas is also well known.

Perdiccas, in an uncertain moment, kept out of the battle and was in charge of the Macedonian camp, when he decided of his own accord to attack the walls at a point where they seemed to be undefended. When Alexander had news of Perdiccas' attack, he had to deploy some of his forces to give support to Perdiccas so that he and his men would not be isolated and in serious danger. So, archers, probably Cretans, since Euribotas the leader of this unit died during this action,[33] and *agrianes* (Paeonian–Thracian javelin men), were ordered by Alexander to go beyond the defensive fortifications of the Theban walls, in order to wait for his arrival. Alexander, with his elite forces, was to come to the aid of Perdiccas. Meanwhile, Perdiccas, who was seriously wounded during the action[34] when he tried to beat the second line of Theban fences, and his men fought against the Theban defenders. In the battle between these two forces (the soldiers of Perdiccas' battalion and the Thebans) the Macedonians were overpowered by the enemy and started a calculated retreat that induced the Thebans to follow them. Encouraged by their success against those experienced warriors, the Thebans left the fences unattended. This false retreat[35] was revealed definitively as dangerous when the defenders came face to face with Alexander and his elite troops. Although the Thebans tried to regain the security of the defensive position they had left just a moment ago, their flight for security allowed the Macedonians to pursue them, to overwhelm the defensive strongpoints, and to enter the city. It seems clear that Perdiccas' initiative played a key role in allowing the Macedonians to overcome the Theban defences and enter the city.

The account of Diodorus marks a clear contrast with that of Arrian in that he writes that Perdiccas' attack was, in fact, a result of Alexander's orders.[36] Indeed, the simultaneous organization, masterly planned, in the different phases of the attack must be considered as an indication that Perdiccas' action was less a consequence of his own will to fight than part of an organized strategy coordinated by Alexander himself.

Likewise, the episode of Perdiccas' attack that led the Macedonians beyond the walls of the city can be linked with some other references and information recorded by other sources. First, we must remember an episode in Polyaenus' work.[37] According to Polyaenus, Alexander

---

[33] Arr. *Anab.* 1.8.4.
[34] Arr. *Anab.* 1.8.1-3.
[35] Antela 2013
[36] Diod. Sic. 17.12.3-4.
[37] Polyaen. 4.3.12.

organized a kind of tricky operation during the attack on Thebes: while the king with almost all his forces attacked a certain point of the walls, probably near the point we have already explained as being next to the "Athenian" gate and the Cadmea fortress, Antipater waited until the peak moment of battle, and profiting from the confusion and roar he started an attack against an undefended point of the Theban wall, breaking the resistance of the defenders and gaining access to the city. No doubt Polyaenus is here confusing Antipater, who scholars used to locate at Pella during the siege of Thebes,[38] with Perdiccas, the main character of the episode in the accounts of Diodorus and Arrian.

We must also have in mind that at the time of Philip II's murder, Perdiccas was part of the *hypaspists*.[39] In addition, the fact that Perdiccas appeared later commanding the battalion (*taxis*) of the Orestians and Lyncestians[40] does not seem to be a good reason for accepting that before the beginning of the campaign against Persia (especially at the siege of Thebes, which happened in a date so near to the death of Philip) he had not maintained close links with the unit with which he had been involved at least until Philip's death. On the other hand, although Diodorus mentions Perdiccas as one of the bodyguards of Philip (*somatophylakes*) during the events that led to his murder,[41] those bodyguards seem in fact to have been *hypaspists*. Also, Arrian says explicitly that the *hypaspists* took part in the attack led by Perdiccas in order to secure the advanced position gained by his first assault beyond the outer fence of the Thebans (perhaps this was the very moment when Perdiccas was seriously wounded).[42] Thus, if we consider that the best elite forces of Alexander's army were involved in what our sources describe as a casual attack, it seems clear that we are not facing an unorganized and spontaneous movement led by Perdiccas, but a strategic move directed by Alexander's command. Luck, then, had nothing to do with the success of the operation.

Another source to support this interpretation can be found in the later siege of Halicarnassus, where the trick of Perdiccas' false retreat was

---

[38] Cf. Heckel 2006, 35-6. Also, the requirement by the Thebans, recorded in Plut. *Vit. Alex.* 11.8, for the delivery to them of Antipater by Alexander, which can be understood as a clue to Antipater's presence at the walls of Thebes, was actually put seriously in doubt: Hamilton 1999, 30.
[39] Diod. Sic. 16.94.4. Cf. McQueen 1995, 179. Heckel 1992, 135-136 and n. 382.
[40] Diod. Sic. 17.57.2; Rzepka 2008.
[41] Diod. Sic. 16.94.4
[42] Arr. *Anab.* 1.8.3.

repeated in order to gain access to the city. Again, as in Thebes, Perdiccas' men are said by our sources to have taken the decision by themselves to attack the enemy without the consent of Alexander. In the case of Halicarnassus, the accounts of Arrian and Diodorus are again the main sources available. Arrian explains that during the night two hoplites from Perdiccas' battalion decided, after a heavy drinking session, to attack by themselves the enemy's walls. The two soldiers began to insult the defenders. When the Halicarnassians discovered that the Macedonians fighting under the walls were only two men, they opened the city gates in order to kill them quickly in retaliation for the insults they were screaming at the walls, but on account of their unexpected and skilful military ability, the two Macedonians, as it seems in the account, not only survived but also resisted their enemies. More people came from the walls, and a night battle began between them and the men from Perdiccas' battalion, who had come to help their two brave (drunk?) comrades. The great number of Halicarnassians involved in this battle finally forced Perdiccas' men to retreat, probably in battle order. More defenders came from the city, and confusion was probably widespread in the dark of the night. Alexander's main army then joined the combat. Although Arrian believed that the reason some reinforcements arrived was that the rest of the Macedonians were alerted by the noise of the fight,[43] it is difficult to believe that the full army could have been ready to fight in the middle of the night in an instant or that Alexander himself would have decided to lead the attack in what seems a very confused situation. Since the city's gates were kept open in order to give passage to the defenders that came and went from the fight, Alexander's attack must have been surprising to the Halicarnassians, and the Macedonians almost got through the city's gates before the defenders could secure them and block access.

Diodorus' account is very similar to that of Arrian,[44] but it adds a key question, in that he says that this episode happened after previous siege activities had broken two towers and two sections of the defensive wall of Halicarnassus.[45] If this is true, we can be sure that this attack at the gates tried to get some advantage at this weak point. Perhaps this is also the reason for the ferocious defence by the Halicarnassians and the need for them to exit beyond the security of the walls in order to face the first attack from Perdiccas' men. This time the strategy of Alexander was not successful, but it almost gained the gates, and a lot of defenders were

---

[43] Arr. *Anab.* 1.21.1-4.
[44] Diod. Sic. 17.25.5-6.
[45] Diod. Sic. 17.25.5.

killed after the arrival of Alexander's reinforcements to the battle.

Although this episode, just as that of Thebes, is recorded in our sources as an example of the indiscipline of Perdiccas' soldiers, it is probably a consequence of the intention of the sources (likely with Ptolemy's account behind the original information) to dismiss Perdiccas' ability to command. The similarity of both cases shows a thorough organization and some pre-planned stratagems of the Macedonian army.

Thus, with the case of Thebes in mind we can suggest that the episode shows another example of the Macedonian strategy of the false retreat: Perdiccas' men, probably an elite squad,[46] began an attack against the enemy with the goal of tempting the defenders away from their defensive walls, and the retreat in battle order was to provoke a pursuit by the enemy and cause confusion, which sometimes led to the gates or the defences being left unattended. After that, a second movement of the Macedonians started, pressuring the enemy with new troops, usually commanded by Alexander himself, the aim of which was to break the enemy's line and gain access to the city. The similarities between the events at Thebes and Halicarnassus are striking and cannot be casual.

Turning our attention back again to Thebes, we know that once the Macedonians had gained the defences of the city, the Theban cavalry that had been fighting outside the city left the battle and fled, even in some cases smashing into their own comrades, who were still trying to protect the city. Nevertheless, the result was a total defeat for Thebes. The Macedonian garrison of the Cadmea came out from its blockaded position and gave support to Alexander's army, which was now on the streets of the city. The Theban defenders inside the walls found themselves under attack on multiple fronts and the number of Macedonians inside the walls was growing at every moment. Chaos spread out over the streets, which became a labyrinth for the defenders, who were gradually being pressed on all sides and surrounded by the enemy.[47] Then the massacre began. Most of the Thebans were slaughtered with no mercy, even the women and children. After the mass rapes and murders, only a few old men, children

---

[46] Like the *hypaspists*, who were mentioned explicitly in the attack on Thebes, the resistance against a numerous enemy force in the case of Halicarnassus made it more probable that the soldiers involved were not ordinary ones (despite the opinion of Diod. Sic. 17.25.5, who describes them as inexperienced troops).
[47] Diod. Sic. 17.12.4-5.

and women survived.[48] Later, our sources say that the city was razed to the ground, as an example to all of Greece of what would happen to those who attempted resistance against Alexander and the Macedonian hegemony. Nevertheless, if we consider the episode of Timoclea,[49] a noble Theban woman who had to quarter some of Alexander's soldiers at her home for some days after the siege, it seems clear that the decision to destroy the city did not happen immediately after it was taken, and at least some days must have passed between the end of the siege and the demolition of the entire city of Thebes. During this time the soldiers were probably allowed to plunder the city for their own profit as a reward for their service, as we can guess also from the story of Timoclea.

After the final destruction of Thebes, the territory was divided among the Macedonian allies, especially those with a vote at the *Synedrion* of the Corinthian League. We know that Plataea, Phocis and Orchomenos were rewarded with lands that had belonged to the Thebans.[50] Our sources also tell us that these *poleis* had taken part in the battle, but we do not know where their forces were during the assault.[51] Because Alexander and his best men were focusing their attention on the tricky action of Perdiccas, it seems probable that the allies were fighting outside the walls, especially against the Theban cavalry.

The surviving Thebans were all sold as slaves.[52] Only the priests, the Theban individuals closely linked with the Macedonians (*proxenoi*), the descendants of Pindar,[53] and possibly some other prominent citizens escaped this sorrowful fate.[54] The sources record that the prisoners numbered 30,000, but, as far as we know, this must be, approximately, the

---

[48] Just. 11.4.2-5.
[49] Timoclea's episode (Plut. *Vit. Alex.* 12; *Mor.* 259C) is our best example about the treatment of the civilians after the siege.
[50] Alexander's own responsibility in deciding to destroy is explicitly mentioned by Polyb. 28.2.13; Plut. *Vit. Alex.* 11.11; Just. 11.3.8, 11-4, 6-8. Alexander's responsibility can be also understood in relation to the actions of the Gods: Squillace 2011, 317. On the other hand, Bosworth 1980, 79, 90 had stressed the fact that there probably was an intention of the ancient contemporary writers about Alexander to exculpate him of the decision to destroy Thebes.
[51] Arr. *Anab.* 1.8.8. Diod. Sic. 17.13.5 writes "Thespians" for "Phocaeans". Just. 11.3.8 mentions the four communities: Phocaeans, Plataeans, Thespians and Orchomenians.
[52] Diod. Sic. 17.13.3; 5-6; 14.1; Plut. *Vit. Alex.* 11. 11-12; Arr. *Anab.* 1.8.6-8.
[53] Arr. *Anab.* 1.9.9; Plut. *Vit. Alex.* 11.12.
[54] This is shown by the episode of Timoclea.

total population of Thebes at that time, and since many Thebans had been killed in the battle, the accuracy of this number is doubtful. It is possible, however, that this number of 30,000 includes people, such as slaves and foreigners, who were not usually considered part of the population of a Greek *polis*, but who we know played an active role in the defence of the city and suffered the same fate as the Theban survivors. The gain for Alexander was around 440 talents of silver.[55]

The destruction of Thebes shows the most ferocious face of Alexander and it functioned as a clear warning to any other polis that might be thinking of rebellion. Fear, then, was the key in the diplomatic relationships between Alexander and the Greeks.[56] Just as Dionysus in Euripides' *Bacchae*, Alexander expected to be recognized by his power, and when this fact was not accepted, this new Macedonian Dionysos reacted like the god did in Euripides' tragedy, destroying and provoking sorrow beyond human limits. But reality always surpasses fiction and Thebes' destruction became a symbol and a monument in the memory of the Greeks for a long time.[57]

BIBLIOGRAPHY

Antela-Bernárdez, B. (2007a) "IG II^2 329: Another View" *ZPE* 160, 177-178.

—. (2007b) "Panhelenismo y Hegemonía: Conceptos políticos en tiempos de Filipo y Alejandro", *DHA* 33, 69-81.

—. (2011) "El día después de Queronea: La liga de Corinto y el imperio macedonio sobre Grecia" in J. Cortés Copete, E. Muñiz & R. Gordillo (eds.) *Grecia ante los imperios*, Sevilla, 187-195.

—. (2012) "Alejandro Magno, *Poliorcetes*", in J. Vidal & B. Antela-Bernárdez (eds.) *Fortificaciones y Guerra de Asedio en el Mundo Antiguo*, Zaragoza, 77-134.

—. (2013) "El carnero macedonio. La táctica de la falsa retirada en tiempos de Filipo y Alejandro", in A. Espino (ed.) Nuevas fronteras de la Historia de la Guerra, Zaragoza, 2013 [in print].

Bonnet, C. (1988) *Melqart. Cultes et Mythes de l'Héraclès tyrien en Méditerranée*, Leuven.

Borza, E. N. (1982) "Athenians, Macedonians, and the Origins of the

---

[55] Diod. Sic. 17.14.4. Cf. Iust. 11.4.8.
[56] Plut. *Vit. Alex.* 11.11.
[57] The cry for the horrors suffered by the Thebans became a topic for the Ancient Greek Writers: Worthington 2003, 65-68; Squillace 2011, 318 n.90.

Macedonian Royal House", *Hesperia Suppl.* 19, 7-13
Bosworth, A. B. (1980) *A historical commentary on Arrian's History of Alexander*, vol. I, Oxford.
—. (1997) *Alejandro Magno*, Cambridge.
Brosius, M. (2003) "Why Persia became the enemy of Macedon", in A. Kuhrt, W. Henkelman (eds.) *A Persian Perspective: Essays in Memory of Heleen Sancisi-Weerdenburg*, Leiden, 227-237.
Cartledge, P. (2004) *Alexander the Great. The Hunt for a New Past*, London.
Cloché, P. (1952) *Thèbes de Béotie. Des origines à la conquête romaine*, Paris.
Fuller, J. F. C. (1958) *The Generalship of Alexander the Great*, London.
Greenwalt, W. (1986) "Herodotus and the Foundation of Argead Macedonia", *AW* 13, 117-122.
Hamilton, J. R. (1999) *Plutarch: Alexander*, London.
Hammond, N. G. L. (1989) *The Macedonian State*, Oxford.
—. (1992) *Alejandro Magno. Rey, general, estadista*, Madrid.
Heckel, W. (1992) *The Marshals of Alexander's Empire*, London.
—. (2006) *Who's who in the age of Alexander the Great*, Malden.
McQueen, E. I. (1995) *Diodorus Siculus: The Reign of Philip II. The Greek and Macedonian Narrative from Book XVI*, Bristol.
Lane Fox, R. (1973) *Alexander the Great,* London.
Rzepka, J. (2008) "The Units of Alexander's Army and the District Division of Late Argead Macedonia", *GRBS* 48, 39-56.
Squillace, G. (2011) "La maschera del vincitore. Strategie propagandistiche di Filippo II e Alessandro Magno nella distruzione di citt`a greche", *Klio* 93, 308-321.
Wallace, S. (2011) "The significance of Plataia for Greek *Eleutheria*in the early Hellenistic period" in A. Erskine & L. Llewellyn-Jones (eds.) *Creating a Hellenistic World*, Swansea, 147-76.
Worthington, I. (2003) "Alexander's Destruction of Thebes", in W. Heckel & L. A. Tritle (eds.) *Crossroads of History: The Age of Alexander the Great*, Claremont, 65-86.
—. (2007) "Encore IG II^2 329", *ZPE* 162, 114-116.

Chapter Seven

Civil War and Counterinsurgency in Greece: Rival Systems of Hegemony during the Fourth Century BC

Konstantinos Lentakis

Introduction

This paper deals with aspects of hegemony in the Greek World from the end of the Peloponnesian War in 404 BC until the completion of the Lamian War in 322, namely the use of terror and counterinsurgency. During the fourth century, the Greek powers competed with each other for the hegemony of the Greek world, by forcing their will upon the weaker city-states. The Archaic ceremonial type of warfare that revolved around the violent clash of armoured hoplites in phalanx formation played a very small role in deciding matters between warring states.[1] During the fourth century, the Greek states experimented with the formation of standing armies, building defensive walls around urban centers, filling their *choras* with fortifications, developing siege engines, placing garrisons in satellite-states, and forming complex alliances based on the allegiance of ruling elites.[2] Routing a phalanx or destroying a naval force was no longer the

---

[1] Hanson 2009, 30-31.
[2] The *chora* was the countryside that surrounded the *asty* (which was the urban centre of each city-state containing all the institutions of government and the *agora*) of the ancient city-state. During the Archaic period, because the population still lived in that part, and had not yet concentrated in an urban centre, this led to the conception that the *chora* was an integral part of the *polis*. Since the *chora* contained all of the city-state's farmland from which it subsisted, it acquired a strategic value that shaped the unique character of hoplite warfare. The city-states fought between themselves by invading the enemy *chora* in order to burn down the

only way to rise to power. Powerful city-states such as Corinth, Argos, and Thebes suffered major defeats in Nemea and Coronea, that did not hinder them from maintaining the war effort, as long as their systems of alliances and client-states remained untouched.[3] Obtaining hegemony was a very complex process that depended a lot on variables other than the outcome of battles between formations of heavy infantry. In the great powers' contest, the Greek cities that competed with each other for leadership in their periphery first, and in the wider Hellenic world second, had to manage issues such as dealing with terror, implementing counterinsurgency strategy in places plagued by civil-war violence, nation-building, and experimenting with city-state integration into confederations. The purpose of this paper is to examine the ways ancient powers used to intervene in the domestic issues of lesser states in order to promote their interests, and provide an overview of how efficient those strategies were and for how long. Political scientist Alexander George suggested studying both cases of success and failure in order to account for their difference, yet in this paper it would be more appropriate to claim that varying degrees of success are compared in order to reach conclusions in regard to strategies of intervention.[4]

TERROR

Terror is the manifestation of mass-scale political violence within a state during peacetime. Political violence signifies the use of homicides against a political group in order to monopolize power within the government, or to silence dissent by an opposition party.[5] In either case,

---

crops before they could be harvested (Wheeler 2011, 235). The defenders would try to prevent that from happening, by sending out their own army to meet with the enemy and engage in pitched battle. The farmland belonging to landowners turned them into the social class with the highest stakes in its defence, which led to the monopoly of warfare by the farmer-hoplites, among the southern Greek city-states, up until the fifth century.
[3] Diod. Sic. 14.82.1-2; Xen. *Hell.* 4.2.1-23, 4.3.3-9, 4.3.14-23.
[4] George 1979, 55.
[5] Political violence is by no means limited to homicide, as it may include pillage, rape, vandalism, and kidnapping, among other forms of coercion. In regard to this paper, homicide is the means used to identify the utilization of terror. The ancient authors paid heed mostly to this form of political violence and that is why it is the best documented amongst all types of force. Xenophon and Aristotle identified political violence with mass-murder, used by the Thirty during their few months' long reign of terror, despite the fact that they also used extensively disenfranchisement, banishment, and seizure of property. Modern day social

terror is the political strategy by a domestic political faction employing mass-murder as the means to secure its political goals. This paper, because it deals with the pursuit of hegemony, uses examples of political violence breaking out within city-states, that was used by third states in order to increase their own influence abroad, either by allying with one of the two sides, or by assisting both of them in reconciling with each other. Political violence, in the form of mass-homicide, was a tactic utilized by a faction against a rival group within the same city-state in order to achieve the strategic goal of political domination. This, however, served the governments of other city-states as an opportunity to enhance their power by intervening as either peace-keepers or in order to promote political violence for their own benefit. To what degree the third actors benefited in regard to claiming hegemony is what this paper aims to find out.

The fourth century was characterized by civil war erupting in many city-states, and such *poleis* also experienced terror and foreign intervention. The accounts of ancient historians, such as Xenophon and Diodorus, are heavily influenced by their own ideological bias.[6] As with all historians who are influenced by political bias, their narratives evolved around the supposed conflict between the two struggling factions of oligarchs and democrats. According to political science, the ideological polarization theory is actually supported by the members of the warring factions, after they have picked sides in the war.[7] Yet members of insurgent movements after extensive interviews tend to change the rationale of their choices from political to personal. Research, on more recent conflicts, shows that those who take part in civil war do not do so because they are subject to the effects of ideological polarization, instead they pursue their private interests in a new way that was not available to them during

---

scientists agree on the prevalence of homicide over other forms of violence, due to its direct, irreversible and conclusive form of annihilation (Sofsky 1998, 53; Straus 2001, 364).

[6] On the epistemological preference, within the fields of history and sociology, to assign ideological motives to civil war combatants see Kalyvas 2006, 38-48.

[7] According to the ideological polarization theory, the motivation of the participants of civil wars, both combatants and non-combatants, seems to be one of the ideologies espoused by the warring factions. Modern-day combatants tend to initially ascribe ideology as the reason why they joined a faction by themselves, notwithstanding after being extensively interviewed they change their motives to personal (cf. Ermakoff 2001, 4 cited in Kalyvas 2006, 46). In the provinces of Revolutionary France, individuals chose sides according to chance or personal ambitions, and afterwards the Parisian elites labeled them politically (Cobb 1972, 123).

peacetime.[8] Antiquity was no exception to the rules that decide the behaviour of individuals in civil wars today. People sought to survive first, and exploit conflict to advance themselves second.[9] Lysias, who took part in the Athenian civil war, also came to the conclusion that people join sides based on their private interests at the time, not on political preferences.[10] All civil war violence being explained as a product of the division between oligarchs and democrats was something that was a tale reconstructed by historians and politicians long after the conflict had erupted, sacrificing the original and complex conditions that enveloped people into domestic conflict for a simpler and ideal explanation of its origins.[11]

The first example of such a case comes from Thucydides in an episode of the Peloponnesian War that took place in Corcyra.[12] He claimed that the democrats invited the Athenian forces to help defend them from being forcefully annexed by the Corinthians. When the Athenian forces arrived at Corcyra, the local democratic faction conspired with them against the oligarchic faction, and as soon as the Athenians departed, the Corcyrean democrats led a bloody purge against those they had designated as oligarchs. The democrats convinced the Athenians to approve of this measure, by claiming that the oligarchs were plotting to join Sparta's alliance. Yet before this purge had taken place, there was no indication of the so called oligarchic faction's activities leading to such a conclusion. The oligarchs were not against opposing Corinth in favour of Corcyrean autonomy, or receiving Athenian aid against their country's enemies. The

---

[8] Kalyvas has researched extensively in the field on the reasons why the inhabitants of the Argolid joined the Germans against the Greek communists, during the formers' counterinsurgent campaign of 1944 (2006, 262-3).
[9] The *crypteia* was a proto-state secret service institution that dealt with domestic threats to the Spartan government (Plut. *Vit. Lyc.* 28.1-6). An example of the similarities between ancient and modern-day political violence is that the Spartan *crypteia* dealt with influential *helots* (Plut. *Vit. Lyc.* 28.2-3) in the same manner that the communist insurgents treated the ruling elites of the Argolid's communities in 1943 (Kalyvas 2006, 257-261), and for the same reasons as well.
[10] Lys. 25.10-11.
[11] The theory of retrospective rationality introduced by social psychologist Eliott Aronson deals with the causes of this behaviour (2007, 120-2). Andrew Wolpert wrote extensively on the reconstruction of the Athenian civil war narrative and the reasons behind it (2002, 119-136). On the Messenian ethno-genesis after the founding of Ithome in 369/8 as a product of the war between the Sparta and Boeotia see Luraghi 2008, 209-248.
[12] Thuc. 3.69-85.

olicarchs joined the Peloponnesian side and fought against their own demos, after the purge against them had taken place.

Xenophon describes a similar case that occurred in the Fourth Century.[13] He claimed that the Corinthian democrats conspired with the Allied Council against the landed citizens of their *polis*. The latter had grown weary of the war, because they had suffered the most from the Peloponnesian League's incursions. Yet although the Corinthian democrats and their Argive allies led a bloody cleansing of the "Peace Party", again there was no indication that the latter were in favour of changing sides, or of pursuing a philo-Laconian policy. The Corinthian landowners did conspire with the local Spartan commander to betray their own city, but only after they had suffered a brutal attack by their own fellow citizens and allies, and that is the reason why they ultimately changed sides.[14]

In both cases, the civil war violence was not pursued due to having a different ideological set of views, but in order to gain more power and money by purging wealthy and influential citizens. Recent research has eroded the polarization theory, by proving that conflict within communities actually depends upon matters of personal differences, caused by private issues, such as settling scores between neighbours, financial disputes among family members, and pursuing an increase in one's own influence and prestige through collaborating with a warring faction by denouncing other members of the local community. Greek city-states were not above such practices, and the civil war violence that took place within their borders had the same origins as its twentieth century counterpart.[15]

Terror was used by powerful city-states to polarize the societies of their client-states and help create elites that were committed to serving the interests of their patrons, in order to continue ruling and to avoid retaliation from the opposition. In both the cases of Corcyra and Corinth,

---

[13] Xen. *Hell.* 4.4.3-5; Diod. Sic. 14.86.1-2.
[14] Xen. *Hell.* 4.4.7.
[15] For this reason Kalyvas in his study of civil war violence in 1940s Greece (2006), frequently brings up as an example Corcyra's civil war described by Thucydides, its progress being a classic example of how foreign intervention functioned as a catalyst in regard to the eruption of political violence, and the fragmentation this caused to the Corcyrean society soon afterwards, as the democratic faction allied with Athens, and the oligarchs joined the Peloponnesian League.

the use of terror as a strategy to establish a satellite-state worked only in the short-term. Corcyra and Corinth had their exiles returned and their city's autonomy restored, while Athens and Argos lost entirely an important ally in their struggle against Sparta.[16] In the long-term their use of terror was a flawed strategy, because this brought ill fame to the two city-states, who were seen as brutes using foul means in order to maintain and expand their sphere of influence, ultimately bringing harm to the cohesion of their alliances.

COUNTERINSURGENCY

In the contest between the great powers, historians have tended to focus on the direct interactions between them, especially on pitched battles between massed armed forces, and on carrying out diplomatic negotiations. However, these were secondary in importance towards deciding which would be the most powerful state in Greece. The process of rising to power involved to a great degree the involvement of powerful *poleis* in the political processes of less powerful states. Since the western interventions in Afghanistan and Iraq during the first decade of the twenty-first century, the term broadly used for this kind of operation is counterinsurgency.[17] In the past counterinsurgency was called small wars strategy because it was identified with western powers carrying out military interventions in weaker countries, either to establish a political equilibrium according to the formers' interests or as part of colonial politics in the context of running empires. Today, for reasons of political correctness, as well as because European colonialism today is associated with western exploitation of third world countries, small wars strategy has been

---

[16] Xen. *Hell.* 5.1.32-34.
[17] Counterinsurgency (COIN) implies strict military operations against armed insurgent forces, yet it has come to involve the provision of security and services to the local population, direct meddling in the normalization of the political process, and even the planning and funding of local infrastructure projects. In fact military operations against insurgent forces are considered secondary in importance, in regard to the aforementioned measures, according to COIN doctrine (Austin 2006, 23-24, 52-54, 66; *Counterinsurgency Field Manual* 2007, 37-50; Kilcullen 2010, 43-45). The Hearts and Minds approach was implemented in order to deal with the backlash caused by the introduction and development of modernity into traditional societies that then experience the fragmentation of old institutions (Austin 2006, x). Ancient powers experienced similar issues. *Poleis* such as Athens and Sparta had to deal with violent opposition to the regimes that they helped install, and had to take similar measures in order to maintain their hegemony across Greece.

replaced with the term counterinsurgency. Yet, for all intents and purposes, since ancient powers carried out military interventions against lesser city-states with the same political goals, to bring stability in the region, and using the same means, such as installing garrisons and forming puppet-governments, counterinsurgency will be the name of the strategy that they used in regard to running their petty empires.

SPARTA

The Spartan model of counterinsurgency focused on the establishment of *decarchies*, the use of *harmosts*, and the placing of garrisons in allied city-states. The *decarchies* were ruling councils comprised of ten-members that had absolute power over the inhabitants of their *poleis*, yet they depended entirely upon Lacedaemonian support in order to maintain power. Since governments handpicked by foreigners did not tend to acquire much popularity from the local population, the Lacedaemonians were forced to send *harmosts* and garrisons in order to maintain their favourites in power. The *harmosts* were Spartan citizens who acted as advisors to the local governments, much in the same way Gylippus did in Syracuse during the Athenian expedition in Sicily, and also served as military commanders to the local Peloponnesian garrison.[18] The Peloponnesian garrisons consisted of small Lacedaemonian forces, mainly *neodamodes*, and their Peloponnesian allies, mostly mercenaries who served instead of citizen-hoplites.[19] The garrisons served a double function. They guaranteed that the *decarchies* stayed in power against local opposition, and provided security from the depredations of foreign states.

The Spartans avoided taking part in internecine conflict and sought instead to maintain political stability within city-states, in order to maintain their puppet-governments and the tribute flowing to their city-state that helped them maintain their costly fleet. Cases that display the Spartans' avoidance of promoting political violence within satellite-states that were suffering from civil strife were Phlius and Mantinea.[20] During the 380s, the Spartans carried out military interventions in the two *poleis*, leading to the installation of puppet governments. Although the governments installed by the Spartans were illegitimate and unpopular,

---

[18] Diod. Sic. 14.10.1-2; Thuc. 6.93.
[19] Diod. Sic. 14.12.1-3; Xen. *Hell*.4.4.14. The *neodamodes* were former *helots* who had joined the Lacedaemonian phalanx as hoplites (Ath. 6.102).
[20] Xen. *Hell*. 5.2.5-6, 5.3.25.

they did not carry out campaigns of terror against the population, but maintained order and stability within their states for as long as Sparta held them under control. Two exceptions have been documented that actually prove the rule of the Spartan model of counterinsurgency focusing on order and stability. In Byzantium and Athens the *harmosts* and their garrisons directly promoted political violence.[21] The fact that the garrisons had violated the Lacedaemonian instructions is proven by the fact that Spartan-led armies soon intervened and put an end to this behaviour by having them removed.[22]

ATHENS

The Athenian Demos learned a lot from its past ordeals in Sicily and Corcyra at the height of the Peloponnesian War. The Athenians stopped committing all of their forces to achieve their aims at the local level, as they had done in the past. In Sicily and at Aegospotami, they suffered tremendous casualties that ultimately cost them their empire and autonomy. Never again in the fourth century did the Athenians concentrate all of their forces in a single place. Even during the Lamian War, with most of the Athenian armed forces operating abroad, when the Macedonians attempted a landing in Attica, the Athenians had their fleet opposing its Macedonian counterpart in the Aegean, while the army was engaged against Antipater in Lamia.[23]

Throughout the fourth century the Athenians would use only limited forces in order to achieve their aims. Even during the 370s, when the Athenians were very militarily active, splinter Athenian fleets would be intervening in foreign *poleis* in both the Aegean and Ionian Seas, while the land forces were committed elsewhere. The bulk of the Athenian army, during the 370s, was annually sent to Thebes, in order to help the latter maintain its autonomy from Sparta, while the Lacedaemonians led brutal incursions into the Theban *chora*.[24] Because of this, the Athenian fleet found itself overextended as the Lacedaemonian control of its maritime empire collapsed very fast, and the Athenians had to intervene quickly with petty forces, in order to reestablish order and make sure that the recently "liberated" city-states found their way into the Second Athenian

---

[21] Diod. Sic. 14.12.3; Xen. *Hell.* 2.3.21.
[22] Diod. Sic. 14.12.4; Xen. *Hell.* 2.4.35.
[23] Plut. *Vit. Phoc.* 25.1-2.
[24] Diod. Sic. 15.32.1-15.34.2; Plut. *Vit. Ages.* 26.2-3; Xen. *Hell.* 5.4.35-5.4.59.

League.[25]

Induction into the Second Athenian League provided city-states with protection from the Spartan-led Peloponnesian League, as well as from piracy, whose rise the Lacedaemonian and Persian fleets had come to ignore. Each member-state of the League had a single vote in the alliance's council, called the *synedrion*, except for Athens. Yet unlike the Delian League, the Athenian Demos was not able to act on its own; every decision had to be approved by the *synedrion* first.[26] Thus the new member-states acquired a greater role in allied decision-making in the Athenian League than they had had before in the Peloponnesian League, where the members of their own governments were hand-picked by the Spartans. Still the member-states had to contribute monies for the alliance's costly naval military operations, which were carried out solely by Athens, in the Aegean and Ionian seas. Yet, as was stated earlier, the Athenians would not force their allies to pay excessive amounts in order to secure their own interests at the cost of their allies' as they had done in the past with the Delian League.[27]

It should be added that the Athenians had learnt a valuable lesson from their ill-fated intervention in Corcyra during the Peloponnesian War. The Athenian Demos had taken sides, and assisted the Corcyrean democrats in cleansing their city-state of the opposition. This ill decision ultimately cost Athens a valuable ally, who had been pivotal in the confrontation with the Peloponnesian League. In fact, Corcyra was considered so valuable that it became the reason why the war began, as the Athenian Demos decided that it was preferable to fight for Corcyrean autonomy than to allow Corinth and its allies to subjugate the Ionian naval power.

During the 370s, Athenian forces overthrew the governments that had been put in place by the Lacedaemonians, and ousted the Peloponnesian garrisons that had helped them to stay in power.[28] In the aftermath of these events, the freshly liberated city-states suffered from civil strife due to the power vacuum created by the loss of the small ruling elites' monopoly of government. The Athenians made certain that they created friendships with both sides competing for power, and assisted those societies going through the process of reconciliation. They did not pick sides as they had done

---

[25] Xen. *Hell*. 6.2.29-38.
[26] Cf. Cargill 1981, 185-6; Hammond 1977, 486-7.
[27] I.G., ii^2, 43.
[28] Diod. Sic. 15.36.5-6.

during the Peloponnesian War; instead they assisted city-states with normalizing their affairs and in restoring the political process. This selfless strategy, implemented from the formation of the Second Athenian League in 378 until the battle of Leuctra in 371, allowed the Athenians to reach the peak of their power in the fourth century. After the battle of Leuctra, the surprising rise in power of Thebes and the collapse of Lacedaemonian influence throughout Greece brought panic to the Athenian demos, which chose to change its successful strategy for realpolitik. This change led to Athens forming alliances with autocratic regimes such as Elis, Syracuse, and Sparta in order to oppose democratic Thebes, and forcing Athenian garrisons into foreign states, ultimately alienating the most important member-states of the Second Athenian League, causing the Social War and the implosion of Athenian influence in the 350s.

THEBES

The Thebans rose to power in the late 370s, after having successfully defeated the Peloponnesian garrisons based in Boeotia in several engagements, and having fended off several massive Lacedaemonian-led incursions into their own *chora*.[29] After the battle of Leuctra in 371, where Thebes replaced Lacedaemon as the greatest land power in Greece, the Theban Demos adopted a very aggressive foreign policy of forceful democratization throughout mainland Greece. The Thebans took advantage of the Athenian failure to replace the power vacuum that had been created by Sparta's fall, and began to assist the Peloponnesian *poleis* in the process of democratization.[30] The Thebans, being full of confidence after their confrontation with the Lacedaemonian phalanx at Leuctra, welcomed the opportunity to confront a weakened Lacedaemon for the prize of the Peloponnesus. The Theban Demos provided assistance to the Peloponnesian *poleis* during their difficult transitions to democracy, and gave them military aid, rescuing them from the threat of Lacedaemonian military intervention.[31] The Lacedaemonians would have attempted to

---

[29] Diod. Sic. 15.37.1-2; Xen. *Hell.* 5.4.42-6.
[30] The Athenians had allied with nearly seventy Peloponnesian city-states after the devastating defeat of the Lacedaemonian army in Boeotia, nevertheless they backed out from assisting their new allies, when it was made clear that if they pursued this policy they would find themselves forced into a direct military confrontation with Sparta (Xen. *Hell.* 6.5.1-3). On whether the Athenians allied with over seventy city-states or merely with twenty-four see Cargill 1981, 46-47.
[31] It should be noted that in Boeotia the Theban Demos followed a completely different foreign policy, being quite brutal towards the Boeotians. The Thebans

prevent the spread of democracy, were it not for Boeotian infantry defending that political experiment.[32]

Still, it should be mentioned that the Thebans, much like their Athenian counterparts at that time, thanks to Epaminondas' influence, decided not to take sides in *poleis* suffering from civil strife.[33] They assisted conflicting sides in reconciling and averted the threat of the eruption of mass violence where they could. However, unlike the Athenians, the Thebans committed their full resources in these enterprises, and because of that they achieved much more than just the peaceful democratization of the Peloponnese.

Thebes throughout the 360s embarked not only on the democratization of the Peloponnese, but also on a project of nation-building. The Thebans assisted the Arcadian and Achaean experiments with confederacy, helped Mantinean communities reunite into a single state, and even caused a civil war within Lacedaemon that culminated with the secession of Messenia and the founding of the heavily fortified city-state of Ithome.[34] The Spartans in the early fourth century had to deal with the threat of civil strife in the state of Lacedaemon on two occasions: The first was with a Lacedaemonian called Cinadon who plotted against the citizenry, and the second was with Lysander who hoped to overthrow the two ruling Spartan dynasties.[35] After the debacle of Leuctra with over four hundred *homoioi* lying dead in Boeotia, it was not very difficult for the Theban Demos to divide Lacedaemonian society.[36] Having failed to cross the Eurotas River

---

displaced the citizenries of disloyal city-states and installed their own colonists, who would then vote in favour of Theban interests at the assemblies of the Boeotian League. An example of this is the destruction of Orchomenus, which took place after the Theban defeat at Mantinea in 361 (Diod. Sic. 15.79.5-6; Paus. 9.15.3). Theban brutality towards the Boeotians ultimately had an extremely high cost for the Thebans. During the siege of Thebes by Alexander in 335, the Boeotians took revenge against their former overlords by committing atrocities while sacking Thebes, and afterwards voted to sell the inhabitants into slavery, to raze the city, and split the former Theban *chora* amongst themselves (Arr. *Anab.* 1.7.8-1.9.10; Diod. Sic. 17.14.2-4).

[32] After the pitched battles of Leuctra and Mantinea, the Thebans installed a formidable garrison in Ithome that stayed behind and defended the city from the Lacedaemonians after the Boeotian army had departed from the Peloponnese (Diod. Sic. 15.67.1).

[33] Diod. Sic. 15.57.1.

[34] Diod. Sic. 15.66.1-6; Plut. *Vit. Pel.* 24; Paus. 4.26.27; Xen. *Hell.* 6.5.6-9.

[35] Diod. Sic. 14.13.3-8; Plut. *Vit. Ages.* 20.3; Xen. *Hell.* 3.3.4-11.

[36] Diod. Sic. 15.33.5-6. Xenophon claimed that several *perioeci* (second-class

due to its swelling, the Boeotian forces crossed Mount Taygetus and "liberated" Messene instead.[37] The Thebans overthrew the oligarchic constitution in the periphery of Lacedaemon, and replaced it with a new democratic regime. The Lacedaemonians, who had been scorned in the past for not being part of the citizenry, and whose political views were largely ignored and unrepresented in Sparta's assemblies, now became full citizens in a democratic republic, and, while Messene's impressive walls were being built, the citizens were granted protection from Spartan reprisals by the Boeotians. The original inhabitants of Ithome, who answered Epaminondas' call, must have been baffled by Epaminondas' claims that they were an enslaved people fallen prey to Spartan imperialism.[38] Yet, as in the coming years, the Lacedaemonian loyalist and secessionist phalanxes clashed against each other time and again, and what Agesilaus had initially viewed as Pythagorean rants in a diplomatic meeting, became state ideology and national history in the coming centuries, as we know from Pausanias' account.[39] The Messenian Lacedaemonians had every reason to avoid admitting that they were traitors who took advantage of a foreign invasion of their own country in order to advance their personal interests. Instead they adopted Epaminondas' narrative that they were the descendants of the original inhabitants who dwelled in Messene before the expansion of Lacedaemon, regardless of which social class they belonged to earlier, and from which community in Lacedaemon they had come.[40]

The double aims of democratization and nation-building in Messene were achieved thanks to Thebes' full commitment to overthrowing the

---

Lacedaemonian citizens above the helots in Lacedaemon's social hierarchy, yet not equal to the Spartans) appealed to Epaminondas not to turn back home with his army, but to invade their country because it was in turmoil (*Hell.* 6.5.25). *Homoioi*, roughly translated as equals, was the term used for Lacedaemonians who enjoyed full citizenship. Before the secession of Messene, Spartans and *homoioi* were synonymous, while after the founding of Ithome the Spartans became more associated as an ethnic group rather than a social class.

[37] Plut. *Vit. Ages.* 32.2; Xen. *Ages.* 2.24. On the participation of Arcadians and Argives in the 369/8 Boeotian invasion of Lacedaemon and the founding of Messene (Paus. 4.26.7, 4.27.7) see Luraghi 2008, 214; Tausend 1992, 155.

[38] Paus. 4.4.4-4.24.6. Epaminondas destroyed the peace talks between Thebes and Lacedaemon when he ranted about the occupation of Messene by the Lacedaemonians (Plut. *Vit. Ages.* 28.1-2). Cf. Cartledge 1987, 379-80; Jehne 1994, 71-4; Keen 1996, 115-17; Rhodes 1999.

[39] Paus. 4.4.4-4.24.6. Cf. Luraghi 2008, 247-8.

[40] Cf. Luraghi 2009, 117-123; Robinson 1987, 138.

Lacedaemonian hegemony with every force available, as well as to the fact that it had just regained dominance in the re-founded Boeotian League. Using a military force, whose size ranged between twenty and forty thousand heavy infantrymen, to invade Laconia and occupy Western Lacedaemon for months until the walls of Ithome were completely built is one of the greatest military achievements of fourth century democracy, and definitely something that Athens could not fulfill at the time even if its Demos had wanted to.[41] Notwithstanding Thebes' success in Messene, the Boeotian city-state lacked an economy as powerful as Athens, and nation-building in South Greece had its toll on it. The Thebans, after suffering defeat at Mantinea, no longer had the resources to run an empire efficiently, and saw their influence wither in Central Greece, leading to autocratic restorations in Euboea, Phocis, and Thessaly.

MACEDON

The Macedonian kings employed all of the aforementioned measures after 338, such as installing garrisons and forcing political stability in Thessaly, imposing democratic government in Asia Minor, or tyrannical regimes on the Greek mainland, and promoting nation-building in Macedon itself.[42] Yet their unique contribution to maintaining stability among their client-states was Philip's introduction of the League of Corinth.[43] The League was an organization supposed to unite the Greek city-states, and mobilize their armed forces against the Persian Empire. It actually served to communicate the demands and problems of the ruling Greek elites to the Macedonian dynasty, and as a way to alleviate the unpopularity caused by the latter's hegemony in Greek affairs. It also provided security to the Greek city-states from a resurgent Sparta subsidized by Persian gold. When Agis III of Sparta returned to the Peloponnese from a successful military campaign in Crete, he led a war

---

[41] The Athenian armed forces at their peak in the fifth century possessed around sixteen thousand hoplites and over a thousand cavalrymen (Thuc. 2.16.3-7). Mobilizing over twenty thousand Boeotian military-age men to go on a campaign far from Boeotia (Plut. *Vit. Ages.* 31.1) remained unprecedented in Greece until the twentieth century, when the Greek nation-state would employ modern institutions in order to mobilize such massive numbers of manpower.

[42] The size of the forces that the Macedonians used for maintaining their empire varied from Thrace to the Peloponnese, making it difficult to claim that they consistently used either great or limited forces to achieve their aims in regard to counterinsurgency.

[43] Diod. Sic. 17.48.1.

against Macedonian hegemony, and became so bold that he asked the Athenian Demos to join in an alliance against Antipater.[44] The League established by Philip functioned quite well, and maintained its cohesion and loyalty to Macedon.[45] In fact, Antipater being devoid of experienced troops, having dispatched most of them to Alexander due to the latter's needs for the escalating military confrontation with the Great King, had to use the forces of the "subjugated" city-states in the Greek mainland. The Greek city-states, being full of painful memories from Sparta's thirty-three years' long hegemony, quickly mobilized as soon as Antipater was able to lead a campaign against the Spartan King. Without the League of Corinth, Sparta would have rampaged throughout the South Peloponnese, destroying Megalopolis and Ithome. The contribution of the Macedonian regent was limited to providing valuable military leadership to the Peloponnesian city-states' armed forces, that would have otherwise stood idle or have been forced to fight against Lacedaemon in detail.[46] The League of Corinth was without a doubt a much more moderate form of control of city-states than garrisons and the promotion of civil-strife were. The League turned out to be very successful in maintaining the Macedonian hegemony in Greece without serious opposition, until Alexander undermined it as his late-reign became more authoritarian, and his meddling into its member-states' affairs more conspicuous.

CONCLUSIONS

The use of terror and counterinsurgency during the fourth century became defining aspects of empire-building for Greek states. Whether the *poleis* seeking to obtain hegemony would take advantage of civil-strife in other city-states or would implement a counterinsurgency strategy, often decided the endurance of their petty empires in time and their success against enemies seeking to topple them. For a few years Argos was similar in size to Lacedaemon, but this created a Corinthian insurgency that would always undermine the complete assimilation of Corinth by Argos.[47]

---

[44] Diod. Sic. 17.62.4-6. Athens since its defeat at the battle of Chaeronea had become a member-state of the League of Corinth (Plut. *Vit. Phoc.*16.4-5).
[45] Agis was joined by the Achaeans, Elis, and several Arcadian city-states, probably bent on looting, but no one from beyond the Peloponnese allied with Sparta (Diod. Sic. 17.62.7).
[46] Diod. Sic. 17.62.1-63.4; Quint. 6.1.21; Fox 1973, 252.
[47] The landowners, who had grown weary of the Corinthian War, were Corinth's finest shock troops, and had dared face the Lacedaemonian phalanx at the battle of Nemea, suffering many casualties among their ranks (Xen. *Hell.* 4.2.18-23). Being

Moreover the insurgents became allies of Sparta, with whom they would always work in tandem against the expanded state, making its survival less likely.[48] Athens and Thebes were more successful than Argos during the 370s and 360s respectively because they refused to take sides in cases of dispute, or to escalate civil strife into civil war, and for this reason they were able to create larger and more powerful empires than Argos. Sparta's imperial model was quite successful, for in only two cases did it break down without foreign intervention.[49] The collapse of the Spartan hegemony was due to its decades-long confrontation with the most advanced Greek *poleis*, Athens and Thebes, taking its toll on the *polis* whose social institutions and economy remained Archaic. Despite the claims of Aristotle and Polybius, as well as quite a few twentieth century historians, that Sparta was unfit for empire-building, the resilience of its hegemony for decades, while being at war with the most powerful Greek states as well as the Persian Empire, is most impressive.[50] Furthermore, Sparta's use of garrisons as a tool for controlling city-states was a proven success, emulated by the Macedonian and Roman Empires in the following centuries.

Philip II of Macedon added to counterinsurgency the use of the panhellenic organization known as the League of Corinth. It was based on the past models of the Delian and Peloponnesian Leagues, yet it proved to be far superior to them, by becoming a way of moderating the Macedonian hegemony, instead of intensifying its less pleasant effects upon the Greek member-states.

Counterinsurgency strategy in the fourth century, much like today, was implemented differently by each state, yet those which were successful connected military efforts to political goals. In contrast to what was the case with states that relied on strict enemy-centric strategies that sought to impose their rule by annihilating the enemy in a single blow, their influence lasted for longer periods. The most successful forms of counterinsurgency, those aiding the patron states to vastly increase in power for very long periods, depended on installing garrisons within client

---

betrayed by their own allies and fellow-citizens (Xen. *Hell.* 4.4.1-4), many Corinthian landowners were forced to commit treason and fight bitterly against their own city-state for the remainder of the war (Xen. *Hell.* 4.4.6-13).
[48] Xen. *Hell.* 4.4.13.
[49] Xen. *Hell.* 2.4.23, 5.4.5-7, 5.4.10-11.
[50] Arist. *Pol.* 2.6.22-3; Polyb. 6.49.6-10; Forrest 1968, 125-6; Michell 1952, 334; Strauss & Ober 1990, 99-101; Toynbee 1969, 298-9.

states and helped bring stability and security, while those who relied on the promotion of intrastate conflict and instability in order to take advantage of their neighbours, saw their power disintegrate sooner rather than later.

BIBLIOGRAPHY

Aronson, E. (2007) *The Social Animal*. New York.
Austin, L. (2006) *On the "Other" War: Lessons from Five Decades of RAND Counterinsurgency Research*. Santa Monica, California.
Cargill, J. (1981) *The Second Athenian League: Empire of Free Alliance?*. Berkeley; Los Angeles; London.
Cartledge, P. (1987) *Agesilaos and the Crisis of Sparta*. London.
Cobb, R. (1972) *Reactions to the French Revolution*. London.
Ermakoff, I. (2001) *Ideological Challenges, Strategies of Action, and Regime Breakdown*. Unpublished paper, Department of Sociology, University of Wisconsin-Madison.
Forrest, W. G. (1968) *A History of Sparta, 950-192 B.C.* London.
Fox, R. L. (1986) *Alexander the Great*. London.
George, A. (1979) "Case studies and Theory Development: The Method of Structured, Focused Comparison", in P. G. Lauren, (ed.) *Diplomacy: New Approaches in History, Theory, and Policy*, New York, 43-68.
Hammond, N. G. L. (1977) *A History of Greece to 322 B.C.* Oxford.
Hanson, V. D. (2009) *The Western Way of War: Infantry Battle in Classical Greece*. Berkeley; Los Angeles; London.
Jehne, M. (1994) *Koine Eirene: Untersuchungen zu den Befriedungs- und Stabilisierungsbemühungen in der griechischen Poliswelt des 4. Jahrhunderts v. Chr.* Stuttgart.
Kalyvas, S., N. (2006) *The Logic of Violence in Civil War*. Cambridge.
Keen, A. G. (1996) "Were the Boeotian poleis autonomoi?", In M. H. Hansen and K. Raaflaub, (eds.) *More Studies in the Ancient Greek Polis*. Stuttgart, 113-125.
Kilcullen, D. (2010) *Counterinsurgency*. London.
Luraghi, N. (2008) *The Ancient Messenians: Constructions of Ethnicity and Memory*. Cambridge, UK; New York.
—. (2009) "Messenian Ethicity and the Free Messenians", in P. Funke and N. Luraghi, (eds.) *The Politics and Ethnicity and the crisis of the Peloponnesian League*. Hellenic Studies 32. Cambridge, Massachusetts; London, 110-134.
Michell, H. (1952) *Sparta*. Cambridge.
Rhodes, P. J. (1999) "Sparta, Thebes and autonomia", *Eirene 35*, 33-40.
Sofsky, W. (1998) *Traité de la violence*. Paris.

Straus, S. (2001) "Definitions and Sub-Types: A Conceptual Analysis of Genocide", *Journal of Genocide Research 3(3)*, 349-375.
Strauss, B. and Ober, J. (1990) *The Anatomy of Error: Ancient Military Disasters and Their Lessons for Modern Strategists*. New York.
Tausend, K. (1992) *Amphiktyonie und Symmachie. Formen zwischenstaatlicher Beziehungen in archaischen Griechenland. Historia Einzelschrift 73*. Stuttgart.
The US Army/Marine Corps Counterinsurgency Field Manual (2007) London.
Toynbee, A. (1969) *Some Problems of Greek History*. Chicago; London.
Wolpert, A. (2002) *Remembering Defeat: Civic War and Civic Memory in Ancient Athens*. Baltimore; London.

Chapter Eight

The Problem of the Four Hundred Wagons: The Provisioning of the Ten Thousand on the March to Cunaxa

Dr. Stephen O'Connor

When the Ten Thousand returned to their camp after the battle of Cunaxa, Xenophon tells us that:

> καταλαμβάνουσι δὲ τῶν τε ἄλλων χρημάτων τὰ πλεῖστα διηρπασμένα καὶ εἴ τι σιτίον ἢ ποτὸν ἦν, καὶ τὰς ἁμάξας μεστὰς ἀλεύρων καὶ οἴνου, ἃς παρεσκευάσατο Κῦρος, ἵνα εἴ ποτε σφόδρα τὸ στράτευμα λάβοι ἔνδεια, διαδιδοίη τοῖς Ἕλλησιν—ἦσαν δ' αὗται τετρακόσιαι, ὡς ἐλέγοντο, ἅμαξαι—καὶ ταύτας τότε οἱ σὺν βασιλεῖ διήρπασαν.

[t]hey found most of their property pillaged, in particular whatever there was to eat or drink, and as for the wagons loaded with wheat-flour and wine which Cyrus had provided in order that, if ever serious need should overtake the army, he might have supplies to distribute among the Greeks (and there were four hundred of these wagons, it was said), these also the King and his men had now pillaged. (1.10.18)[1]

---

[1] All text references in this chapter will be to Xenophon's *Anabasis*, unless otherwise indicated. All translations are taken from the Loeb edition of the *Anabasis*. I would like to thank the editors, and the two anonymous referees engaged by the editors, for their constructive comments on this chapter. I would also like to thank Kelly Donovan, Graphic Artist at the Faculty Development Center, California State University, Fullerton, for producing the map and tables accompanying the chapter. Finally, I would like to thank again Geoff Lee for being the driving force behind such a successful and stimulating 2013 IAWC in Aberystwyth.

The role of these wagons in the provisioning of the Greek mercenaries hired by Cyrus has been the source of much controversy. Some scholars have denied that the wagons existed at all,[2] basing this view primarily on the fact that Xenophon used the phrase "ὡς ἐλέγοντο" ("as it was said") in reporting the number of the wagons prepared by Cyrus. But Xenophon states in his own voice that Cyrus provided the wagons—therefore they must have existed—and the words "ὡς ἐλέγοντο" here, far from expressing doubt as to the existence of the four hundred wagons prepared by Cyrus, are, in fact, used by Xenophon to authorize the extremely large figure given for their number.[3]

Other scholars have taken the position that the wagons did exist and that they accompanied most or all of Cyrus's march to Cunaxa.[4] Griffith, for example, took the presence of the four hundred wagons in the camp of the Greeks after the battle of Cunaxa as evidence to support the view that the mercenaries were provisioned from the start of their march primarily through rations in kind provided by Cyrus and transported on the wagons.[5] Descat took the mention of the wagons at 1.10.18 as evidence supporting a hypothesis that, from Thapsacus onwards, the mercenaries were provisioned in kind from imperial stores of grain carried on the wagons.[6]

---

[2] Roy 1967, 311 n. 93; Krasilnikoff 1993, 83-84; Lendle 1995, 90 (more doubting than denying); Lee 2007, 134, 215. Roy (1967, 311 n. 93) is cited by each of the last three scholars in support of their position, but Roy has recently changed his position on the wagons and now believes that they did, in fact, exist: see Roy 2004, 277 and n. 27, following Gabrielli 1995 with an important reservation (see n.17 below).

[3] See Gray 2003, 116 (with n. 29 citing 1.10.18 as an example): "The major function of citations [in Xenophon] is to validate content that the the reader might find too great to be believed. The writer engages with the reader to authorize... excessively large or small numbers..." Cf. Gray 2003, 123. See also Gray 2003, 117: "The citations [in Xenophon's *Anabasis* and *Hellenica*] do not authorize entire stories, only details in a larger story that the narrator tells in his own voice... [Xenophon] does not use citations where his knowledge falls short, or because he disbelieves the report, or for any other straight research reason."

[4] See the accompanying map – Fig. 8.1 – for the location of all place names between Myriandros and Cunaxa mentioned in this chapter. The outline of the march route presented there follows Lee 2007, 20-21.

[5] See Griffith 1935, 266 (followed by Dillery 1995, 67; Loomis 1998, 47-48, esp. 48 n.65).

[6] Descat 1995, 104.

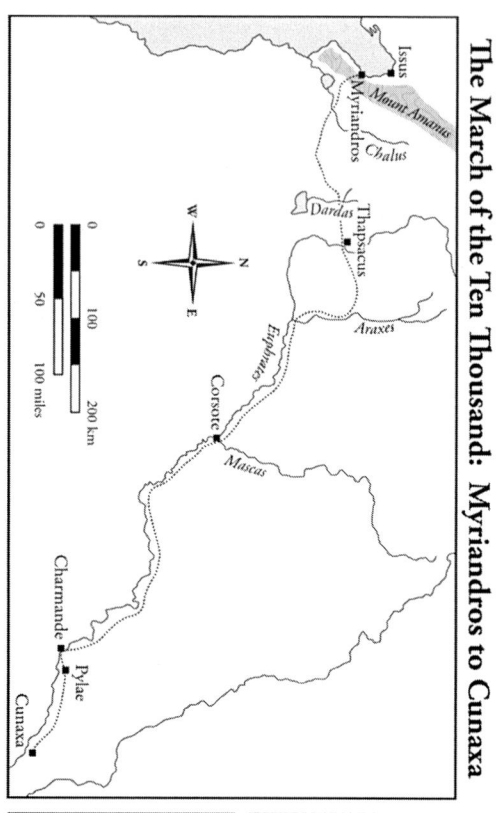

The March of the Ten Thousand: Myriandros to Cunaxa

Fig. 8.1

March Halts: Myriandros to Cunaxa

1. Myriandros (1.4.6)
2. Chalus River/Villages of Parysatis (1.4.9)
3. Dardas River/Palace of Belesys (1.4.10)
4. Thapsacus/Euphrates (1.4.11)
5. Araxes River/Villges (1.4.19)
6. Corsote/Mascas River (1.5.4)
7. Charmande/Euphrates (1.5.10)
8. Pylae/Euphrates (1.5.5)

March Rates: Myriandros to Cunaxa

March Stage	Number of March Days	Number of Parasangs	Average Daily March Rate (kms)
Myriandros to Chalus River	4	20	25-30
Chalus to Dardas River	5	30	30-36
Dardas River to Thapsacus	3	15	25-30
Thapsacus to Araxes River	9	50	28-33
Araxes River to Corsote	5	35	35-42
Corsote (via Charmande) to Pylae	13	90	35-42

Gabrielli has also argued that the wagons did, in fact, exist and that they provisioned the mercenaries on the march, starting from Myriandros or Issos.[7]

But if the scholars who deny or doubt the existence of the four hundred wagons described at 1.10.18 are incorrect, so, too, are those who think that the wagons were present throughout the march through Asia.[8] The key text here is 1.5.6. After provisioning at Corsote,[9] the journey from that city to Charmande—at eleven or twelve days[10]—was the army's longest single march between settlements before Cunaxa, and was through desert terrain which Xenophon tells us was "absolutely bare" of living things and thus offered no opportunity to provision through foraging.[11] The Greeks did not bring enough food to cover this extraordinarily long and barren march from Corsote through the desert, there were no settlements to re-provision in, and so:

τὸ δὲ στράτευμα ὁ σῖτος ἐπέλιπε, καὶ πρίασθαι οὐκ ἦν εἰ μὴ ἐν τῇ Λυδίᾳ ἀγορᾷ ἐν τῷ Κύρου βαρβαρικῷ, τὴν καπίθην ἀλεύρων ἢ ἀλφίτων τεττάρων σίγλων.

---

[7] Gabrielli 1995.
[8] In addition to the arguments that follow here, see O'Connor 2011, 637-648 for a full discussion of the many methodological errors, false assumptions, and contradictions contained in Gabrielli's paper which mean that his arguments that the wagons accompanied the march of Cyrus's army from Issos or Myriandros should be rejected.
[9] See n. 29 below for further discussion of the provisioning at this halt.
[10] See 1.5.5: Xenophon states that the march from Corsote to Pylae took thirteen days, covering ninety parasangs. There were not, however, thirteen days of straight marching between Corsote and Pylae, but more probably eleven (or twelve), since in the course of the march through the desert to Pylae the soldiers halted at the city of Charmande (1.5.10), which was probably a day's march away from Pylae (see Lendle 1995, 48). Even at eleven days, however, the march from Corsote to Charmande was still two days longer than the next longest march on the journey to Babylonia (that from Thapsacus to the Araxes (1.4.19)) and six days longer than the next longest after that (see Lee 2007, Table 1 for a table conveniently listing the lengths and duration of the Cyreans' marches).
[11] 1.5.5: "ἐν τούτοις τοῖς σταθμοῖς πολλὰ τῶν ὑποζυγίων ἀπώλετο ὑπὸ λιμοῦ· οὐ γὰρ ἦν χόρτος οὐδὲ ἄλλο οὐδὲν δένδρον, ἀλλὰ ψιλὴ ἦν ἅπασα ἡ χώρα", "[i]n the course of these stages many of the baggage animals died of hunger, for there was no fodder and, in fact, no growing thing of any kind, but the land was absolutely bare". See pp.137-139 for more on the role of foraging in the provisioning of the army during the march to Cunaxa.

> [t]he army's supply of grain gave out, and it was not possible to buy anywhere except in the Lydian market situated in the barbarian part of Cyrus's army, at the price of four sigloi [=30 Attic obols] for a kapithē [=2 choinikes] of wheat flour or barley meal. (1.5.6)

Rather than buy grain at inflated prices in the Lydian market, the Greeks subsisted instead during this part of the march on meat (most likely of their dead baggage-animals).[12]

If Cyrus had already prepared, in case of serious need among the Greeks, the four hundred wagons full of wheat-flour and wine by this point of the march, "it would have made no sense" for him to hold back the flour from the soldiers when they had no other means of acquiring it—when they were, in fact, suffering a serious need of grain.[13] In addition, despite the desperate situation facing the mercenaries on the march between Corsote and Charmande, Xenophon does not mention in his description of the famine any intervention by Cyrus to alleviate the lack of grain or, more specifically, any failure by Cyrus to distribute the flour carried on the four hundred wagons.[14] Rather, at 1.5.6 he states that the men were suffering famine because they had no opportunity to purchase grain other than in the Lydian market. When the option to purchase grain was no longer available to them (due to the inflated prices in the Lydian market and the absence of any nearby settlements), they were reduced to eating meat. The absence, then, in Xenophon's description of the famine of any mention of the four hundred wagons—and specifically of any mention of Cyrus's failure to distribute grain from them[15]—in a situation where the Greeks were reduced to eating unusual food,[16] makes it certain

---

[12] See Anderson 1970, 51; Lee 2007, 222. Xenophon gives the conversions for the sigloi and kapithē into Attic measures a little later at 1.5.6.
[13] Roy 1967, 311 n.93.
[14] Cf. Tänzer 1912, 53.
[15] Some scholars arguing for the presence of the four hundred wagons before Charmande have resorted, in order to explain the dearth of grain described by Xenophon at 1.5.6, to thinking that Cyrus miscalculated the amount of supplies needed for the march from Corsote to Charmande and therefore that there was flour distributed from the wagons during this part of the march, but not enough: see Kelsey and Zenos 1895, 18, 28; Mather and Hewitt 1938, 269; cf. Gabrielli 1995, 119-120. The lack of any mention at 1.5.6 of the wagons and the implication from the passage that purchase was the regular means of acquisition of grain for the mercenaries renders this position untenable (see further on this point p.132 below).
[16] The only two other occasions when the Cyreans subsisted exclusively on meat were in similarly desperate circumstances: 2.1.6-7 (the day after the battle of

that the four hundred wagons were not present before Charmande.[17]

Xenophon's description at 1.10.18 of the wagons' function—that they had been provided by Cyrus so that, if ever serious need (of food) should ever overtake the army, he might have supplies to distribute to the Greeks—confirms the point that the wagons had not been used to provision the mercenaries before Cunaxa.[18] The use of a future less vivid construction (εἴ... λάβοι... διαδιδοίη...) ("if serious need *should*... he *might* have supplies...") here shows that the serious need and the subsequent distribution might have come about at some point in the future—but, as it happened, did not because of the pillaging of the wagons by the King's men. The implication of the description of the purpose of the wagons at 1.10.18, then, must be that a serious need for grain had not arisen after they had been prepared and that the wagons had never been used to distribute grain to the Greeks.[19] In other words, 1.10.18 provides evidence that the four hundred wagons had been prepared after the famine in the desert, and that the flour and wine transported on them had not

---

Cunaxa, in the absence of grain or any other food (see 1.10.18, 2.2.3), the Cyreans provided themselves with food as best as they could by slaughtering animals from the army's baggage-train); 4.7.17 (in the land of the Chalybes, the Cyreans subsisted on the cattle they had taken from the Taochians (4.7.14), since their provisions had given out (4.7.1) on their arrival in the land of the Taochians (the territory they passed through before entering the land of the Chalybes), and they were unable to steal any grain or any other provisions from Taochian or Chalybian territory, since both of these peoples kept their provisions stored away in strongholds (4.7.1, 4.7.17)).

[17] Neither Griffith nor Descat deal with the fatal implications of 1.5.6 for their arguments that the wagons existed before the army's march from Corsote to Charmande. Neither does Gabrielli explain why grain from the wagons was not distributed by Cyrus in the desert (as noted by Roy 2004, 277) or why Xenophon does not mention the wagons at 1.5.6. Other scholars accepting the presence of the wagons before Charmande confess that they have no idea why the grain was not distributed on the march between Corsote and Charmande (Anderson 1970, 52; Harthen 2001, 128)—since it simply does not make sense that there should be no grain distributed if the wagons were already present.

[18] Cf. Tuplin 1999, 345:"X[enophon] might be right to state that the wagons were intended for the Greeks alone and/or to imply that they were not the principal regular source of supplies. Indeed, X[enophon]'s description of them *is* rather peculiar if they were actually the ones which had fed them for at least half of the hard stages after Corsote".

[19] This provides another reason why the view that some (but enough) grain was distributed from the four hundred wagons in the desert between Corsote and Charmande (see n. 15 above) should be rejected.

needed to be distributed to the Greeks between their preparation and the battle at Cunaxa.

A final confirmation that the wagons were not present on the desert marches is the fact that the pace of these marches was much too high for wagons heavily laden (μεστὰς) with wheat-flour and wine.[20] The speed of the march between the Araxes River and Pylae—some thirty-five to forty-two kilometres a day[21]—was exceptionally high by the standards of pre-industrial armies. Twenty-six kilometres per day was "a reasonable maximum" for contemporary Greek armies;[22] and generally, although armies were sometimes capable of much longer marches, nineteen and a half to twenty-two kilometres a day serves as a reasonable average for the march rates of pre-industrial armies operating in the eastern Mediterranean and Near East.[23] The exceptional speed of Cyrus's march from Corsote to Pylae is further illustrated by comparison with a march led by the Assyrian king Tukulti-Ninurta II in 884 BCE over the same route: while Tukulti-Ninurta's army, marching at a normal pace, took twenty-three days to complete the journey, Cyrus's army completed it in thirteen.[24] Clearly,

---

[20] See already Roy 1967, 311 n.93.
[21] See the table with average daily march rates at Fig. 8.1. The sources for this table: Lee 2007, Table 1, 283-284 for the lengths and duration of the marches from Myriandros to Cunaxa. Regarding the march rates recorded in the table: the parasang was a Persian unit of distance. See Tuplin 1997, 404-417 for the probability that the parasang as used by Xenophon in the *Anabasis* was "a spatially measured distance". Herodotus states that the parasang equalled thirty stades (2.6, 5.53, 6.42). Xenophon was almost certainly thinking in terms of Attic stades (see 1.5.6 for his conversion of local standards and measures into their Attic equivalents) which were 177.6 meters in length (Lewis 2001, 19). We cannot, however, expect complete precision in Xenophon's measurements of distance along the march (Tuplin 1997, 404-405). I will therefore use a figure of five to six kilometres for Xenophon's parasang (hence the use of ranges, rather than specific distances, for the average daily march rates in the table (cf. Paradeisopoulos 2013, 669-670)).
[22] Krentz 2007, 161.
[23] Haldon 2006, 143. See also, e.g., Bachrach 2006, 44-45: over short periods of time, the forces of the First Crusade could average thirty kilometres per day; their normal march rate, however, including all stops, was ten kilometres per day. See, e.g., too, Engels 1978, Appendix 5, Table 7 (with note): the highest recorded march rate for Alexander's army marching as a whole was just over thirty-one kilometres per day; his army's average march rate over long distances, including day-long halts every five to seven days, was about twenty kilometres per day (= twenty-four kilometres per day with one day's halt in seven).
[24] See Joannès 1995, 182-186.

then, the extraordinary speed of the march from Corsote to Charmande (and from the Araxes to Corsote) would have been too fast for hundreds of wagons carrying hundreds of kilogrammes of wheat-flour and wine.[25]

We can state with certainty, then, that the four hundred wagons mentioned by Xenophon at 1.10.18 were not used to provision the Greeks at any point on their march to Cunaxa. The wagons were present at Cunaxa, but they were not present on the march through the desert, or at any point on the army's march before Charmande or Pylae (the last settlement the army met before Cunaxa). So, when and why did the wagons join the march—or, to put it another way, when and why did Cyrus decide to prepare four hundred wagons full of wheat-flour and wine for the Greeks in his army? The answer to these questions lies in, firstly, understanding the Greeks' usual means of acquisition of food supplies on their march under Cyrus, and, secondly, in understanding the roles played by supply-trains (which is what the four hundred wagons were) in the provisioning of pre-industrial land campaigns.

Cyrus's army acquired its food supplies on the way to Cunaxa in the settlements it passed during its march. 1.5.9, where Xenophon comments on the nature of the march, is crucial in establishing this point:

τὸ δὲ σύμπαν δῆλος ἦν Κῦρος ὡς σπεύδων πᾶσαν τὴν ὁδὸν καὶ οὐ διατρίβων ὅπου μὴ ἐπισιτισμοῦ ἕνεκα ἢ τινος ἄλλου ἀναγκαίου ἐκαθέζετο...

In general, it was clear that Cyrus was in haste throughout the whole journey and was making no delays, except where he halted to procure provisions or for some other necessary purpose...

---

[25] Xenophon does note the presence of wagons on the march between Corsote and Charmande, but it appears that they were few in number and were not heavily laden, since all of them could be lifted "high and dry" out of the mud of the Euphrates by the (few) Persian nobles accompanying Cyrus on his campaign against the King (1.5.7-8). These wagons probably carried Cyrus's personal belongings. At any rate, to whomever they belonged, they were a completely different entity from four hundred wagons heavily laden with wheat-flour and wine, as were the wagons some soldiers were using to carry their weapons just before the battle at Cunaxa (1.7.20). Gabrielli (1995, esp. 117) argues that the four hundred wagons were lightly laden and so could keep up with the rapid pace of the army's marches. This is demonstrably incorrect: see O'Connor 2011, 641-648.

The army, then, stopped at settlements in order to re-provision. The institutional means the army used to acquire its provisions during its halts differed according to the differing settlement patterns, ecologies, and relations with Cyrus of the regions through which it passed.[26] In urbanized regions (almost certainly between Myriandros and Cunaxa, and very probably from Sardis to Myriandros), the primary means of provisioning, however, was purchase from markets provided by the cities they found along the route of their march. This can be said for three reasons. Firstly, to return to Xenophon's description of the extreme scarcity of food that afflicted the Greeks in the desert between Corsote and Charmande when their grain had given out (1.5.6), he states there that "καὶ πρίασθαι οὐκ ἦν εἰ μὴ ἐν τῇ Λυδίᾳ ἀγορᾷ ἐν τῷ Κύρου βαρβαρικῷ", "and it was not possible to buy anywhere except in the Lydian market in the barbarian part of Cyrus's army". The necessary implication from this statement is that it was usual during this part of the march for the Cyreans to buy provisions elsewhere than in the Lydian market:[27] that is, that the mercenaries usually bought their provisions in the settlements they passed through.

Secondly, the provisioning of the mercenaries under Cyrus is taken for granted in Xenophon's narrative, mentioned only when it took place under exceptional circumstances or by methods that might be considered unusual: there are only five explicit references to (actual) provisioning in Xenophon's description of the six months from the beginning of the march in Sardis to the battle of Cunaxa (1.4.19, 1.5.4, 1.5.6, 1.5.9, 1.5.10) and all refer to exceptional circumstances. In the rest of the *Anabasis*, the provisioning of the mercenaries is assumed in the narrative in two circumstances only. In those cases when the mercenaries were explicitly guaranteed availability of supplies in an agreement with a state agent or employer, and this source of supplies was explicitly described before a part of a march (or a campaign) (as in the cases of Tissaphernes (2.3.26-27) and Seuthes (7.3.10)), their provisioning is not mentioned at all or only in unusual circumstances (or when it serves to clarify the narrative) in the

---

[26] Cf. Marinovic 1988, 160: "la situation concrète comptait pour beaucoup, et en particulier les possibilités du pays traversé par l'armée…"

[27] Note that Xenophon states that "there was nowhere else to buy...", not "there was nowhere else to get food": the default mode of supply is purchase. Incidentally, 1.5.6, together with the arguments presented here demonstrating that provisioning in settlements was the primary means of acquiring food for the Cyreans, shows that the Lydian market mentioned at 1.5.6 (and 1.2.18, 1.3.14) played no important part in the provisioning of the Ten Thousand on their march to Cunaxa.

subsequent narrative of the march or campaign. The provisioning of the mercenaries is also assumed (and thus only mentioned exceptionally) in those months when they were moving within a world of Greek cities and were purchasing their provisions at markets provided by friendly (Greek) cities or foraging for them from hostile non-Greek territory. Otherwise, when the mercenaries were moving through strange, hostile and non-Greek territory without a state agent or employer who could guarantee access to provisions, their food supply was always precarious, and since they could not take it for granted, it was not taken for granted in Xenophon's narrative, either.[28] The march from Sardis to Cunaxa took place mainly within a world of friendly cities, too: the rhythm of the march in Anatolia was from city to city and, after Anatolia, the march stopped and was received at the cities of Issos, Myriandros, Thapsacus, Corsote,[29] Charmande, and Pylae. It appears most probable, then, that purchase at markets in cities was the assumed means of acquiring provisions for the mercenaries when they marched through urbanized regions on their way to Cunaxa.

---

[28] Thus, in the three days from the battle of Cunaxa to the mercenaries' temporary truce with the King (2.1.1-2.3.26-27), there are fifteen explicit mentions of provisions and the act of provisioning, compared to five for the previous six months. On the narrative of the march from the Zapatas (after the murder of the generals and the break with Tissaphernes) to Trapezos (3.1.1-4.8.21), see Nussbaum 1967, 148: the narrative of this part of the march is "completely dominated by the external physical emergency in which the Army finds itself – the immediate need to procure subsistence and to ward off an active enemy and in general overcome every physical danger and obstacle..." Cf. Woronoff (1987, 13) on Xenophon's descriptions of the food resources of the villages the army comes across between the Zapatas and Trapezos: "si Xénophon s'attarde aussi longuement sur la prospérité de ces villages, c'est que les questions d'intendance sont primordiales".

[29] Xenophon at 1.5.4 describes Corsote as a "πόλις ἐρήμη, μεγάλη". On the basis of the parallels at 3.4.7 (the once inhabited Larisa described as a deserted (ἐρήμη) city) and 3.4.10 (a deserted (ἔρημον) stronghold by the formerly inhabited city of Mespila), Corsote has been taken to have been a deserted city: thus, see, e.g., Masqueray 2000, 66; Joannès 1995, 176; Lendle 1995, 46; Tuplin 1999, 353. Walpole (1963, 69), however, translates "a large, desert city" on the grounds that "πόλις ἐρήμη" form a compound word, and so the second epithet is allowable (cf. the Loeb translation: "in the desert... a large city"). This would make sense of the fact that Xenophon narrates that the Greeks "ἐπεσιτίσαντο" at Corsote (1.5.4) (cf. Mather and Hewitt 1938, 269 ad 1.5.4, ἐρήμη: "not 'deserted,' for Cyrus took in provisions there... rather, *a desert city, a city in the desert*" [emphasis in the original]). It should be taken therefore that the Greeks provisioned themselves in the city of Corsote.

Thirdly, the conclusion that the army primarily acquired its food from markets provided by friendly cities gains support from the one incidental mention in the narrative of purchasing in a market provided by a city during the march to Cunaxa, at Charmande (1.5.10, cf. 1.5.12). Here, the purchasing of food is described by Xenophon because of the unusual means of transport necessary for the soldiers to get to the market in the city (the soldiers used skins filled with hay and then sewn up to cross the Euphrates), the unusual (for classical Greeks) food purchased there (wine made from dates and bread from millet), and because Clearchus was nearly killed on his way back from inspecting the market (1.5.11-12). That is, the purchase of food in the market at Charmande is mentioned by Xenophon because of the unusual circumstances under which the purchasing took place in the city and because of the unusual products bought in the market, but the means of acquisition—purchasing in a market—is not presented (in any way) as unusual.[30]

---

[30] Krasilnikoff 1993, now sometimes cited as the standard work on the pay of the Ten Thousand (Descat 1995, 101; Roy 2004, 265 n.2, 269), also argues that the Ten Thousand usually obtained their food by purchase from cities (and villages) throughout the course of the march to Cunaxa. He cites (1993, 84-85 and n.21) 1.5.6, and 1.2.18, 1.2.24, 1.5.10 in support of this view (without further argumentation for why we should or can extrapolate from the few mentions of provisioning on the march to Cunaxa to the army's normal provisioning practices) but only the last passage refers to the purchase of supplies at a city (at 1.2.18, in contrast, there is a mention of the (Lydian) traders accompanying the army; at 1.2.24, Xenophon notes that the tavern-keepers ("οἱ τὰ καπηλεῖα ἔχοντες") remained at Tarsus after the rest of its inhabitants had fled. While it is possible that the Greeks may have bought some provisions from these tavern keepers, it cannot have been significant; at least Menon's soldiers could have lived off the plunder they took in the city (1.2.20); and, at 1.3.14, when the troops were still at Tarsus, the assumed place of purchase of provisions is the Lydian market in the non-Greek part of the army (although this is meant as a deliberately absurd proposal); and finally, Krasilnikoff does not explain how 1.5.6 can be used to support the point that the Cyreans bought their supplies in the cities and villages they passed). Krasilnikoff (1993, 86-87) also cites 1.3.9 and 1.3.21, together with 5.6.19-23 and 7.1.7, in support of the view that the Cyreans provisioned themselves by purchases in cities and villages from $\mu\iota\sigma\theta\delta\varsigma$ provided by Cyrus before the battle of Cunaxa. The first two passages, however, refer only to the provision of $\mu\iota\sigma\theta\delta\varsigma$ by Cyrus, and cannot be taken (in the absence of further argument, not provided by Krasilnikoff) as supporting the view that the Cyreans purchased their food supplies in cities and villages before Cunaxa. While 5.6.19-23 and 7.1.7 do refer to the purchase of provisions from $\mu\iota\sigma\theta\delta\varsigma$, these arrangements for payment (and purchase) made with (prospective) employers at Cotyora and Byzantium cannot tell us anything by themselves (i.e. without further argument, which Krasilnikoff

There are very good reasons to think, then, that purchasing in markets provided by cities was the principal means of food supply for the Cyreans in urbanized regions along their march route. It cannot be stated conclusively that purchase in markets provided by cities was their principal means of provisioning in the settlements they passed on their march through Cyrus's sphere of control in Anatolia, however, since there is evidence for the presence of sizeable reserves of tax grain available to satraps in Anatolia in the fourth century,[31] and it is possible that Xenophon may have felt his readers sufficiently familiar with Persian institutions to take for granted in his narrative the distribution of provisions by Cyrus to the army during the march in Anatolia until the border of Lycaonia (which marked the limit of his satrapal power).[32] There almost certainly would have been satrapal reserves of grain at Cyrus's capital of Sardis and at Celaenae, for example, where the march paused for thirty days and which was a centre of satrapal administration,[33] and probably there would have been some also at Ceramon Agora (1.2.10), where, because of its situation on the Royal Road, there would have been imperial stores of provisions stockpiled.[34] As long as the army marched through Cyrus's sphere of control in Anatolia, then, there is a possibility that the men may have been provisioned from satrapal reserves of grain. The evidence of 1.5.6 and 1.5.10, however, taken together with the fact that it is very unlikely that there were significant imperial resources in grain stored on the route Cyrus

---

does not provide) about the arrangements for pay and provisioning under Cyrus. In sum, Krasilnikoff's arguments that the Greeks on their march to Cunaxa usually obtained their food by purchase from the settlements on their way provide no firm basis at all for that position.

[31] See Briant 1994, esp. 71-72 (cf. Briant 1986, 37, 47-48 n.23). For other evidence of possible Persian use of satrapal/imperial stores in Anatolia in the fourth century: see Dem. 23.155, Diod. 15.3.3, Polyaen. *Strateg.* 7.33.2.

[32] See Briant 1987, 4-5 for classical Greek literary audiences being relatively familiar with Persian customs and institutions.

[33] See Briant 2002, 625, 705 and 1.2.7-9.

[34] Though whether the staging-posts along Royal Roads could provision large armies is a matter of some doubt (Tuplin 2004, 173), set up, as they were, mainly for individual travellers and messengers or small groups of the same (see, e.g., Briant 2002, 364-368; Debord 1995, 90; see, however, [Arist.] *Oec.* 2.2.38a, 1353a25-28 with Briant 2002, 364-365, 452-453 for the possibility of storehouses on the Royal Road being able to feed passing armies in Alexander's time). Ceramon Agora was the only point at which Cyrus joined the Royal Road, before leaving it again to march to Iconium (Debord 1995, 95) (though, outside of the Royal Road, there is the possibility that Cyrus could have ordered communities on the route of the march through the areas he controlled in Anatolia to prepare provisions for the (ostensible) purpose of the march against Phrygia).

took to Babylonia, since he did not take the Royal Road to Cunaxa (but instead took an unusual route down the left bank of the Euphrates),[35] makes it (almost) certain that purchase in markets provided by cities was the main means of acquisition of provisions for the Greeks when they marched through urbanized regions during their journey from Myriandros to Cunaxa.

On those parts of the journey from Myriandros to Cunaxa outside urbanized regions, groups of villages were the primary source of supplies for the army. The soldiers had to provision in the villages they encamped in at the Chalus River because it was the last settlement before five days of marching through unpopulated (and infertile) country;[36] and in the villages they found at the Araxes River[37] because, during their march along this part of the middle Euphrates, these were the only settlements in this non-urbanized and desert region, and thus the only places that offered them opportunities to provision.[38] We can presume that the army was able to requisition food from the villages belonging to Cyrus's mother on the Chalus (since Cyrus would be able to treat the surpluses of these villages as his own). There is no way of ascertaining, however, the institutional means the mercenaries used to acquire their food in the villages at the

---

[35] Joannès 1995, 173, and esp. 182-183; Tuplin 1999, 343; Briant 2002, 628; Tuplin 2004, 171. Still only "(almost) certain" because of Cyrus's requisitioning at Pylae of the wheat-flour and wine for the four hundred wagons: see n. 56 below.

[36] At 1.4.9, Xenophon tells us that the army encamped ("ἐσκήνουν") in some villages at the Chalus River belonging to Parysatis, the mother of Cyrus. It seems certain, on the basis that the stop here resembled those made later in the march to and from Mesopotamia—made at a settlement with provisions and a water supply during and before a march through desert (and unpopulated) territory—that Cyrus halted in these villages for the sake of provisioning his troops. The journey between Myriandros and Thapsacus was a march through a "*polis*-free zone" (Lee 2007, 38) of twelve days and 350 kilometres (see Fig. 8.1) (furthermore, although the Amiq plain west of the Chalus is fertile (Lendle 1995, 38), the "country eastwards from the River Chalus/Afrin is for the most part arid and stony downland broken by steep and rough limestone ridges" (Farrell 1961, 154)). The stop at the Chalus River, then, provided the only opportunity in nine days of rapid marching to re-provision; Xenophon probably did not specify that the troops provisioned in the villages of Parysatis because it could be taken for granted that Cyrus's troops would be able to requisition food from villages belonging to his mother.

[37] See 1.4.19: at the end of a nine-day march from Thapsacus, the army halted for three days at the Araxes river, where the soldiers found many villages full of grain and wine and provisioned themselves ("ἐπεσιτίσαντο").

[38] See Joannès 1995, 174-176; Tuplin 1999, 353.

Araxes. As other scholars have pointed out,[39] the term "ἐπεσιτίσαντο" used by Xenophon at 1.4.19 tells us nothing by itself about the institutional means by which the Cyreans provisioned themselves at the Araxes; the verb simply refers to the act of providing food for oneself and tells us nothing without context (lacking here) about the means used to provide that food.[40] There is nothing in Xenophon's narrative, however, that indicates the army took the villages at the Araxes to be hostile: either requisitioning or purchase (as opposed to pillaging) was therefore the mode of provisioning in them.[41]

The Greeks stopped to pillage food from settlements on at most two occasions. The fact that the mercenaries only rarely passed through hostile territory greatly limited the role played by pillaging in the provisioning of the march to Cunaxa. It is almost certain that the Greeks were able to plunder food when Cyrus cut down the *paradeisos* of Belesys (which contained "all the products of the seasons") and burned down his palace, both of which were located at the sources of the Dardas River (1.4.10).[42] Xenophon's description of the provisioning arrangements of the army at Tarsus implies strongly, too, that at least some of the mercenaries stole provisions in that city or its surrounds.[43]

Outside of settlements, passing into Lycaonia, Cyrus, in accordance with convention, gave the country over to the Greeks to pillage on the grounds that it was hostile territory ("ὡς πολεμίαν οὖσαν") (1.2.19). The army also foraged for food as it marched down the Euphrates.[44] On the march from the Araxes to Corsote, the soldiers hunted the wild animals and birds found in the country (1.5.1-3).[45] The bustards that were caught were eaten as a "delicious" supplement to the soldiers' grain-based diet

---

[39] Marinovic 1988, 160; Tuplin 2004, 171.
[40] Thus, "ἐπισιτίζομαι" and its derivatives can refer in the *Anabasis* to the stealing or seizing of provisions (3.4.18, 4.7.18, 6.2.4, 7.7.1), as well as to the purchase (7.1.7, 7.1.9) and requisitioning of food (2.4.5, 2.5.37).
[41] Krasilnikoff (1993, 85) and Trundle (2004, 88) mistakenly assume, without evidence, that the Greeks bought their provisions in the villages at the Araxes.
[42] Lee 2007, 23. *Paradeisoi* ("paradises") were parks created by the Persian king or his satraps for their pleasure; they were hunting preserves and also contained gardens (see, e.g., Briant 2002, 201-202, 233-239).
[43] See n. 30 above.
[44] Cf. Lee 2007, 222-223 on the soldiers' foraging for meat.
[45] They had also probably made an attempt earlier (at the Chalus River) to supplement their diet with fish and doves but were prevented from doing so by the Syrian inhabitants on religious grounds: see 1.4.19 and Lee 2007, 223.

(1.5.3).[46] The day after the battle of Cunaxa, when the Greeks discussed with Ariaeus, the commander of Cyrus's barbarian troops, how they should return to Ionia (2.2.10-12), he was of the opinion that they should return by a route different from that which they had taken to get to Cunaxa: "For even on our way hither we were not able to get anything from the country during the last seventeen stages; and where there was anything, we consumed it entirely on our way through" (2.2.11).[47] Ariaeus's statement is supported by Xenophon's narrative: the army can be calculated to have been, seventeen stages before the meeting of the Persian with the Greek commanders, in the midst of the march to Corsote to Charmande (Pylae);[48] in the course of this march, Xenophon tells us, there was no fodder or any growing thing of any kind (1.5.5); and from Charmande, the Persians had adopted a "scorched earth" strategy, burning up "καὶ χιλὸν καὶ εἴ τι ἄλλο χρήσιμον ἦν", "fodder and everything else that was of any use" (1.6.1). One can infer from the implicit contrast in Ariaeus's statement with the rest of the march before the ordeal from Corsote to Charmande (Pylae) that the army, including the Greeks, had been able to forage for provisions from the country it passed through previously. This foraging, however, was limited in scope for two main reasons. Firstly, it took place mostly in infertile and unpopulated (and therefore uncultivated) territory. Secondly, the exceptionally rapid speed of the march from the Levant to Pylae—some twenty-five to forty-two

---

[46] And see again 1.5.6: on the most barren part of the entire march—from Corsote to Charmande—the Greeks, when their grain gave out, subsisted on meat obtained by butchering the baggage-animals who had died on this stage of the march.

[47] "ἑπτακαίδεκα γὰρ σταθμῶν τῶν ἐγγυτάτω οὐδὲ δεῦρο ἰόντες ἐκ τῆς χώρας οὐδὲν εἴχομεν λαμβάνειν· ἔνθα δέ τι ἦν, ἡμεῖς διαπορευόμενοι κατεδαπανήσαμεν." (Diod. 14.25.8 is a summary of 2.2.11 and thus offers no information additional to that passage.)

[48] Calculated from Lee 2007, Table 1, 284. Roy (1967, 311 n. 93) also argued against the existence of the four hundred wagons on the grounds that 2.2.11 showed that there were no opportunities for the army to re-provision after Charmande and therefore no opportunity to acquire four hundred wagon loads of food after Charmande. But the start of the seventeen march days can be calculated to have been in the middle of the march between Corsote and Charmande, and the mercenaries bought provisions at Charmande (1.5.10), i.e. after the start of the seventeen march days referred to by Ariaeus. Thus, when Ariaeus stated at 2.2.11 that there were no opportunities to provision "ἐκ τῆς χώρας" ("from the country") in the seventeen march days previous to his meeting with the Greeks, he meant that there were no opportunities for the army to provision from foraging from the countryside they passed through, and not that there were absolutely no opportunities for the army to provision itself. 2.2.11 therefore does not rule out the preparation of the four hundred wagons after Charmande.

kilometres per day,[49] a rate of march which, as I have shown, was exceptionally high for a pre-industrial army operating in this region—would have prevented the army from gathering any very large amount of food through foraging, even if there had been any, since gathering large supplies of food through foraging was a process that took significant amounts of time and would have slowed down the march considerably.[50] In sum, then, on the march to Cunaxa, foraging from the countryside through which the army passed was an occasional source of food to enliven otherwise monotonous grain-based meals. Foraging functioned, in other words, just as the Lydian market did: as a supplementary source of provisions to those acquired in settlements (whether cities or villages).[51]

Cyrus's army, then, acquired (and could rely on acquiring) its food supplies (primarily through purchase, perhaps occasionally through requisitioning, but rarely through pillaging) on its way to Cunaxa in the settlements it passed during its march, including Pylae, the last settlement Xenophon mentions the army passing before Cunaxa (1.5.5). This can be stated with certainty since, given that the four hundred wagons were not present on the march to Babylonia (or at any time before), but were present at the battle of Cunaxa, the wagons must have been acquired and

---

[49] See accompanying table of average daily march rates at Fig. 8.1.
[50] Roth 1999, 294; Harari 2000, 306.
[51] There is almost no evidence for the means by which the non-Greek part of Cyrus's army was provisioned throughout the march to Cunaxa. The Lydian market was in the barbarian part of the army (see again 1.2.17-18, 1.3.14, 1.5.6) but this travelling market probably did not play any major role in the provisioning of the non-Greek part of the army for the reasons outlined at n. 27 above. Ariaeus, in speaking of the strategic situation that faced the non-Greeks in the army that survived the battle of Cunaxa and the Greek mercenaries, uses the first person plural in addressing the Greeks and speaking of the army's provisioning in the seventeen days before the battle and of his plan for the joint forces' sources of provisions in the upcoming march home (2.2.11-12, and see above). This suggests that Greeks and non-Greeks in Cyrus's army provisioned themselves on the march before Cunaxa by the same means, though, frustratingly, in the negotiations and descriptions concerning provisioning that follow Ariaeus's speech, Xenophon only tells us of the Greeks' negotiations with the Persians and of how the Greeks provisioned themselves (2.3.5-6, 2.3.14, 2.3.24-28); this is despite the fact the Greeks and the force under Ariaeus continued to encamp near each other for twenty days after the agreement with Tissaphernes (2.4.1) before Ariaeus's force started to encamp with Tissaphernes (2.4.9). Thus, although there are some indications that non-Greek forces of Cyrus provisioned themselves using the same methods as his Greek mercenaries, certainty (or even probability) on this question is impossible.

loaded with wheat-flour and wine at Pylae, the last city the army stopped at before the battle.[52] Although Xenophon does not mention provisioning at Pylae,[53] this is unsurprising since provisioning is taken for granted throughout Xenophon's narrative of the army's experiences before Cunaxa.[54] The implication drawn earlier from 1.5.6 and 1.10.18—that the wagons were prepared at Pylae—remains necessary and valid, then, especially as there would have been the resources in Pylae to load the wagons: the area around Pylae was fertile[55] and one of the few places in Mesopotamia where viticulture was possible.[56]

But why did Cyrus prepare the four hundred wagons at Pylae? Why

---

[52] Cf. Kelsey and Zenos 1895, 264 ad 1.10.18: after noting the supply crisis at 1.5.6, stating that "Cyrus must have obtained these supplies [on the wagons] after leaving the desert...." Since the wagons were not present before Charmande, but were at Cunaxa, they could have been loaded at either Charmande or Pylae. Given the rapid pace of the march from Corsote to Pylae, however, it is most unlikely that the army spent more than a day at Charmande (cf. n. 10 above), which was probably insufficient time for the preparation of the four hundred wagons.

[53] Tuplin (1999, 346) notes that there is no mention of provisioning at Pylae.

[54] As noted earlier at pp.132-133. As for the lack of a description of a halt at Pylae: at 1.7.18, Xenophon narrates that, four days' march out of the city, Cyrus gave Silanus three thousand darics for correctly forecasting, eleven days earlier, that there would not be a battle within ten days. Xenophon specifies at 1.7.18 that Cyrus thought that the King would fight within ten ἡμέραι and not ten σταθμοί, i.e. within ten days and not ten march-days. It is likely that the army spent around six or seven days at Pylae, and that Xenophon did not describe the army's halt at the city because little unusual or of consequence happened there. Six or seven days would give plenty of time to prepare the four hundred wagons, but because the soldiers and Xenophon played no role in their preparation, and the wagons played no role in their provisioning, they did not enter the narrative until after the battle, at the moment when they impinged on the soldiers' and Xenophon's consciousness (at 1.10.18). (I note here, that envisioning a six or seven day break at Pylae does not have any implications for my treatment of 2.2.11 above (esp. n.48), since the question here is of ἡμέραι, not σταθμοί.) See also Lendle 1995, 61 (with below): a halt of several days at Pylae should be assumed since Cyrus and his army needed (after a long and gruelling march through the desert) to make final preparations for their march into Babylonia and the imminent battle with the King.

[55] Joannès 1995, 175.

[56] See Joannès 1995, 179 with Tuplin 1999, 346, 354 n. 39. One more important point on the loading of the wagons at Pylae: Cyrus almost certainly requisitioned at Pylae the provisions loaded on the four hundred wagons. His power to do this means that we can only be "almost certain" that purchases at markets were the main means of supply for the mercenaries in other cities on the march from Myriandros onwards (see n. 35 above).

now and not before? To answer the last question first, the fact that, up to (and including) Pylae, Cyrus knew that the Greeks could re-provision in the settlements which they passed meant there was no need for the army to be accompanied by hundreds of wagons full of food. It was not logistically necessary to prepare the four hundred wagons before Pylae: the re-provisioning opportunities offered by the cities and villages the army halted at on the way to Babylonia meant that wagons piled high with wheat-flour and wine containers would have served no useful purpose for the army.

Not only was there no need for hundreds of wagons to be present before Pylae, but the presence of a substantial supply-train on the march before that city would have threatened a key strategic goal of Cyrus's: Xenophon states explicitly that Cyrus was making haste throughout the whole journey to Babylonia, in an effort to find the King as unprepared as possible for the eventual confrontation between the two (1.5.9). This was why the march from Myriandros to Cunaxa was so exceptionally fast, and why Cyrus did not take the Royal Road to Babylonia, but instead took a rarely used—but shorter—route down the left bank of the Euphrates.[57] The presence of a substantial supply-train—four hundred wagons of wheat-flour and wine—would have slowed down the march unnecessarily and jeopardized Cyrus's goal of catching his brother unawares. The necessity for speed throughout the march to Pylae meant, therefore, that not only would the wagons have served no useful purpose before that city, but also that their presence in the army before Pylae would have also endangered the entire purpose of the march.

At Pylae, however, the strategic situation facing Cyrus changed completely, and necessitated the preparation in this city of a supply-train for the Greeks. Cyrus was expecting battle with the King soon after he left Pylae. Xenophon states that, three days' march out of the city, Cyrus expected that Artaxerxes would come to give battle at dawn of the following day (1.7.1), and that Cyrus marched with his whole army drawn up in line of battle on the following day since he was expecting his brother to give battle that day (1.7.14). Furthermore, at 1.7.18 (as already noted at n. 54), Xenophon tells us that, four days' march out of Pylae, Cyrus gave Silanus three thousand darics for correctly forecasting, eleven days earlier, that there would not be a battle within ten days: Cyrus had expected that the King would fight within ten days or not at all. This confirms that Cyrus (since the prophecy was made at some point during the period of the

---

[57] See again n. 35 for references; see also Tuplin 1999, 354 and n. 40.

army's halt at Pylae)[58] was expecting battle with his brother soon after leaving Pylae. But, after the army had departed from Pylae, there were no settlements on the march out from the city from which the mercenaries could acquire new sources of supplies.[59] Cyrus could not expect, either, that his army would be able to rely on foraging for their provisions. There was little or nothing to forage in the countryside outside of Pylae;[60] and, in any case, tactical considerations (the expected approach of Artaxerxes's army) meant that the soldiers could not be allowed to spread out in order to forage.[61] Therefore, in the time between the departure of the army from Pylae and the imminent battle, Cyrus could not rely on any new means of acquiring provisions for the mercenaries to supplement the supplies they had each taken from Charmande and/or Pylae for the upcoming march.[62]

Given the new tactical and logistical situation facing the army on the march out of Pylae—the imminent battle and the absence of any source of means of re-provisioning for the army—Cyrus's preparation in that city of the four hundred wagons full of provisions will have had two linked functions. Firstly, the wagons would have acted as a "safety net" for the Greeks,[63] which the mercenaries could have relied upon if a greater

---

[58] See again n. 54.
[59] There is no mention of any settlements in Xenophon's account of the five days of marching from Pylae before the battle at Cunaxa. See also 2.2.12-13: the first villages in Babylonia were a long day's march away from the halt the army departed from on the day of the battle.
[60] See p.138 on Ariaeus's statement at 2.2.11 as evidence for limited foraging opportunities on the march out of Pylae. Cyrus probably expected, too, that the King's force would employ a "scorched earth" strategy in the countryside outside of Pylae since they had done so outside Charmande (1.6.1) (in the event, Xenophon does not mention the King's forces engaging in this strategy on the march out of Pylae).
[61] In addition, the expected presence of the King's (vast) forces nearby meant that Cyrus would have been expecting to compete for whatever supplies there were in the area of operations with another (large) army.
[62] See again 1.10.18: the food and drink that belonged to individual Greeks were among the items in the army's camp that were plundered by the Persians after the battle ("καταλαμβάνουσι δὲ τῶν τε ἄλλων χρημάτων τὰ πλεῖστα διηρπασμένα καὶ εἴ τι σιτίον ἢ ποτὸν ἦν" "they found most of their property pillaged, in particular whatever there was to eat or drink"). Given the straits that the Greeks found themselves in on the march to Charmande, this food and drink must have been purchased at Charmande or Pylae (or both cities). Incidentally, the fact that the Greeks still had personal supplies of food at the time of the battle explains why Cyrus had not distributed the wheat-flour and wine on the wagons before the battle.
[63] See Harari 2000, 319 for this concept.

amount of time than Cyrus expected elapsed between the departure from Pylae and the battle: if the mercenaries' personal supplies ran out because of a later (than expected) arrival of the King's forces, or because the armies' manoeuvring for position before battle took up a large amount of time, the wheat-flour and wine on the wagons would ensure that they would not starve.[64] Secondly, the four hundred wagons "increased the tactical flexibility" of Cyrus' army.[65] The flour and wine carried on the wagons gave Cyrus considerable manoeuvring room before the imminent battle: any decisions he might make on whither and when to march could be made now for solely tactical rather than supply considerations.[66] Whereas the necessity for speed earlier on the march had discouraged the preparation of a substantial supply-train to accompany the army—and the fact that the army was able to acquire provisions from the settlements it passed during the march had meant that such a supply-train was previously unnecessary—the new tactical situation (manoeuvring before an expected battle) confronting Cyrus at Pylae, and especially the freedom of action which the presence of the wagons in the army would give in that situation, now compelled the preparation of a sizeable supply-train at that city.[67] With the addition of the wagons, Cyrus was able to lead his army out of Pylae without the worry that logistical pressures might force him into a tactically unfavorable situation.

---

[64] Cf. 1.10.18 (Cyrus provided the wagons in case "serious need should overtake the army") to Harari 2000, 319 (the "safety net" of a supply-train permitted armies to operate "without fear that a sudden supply crisis would bring immediate starvation"). The straits to which the army had been reduced on the march from Corsote to Charmande doubtlessly reinforced in Cyrus's mind the potential advantages of having a supply-train accompany the army on the last days before the battle.

[65] Erdkamp 1998, 22.

[66] See again Harari 2000, 319: "Trains were also of great importance during military crises, for instance when a battle was imminent, because they enabled armies to maneuver freely at least for a few days, unimpeded by supply considerations."

[67] Note, in this regard, that on the first three days of marching through Babylonia from Pylae, the average number of parasangs covered a day dropped to four (equalling roughly twenty to twenty-four kilometres a day) (1.7.1), the slowest rate at any point on the march from Sardis (see again Lee 2007, Table 1, 283-284) (the fourth day of marching from Pylae only covered three parasangs (though this is probably to be explained by the fact that the army was expecting battle and by the difficulty of marching through the narrow passage between the Euphrates and a huge ditch dug by the King (see 1.7.14 with Anderson 1974, 100)). The decrease in marching rates after Pylae would be consistent with the addition of four hundred wagons heavily laden with wheat-flour and wine to the train of the army.

In conclusion, this explanation of the function of the four hundred wagons provided by Cyrus for the Greeks—which Cyrus prepared so that he could "operate freely"[68] in the barren, unpopulated territory outside Pylae without the fear that a supply crisis could render the Greeks militarily unable or constrain his tactical options—has the following advantages. Firstly, it is consistent with Xenophon's statement at 1.10.18 that Cyrus's intention in providing the wagons was to have supplies distributed to the Greeks in case of serious need in the army. Secondly, it is also consistent with Xenophon's description of provisioning throughout the march to Cunaxa, and explains why the wagons were present at Cunaxa but not at any point on the march before Pylae. Finally, and crucially, it gives us a convincing logistical and tactical rationale for the addition of the wagons to the army—something lacking from all previous treatments of the four hundred wagons prepared by Cyrus.

BIBLIOGRAPHY

Anderson, J. K. (1970) *Military Theory and Practice in the Age of Xenophon*. Berkeley and Los Angeles.
—. (1974) *Xenophon*. New York.
Bachrach, B. S. (2006) "Crusader logistics: from victory at Nicaea to resupply at Dorylaion," in J. H. Pryor (ed.) *Logistics of Warfare in the Age of the Crusades*, 43-62, Aldershot.
Briant, P. (1986) "Guerre, tribut et forces productives dans l'Empire achéménide," *Dialogues d'Histoire Ancienne* 12, 33-48.
—. (1987) "Institutions perses et histoire comparatiste dans l'historiographie grecque," in H. Sancisi-Weerdenburg and A. Kuhrt (eds.) *The Greek Sources: Proceedings of the Groningen 1984 Achaemenid History Workshop* (*Achaemenid History vol.2*), 1-10, Leiden.
—. (1994) "Prélèvements tributaires et échanges en Asie Mineure achéménide et hellénistique," in J. Andreau, P. Briant, and R. Descat (eds.) *Économie Antique: Les échanges dans l'Antiquité: le rôle de l'État*, 69-81, Saint-Bertrand-de-Comminges.
—. (ed.) (1995) *Dans les pas des Dix-Mille* (= *Pallas* 43). Toulouse.
—. (2002) *From Cyrus to Alexander: a history of the Persian Empire* (transl. P. T. Daniels). Winona Lake, IN.
Debord, P. (1995) "Les routes royales en Asie Mineure Occidentale," in Briant, 89-97.

---

[68] Erdkamp 1998, 22.

Descat, R. (1995) "Marché et tribut: l'approvisionnement des Dix-Mille," in Briant, 99-108.

Dillery, J. (1995) *Xenophon and the History of his Times.* London and New York.

Engels, D. W. (1978) *Alexander the Great and the Logistics of the Macedonian Army.* Berkeley and Los Angeles.

Erdkamp, P. (1998) *Hunger and the sword: warfare and food supply in Roman Republican wars (264-30 B.C.).* Amsterdam.

Farrell, W. J. (1961) "A revised itinerary of the route followed by Cyrus the Younger through Syria, 401 BC," *Journal of Hellenic Studies* 81, 153-155.

Gabrielli, M. (1995) "Transports et logistique militaire dans l'*Anabase*," in Briant, 109-122.

Gray, V. J. (2003) "Interventions and Citations in Xenophon, *Hellenica* and *Anabasis*," *Classical Quarterly* 53, 111-123.

Griffith, G. T. (1935) *The Mercenaries of the Hellenistic World.* Cambridge.

Haldon, J. F. (2006) "Roads and communications in the Byzantine Empire: wagons, horses, and supplies," in Pryor, 131-158.

Harari, Y. N. (2000) "Strategy and Supply in Fourteenth-Century Western European Invasion Campaigns," *Journal of Military History* 64, 297-333.

Harthen, D. (2001) *The Logistics of Ancient Greek Land Warfare.* Ph.D. Diss., University of Liverpool.

Joannès, F. (1995) "L'itinéraire des Dix-Mille en Mésopotamie et l'apport des sources cunéiformes," in Briant, 173-199.

Kelsey, F. W. and A. C. Zenos (eds.) (1895) *Xenophon's Anabasis, Books I.-IV.* Boston and Chicago, 5th edn.

Krasilnikoff, J. A. (1993) "The Regular Payment of Aegean Mercenaries in the Classical Period," *Classica et Mediaevalia* 44, 77-93.

Krentz, P. (2007) "Part I: Archaic and Classical Greece: War," in P. Sabin, H. van Wees and M. Whitby (eds.) *The Cambridge History of Greek and Roman Warfare, Vol. I: Greece, the Hellenistic World and the rise of Rome*, 147-185, Cambridge.

Lendle, O. (1995) *Kommentar zu Xenophons Anabasis: Bücher 1-7.* Darmstadt.

Lee, J. W. I. (2007) *A Greek Army on the March: Soldiers and Survival in Xenophon's* Anabasis. Cambridge.

Lewis, M. J. T. (2001) *Surveying Instruments of Greece and Rome.* Cambridge.

Loomis, W. T. (1998) *Wages, Welfare Costs and Inflation in Classical*

Athens. Ann Arbor.

Marinovic, L. (1988) *Le Mercenariat grec au IVe siècle et la crise de la polis* (transl. J. & Y. Garlan, intro. Y. Garlan). Paris.

Masqueray, P. (ed.) (2000) Xénophon, *Anabasis.* Paris, 6th edn. (1st edn. 1930/31).

Mather, M. W. and J. W. Hewitt (eds.) (1938) *Xenophon's Anabasis, Books I-IV.* New York; Cincinnati; Chicago.

Nussbaum, G. B. (1967) *The Ten Thousand: a Study in Social Organization and Action in Xenophon's Anabasis.* Leiden.

O'Connor, S. (2011) *Armies, Navies and Economies in the Greek World in the Fifth and Fourth Centuries B.C.E.* Ph.D Diss., Columbia University.

Paradeisopoulos, I. K. (2013) "A Chronology Model for Xenophon's Anabasis," *Greek, Roman, and Byzantine Studies* 53, 645-686.

Roth, J. P. (1999) *The Logistics of the Roman Army at War (264 B.C. – A.D. 235).* Leiden.

Roy, J. (1967) "The mercenaries of Cyrus," *Historia* 16, 287-323.

—. (2004) "The Ambitions of a Mercenary," in R. Lane Fox (ed.) *The Long March: Xenophon and the Ten Thousand,* 264-288, New Haven and London.

Tänzer, K. (1912) *Das Verpflegungswesen der griechischen Heere bis auf Alexander d. Gr.* Jena.

Trundle, M. (2004) *Greek Mercenaries: From the Late Archaic Period to Alexander.* London and New York.

Tuplin, C. J. (1997) "Achaemenid arithmetic: numerical problems in Persian history," *Topoi* (supplement 1), 365-421.

—. (1999) "On the track of the Ten Thousand," *Revue des Études Anciennes* 101, 331-366.

—. (2004) "The Persian Empire," in Lane Fox, 154-183.

Walpole, A. S. (1963) *Xenophon. The first book of the Anabasis.* London.

Woronoff, M. (1987) "Villages d'Asie Mineure et promenade militaire dans l'*Anabase* de Xénophon," *Ktèma* 12, 11-17.

CHAPTER NINE

WAR AS TRAINING, WAR AS SPECTACLE: THE *HIPPIKA GYMNASIA* FROM XENOPHON TO ARRIAN

DR. ANNA BUSETTO

Ancient authors typically tended to legitimize their interest in a specific topic by inserting it into a consolidated literary tradition, and this is particularly evident in Greek military treatises; here the author often outlines his "bibliographical and ideological genealogy" at the beginning,[1] or the whole treatise echoes – or recalls precisely – the structure and contents of a previous work. Arrian, versatile philosopher, intellectual, politician, and man of arms, wrote what is perhaps the most unique military treatise from this point of view, for it appears to both retrieve the past and value the present age. It shows, in fact, a bipartite structure: the first section (ch. 1-32.2) concerns the organization and drills of ancient Greek and Macedonian formations and seems to follow a literary trend, as represented by Asclepiodotus's and Aelian's works.[2] On the other hand, the second part (ch. 33-44) constitutes, for the Latin world, the only detailed literary evidence of a contemporary practice, the Roman cavalry exercises (*hippika gymnasia*). Arrian actually regards this as a completely different part and the end (*telos*) of his treatise, as he clearly states in *Tact.* 32.2-3, indeed appearing conscious of such a thematic innovation:[3]

---

[1] Cf. Ael. *Tact.* 1.1-3.
[2] The cogent verbal and content similarities between the first section of Arrian's manual and Aelian's and Asclepiodotus' *Tactica* have been the subject of much research since the mid-19th century: cf. Köchly 1851; Förster 1877; Dain 1946, 26-44; Devine 1993, 316-30 and 333-34; Devine 1995. The description of the Greek and Macedonian formations also in the works of Aelian and Asclepiodotus, seems to have become, therefore, a conventional topic in military treatises.
[3] Cf. Stadter 1980, 43. Yet the connection between the two sections of the treatise is not very clear nor appears sustained by any programmatic intent; a

Τάδε μέν, ὥσπερ ἐν τέχνῃ, δι'ὀλίγων ἐδήλωσα ἱκανὰ ὑπέρ γε τῶν πάλαι Ἑλληνικῶν καὶ Μακεδονικῶν τάξεων, ὅστις μηδὲ τούτων ἀπείρως ἐθέλοι ἔχειν· ἐγὼ δὲ τὰ ἱππικὰ γυμνάσια, ὅσα Ῥωμαῖοι ἱππῆς γυμνάζονται, ἐν τῷ παρόντι ἐπεξελθών [...] τόδε μοι ἔσται τέλος τοῦ λόγου τοῦ τακτικοῦ.[4]

Yet the description of the cavalry exercises, although certainly not common among ancient authors as a "monographic" interest, was not a brand new topic as a superficial consideration of the second section of the *Tactica* would lead the modern reader to think: such a theme sank its roots in classical Greece and followed an irregular, "Karstic" trend in ancient literature, sometimes being neglected, while sometimes peeking out in historiographical works,[5] and emerging decisively in the 2nd century CE, in a presumably not accidental conjunction with Hadrian's reign.[6]

The aim of the present article is, actually, briefly to trace the development of this theme and to show the "red thread" which links Arrian's *Tactica* with the other main literary evidences of it, by a thorough survey of their textual and lexical similarities.

THE *TACTICA* AND XENOPHON

Despite their thematic uniqueness, chapters 33-44 actually show several Xenophontean echoes, which could be easily explained in light of the admiration for Xenophon always shown by Arrian, who perceived (and sometimes even called) himself as νέος Ξενοφῶν ("young/new Xenophon") and, as such, would be remembered in future tradition.[7] In the

---

problem made greater by a lacuna which obscures a critical passage in *Tact.* 32.3: cf. Bosworth 1993, 254 (and in general 253-55 for the discussion on the bipartite structure of the treatise) and Petrocelli and Pitagora 2005, 145.

[4] Arr. *Tact.* 32.2-3: "I have adequately and briefly revealed these things, as in a technical manual, about the old Greek and Macedonian formations, for anyone who would want not to be ignorant of them. At present I will go through the cavalry exercises which Roman horsemen perform [...] this will be the end of my tactical discourse".

[5] Cf. for example Liv. 40.6.5-6 and 44.9.4-5 or (later) Suet. *Iul.* 39.

[6] On the possible occasional nature of Arrian's *Tactica* see further the chapter "The *Tactica* and Hadrian".

[7] Cf. Arr. *Cyneg.* 1.4 (see below, fn. 15); Phot. *Bibl.* 58.17b.11-15 (Οὗτος ὁ Ἀρριανὸς φιλόσοφος μὲν ἦν τὴν ἐπιστήμην, εἷς τῶν ὁμιλητῶν Ἐπικτήτου, κατὰ δὲ τοὺς χρόνους Ἀδριανοῦ καὶ Ἀντωνίνου τοῦ Πίου καὶ Μάρκου τοῦ Ἀντωνίνου ἐγνωρίζετο. Ἐπωνόμαζον δὲ αὐτὸν Ξενοφῶντα νέον, "This Arrian was a philosopher as for his knowledge, one of Epictetus's disciples, and gained

Latin world, Xenophon was widely read during the late Republic, though less so in the Imperial era, when he was mentioned more as a philosopher.[8] At the same time, the Greek world experienced a new interest in him, an interest linked to the Cynic, Stoic and Atticist movements,[9] which held him up as a model of style.[10] Arrian probably first encountered Xenophon's works at the school of Epictetus, who mentions – in one of his dissertations collected by Arrian himself – a pupil striving to write *μεγάλως εἰς τὸν Ξενοφῶντος χαρακτῆρα* ("greatly in Xenophon's style").[11] Therefore, this practice was probably not unusual in his entourage.

Arrian and Xenophon shared an early philosophical education under the guidance of a great teacher, an education which would later be moved into the background – yet without being disowned or completely abandoned – due to biographical and literary choices. Even though Arrian never mentions explicitly Xenophon's philosophical writings in his works, his notes to Epictetus's lessons seem to recall the *Memorabilia,* and his connection to Hadrian[12] could parallel the relationship between Xenophon and Agesilaus, as already noticed by Bosworth and Devine:[13] we can thus rightly say with Petrocelli and Pitagora (who recall a previous Bosworth statement), that Xenophon's influence seems to surface constantly in Arrian's life as much as in his literary activity.[14] In *Cynegeticon* 1.4 Arrian claims that since his youth he had had the same interests as his model: hunting, strategy, and the pursuit of knowledge.[15] The first two, in

---

popularity at the times of Hadrian, Antoninus Pius and Marcus Antoninus. They called him 'the new Xenophon'") and Suid. A 3868 (*Ἀρριανός, Νικομηδεὺς, φιλόσοφος Ἐπικτήτειος, ὁ ἐπικληθεὶς νέος Ξενοφῶν*, "Arrianus, Nicomedian, Epictetan philosopher, called 'the new Xenophon'"). On this homonymy already claimed by Arrian cf. in detail Stadter 1967 (who actually posits that "Xenophon" was part of Arrian's name, not a nickname); Ameling 1984. On the close connection between Arrian and Xenophon cf. also Tonnet 1988, I, 225-81 (general discourse on Arrian's imitation of Xenophon); Bosworth 1988, 25-7; Bosworth 1993, 272-75; Devine 1993, 314; Petrocelli and Pitagora 2005, 141-42. For possible archaeological evidence cf. Oliver 1972.

[8] Cf. e.g. Quint. *Inst.* 10.1.75. See the previous footnote for the bibliography on this theme (especially Tonnet 1988, I, 229-30).
[9] Cf. Tonnet 1988, I, 232-33.
[10] Cf. for example Plut. *Mor.* 5.79d.
[11] Arr. *EpictD.* 2.17.35.
[12] See below, at the end of the section "The *Tactica* and Hadrian".
[13] Cf. Bosworth 1993, 275 and Devine 1993, 315.
[14] Cf. Bosworth 1993, 274 and Petrocelli and Pitagora 2005, 142.
[15] Arr. *Cyneg.* 1.4 ὁμώνυμός τε ὢν αὐτῷ [Ξενοφῶντι] καὶ πόλεως τῆς αὐτῆς καὶ

particular, might have oriented Arrian's study towards Xenophon's historiographical works and minor treatises, as his use of some Xenophontean titles (like *Anabasis* – although this may be not the original Arrianic title, but a Byzantine accretion[16] – and *Cynegeticon*) as his own works would prove. Arrian thus seems to have aimed at creating a parallel and establishing an explicit link, even on formal grounds, with Xenophon's works. In the first section of the *Tactica*, the albeit derivative material shows some original embellishments, one of which (description of the size of the contingent called *enomotia* in ch. 6.3) is drawn verbatim on Xenophon's *Anab*. 4.3.26, as clearly highlighted by Bosworth.[17] Furthermore, in the second part of the treatise, Xenophontean echoes are related to the equestrian theme, which was another topic shared by the two authors. The reminiscences of the manual *On cavalry commander* (or *Hipparchicus*, so hereafter) especially in the description of the *hippika gymnasia*, are so many that it is impossible to think that Arrian did not know of such a handbook.[18]

For the comparisons with the second part of the *Tactica*, the most relevant chapters of the *Hipparchicus* are the first three. They are focused on the theme of *askeîn* and *meletân* – i.e. the importance of a continuous military training and the mastery acquired through practice[19] – with an invitation to exercise which is explicit in ch. 1.18-19,[20] and alluded to in

---

ἀμφὶ ταὐτὰ ἀπὸ νέου ἐσπουδακώς, κυνηγέσια καὶ στρατηγίαν καὶ σοφίαν ("as I have his [Xenophon's] same name and come from the same city, and have been loving from my youth the same things: hunting, strategy, knowledge"). About Arrian's link as Xenophon, cf. the bibliography cited in n. 7.
[16] This is the position shared by Bosworth 1993, 275 and Devine 1993, 314, since the title of the work is first attested by Stephanus of Byzantium (cf. St. Byz., 135, 20-21).
[17] Bosworth 1993, 262.
[18] These suggestions have been noticed by scholars, but not analysed: cf. the only general statement by Stadter 1967, 156 ("The *Hipparchicus* of Xenophon, on the duties of the cavalry commander, is similar to Arrian's *Tactica*"), and, for a more thorough discussion, Petrocelli and Pitagora 2005, 151-55.
[19] Petrocelli 2001, 62 (no. 33) states that *meletân* is a technical verb indicating military training, especially of cavalry, specialized corps (e.g. archers, javelin-throwers), or concerning specific tasks (e.g. to pilot a boat).
[20] Xen. *Hipp*. 1.18-19 συγκαλέσαντα δὲ χρὴ τοὺς ἱππέας συμβουλεῦσαι αὐτοῖς μελετᾶν [...]. Ταῦτα γὰρ ἐνθυμουμένους εἰκὸς καὶ τοὺς ἱππέας μᾶλλον <ἂν> ἀσκεῖν τὴν ἱππικήν, ὅπως, ἢν πόλεμος ἐγείρηται, μὴ ἀμελετήτους ὄντας ἀγωνίζεσθαι δέῃ περί τε τῆς πόλεως καὶ περὶ εὐκλείας καὶ περὶ τῆς ψυχῆς. ("It is necessary, when you have called the men together, to recommend them to practise [...]. With these thoughts in mind, it is obvious that the horsemen are likely to practise their

the whole of Arrian's section about the *hippika gymnasia*. In addition, a deeper, more sophisticated and erudite echo of the *Hipparchicus* in the syntactic plot of the *Tactica* could be recognised in the use – moreover perfectly alternated – of the same two Xenophontean key-verbs in the final chapter of the treatise:

Ταῦτα μὲν τοῖς Ῥωμαίων ἱππεῦσι τὰ ξυνήθη τε καὶ ἐκ παλαιοῦ **ἀσκούμενα**· βασιλεὺς δὲ προσεξεῦρεν καὶ τὰ βαρβαρικὰ **ἐκμελετᾶν** αὐτούς, ὅσα τε ἢ Παρθυαίων ἢ Ἀρμενίων ἱπποτοξόται **ἐπασκοῦσι** [...]. Καὶ τάφρον δὲ διαπηδᾶν **μελετῶσιν** αὐτοῖς οἱ ἵπποι καὶ τειχίον ὑπεράλλεσθαι, καὶ ἑνὶ λόγῳ, οὐκ ἔστιν ὅ τι Ῥωμαίοις τῶν τε παλαιῶν ἐπιτηδευμάτων, ὅ τι περ ἐκλελειμμένον, οὐκ ἐξ ὑπαρχῆς **ἐπασκεῖται**[21]

Furthermore, the Xenophontean invitation to enhance the attractive aspects of cavalry is vivid and acts to provoke the emulation of young people and the admiration of spectators, as is clear from the following passages:

Ἔστι δὲ καὶ οὓς ἄν μοι δοκεῖ τις νέους μὲν τὰ ἐν ἱππικῇ λαμπρὰ λέγων εἰς ἐπιθυμίαν καθιστάναι τοῦ ἱππεύειν,[22]

Τῶνδέ γε μὴν αὐτῷ ἤδη μέλειν δεῖ τῷ ἱππάρχῳ· [...] ἔπειτα ὅπως τὰς πομπὰς ἐν ταῖς ἑορταῖς ἀξιοθεάτους ποιήσει, ἔτι δὲ καὶ τἆλλα ὅσα ἐπιδεικνύναι δεῖ τῇ πόλει ὅπως ᾗ δυνατὸν κάλλιστα ἐπιδείξει,[23]

---

horsemanship, so that when war breaks out they may not have to fight untrained for the state, for glory and for their life". Transl. adapted from Marchant 1946, 243).
[21] Arr. *Tact.* 44.1-2: "These are the traditional exercises which the Roman cavalry have practised (ἀσκούμενα) since ancient times. But the emperor has also introduced the practice (ἐκμελετᾶν) of barbarian manoeuvres such as the Parthian and Armenian horse-archers carry out (ἐπασκοῦσι) [...]. The horses are also trained (μελετῶσιν) in jumping across a ditch and leaping over a wall and, in a word, there are none of their ancient practices which have become obsolete that have not been revived and are now practised (ἐπασκεῖται) by the Romans [...]" (transl. Hyland 1993, 77). Cf. n. 90. The emboldenings in the Greek text are mine, in order to better highlight Arrian's re-use of the Xenophontean key-verbs *askeîn* and *meletân*.
[22] Xen. *Hipp.* 1.11: "I think, too, that by dwelling on the brilliancy of horsemanship, you might fire some of the young men with ambition to serve in the cavalry" (transl. Marchant 1946, 239).
[23] Xen. *Hipp.* 3.1: "Now we come to duties that the cavalry commander must perform himself: first, he must sacrifice to propitiate the gods on behalf of the cavalry; secondly, he must make the processions during the festivals worth seeing; further, he must conduct all the other obligatory displays before the people with as much splendour as possible" (transl. Marchant 1946, 251).

This is also Arrian's goal in the description of the exemplar display for – most likely – Hadrian: the valuable armour exhibited by the cavalrymen and their expertise in the manoeuvres were mainly used to cause "astonishment in the spectators" (ἔκπληξις τῶν ὁρώντων).[24] The cavalrymen's ability to display themselves in formation and ride elegantly is paramount both in the – paradigmatic – Xenophontean training and in Arrian's description, where the κάλλιστα ἱππάσονται ("they will ride in the most beautiful manner") of *Hipp.* 2.1 becomes the maintenance of an "elegant and straight posture" (καθέδρα [...] εὐσχήμων καὶ ὀρθὴ) and a demonstration of "the brilliance of the weapons" (τῶν ὅπλων ἡ λαμπρότης).[25] Arrian's recommendation to grant honour to those respecting discipline and to censure and punish unruly riders is already a Xenophontean suggestion, as the following passages clearly reveal:[26]

ἀλλὰ χρὴ τοῦ ξυνεχοῦς σῳζομένου τόν τε ἔπαινον τῷ ἀγαθῷ σῷον εἶναι καὶ πρέποντα, καὶ τῷ κακῷ τὸ ὀφειλόμενον ὄνειδος ἀποδίδοσθαι.[27]

μέγα δὲ καὶ τὸ ἔργῳ [κατὰ τὸν νόμον] πλεονεκτεῖν μὲν ποιεῖν τοὺς εὐτάκτους, μειονεκτεῖν δὲ ἐν πᾶσι τοὺς ἀτακτοῦντας.[28]

Moreover, considering the time span between the two authors, the affinity between the training as suggested by Xenophon and that described by Arrian (consisting of raids, flights, gallop pursuits,[29] javelin throwing,[30]

---

[24] About the link between Hadrian and the second part of the *Tactica* (with the possible reasons for the Arrianic account) see in detail the chapter "The *Tactica* and Hadrian". About the insistence on the *sight* (and the text of Arr. *Tact.* 40.12 from which the quotation between parenthesis is taken), see also the fourth table in the same chapter "The *Tactica* and Hadrian".

[25] Arr. *Tact.* 38.3.

[26] Petrocelli and Pitagora 2005, 155, state that the two authors shared the belief that rewarding those who offer good evidence during the spectacular training could provoke emulation and keep up the troops' morale – the latter being an essential condition to get the maximum efficiency from soldiers.

[27] Arr. *Tact.* 38.5: "It is essential, while maintaining the continuity, to ensure that the good rider receives the appropriate praise which is his due and to give the bad one the censure he deserves" (transl. Hyland 1993, 74).

[28] Xen. *Hipp.* 1.24: "In practice, it is important to give advantage to those who carry out orders properly and inflict instead all manner of punishment on those who are unruly".

[29] Cf. Xen. *Hipp.* 1.20 and 3.11, and Arr. *Tact.* 35.1, 36, 38, 40.

[30] Cf. Xen. *Hipp.* 1.6, 25, and Arr. *Tact.* 36.4, 37.

vaulting onto a horse's back[31]) seems somewhat noteworthy.

The ties between Xenophontean and Arrianic suggestions and directives seem justified by a somewhat similar military background. The *Hipparchicus* was probably composed between 362 BCE and 355 BCE,[32] even if Gustave Delebecque, after suggesting a period slightly later than 362 BCE, indicates a precise date: the spring of 357, when Athens saw a concrete threat to the borders of Attica due to unrest on Euboea, which ultimately led the Thebans to send troops to the island in the summer of that year.[33]

At the crux of the genesis of the *Hipparchicus* – that is, of Xenophon's desire to make a statement on the training of an expert cavalry commander – lie two related and specifically Athenian problems: the imminent Theban threat and the significant reduction in enlistments.[34] The author's proposed solution interweaves the purely technical aspect of military preparation and scrupulous training of the *hipparchos* and his men with the more "epic-propagandistic" aspect that appeals to the prestige and glory of the horseman, along with his love of, and sense of duty towards, his country. Xenophon understood that the lure of the cavalry for young men found a sure ally in the mythical, epic presentation of the horseman, that the

---

[31] Cf. Xen. *Hipp.* 1.5 and Arr. *Tact.* 43.4.

[32] It is widely accepted that the manual is to be dated after Leuctra, since the Theban threat is clearly noticeable, and there is explicit reference to the Boeotians in ch. 7.3. On the other hand, the identification of the date before which it must have been written is not so clear and unequivocal: the use of "Du Stil" (i.e. of the second person singular when speaking to the addressee of the manual), which gives way to a reference to a generic figure of cavalry commander (*hipparchos*) from *Hipp.* 5.9, led Erik Ekman to suggest that Xenophon intended to address his manual to his sons or to Grillus only, and that the latter's death obliged him to revise the original project (cf. Ekman 1933 and in general Petrocelli 2001, XII, in relation to the question of the addressees of the *Hipparchicus*). Delebecque 1973, 20, who shares Hatzfeld's position (cf. Hatzfeld 1946-1947, 58, no. 1), sets a 'date after which' for the writing of the manual in 362 BCE, because, at the time of Leuctra, the Spartan cavalry, taken as a model by Xenophon (cf. *Hipp.* 9.4), had not yet shown the organisation later revealed at Mantinea (cf. Petrocelli 2001, 96-7, no. 153); the 'date before which' would therefore drop to 355 BCE (date of composition of *Poroi*), because that year the Theban threat appeared to have ceased.

[33] Delebecque 1973, 19-21.

[34] Contemporary Athens emerges from numerous references to the Boulè (e.g. 1.8,13; 3.9,12,14) and the "land survey" of the main urban sites (ch. 3): the Academia, the Liceum, the Phalerus, the Hermai, the Eleusinion.

historically urgent problem of a very strong Thebes at the gates of a weaker Attica could (and had to) be a source of appeal to discipline and training without overlooking the more gratifying aspect of the equestrian arts. So, he appeals more to the beauty, prestige, and pomp of the religious processions than to demanding continuous training; furthermore, the manual does not teach how to administer first aid to fallen comrades or protect oneself from injury. Even though the darkest aspects of warfare do not traditionally fit into ancient military treatises, the nature and background of the *Hipparchicus* make it plausible that Xenophon felt the demands of propaganda, thus preferring to overlook, or merely suggest, the less pleasant elements of discipline in favour of exalting the more spectacular ones, which find their culmination in the grand parades.[35] The cavalry, therefore, in addition to being an instrument of war, was a means of pride and a symbol of aristocratic prestige, even if the aim was always "to urge all Athenians to emulation".[36] Moreover, efficient preparation through practice seemed to be the only way to restrain spreading dilettantism. For this reason, the most important quality in a *hipparchos* is versatility, "completeness":[37] τὸν ἵππαρχον προσήκει ἀποτετελεσμένον

---

[35] Cf. Salomone 1986, 200-2. The counterpart of this attitude appears in Dem. *Phil*. 1.26, where the orator complains that *hipparchoi* and *philarchoi* ("squadron leaders") are concerned too much with parades and too little with war.

[36] Xen. *Hipp*. 1.26 εἰ δὲ καὶ ἆθλά τις δύναιτο προτιθέναι ταῖς φυλαῖς πάντων ὁπόσα ἀγαθὰ νομίζουσιν ἀσκεῖσθαι ἐν ταῖς θέαις ὑπὸ τοῦ ἱππικοῦ, τοῦτο πάντας οἶμαι Ἀθηναίους γε μάλιστ' ἂν προτρέπειν εἰς φιλονικίαν ("And if you could offer prizes to the regiments for skill in all the feats that the public expects the cavalry to perform at the spectacles, I think this would appeal strongly to the spirit of emulation in every Athenian", transl. Marchant 1946, 245-7).

[37] I prefer "completeness", because it expresses perfectly the meaning of the Greek verb *apoteleo*. "Completeness" brings together resistance (*[δεῖ] αὐτὸν πονεῖν ἱκανὸν εἶναι*, "The cavalry commander has to be able to stand hard work", *Hipp*. 7.5), speech and action (*Δεῖ γὰρ καὶ λέγειν αὐτὸν ἱκανὸν εἶναι καὶ ποιεῖν*, "The cavalry commander has to be able to speak and act", *Hipp*. 8.22), intelligence and ability (*Ἀλλὰ μὴν φρονίμου γε ἄρχοντος καὶ τὸ μήποτε κινδυνεύειν ἑκόντα*, "A prudent commander never takes risks unnecessarily", *Hipp*. 4.13; *Παντὶ μὲν οὖν προσήκει ἄρχοντι φρονίμῳ εἶναι*, "Every commander, then, should have intelligence", *Hipp*. 7.1). The latter must be accompanied by devotion to the gods and military abilities (*τὸν Ἀθηναίων ἵππαρχον διαφέρειν δεῖ καὶ τῷ τοὺς θεοὺς θεραπεύειν καὶ τῷ πολεμικὸν εἶναι*, "The Athenian cavalry commander, however, should excel greatly both in the observance of his duty to the gods and in the qualities of a warrior" [transl. Marchant 1946, 273], *Hipp*. 7.1). This 360-degree mastery was also a formidable means of guaranteeing obedience by imitation in soldiers (cf. *Hipp*. 6.4-6). On this subject, cf. Petrocelli 2001, XXXI-XXXIV. That a vast number of qualities – expertise above all – is necessary to hold an important

ἄνδρα εἶναι ("the cavalry commander has to be a most versatile man", *Hipp*. 7.4).

THE *TACTICA* AND HADRIAN

Arrian wrote the *Ars Tactica* in 136/7 CE, in the twentieth year of Hadrian's reign,[38] a date full of implications about the content, the occasion and the purpose of the treatise, as we will see. According to the testimony, perhaps not entirely impartial, of Fronto's *Principia Historiae*, the period of Hadrian's reign was characterised by a general weakening in military discipline,[39] possibly the result of the generally peaceful foreign situation.[40] This allowed the Emperor to institute a policy of consolidation and maintenance contrary to that of his predecessor[41], which may well be read as a realistic assessment of the inability to expand an already vast empire that had begun to show signs of weakness. Nevertheless, Hadrian reacted to the weakening discipline with reforms that contemplated, on the one hand, the introduction of new weapons and combat techniques[42] and, on the other, maximum attention to *askesis* ("exercise", "training") and *katakosmesis* ("arrangement", "order"), through the personal example of a sober and austere lifestyle.[43]

---

position is a conviction derived from Socratic teaching.
[38] This can be inferred from ch. 44.3: ἐς τήνδε τὴν παροῦσαν βασιλείαν, ἣν Ἀδριανὸς εἰκοστὸν τοῦτ'ἔτος βασιλεύει ("So that in our present empire, in the twentieth year of Hadrian's reign").
[39] For bibliography on this cf. n. 41.
[40] Fronto 208, 9-11 van den Hout. Fronto's judgment was influenced perhaps by encomiastic intention towards Lucius Verus, who had resumed the war against the Parthians.
[41] Cf. Giannelli and Mazzarino 1956, II, 205-6; Petit 1975, 357; Thornton 1975, 433-35 (who highlights the link with Augustus's policy of containment).
[42] For example, cf. SHA, *Vita Hadr.* 10.7 *arma postremo eorum [militum] suppellectilemque corrigeret* ("lastly he enhanced the weapons and equipment of soldiers"). If the institution of *numeri* (ethnic units which fought maintaining their native equipment and tactics), *contarii* ("pike-bearers") and *sagittarii* ("arrows-bearers") fluctuates in the eras of Trajan and Hadrian, it was likely Hadrian himself who created the *ala I Gallorum et Pannoniorum catafractata* (cf. *CIL* XI, 5632) – apparently the first and only case of official introduction of cataphract cavalrymen until Severus Alexander. On the transformations of the Roman army and the introduction of new corps under Hadrian cf. Ensslin 1938, 367-70; Speidel 1975, esp. 202-8; Thornton 1975, 453-54; Le Bohec 1989, 28; Levi 1994, 56-8; Le Bohec 2003a, 16-17; Fields and Hook 2006, 10-12.
[43] For example, cf. Eutr. 8.7.2 *diligentissimus [...] circa [...] militum disciplinam* ("most scrupulous about soldiers' discipline"); SHA, *Vita Hadr.* 10.3 *post*

In reality, the Romans had perceived the convenience of on-going training well before Hadrian, whose innovative merit lay rather in having rendered it, together with rigorous discipline, the keystone of his domestic policy. An emphasis on *exercitium* can be found already in Varro, who states *exercitus, quod exercitando fit melior* ("'exercitus', because it improves through exercise", *ling*. 5.87). Other evidence, traceable to the Republican period, can be found in Polybius (who describes Scipio's rigorous training of his forces in Spain, interestingly quoting Xenophon),[44] and later on in Vegetius[45] and in Frontinus (who attests to practices that even date to the time of the First Punic War).[46] Furthermore, since the late Republic or the early Augustan age at least, the Romans had had *ludi castrenses* or *armaturae*, intense and spectacular forms of training, often with connotations of entertainment,[47] which found their mythical-literary

---

Caesarem Octavianum labantem disciplinam incuria superiorum principum retinuit ("after Caesar Octavianus he restrained discipline which was fading due to the negligence of previous emperors"); Dio Cass., *Hist*. 69.9.3-4 Ἐγύμναζέ τε αὐτοὺς πρὸς πᾶν εἶδος μάχης, καὶ τοὺς μὲν ἐτίμα τοὺς δὲ ἐνουθέτει, πάντας δὲ ἐδίδασκεν ἃ χρὴ ποιεῖν. Καὶ ὅπως γε καὶ ὁρῶντες αὐτὸν ὠφελοῖντο, σκληρᾷ τε πανταχοῦ τῇ διαίτῃ ἐχρῆτο, καὶ ἐβάδιζεν ἦ καὶ ἵππευε πάντα, οὐδ' ἔστιν ὁπότε εἴτε ὀχήματος τότε γε εἴτε τετρακύκλου ἐπέβη· οὐδὲ τὴν κεφαλὴν οὐκ ἐν θάλπει, οὐκ ἐν ῥίγει ἐκαλύφθη, ἀλλὰ καὶ ἐν ταῖς χιόσι ταῖς Κελτικαῖς καὶ ἐν τοῖς καύμασι τοῖς Αἰγυπτιακοῖς γυμνῇ αὐτῇ περιῄει. Συνελόντι τε εἰπεῖν, οὕτω καὶ τῷ ἔργῳ καὶ τοῖς παραγγέλμασι πᾶν τὸ στρατιωτικὸν δι' ὅλης τῆς ἀρχῆς ἤσκησε καὶ κατεκόσμησεν ὥστε καὶ νῦν τὰ τότε ὑπ' αὐτοῦ ταχθέντα νόμον σφίσι τῆς στρατείας εἶναι ("He drilled the men for every kind of battle, honouring some and reproving others, and he taught them all what should be done. And in order that they should be benefited by observing him, he everywhere led a rigorous life and either walked or rode on horseback on all occasions, never once at this period setting foot in either a chariot or a four-wheeled vehicle. He covered his head neither in hot weather nor in cold, but alike amid German snows and under scorching Egyptian suns he went about with his head bare. In fine, both by his example and his precepts he so trained and disciplined the whole military force throughout the entire empire that even to-day the methods then introduced by him are the soldiers' law of campaigning", transl. Cary 1925, VIII, 441-3). The mention of how the Emperor honoured some of his men and reproved others is interesting: this behaviour is the same suggested both by Xenophon and Arrian (see above in the chapter "The *Tactica* and Xenophon"). About Hadrian's reaction to the weakening of military discipline cf. at least– Davies 1968; in general, all the essays included in Le Bohec 2003 (esp. Le Bohec 2003c); Galimberti 2007, 73-121, esp. 100-2.

[44] Pol. *Hist*. 10.20 (especially par. 7 for Xenophon's quotation).
[45] Veg. *Mil*. 1.9.8.
[46] Frontin. *Strat*. 3.1.2.
[47] See e.g. Livy's passages mentioned in n. 5.

model from the funeral games for Anchises described in the fifth book of the *Aeneid* (545-603).[48] Hadrian then moved along a path that had already been laid out, where the true extent of his innovations lay in adaptation to a political panorama, which, both internally and externally, had undergone deep changes compared to that of the Republican era or the first century of the Empire.[49]

The close connection between *exercitium* and entertainment, which emerges forcefully also in the part of Arrian's *Tactica* on the *hippika gymnasia*, was supposed to, on the one hand, stimulate effort in soldiers (especially in the case of exhibitions before prominent figures) and, on the other, encourage – given the truthful resemblance to manoeuvres and engagement – the interest and involvement of the public, like that of ancient Rome, always eager for spectacular entertainment.

The last eleven chapters of the *Tactica* seem, moreover, to not simply reveal the climate of Hadrian's epoch, but to be explicitly conditioned by the key text of his military policy: the *Adlocutio Hadriani*, an inscription (carved on an altar discovered in the sanctuary of the insignia of the garrison) recording a speech he gave in Lambaesis[50] – the headquarters of the *III legio Augusta* stationed in Northern Africa since the time of Trajan[51] – in 128 CE at the latest.[52] In Lambaesis Hadrian attended a spectacular military exercise by the divisions stationed there to which, apparently, he gave orders and directives with a pragmatic goal in mind: to provide a clear example of the various modes of military formation, which

---

[48] They became the legitimising model of the *lusus Troiae*, the most elite form of equestrian competition, practiced by young nobles. For example, cf. Suet. *Iul.* 39.2, *Nero* 7.1 and Dio Cass. *Hist.* 51.22.4. On this subject cf. at least Petrikovits 1939; Pfister 1993; Freyburger-Galland 1997.

[49] In this perspective, we should also analyse the ideological (and practical) value attributed to discipline, which had always been – and would always be – perceived as an essential element for the stability of the military apparatus. Hadrian, however, went much further: he promoted it to divine status and fostered its cult through coins and inscriptions (cf. Ziołkowski 1990).

[50] Cf. *CIL* VIII, 2532 and *CIL* VIII, Suppl. Prov. Numidiae, 18042; a new edition of the text of the inscription (now very damaged) can be found in Speidel 2006. On the content of the *Adlocutio Hadriani* and its relation to Arrian's *Tactica* cf. Le Bohec 2003 and Zaroski 2009.

[51] On the history of *III legio Augusta* cf. Gonzalez 2003, 114-31 and Le Bohec 1989.

[52] Cf. Chowen 1970.

he required and approved of.[53]

The section of the *Tactica* concerning the *Rhomaia hippika gymnasia* shows such an overlap of content with this inscription – beyond more or less explicit references to Hadrian's military policy[54] – that it seems difficult to think of a completely independent genesis of the two texts. In fact, since the *Tactica* clearly dates from after the Lambaesis speech, it would be easy to think of the treatise as a literary re-working of the *Adlocutio* (whether or not Arrian himself had attended the Lambaesis exercises), and to assign to it an occasional nature.[55]

For example, the normative intent of frg. B a seems to be echoed in *Tact.* 42.2, where Arrian insists on the need to respect imperial directives during the exercises:

Adlocutio Hadriani	Arrian's *Tactica*
frg. B a: [*ex*]*ercitationes militares quodam modo suas leges* [*ha*]*bent*[56]	ch. 42.2: πρὸς βασιλέως τεταγμένα [...] κατὰ πρόσταξιν βασιλέως[57]

---

[53] The official and normative aim is revealed in the statement [*ex*]*ercitationes militares quodam modo leges suas* [*ha*]*bent* in frg. B a (please note that I quote text and numbers of the fragments of the *Adlocutio* according to the *CIL*), about which see the following table. That the *Adlocutio* appears as "una sorta di 'regolamento' della 'disciplina' intesa [...] nella accezione di fissazione delle regole d'addestramento e di vita" ("a kind of 'guideline' for the 'discipline' intended as a scheduling of rules for training and life", Giuffrè 2003, 161) is proved by the detailed references to the *munitiones* ("defensive works"). Building walls and moats, knowing how to procure food and weapons – even better by accomplishing in one single day what *alii* [*per*] *plures dies divisis* [*sent*...] ("others had divided in several days", frg. B b) – is part of the show of troop efficiency, as much as the activities relating to mock battles. On the Lambaesis inscriptions as a document of Hadrian's new doctrine of defence cf. Levi 1994, 44-53.
[54] See below, at the end of the current chapter.
[55] On the possible dedication of the *Tactica* to Hadrian, cf. essentially Wheeler 1978 (who though maybe goes too far when stating that the treatise was a gift for Hadrian's *vicennalia*: without a surviving dedication revealing the purpose of the work, this is just a – yet likely – guess); Devine 1993, 315-16; Bosworth 1993, 259. On this subject see also the end of the current chapter.
[56] "Military exercises have their own laws, so to speak".
[57] Both expressions mean "by the instruction(s) of the Emperor".

In frg. C b of the *Adlocutio*, Hadrian praises Catullinus for "a training which looked like a real battle".[58] The beginning of chapter 41 and the end of chapter 42 of the *Tactica* are almost to be considered as a ring composition on the same topic: Arrian describes the soldiers who "arm themselves as to go to war"[59] and ends with praise for training resembling real battle:

Adlocutio Hadriani	Arrian's *Tactica*
frg. C b: ...*ad hanc exercita[tionem, quae verae di]micationis imaginem accepit*	ch. 41.1: ὡς ἐς μάχην ὁπλίζονται ch. 42.5: ταύτην <δεκαδαρχίαν> ἐγὼ μᾶλλον ἤ τινα ἄλλην ἐπήνεσα ὡς πρὸς ἀλήθειαν τῶν πολεμικῶν ἔργων ἠσκημένην[60]

Moreover, in the description of the *exercitatio* performed by the cavalrymen of the sixth Commagenian cohort (*equites cohortis VI Commagenorum*, frg. A a), Hadrian mentions that they have demonstrated good abilities in throwing missiles and stones with slings and in mounting horses very quickly. In *Tact.* 43.1 Arrian mentions various forms of shooting, among which there is the same stone-throwing, launched either by hand or by sling. Arrian then concludes the account on the *hippika gymnasia* by mentioning the vault onto a horse's back while it is moving:[61]

Adlocutio Hadriani	Arrian's *Tactica*
frg. A a: *addidistis ut et lapides fundis mitteretis et missilibus confligeretis*[62]	ch. 43.1: πολύτροποι ἐξακοντισμοὶ γίγνονται ἤ κούφων παλτῶν ἤ καὶ βελῶν, οὐκ ἀπὸ τόξου τούτων γε ἀλλ' ἀπὸ μηχανῆς ἀφιεμένων, ἤ λίθων ἐκ χειρὸς ἤ ἐκ σφενδόνης[63]

---

[58] See the following table for the Latin text corresponding to this translation.
[59] See the following table for the Greek text (ch. 41.1) corresponding to this translation.
[60] "I would praise, more than anyone else, this unit, because of the proximity to the real deeds of war she showed in her training".
[61] These similarities have been pointed out already in the critical edition of the *Tactica*: cf. the apparatus in Roos and Wirth 1968, 175.
[62] "You added throwing stones with slings and fighting with javelins".
[63] "There are, furthermore, various forms of shooting, employing light javelins or missiles, the latter shot not from a bow but from a machine, or stones thrown from the hand or from a sling" (transl. Hyland 1993, 76).

frg. A a: *saluistis ubique expedite*[64] frg. 35, *AE*, 1900: *saluistis et hic agiliter et heri velociter*[65]	ch. 43.4: *τὴν ἐνόπλιον πήδησιν ἐπιδεικνύουσι θέοντος τοῦ ἵππου [...] ἥν τινες ὁδοιπορικὴν ὀνομάζουσιν*[66]

The *Tactica* also contains detailed descriptions of some manoeuvres which, in the *Adlocutio Hadriani,* are concisely pinpointed by a term or a phrase: this is the case of the first *epelasis* ("charge"), "arranged [...] so to give the impression of breaking in from the dark (*ἐκ τοῦ ἀφανοῦς*)" (ch. 35.1), which could be identified with the expression "*e tecto transcurrat eques*" of frg. C b.[67] Another connection between the two texts could be Arrian's reference to the turn to the right, almost in a circle,[68] so as not to hamper shooting arrows, which perhaps corresponds, in the *Adlocutio,* to the *hapax 'dextrator'* (frg. A a).[69] In the *Tact.* 40.6 there is a *hapax* – Καντάβρικὸς κύκλος (*Kantabrikos kyklos*)[70] – which might be related to the *Cantabricus densus* – another *hapax,* as a phrase – mentioned by Hadrian (frg. A a).[71] The appeals to elegance and order also demonstrated by the *ala I Pannoniorum,* with their prescriptive force, seem corroborated by Arrian's statement on the pleasure elicited in spectators at the sight of perfect manoeuvres and splendid armour:

---

[64] "You promptly jumped everywhere".
[65] "You jumped nimbly now and quickly yesterday".
[66] "They demonstrate leaping in full armour onto a galloping horse which some call the 'traveller's leap" (transl. Hyland 1993, 76-7).
[67] "Let the cavalryman go through from a hidden spot". For a survey of this similarity, cf. also the apparatus in Roos and Wirth 1968, 166.
[68] Arr. *Tact.* 36.5: *ἡ κλίσις δὲ αὐτοῖς ἐπὶ τὰ δεξιὰ σφῶν γίγνεται ἐπί δόρυ* ("Their veering is to their right [i.e.] to spear", (transl. DeVoto 1993, 87).
[69] The interpretation of Pérez Castro 1982, who thinks that *dextrator* refers to outstanding horsemanship rather than skilled sharp-shooting on horseback (denying a connection with Arr. *Tact.* 36.5), and that "Cantabricus" would mean "pugnacious, war-loving", in the *Adlocutio Hadriani* bearing no relation to the drill called *Kantabrikè epelasis,* is not very convincing. A *hapax* (extensively *hapax legomenon,* ἅπαξ λεγόμενον) is a word appearing only once in a work, an author, or in the entire surviving literature; this last is the case of *dextrator,* and it will be for *Kantabrikos kyklos/Cantabricus densus* as well (see further in the text).
[70] In *Tact.* 40.1 there is a synonym: Καντάβρικὴ ἐπέλασις (*Kantabrike epelasis*).
[71] Both the expression means "Cantabrian circle" (cf. Dixon and Southern 1992, 133, and, on what this manoeuvre exactly consisted, Hyland 1993, 133-41). For a survey of this similarity, cf. also the apparatus in Roos and Wirth 1968, 171.

Adlocutio Hadriani	Arrian's *Tactica*
	ch. 34.2: *Αὐτοὶ δὲ ὡπλισμένοι παριᾶσι κράνεσι μὲν σιδηροῖς ἢ χαλκοῖς κεχρυσωμένοις, ὅσοι κατ' ἀξίωσιν αὐτῶν διαπρεπεῖς ἢ καθ' ἱππικὴν διαφέροντες, ὡς καὶ αὐτῷ τούτῳ ἐπάγειν ἐπὶ σφᾶς τῶν θεωμένων τὰς ὄψεις*[73]
frg. 35, *AE*, 1900: *Omnia per ordinem egistis* [...] *non ineleganter*[72]	ch. 35.1: *Πρῶτον μὲν δὴ ἐπέλασις γίνεται ὡς διαπρεπέστατα ἐς κάλλος καὶ λαμπρότητα ἠσκημένη* [...][74]
	ch. 38.2-3: *Οὐδὲ γὰρ ἄλλου τινὸς θέαν [scil. οἱ μέν γε ἀπὸ τῶν δεξιῶν τοῦ βήματος ἀρχόμενοι] παρέχουσι τοῖς ἐπὶ τοῦ βήματος ὁρῶσιν* [...] *ὅτι ἐπελαυνόντων ὁρᾶται καὶ τῶν ὅπλων ἡ λαμπρότης*[75]
	ch. 40.12: *Ἀλλ' ἔγωγε πολὺ μᾶλλον ἐπαινῶ τὸ ἐννόμως δρώμενον ἤπερ τὸ ἐς ἔκπληξιν τῶν ὁρώντων σοφιζόμενον*[76]

---

[72] "You accomplished every task, one by another [*or* unit by unit] elegantly".
[73] "Those of the troopers who are distinguished in rank (*or* reputation) or are outstanding in horsemanship, come past armed with gilded iron or bronze helmets, so that in this way they draw the gaze of the spectators upon themselves" (transl. Hyland 1993, 72).
[74] "Firstly the charge is performed so to be the most beautiful and brilliant possible".
[75] "They [Those starting from the left of the tribune] provide those watching on the tribune a view of anything else [...] because, of the charging men, just the weapons' brilliance and the horses' swiftness are seen" (transl. adapted from DeVoto 1993, 89).
[76] "For my own part I hold in much greater esteem a performance which sticks to the rules rather than a clever show designed to impress the spectators" (transl. Hyland 1993, 75).

This forceful insistence on the spectacular elements of the training and display leads us to believe that the *hippika gymnasia* described by Arrian did not constitute ordinary exercises,[77] but rather highly spectacular sport competition.[78]

Moreover, the description of the roll call at ch. 42.1, though a bit convoluted, allows us to identify a *decurio* (δεκαδάρχης, *dekadarches*),[79] a *duplicarius* (διμοιρίτης, *dimoirites*)[80] and a *sesquiplicarius* (ὅστις ἐν ἡμιολίῳ μισθοφορᾷ, *hostis en hemiolio misthophora*):[81] these are the first three figures of importance in a *turma*, the basic unit of *alae* and *cohortes*.[82] Therefore, it emerges that the "companies" of horsemen in the *hippika gymnasia* described by Arrian were not generic formations, but rather units of the auxiliary cavalry. And in the *Adlocutio Hadriani* a *cohors II Hamiorum* ("second cohort of the *Hamii*")[83] an *ala I Pannoniorum* ("first

---

[77] The same could be said for the exercises Hadrian presided over – assuming that we are dealing with two different events, which seems unlikely for a variety of reasons, as emerging from the analysis here conducted.

[78] Cf. Wheeler 1978, 357; Dixon and Southern 1992, 126: "The participating riders and their mounts wore and used special equipment. Many books refer to these items as 'parade equipment'. In this book, however, the term 'sports equipment' is used. (…) Parade equipment' was a soldier's entire kit which was worn during static inspection parades; all of this kit *could* be worn in combat. 'Sports equipment' (…) included highly decorative items, designed specifically for displays; although some of these items could conceivably have been worn in combat, it seems highly unlikely that they would have been". According to the opinion of Devine 1993, 332, "Arrian's object is clearly that of describing a mere festive display, not of instructing his readers in the mechanics of cavalry drill".

[79] The *decurio* (corresponding to Greek *dekadarchos*) is an officer of the Roman army, commanding a troop of ten men (a *decuria*) in the early Republic, and a unit of auxiliary cavalry of 32 men (a *turma*) during the late Republic and the Empire. It is noteworthy that δεκάδαρχος (variant of δεκαδάρχης) is attested first in Xenophon's works, specifically in *Cyropaedia* and *Hipparchicus*; in the latter, it occurs six times (ch. 2.2, 4, 6, 7; 4.9).

[80] Literally "who receives a double pay" (cf. Varro *ling*. 5.90); he's an official holding the second rank in the command of a *turma*.

[81] Literally "who receives one and a half pay"; he's an official holding the third rank in the command of a *turma*. On *decurio, duplicarius, sesquiplicarius* see in detail Cheesman 1914, 37-41.

[82] About the *alae* and *cohortes* (respectively, the auxiliary cavalry and infantry units), see Cheesman 1914, 22-5. For the text and a deeper analysis (also of the terminology) of ch. 42.1 cf. Busetto 2013, 235-37.

[83] Speidel's integration *Ha*[*miorum*] in Speidel 2006, 48 (frg. 33) is preferable to *Hi*[*spanorum*] proposed in *CIL* VIII, Suppl. Prov. Numidiae 18042, frg. D.

wing of the Pannonians")[84] and a *cohors VI Commagenorum* ("sixth cohort of the Commagenians")[85] are mentioned.[86]

Despite the fact that the beginning of the *Tactica*, which perhaps contained the dedication of the work,[87] is mutilated and that Arrian never refers directly to Hadrian in the surviving part,[88] it does seem possible to discern, on closer scrutiny, some allusions (perhaps of an encomiastic intent) directed at the Emperor, beyond mere similarities of content between the *Tactica* and the *Adlocutio*. For example, the celebration of the opening of Rome to foreign elements in ch. 33 is a topical theme, but it could be updated in light of Hadrian's love of foreign things.[89] In a kind of thematic ring composition, Arrian concludes the treatise by calling attention to the introduction, by a formally unnamed *basileus* ("emperor"), of foreign military practices and divisions, like the Parthian and Armenian *hippotoxotai* ("horse-archers") and Sarmatian and Celtic *contoforoi* ("pike-bearers").[90] Such a reference reveals the paradigmatic importance, for the

---

[84] *AE*, 1900, 35.

[85] *CIL* VIII, Suppl. Prov. Numidiae 18042, frg. A a and C b.

[86] Other than the *III legio Augusta*, the African military contingent was made up of auxiliary divisions: three *alae quingenariae* (*alae* composed by 16 *turmae* of 32 men, for a total amount of 512 men) and six or more *cohortes equitatae* (cohorts composed by both cavalry and infantry, introduced in the Roman army during the Julio-Claudian age). Cf. Cheesman 1914, 25-30 (general discourse on the size of auxiliary regiments); Hyland 1993, 78; Le Bohec 2003b; Speidel 2006, 3 (with useful bibliography).

[87] This is the case with Aelian's *Tactical Theory* (*praef.* 4-7), which shows many structural and thematic similarities with Arrian's *Tactica*, as noted previously (in addition to the bibliography cited above, n. 2, cf. in particular Devine 1989, 32).

[88] The only mention of Hadrian's name occurs in the third person in *Tact.* 44.3 (for the text see above, n. 38). Apart from that, there are only generic references to the emperor (*basileus*).

[89] Cf. *Tact.* 33.2 Εἰ γάρ τοι ἐπ' ἄλλῳ τῳ, καὶ ἐπὶ τῷδε ἄξιοι ἐπαινεῖσθαι Ῥωμαῖοι, ὅτι οὐ τὰ οἰκεῖα καὶ πάτρια οὕτως τι ἠγάπησαν, ὡς τὰ πανταχόθεν καλὰ ἐπιλεξάμενοι οἰκεῖα σφίσιν ἐποιήσαντο ("For if for any other reason the Romans merit praise, they do so especially on this account, that their devotion to their own native institutions has not been such as to prevent them from taking over good customs from every source and making them their own", transl. Hyland 1993, 72). As Kiechle 1964, 126 had already pointed out, this panegyric of ch. 33 reveals Arrian's "complete support for Hadrian's introduction of barbarian tactics, for which *exempla maiorum* are cited as a proof that Hadrian's policy is not revolutionary" (quotation from Wheeler 1978, 362).

[90] *Tact.* 44.1-2 Βασιλεὺς δὲ προσεξεῦρεν καὶ τὰ βαρβαρικὰ ἐκμελετᾶν αὐτούς, ὅσα τε ἢ Παρθυαίων ἢ Ἀρμενίων ἱπποτοξόται ἐπασκοῦσι καὶ ὅσας οἱ Σαυροματῶν ἢ

Roman *gymnasia*, of these foreign contingents, which cannot be dated before the end of the 1st and beginning of the 2nd centuries CE: it therefore determines an easy connection to Hadrian's military policy, which actively encouraged the assimilation of eastern elements into the Roman army.[91] In the end, an encomiastic seal of the treatise can be found in the final citation of Terpander's couplet (of which Arrian is, moreover, the only complete source).[92] As suggested by Everett L. Wheeler: "the verses apply very well to Hadrian and reflect his interests in military training, Hellenic culture and law. Even the selection of Terpander fits Hadrian's preference for archaic authors".[93] Therefore, positing that the

---

Κελτῶν κοντοφόροι ἐπιστροφάς τε καὶ ἀποστροφάς, [...] καὶ ἀκροβολισμοὺς [...] καὶ ἀλαλαγμοὺς πατρίους ἑκάστῳ γένει, Κελτικοὺς μὲν τοῖς Κελτοῖς ἱππεῦσι, Γετικοὺς δὲ τοῖς Γέταις, Ῥαιτικοὺς δὲ ὅσοι ἐκ Ῥαιτῶν ("But the emperor has also introduced the practice of barbarian manoeuvres such as the Parthian and Armenian horse-archers carry out, together with the turns and feigned retreats of the Sarmatians and Celtic stave-bearers […], varieties of skirmishing […], and the war-cries native to each race: Celtic for Celtic cavalry, Getic for Getic and Rhaetic for those from Rhaetia", transl. Hyland 1993, 77). This thematic ring composition could lead to "interpret Hadrian's policy as not revolutionary, for being deeply rooted in ancient tradition" (Petrocelli and Pitagora 2005, 147). Wheeler 1978, 357 points out how, here, Arrian "extols Hadrian's cavalry reforms, carefully noting their consistency with the *mos maiorum*".

[91] See previous note. This seems an interesting connection to the *Hipparchicus*, where Xenophon relates the prestige and the high reputation of the Spartan cavalry to the introduction of foreign cavalrymen and states that the latter are held in high esteem everywhere in the other *poleis* (οἶδα δ' ἔγωγε καὶ Λακεδαιμονίοις ἱππικὸν ἀρξάμενον εὐδοκιμεῖν, ἐπεὶ ξένους ἱππέας προσέλαβον. Καὶ ἐν ταῖς ἄλλαις δὲ πόλεσι πανταχοῦ τὰ ξενικὰ ὁρῶ εὐδοκιμοῦντα, "I do know that the fame of the Lacedaemonian cavalry dates from the introduction of foreign cavalrymen. And in the other states everywhere I notice that the foreign contingents enjoy a high reputation" [transl. adapted from Marchant 1946, 291], *Hipp*. 9.4).

[92] Terp. *frg*. 6 Bergk (*frg*. 4 Diehl) ἔνθ' αἰχμά τε νέων θάλλει καὶ μῶσα λίγεια, / καὶ δίκα εὐρυάγυια καλῶν ἐπιτάρροθος ἔργων ("There flourishes both the spear of the brave and the sweet-voiced Muse / and Justice in the wide open streets, the defender of fine actions", transl. Hyland 1993, 77). This fragment from Arrian is particularly valuable because it is the only alternative to Plutarch's citation of the couplet (*Lic*. 21.3), which ends with εὐρυάγυια (literally "with wide streets") and bears the (less likely) ionic-attic variant μοῦσα instead of μῶσα (both meaning "muse").

[93] Wheeler 1978, 354. Also in the *Historia Augusta* Hadrian is often said to be interested in the art of war and military exercises, which he himself attended (e.g. SHA, *Vita Hadr*. 14.10), in literature and culture (e.g. SHA, *Vita Hadr*. 14.8-9), and in law, which he was attentive to, in order to uphold civic balance and social justice (cf. the legal actions listed in SHA, *Vita Hadr*. 18).

exercises mentioned in the *Adlocutio* are the same as those witnessed by Arrian, the *Tactica* would constitute a means to further record the Lambaesis events, becoming an opportunity for a refined praise of Hadrian's reforms and interests.[94]

Following Wheeler's position, it seems plausible that the encomiastic allure of the *Tactica* could be tied to the fact that Arrian's political and public career reached its culmination under Hadrian: he was consul and imperial legate (*legatus Augusti pro praetore*)[95] in Cappadocia from 130 to 138 CE and he must have enjoyed a certain familiarity with the Emperor, as shown by two passages from the *Periplus Ponti Euxini* (written in the form of a letter addressed to Hadrian), which would demonstrate that they knew each other.[96] This suggests the possibility that Hadrian read the *Tactica* with interest even without Arrian's having been specifically commissioned to produce the work, and its lack of a specific dedication to the Emperor, which nevertheless could have been in the lost introduction of the treatise. Moreover, a literary re-working of the *Adlocutio* – as the *Tactica* definitely appears to be from the thematic and lexical similarities with the Lambaesis speech that have been pointed out here – may have made it possible for Arrian's work to attract imperial attention and approval, all the more so for the possibility that it might offer a greater echo of Hadrian's desires than epigraphy and, as such, create a further propaganda tool for his military policies. Furthermore, the composition of the *Tactica* occurred at a delicate moment in Arrian's political career: after the end of his governorship in Cappadocia, such an exhibition of loyalty and absolute adherence to Hadrian's political strategy may have been accompanied by the hope of greater appointments in the future.[97]

---

[94] Cf. Wheeler 1978, 364 and Stadter 1980, 44-5.
[95] About this figure of provincial governor see Richardson 1976, 61.
[96] In ch. 1.3-4 Arrian mentions a statue that does not resemble Hadrian (so this would prove that Arrian must have seen the Emperor at least once). In ch. 2.4 he states deep gratitude for the benefits received from Hadrian. The two may have met in 123/124 (during one of Hadrian's trips across Bithynia and a stay in Athens): cf. Tonnet 1988, I, 34.
[97] Cf. Wheeler 1978, 364-65. A recent summary of the stance of the critics can be found in Petrocelli and Pitagora 2005, 157: "Che l'*Ars tactica* possa considerarsi nel suo insieme un omaggio ad Adriano in occasione dei suoi *vicennalia* è opinione condivisa dalla maggior parte degli studiosi, anche in considerazione del fr. 5 Page di Terpandro programmaticamente citato in chiusura, incentrato sulla connessione tra valore militare, poesia e diritto: tutte attività particolarmente care all'imperatore spagnolo" ("That the whole *Ars Tactica* can be considered as a tribute to Hadrian on the occasion of the twenty years of his reign is a view shared by most of the

AS A CONCLUSION: NEW EVIDENCE

It seems noteworthy that the same insistence on spectacular cavalry training in Xenophon, Arrian, and Hadrian is attested by Arrian's contemporary, Appian, even though in reference to a past personality, Pompey the Great:

> ὁ δὲ Πομπήιος [...] τόν τε στρατὸν ἐγύμναζε, συντρέχων καὶ συνιππεύων καὶ παντὸς ἐξάρχων πόνου παρ' ἡλικίαν· ὅθεν αὐτῷ ῥᾳδίως εὔνοιά τε ἦν, καὶ συνέθεον ἐπὶ τὰ γυμνάσια Πομπηίου πάντες ὡς ἐπὶ θέαν. App. Hist. 2.49.200

The historical background of this report is the eve of the Civil War (49 BCE), when Pompey "disciplined his army and took part in the exercises of both infantry and cavalry, and was foremost in everything, notwithstanding his age. In this way he readily gained the good-will of his soldiers; and the people flocked to see Pompey's military drills as to a spectacle."[98] Also in Plutarch's biography, Pompey is described, and at greater length, as directing the training of the army and offering an admirable example in person of both the infantry and cavalry exercises:[99]

---

scholars. Noteworthy is also frg. 5 Page of Terpander – cited at the end of the treatise – which is focused on the connection between military prowess, poetry and law: all activities that the Spanish emperor would most appreciate"). In this same perspective Devine 1993, 333 had softened Bosworth's estimation of the treatise as an original and valuable source for Roman tactics (cf. Bosworth 1993, 253-64) and judged the *Tactica* a "superficially Romanized manual", "a conventional, 'philosopher's' way of ingratiating [...] the reigning emperor, rather than an attempt at genuine originality or the production of a tactical guide of practical utility to contemporary commanders". Even if it could be true that, in this last respect, the *Tactica* appears to differ strongly from the *Hipparchicus*, the negative remark emerging from Devine's statement seems to misunderstand the ancient notion of "originality", which is related not to the absence of a model, but to the terms of its adaptation.

[98] Transl. White 1899, II, 122. The phrase στρατὸν γυμνάζειν ("training the army") is Appian's coinage, unless we consider the title (unlikely the original, at any rate) in Onasander, *Strateg.* 10 περὶ τοῦ δεῖν γυμνάζειν τὸν στρατὸν ἀδείας οὔσης ("how to train the army in times of peace").

[99] Plut. *Vit. Pomp.* 64.1-2: Ἐν δὲ τῷ χρόνῳ τούτῳ μεγάλη συνέστη Πομπηΐῳ δύναμις [...]· τὴν δὲ πεζὴν σύμμικτον οὖσαν καὶ μελέτης δεομένην ἐγύμναζεν ἐν Βεροίᾳ καθήμενος οὐκ ἀργός, ἀλλ' ὥσπερ ἀκμάζοντι χρώμενος αὐτῷ πρὸς τὰ γυμνάσια. Μεγάλη γὰρ ἦν ῥοπὴ πρὸς τὸ θαρρεῖν τοῖς ὁρῶσι Πομπήιον Μάγνον ἑξήκοντα μὲν ἔτη δυεῖν λείποντα γεγενημένον, ἐν δὲ τοῖς ὅπλοις ἁμιλλώμενον πεζόν, εἶτα ἱππότην αὖθις ἑλκόμενόν τε τὸ ξίφος ἀπραγμόνως θέοντι τῷ ἵππῳ καὶ

this aspect of Pompey's attitude and behaviour, therefore, was not new.

The mention that 'συνέθεον ἐπὶ τὰ γυμνάσια Πομπηίου πάντες ὡς ἐπὶ θέαν' ("flocked to see Pompey's military drills as to a spectacle") can now be found only in Appian.[100] It now may be of use to remember that Appian was roughly a contemporary of Arrian's, and, like him, was from the provinces (Appian was from Alexandria, Arrian from Nicomedia); moreover, he also achieved a considerable career both in Egypt and in Rome at the time of the Antonine Emperors,[101] an era which became the point of reference for his literary activity, centred on Roman history. So, beyond the usual Roman susceptibility to the visual power of spectacle and any kind of public performance, it seems at least possible that the

---

κατακλείοντα πάλιν εὐχερῶς, ἐν δὲ τοῖς ἀκοντισμοῖς οὐ μόνον ἀκρίβειαν, ἀλλὰ καὶ ῥώμην ἐπιδεικνύμενον εἰς μῆκος, ὃ πολλοὶ τῶν νέων οὐχ ὑπερέβαλλον ("In the meantime a great force was gathered by Pompey. [...]; and his infantry, which was a mixed multitude and in need of training, he exercised at Beroea, not sitting idly by, but taking part in their exercises himself, as if he had been in the flower of his age. And indeed it was a great incentive to confidence when they saw Pompey the Great, who was now sixty years of age less two, but who nevertheless competed in full armour as a foot-soldier, and then again, as a horseman, drew his sword without trouble while his horse was at a gallop and put it back in its sheath with ease; while in hurling the javelin he not only displayed accuracy, but also vigour in the length of his cast, which many of the young men could not surpass", transl. Perrin 1917, 281-3). As Carsana 2007, 168-169 highlights, "l'attività di addestramento delle truppe svolta personalmente dal generale rispondeva evidentemente a tale scopo: esse avevano bisogno della preparazione e della sicurezza ispirate da una guida eccezionale e Pompeo provvide ad entrambe" ("the activity of training troops carried out by the general himself obviously had this purpose: they needed that preparation and security which only an outstanding guide could inspire, and Pompey provided both").

[98] Carsana 2007, 168 (comm. to "τὸν τε στρατὸν...θέαν") states that this event is reported by Plutarch using the same terms (but this is not correct: see previous note), which would suggest a common source, and that an ironical hint might be noticed in 'ὡς ἐπὶ θέαν' ("as to a spectacle"). However, her position does not seem very convincing.

[101] Cf. App. Hist. praef. 62: τίς δὲ ὢν ταῦτα συνέγραψα, πολλοὶ μὲν ἴσασι καὶ αὐτὸς προέφηνα, σαφέστερον δ᾽ εἰπεῖν, Ἀππιανὸς Ἀλεξανδρεύς, ἐς τὰ πρῶτα ἥκων ἐν τῇ πατρίδι καὶ δίκαις ἐν Ῥώμῃ συναγορεύσας ἐπὶ τῶν βασιλέων, μέχρι με σφῶν ἐπιτροπεύειν ἠξίωσαν ("Who I am, who have written these things, many indeed know, and I have already indicated. To speak more plainly I am Appian of Alexandria, having reached the highest place in my native country, and having been, in Rome, a pleader of causes before the emperors, until they deemed me worthy of being made their procurator", transl. White 1899, I, 8). On Appian's biography and literary activity, cf. in general RE II₁, 1895, 216-237.

appeal of the spectacular nature of Pompey's exercises is not accidental, but rather the update of an ancient episode in light of modern practice, that is, the resurgence of the new impulse and normative value that Hadrian had attributed to the magnificence of military training.

BIBLIOGRAPHY

Ameling, W. (1984) "L. Flavius Arrianus Neos Xenophon", *Epigraphica Anatolica* 4, 119-22.

L'année épigraphique. Revue des publications epigraphiques relatives a l'antiquité romaine (1888-). Paris.

Bosworth, A. B. (1988) *From Arrian to Alexander: Studies in Historical Interpretation*. Oxford.

—. (1993) "Arrian and Rome: the Minor Works", in *Aufstieg und Niedergang der römischen Welt*, 34.1: *Sprache und Literatur*, 226-75.

Busetto, A. (2013) "Linguistic Adaptation as Cultural Adjustment: Treatment of Celtic, Iberic, and Latin Terminology in Arrian's *Tactica*", *Journal of Ancient History* 1, 230-241.

Carsana, C. (2007) *Commento storico al libro II delle* Guerre Civili *di Appiano*. Pisa.

Cary, E. (1925) *Dio's Roman History in nine volumes*, with an English Translation by E. C., vol. VIII. London – New York.

Cheesman, G. L. (1914) *The Auxilia of the Roman Imperial Army*. Hildesheim – New York. [Repr. Facs. Oxford 1971]

Chowen, R. H. (1970) "The Problem of Hadrian's Visits to North Africa", *Classical Journal* 65, 323-24.

Corpus Inscriptionum Latinarum (1863-), consilium et auctoritate Academiae litterarum regiae Borussicae editum [postea: Academiae scientiarum Rei Publicae Democraticae Germanicae]. Berolini.

Dain, A. (1946) *Histoire du texte d'Elien le Tacticien - des origines à la fin du Moyen age*. Paris.

Davies, R. W. (1968) "Fronto, Hadrian and the Roman Army", *Latomus* 27, 75-95.

Delebecque, E. (ed.) (1973) *Xenophon. Le commandant de la cavalerie*. Paris.

Devine, A. M. (1989) "Aelian's *Manual of Hellenistic Military Tactics* – A New Translation from the Greek with an Introduction", *Ancient World* 19, 31-64.

—. (1993) "Arrian's 'Tactica'", *Aufstieg und Niedergang der römischen Welt*, II, 34.1: *Sprache und Literatur*, 312-37.

—. (1995) "Polybius' Lost *Tactica*: The ultimate source for the tactical

manuals of Asclepiodotus, Aelian and Arrian?", *Ancient History Bulletin* 9, 40-4.
DeVoto, J. G. (ed.) (1993) *Flavius Arrianus, Techne Taktika <sic> (Tactical Handbook) and Ektaxis kata Alanōn (The Expedition Against the Alans)*. Chicago.
Dixon, K. R. and P. Southern (1992) *The Roman Cavalry: from the first to the third century AD*. London.
Ekman, E. (1933) *Zu Xenophons Ipparchikos*. Uppsala.
Ensslin, W. (1938) "Zu den symmachiarii", *Klio* 31, 365-70.
Fields, N. and A. Hook (2006), *Roman Auxiliary Cavalryman – AD 14-193*. Oxford.
Förster, R. (1877) "Studien zu den griechischen Taktikern, I: Über die Tactica des Arrian und Aelian", *Hermes* 12, 426-29.
Freyburger-Galland, M.-L. (1997) "Dion Cassius et le carrousel troyen", *Latomus* 56, 619-29.
Galimberti, A. (2007) *Adriano e l'ideologia del principato*. Roma.
Giannelli, G. and S. Mazzarino (1956) *Trattato di Storia romana*. I-II. Roma.
Giuffrè, V. (2003) "'*Armorum exercitio*' e '*castrorum disciplina*' secondo Adriano", in Le Bohec, 159-163.
Gonzalez, J. R. (2003) *Historia de las legiones romanas*. Madrid.
Kiechle, F. (1964), "Die 'Taktik' des Flavius Arrianus", *Bericht der Römisch-Germanischen Kommission* 45, 87-129.
Köchly, H. (1851) *De libris Tacticis, qui Arriani et Aeliani feruntur, dissertatio, Index Lectionum*. Turici.
Hatzfeld, J. (1946-1947) "Note sur la date et l'objet du *Hiéron* de Xenophon", *Revue des Études Grecques* 59-60, 54-70.
Hyland, A. (1993) *Training the Roman Cavalry – From Arrian's Ars Tactica*. Phoenix Mill – Dover (NH).
Le Bohec, Y. (1989) *La troisième légion Auguste*. Paris.
—. (ed.) (2003) *Les discours d'Hadrien à l'armée d'Afrique. Exercitatio*. Paris.
—. (2003) "Hadrien et l'armée", in Le Bohec, 9-19. [= Le Bohec 2003a]
—. (2003) "L'armée d'Afrique au temps d'Hadrien", in Le Bohec, 41-51. [= Le Bohec 2003b]
—. (2003) "L'exercice militaire et l'armée romaine", in Le Bohec, 123-32. [= Le Bohec 2003c]
Levi, M.A. (1994), *Adriano*. Milano.
Marchant, E. C. (ed.) (1946) *Xenophon. Scripta minora*, with an English translation by E.C.M., London – Cambridge, MA.
Oliver, J. H. (1972) "Herm at Athens with portraits of Xenophon and

Arrian", *American Journal of Archaeology* 76, 327-28.
Paulys Realencyclopädie der Classischen Altertumswissenschaft (1893-1978), neue Bearbeitung begonnen von G. Wissowa, fortgeführt von W. Kroll und K. Mittelhaus, herausgegeben von K. Ziegler, I1-XA. Stuttgart-München.
Pérez Castro, L. C. (1982) "Dextrator", *Emerita* 50, 301-3.
Perrin B. (1955), *Plutarch's Lives*, with an English Translation by B. P., vol. V (Agesilaus and Pompey, Pelopidas and Marcellus). London – Cambridge, MA.
Petit, P. (1975), "Le IIe siècle après J.-C.", *Aufstieg und Niedergang der römischen Welt*, II.2, 354-80.
Petrikovits, H. von (1939) "Troiae lusus", *Klio* 32, 209-20.
Petrocelli, C. (ed.) (2001) *Senofonte. Ipparchico - Manuale per il comandante di cavalleria*. Bari.
Petrocelli, C., and A. Pitagora (2005) "Scrivere di militaria. Due storici, un imperatore e i ludi equestri", *Quaderni di Didattica della Scrittura* 4, 141-62.
Pfister, G. (1993) "Lusus Troiae", in K. Dietz, D. Hennig and H. Kaleisch (eds.) *Klassisches Altertum, Spätantike und frühes Christentum: Adolf Lippold zum 65. Geburtstag gewidmet*. 177-89. Würzburg.
Richardson, J. (1976), *Roman provincial administration, 227 BC to AD 117*. London.
Roos, A. G., and G. Wirth (eds.) (1968) *Flavii Arriani quae exstant omnia*, II, *Scripta minora et fragmenta*. Lipsiae.
Salomone, S. (1986) "Letteratura, tradizione e novità tattico-strategiche nello *Hipparchikos* di Senofonte", *Maia* 38, 197-205.
Speidel, M. P. (1975) "The rise of ethnic units in the Roman Imperial Army", *Aufstieg und Niedergang der römischen Welt*, II, 3, 202-31.
—. (2006) *Emperor Hadrian's speeches to the African army: a new text*. Mainz.
Stadter, P. A. (1967) "Flavius Arrianus: the New Xenophon", *Greek, Roman and Byzantine Studies* 8, 155-161.
—. (1978) "The *Ars Tactica* of Arrian. Tradition and originality", *Classical Philology* 73, 117-28.
—. (1980) *Arrian of Nicomedia*. Chapel Hill.
Thornton, M. K. (1975) "Hadrian and his Reign", *Aufstieg und Niedergang der römischen Welt*, II, 2, 432-76.
Tonnet, H. (1988) *Recherches sur Arrien, sa personnalité et ses écrits atticistes*, I-II. Amsterdam.
Wheeler, E. L. (1978) "The Occasion of Arrian's *Tactica*", *Greek, Byzantine and Roman Studies* 19, 351-65.

White, H. (1899) *The Roman History of Appian of Alexandria*. I-II. London.
Zaroski, G. (2009) *Adlocutiones: Imperial Addresses to the Roman Army (27 B.C. - A.D. 235)*, Open Access Dissertations and Theses. Paper 4338, retrievable at:
http://digitalcommons.mcmaster.ca/opendissertations/4338
Ziołkowski, M. (1990) "Il culto della Disciplina nella religione degli eserciti romani", *Rivista di Storia dell'Antichità* 20, 97-107.

CHAPTER TEN

TROUBLE COMES IN THREES: FROM CHARIOT TO CAVALRY IN THE 'CELTIC' WORLD[1]

ALBERTO PÉREZ-RUBIO

The *trimarkisia* always gets a passing mention when tackling the Galatian onslaught against Greece in 280/279 BC, without further delving into the matter. A careful analysis of this cavalry fighting unit within the context of contemporary 'Celtic' societies has been lacking. However, such an analysis can shed light on several aspects of the European Iron Age. This paper analyses just one: how the *trimarkisia* gives us insight into the evolution from chariotry to cavalry in Iron Age temperate Europe.

I have chosen, advisedly, to include the adjective 'Celtic' in the title and therefore employ it in the text. There is neither need nor space to dwell on a debate that has generated much literature in the last two decades.[2] But I consider that the term 'Celtic' is still useful and appropriate when analyzing certain European Iron Age societies that, notwithstanding their differences and distinctive features, shared some linguistic, cultural and social traits.[3] In the same vein, I will resort to parallels in ancient Irish literature if appropriate; even if Jackson's[4] fruitful metaphor of Irish

---

[1] Research project: "*Entre la paz y la guerra: alianzas, confederaciones y diplomacia en el Occidente Mediterráneo (siglos III-I aC)*", HAR2011-27782, National Plan for Scientific Research, Development and Innovation, State Secretary of Research, Development and Innovation, Ministry of Economy and Competitiveness, Government of Spain.
[2] Fitzpatrick 1996; Collis 1996, 1997, 2003; Megaw and Megaw 1996, 1998; James 1998, 1999; Karl 2004; Ruiz Zapatero 2004, 2010; Karl and Stifter 2007; Anthoons and Clerinx 2007.
[3] Ruiz Zapatero 2010, 110.
[4] Jackson 1964.

literature as a "window on the Iron Age" has been downplayed lately, I agree with Karl[5] that it provides an indigenous approach to shared cultural practices.

The only extant quote in the classical sources that explicitly mentions the *trimarkisia* is in book ten of Pausanias' *Description of Greece*, in a passage which deals with the Galatian invasion of Greece in 279 BC led by Brennus and Acichorius. This mention is absent in the two other surviving sources which recount this event, namely the *Histories* of Diodorus Siculus (22.9.1-5) and the *Epitome* of Pompeius Trogus via Justin (24.4-8). The text reads as follows:

> For to each horseman were attached two servants, who were themselves skilled riders and, like their masters, had a horse. [...] This organization is called in their native speech *trimarkisia*, for I would have you know that *marka* is the Celtic name for a horse. (Paus. 10.19.9-11)

Although Pausanias' sources are not totally clear, he relied on third century BC historians' narrations about the Galatian attack against Greece and their later crossing to Asia, as we know about the existence of several *Galatica*.[6] So we can state that Pausanias' description of the *trimarkisia* probably reflects a real cavalry institution observed amongst the Galatians. This was probably familiar to his unknown source because of the pervading presence of Galatian mercenaries in Eastern Mediterranean armies at the time.[7]

ETYMOLOGY AND SYMBOLISM

The etymology of the word *trimarkisia* does not present much of a problem for Celtic philologists. It can be deconstructed in two words, *tri-* and *marcos*.[8] *Tri-* is the Celtic numeral for 'three', in accordance with the Indo-European languages and which appears in many compound words.[9] The number three has a major significance in 'Celtic' cosmology, where the iconography is pervaded by triplism: Triple-faced images, triads as the Matres or triplication in animals.[10] The triple repetition enhances and

---

[5] Karl 2005, 257.
[6] Nachtergael 1975, 49-93; Rankin 1987, 71-2.
[7] Mitchell 2003, 288; Pérez-Rubio 2009.
[8] Delamarre 2003, 301.
[9] Delamarre 2003, 300.
[10] Aldhouse-Green 1991; 1992a, 169-205; 2004, 202.

intensifies the symbolism embodied in the number itself.[11] This prevalence of the number three is endorsed by its importance in Welsh and Irish literature.[12] In fact there is a passage in Irish literature that reflects Pausanias' *trimarkisia,* at least linguistically. The *Togail Bruidne Da Derga*, or *The Destruction of Da Derga's Hostel*, is an Irish epic tale. Although the oldest surviving manuscript dates from the eleventh century AD, its content can be dated several centuries earlier.[13] In section 30 of the manuscript, three dreadful horsemen (*triar marcach*) appear when Conaire was journeying along the Road of Cualu:

> He marked before him three horsemen [*triar marcach*], riding towards the house. Three red frocks had they, and three red mantles: three red bucklers they bore, and three red spears were in their hands: three red steeds they bestrode, and three red heads of hair were on them. (*The Destruction of Da Derga's Hostel,* 30)

The enumeration of the triads sounds almost as a magic spell. These horsemen are messengers from the Netherworld, the *Sidh*, and carriers of terrible omens (*The Destruction of Da Derga's Hostel,* 35).

On the other hand, *marcisia* is a derivate in *-isiā* from *marcos*, 'horse'. Horse is *marc* in Old Irish and *march* in Welsh, Cornish and Breton.[14] *Marcos* has parallels in Germanic, as the Old High German *marh-*, the Old English *mearh* and nowadays *mare*,[15] and it represents a Celto-Germanic isogloss.[16] But *marcos* was not the only Celtic noun for horse.[17] There were several words for the animal and each one seems to have had a correspondence with a certain function or a certain kind of horse. For example *mandus* was a pony,[18] *caballos* was a work horse,[19] *cassica* was a mare,[20] and *ueredus* was a post-horse.[21] That all of these words were

---

[11] Aldhouse-Green 1992, 170.
[12] The *Triads of the Horses* (*Trioedd y Meirch*) found as a distinctive group of 'Triads' in Welsh literature do not seem to have any relationship with the *trimarkisia*, being the Triad, a mnemonic device employed by traditional poets (Bromwich 1997,102-3).
[13] O'Connor 2008, 56.
[14] Delamarre 2003, 216.
[15] Raulwing 2000, 108; Delamarre 2003, 301.
[16] Kelly 1997, 45; Raulwing 2000, 108; Mikhailova 2007, 6.
[17] Kelly 1997.
[18] Kelly 1997, 52; Delamarre 2003, 214; Blažek 2008, 49.
[19] Delamarre 2003, 95.
[20] Kelly 1997, 56; Delamarre 2003, 109-110.
[21] Delamarre 2003, 314; Blažek 2008, 50.

incorporated into Latin is an indicator of 'Celtic' proficiency in horsemanship.[22]

However, the most common term for 'horse' was *epos*. *Epos* derives from **eḱuos*, the ancient Indo-European name for 'horse' – as Latin *equus* or Greek *hippos*[23] – while there is no agreement about the root for *marcos*. Most scholars admit it was a *Wanderwort*, a 'travelling word,' although there are discrepancies about its origin. Gamkrelidze and Ivanov suggest an Altaic origin (from Altaic **morV-*), a borrowing explained by early contacts between both Indo-European and Altaic tribes. However, as Tatyana A. Mikhailova[24] has pointed out, this does not match with the absence of *marcos* in West Indo-European languages apart from Celtic and Germanic.[25] Birkhan proposes a pre- Indo-European word incorporated via the Thracians, who would have maintained the element *mark-* in some anthroponyms.[26] The most convincing thesis is that of Mikhailova,[27] who argues that **mark* would have been borrowed by Celtic and Germanic speakers from Eastern communities skilled in horsemanship, such as the Scythians. *Marcos* would have been used in Celtic languages for 'mounted horse' (and particularly for 'war horse') as advanced by Joseph Loth,[28] so it is plausible that it was a borrowing from the communities that probably introduced horse riding into temperate Europe, as Mikhailova argues. In this respect, it is worth mentioning that according to Pliny (*Nat. Hist.* 8.66) "the Scythians prefer mares for the purposes of war, because they can pass their urine without stopping in their career." In contrast, most Scythian equine iconography seems to depict stallions, although according to Herodotus (7.4.8) the Scythians and Sarmatians used to castrate their horses in order to make them more tractable. This is deemed implausible by Renate Rolle,[29] as it would deplete the vigor of the animal, much needed in warfare. The mention in Trogus (Justin 9.2) of the 20,000 mares that Philip II of Macedon captured from the Scythians and sent to Macedon for breeding is an indicator of the importance of the animal. In any case, if the **mark* root lies in the Scythian word for mare (and hence

---

[22] On the excellence of 'Celtic'horsemanship, Str. 4.4.2, Plut. *Vit. Marc.* 6.4, Arr. *Tact.* 33.
[23] Kelly 1997, 44; Delamarre 2003, 163.
[24] Mikhailova 2007, 6.
[25] Kelly 1997, 45.
[26] Mikhailova 2007, 7.
[27] Mikhailova 2007, 6-7.
[28] Loth 1925, 113; 1927, 410; Mikhailova 2007, 5.
[29] Rolle 1989, 101.

for war horse according to Pliny), Mikhailova's thesis could be strengthened; the word travelling into Celtic as 'mounted (or war) horse.'

The meaning of *marcos* as 'mounted horse' and its use confined to Celtic and Germanic languages in contrast with *epos/*eḱuos*, which is present in almost all languages of the Indo-European family,[30] fit well with a later borrowing. For Loth,[31] *epos* would have been the word for 'yoked horse,' only displaced by *marcos* when cavalry superseded chariots, but remained prevalent in Celtic onomastics and toponymy.[32] The linguistic data matches with what we know about chariotry and cavalry in Iron Age temperate Europe. Indeed, the depictions of chariots pulled by horses in Europe predate by several centuries those of horsemen,[33] and from the middle of the second millennium BC onwards the chariot was part of the European mindset.[34] By contrast, the first depictions of ridden horses in temperate Europe date from the Hallstatt C period, around the sixth century BC.[35] True horse riding only began in temperate Europe around the seventh century BC.[36] Iron Age chariots pulled by horses seem to have inherited, in some ways, the symbolic significance of the four wheeled carts drawn by oxen and associated with burial practices from 3000 BC onwards.[37] The highest symbolic value and prestige of the chariot over the single horse could also have had a reflection in the much higher number of personal names composed with *epos* (even the theonym Epona) than with *marcos*.[38]

THE CHARIOT

In Iron-Age temperate Europe two-wheeled chariots pulled by horses appear in the La Tène period,[39] from the fifth until the first centuries BC,

---

[30] Delamarre 2003, 163.
[31] Loth 1927, 410.
[32] Delamarre 2003, 163.
[33] The first depictions of war chariots in Europe are those of the stelai of the Shaft Graves of Mycenae, c. 1600 BC, while the first image of an armed horseman is a terracotta figure, also from Mycenae, from the thirteenth century BC (Renfrew 1998: 202-5).
[34] Renfrew 1998, 204.
[35] Renfrew 1998, 280. A rock carving in at Tegneby in Bohuslän, Sweden, dated to the second quarter of the first millennium BC may well be the earliest depiction of mounted combat in temperate Europe (Drews 2004, 62).
[36] Powell 1971, 5.
[37] Renfrew 1998, 204-5.
[38] Loth 1927, 410; Kelly 1997, 45; Delamarre 2013, 216.
[39] Piggott 1983, 195-239.

replacing the four-wheeled wagons present in aristocratic Hallstatt burials[40] between 750-500 BC.[41] The La Tène chariot was a status symbol,[42] employed for travel[43] and war (Diod. 5.29), the vehicle in which the high-ranking deceased were transported to the tomb and their vehicle to the Netherworld.[44] Such burials are found from Britain to Thrace, being especially frequent from the fifth and fourth centuries BC in Champagne and the Rhineland, with fewer finds from the third and second centuries BC, and almost disappearing in the first century BC.[45] The last mention of fighting chariots on mainland Europe is from 121 BC, when king Bituitus of the Arverni was routed by the Romans (Flor. 1.37.5). In Britain the chariot would still be in use during the following century, and even as late as AD 83 in the battle of Mons Graupius (Tac. *Ag.* 35.3). According to Diodorus (5.29), in travel and in war:

> The Gauls use chariots drawn by two horses, which carry the charioteer and the warrior; and when they encounter cavalry in the fighting they first hurl their javelins at the enemy and then step down from their chariots and join battle with their swords. [...] They bring along to war also their free men [ἐλευθέρους] to serve them, choosing them out from among the poor, and these attendants they use in battle as charioteers [ἡνίοχοι] and as shield-bearers [παρασπισταῖ]

Most probably Diodorus' account derives from Posidonius,[46] who visited southern Gaul personally in the first decade of the first century BC.[47] His first-hand knowledge was perhaps limited to the area surrounding Massalia,[48] although he could also have gathered information from the inner regions.[49] Brunaux[50] even thinks that Posidonius' information does not reflect the customs of Massalia's Gallic neighbors at the start of the first century BC, but rather those of northern Gaul two centuries earlier (suggesting that Posidonius was relying on older sources).

---

[40] Piggott 1983, 138-194; Pare 1993.
[41] Quesada Sanz 2005a, 56-60.
[42] Piggott 1986.
[43] Raimund Karl (2001) argues for some kind of road networks in "Celtic" Europe.
[44] Quesada Sanz 2005a, 59.
[45] Furger-Gunti 1991, 356; Karl 2003, 3-4.
[46] Tierney 1960, 113.
[47] Ruggeri 2000.
[48] Kidd 1988, 16.
[49] Webster 1999, 8.
[50] Brunaux 2004, 10.

For example, the chain-belt mentioned by Diodorus (5.30)[51] disappeared towards the end of the third century BC.[52] On the specific issue of chariots, even if we have the mention of king Bituitus and some numismatic iconography from the first century BC, Diodorus / Posidonius reflect a bygone era. In fact, Caesar did not meet chariots during his conquest of Gaul, although he did in Britain. There he describes the Britons using their war chariots in a way reminiscent of Diodorus, both as mobile missile platforms and as battle-taxis.[53] Although Caesar does not mention explicitly foot retinues fighting alongside chariots, their presence is highly plausible. Indeed, speaking about British chariots, Tacitus (*Ag.* 12.1) states that "some tribes fight also with the chariot. The higher in rank is the charioteer; the dependents fight." The roles are reversed in Diodorus' text. On the contrary, in Irish literature the highest in rank is the warrior and the charioteer is his dependent (as Cú Chulainn and his charioteer Láeg on the *Táin Bó Cúailnge*), the same as in Diodorus.

Diodorus' description of the chariot in battle mentions the warrior, the charioteer and the shield-bearer, the latter two as dependents of the former. A warrior triad is also suggested by Athenaeus in *The Deipnosophists* (4.152), quoting directly Posidonius, although instead of charioteers [ἡνίοχοι] and shield-bearers [παρασπισταῖ] he speaks about armour-bearers [ὁπλοφοροῦντες] and spear-bearers [δορυφόροι]. In his description of Gallic feasting, a hierarchy determined by skill in warfare, family or wealth dictated how guests sat. Accompanying each guest:

> Armed men bearing oblong shields [ὁπλοφοροῦντες] stand behind the guests, and their bodyguards [δορυφόροι, better translated as 'spear-bearers'] sit opposite them in a circle, just like their masters, and eat together.

Posidonius is describing the feasting of a group of warriors, highly ritualized and employed as a way to strengthen their bonds.[54] There is a clear hierarchy, with a main warrior with his armour-bearer and his spear-bearer. It is plausible that this passage would have figured alongside Diodorus' text on Gallic feasting[55] in the original Poseidonian work. And

---

[51] "They carry long broad-swords which are hung on chains of iron or bronze and are worn along the right flank"
[52] Rapin 1996, 516; 1999, 59.
[53] Bradley 2009, 1088.
[54] Brunaux 2004, 43.
[55] " When they dine they all sit, not upon chairs, but upon the ground, using for cushions the skins of wolves or of dogs. The service at the meals is performed by

although Athenaeus does not refer to chariots, my guess is that this kind of ritual feasting would have been attended by high-status warriors, such as those who fought in chariots. The warrior triad can also be inferred in another text by Diodorus (5.32) (probably using again Posidonius as his source) about the intercourse amongst Celtic men:

> The Celts [...] abandon themselves to a strange passion for other men. They usually sleep on the ground on skins of wild animals and tumble about with a bedfellow on either side.

Although Diodorus' interest dwelt on the sexual overtones of the practice,[56] the passage could, in fact, reveal some kind of ritual bonding amongst three men. The 'skins of wild animals' (also mentioned as cushions in Diodorus' passage on feasting) are highly reminiscent of the skins employed by some *mannerbunde* of young warriors in certain Indo-European societies,[57] and it has been suggested that homosexual intercourse could be a form of warrior bonding in 'Celtic' and 'Germanic' societies.[58]

The iconography displaying 'Celtic' chariots normally shows a warrior and a charioteer, as found in early Irish literature.[59] A funerary stele from Albinagsego dated in the third century BC depicts a chariot[60] carrying two persons, one upright and the other seated on the rear of the vehicle. According to Otto-Herman Frey,[61] the former would be a warrior holding the reins and a whip, and the latter would be his wife. However, the presence of an oval shield on the side of the chariot, and a spear protruding from the back of the upright character, indicates that we should consider this instead as a depiction of a 'driver and warrior' couple. Moreover, the inscription on the gravestone, in Venetic, includes the two names of the

---

the youngest children, both male and female, who are of suitable age; and near at hand are their fireplaces heaped with coals, and on them are caldrons and spits holding whole pieces of meat. Brave warriors they reward with the choicest portions of the meat" Diod. 5.28.

[56] See also Aristotle *Pol.* 1269b.
[57] Speidel 2004, 10-49.
[58] Neill 2009, 121-2.
[59] Greene 1972, 62.
[60] A bird flies over the chariot, bringing to mind a verse from one of the earliest poems in the Ulster cycle, the *Ro-mbáe*: "There were wild geese on the left side [of the chariot], swans on the right side; our chariot was all red, the space between the seats was full of heads" (Ó Cróinín 1998, 154-5)
[61] Frey 1968, 317-20.

deceased - both masculine, and the word *ekupetaris*, tentatively defined as 'charioteer.'[62] On the reverse of the denarius issued by L. Hostilius Saserna *c.* 48 BC,[63] the driver appears seated on the front of the chariot box, while behind a warrior stands upright brandishing a spear and an oval shield. It is likely that Saserna went to Gaul with Caesar,[64] and he perhaps watched the British chariots in action. Some medieval Irish depictions of chariots bear a striking resemblance to these Iron Age images. The image on the Ahenny high cross, dating approximately to the 9th century AD, is very similar to the Paduan stele.[65] Other examples come for the Clonmacnoise and the Monasterboice high crosses. Moreover, old Irish words for the 'chariot warrior' and his *auriga* clearly point towards two men manning the vehicle. The noun for the 'chariot warrior' was *eirr*,[66] a word that originally meant 'he who sits behind' *(*er-seds)*, while the noun for the 'charioteer,' *arae,* meant 'he who sits in front' *(*are-seds).*[67]

However, we also have some depictions with only a single man on the vehicle. The reverse of the denarii issued by L. Licinus Crassus, Cn. Domitius Ahenobarbus and his associates, probably minted in Narbo in, or shortly after 118 BC,[68] depicts a chariot driven by an upright warrior, holding the reins and a shield in his left hand and brandishing a spear in his right. A carnyx appears behind the warrior. J. de Witte[69] suggested that the image could represent king Bituitus, routed and captured in 121 BC by the father of Cn. Domitius Ahenobarbus. Indeed, during the celebration of Fabius Maximus' triumph, "The most conspicuous figure in the triumph was king Bituitus himself, in his vari-coloured arms and silver chariot, just as he had appeared in battle" (Flor. 1.37.5). A single, winged, *auriga*, appears on the reverse of a bronze issue of the Remi tribe, which can be dated before 52 BC as some examples come from Alesia. The prototypes for his image would be found on Hellenistic coins with Nike depictions. In another Gallic issue of the first century BC, a stater of the Redones, a woman drives a chariot pulled by a human-headed horse.[70] A single, upright warrior armed with spear and shield appears in a Galatomachy

---

[62] Kispert 1971, 231-3.
[63] Crawford 1974, 463.
[64] Desnier 1991, 612.
[65] Karl 2003, 13.
[66] Greene 1972, 61: Also *cairptech*, derived from *carpat*, "chariot".
[67] Green 1972, 62.
[68] Crawford 1974, 298-9.
[69] De Witte 1882, 342.
[70] Aldhouse-Green 1992b, 81.

featured on the lower part of an Etruscan sarcophagus from Chiusi, dated to the first century BC.[71] The chariot from the frieze of Civitalba, dated around the end of the second century BC,[72] is also driven by just one man, but according to Stead,[73] the chariot depicted is more similar to Etruscan or Greek models than to 'Celtic' ones. Although probably inspired by the Hellenistic iconography about the sack of Delphi and consciously seeking a parallel with that event, the frieze perhaps reflects some local conflict with the Cisalpine Gauls.[74] It is interesting to note that two Gallic warriors are depicted running alongside the chariot, with another one being trampled by the horses. However, these examples do not mean that chariots were single manned. In fact, although a single warrior could control the chariot with the reins tied around his hips, as is sometimes the case in depictions of Egyptian pharaohs and was sometimes practiced by Etruscan and Roman race charioteers,[75] it was a very hazardous feat and it is difficult to believe this was the practice in battle.[76] Both Caesar and Tacitus make clear that charioteers and warriors manned the British chariots. The examples we have just described owe more to ideal or mythic equivalents (as the winged Nike on the Remic issue or the female charioteer driving an androcephalic horse on the Redones' stater suggest) than to reality. This heroic, upright single driver is also doubtful if we take a look at the etymology of the Gallic word for chariot, *essedon* (Latin *essedum*), that would simply mean 'what is sat in.'[77]

Besides the warrior and the driver, the reading of Diodorus' and Athenaeus' texts suggests that a third man would have been part of the chariot fighting team. His absence in the iconographic record (except perhaps in the Civitalba frieze), scarce as this is, was probably due to his lower status and his minor importance in regard to the warrior and the charioteer. Also Caesar, in his detailed description of British chariots, does not make any mention of a third member of the chariot team. Perhaps these fighters went unnoticed to his sharp military eye, unaccustomed as he was to this kind of warfare? Perhaps the three-man chariot fighting team was a peculiarity of mainland Europe when chariots still played a part in war? In fact, the presence of this third man in battle makes sense. In

---

[71] Stead 1965, 263-4.
[72] Marszal 2001, 215.
[73] Stead 1965, 265.
[74] Marszal 2001, 216.
[75] Anthony 2007, 400.
[76] Quesada Sanz 2005a, 30.
[77] Greene 1972, 62; Delamarre 2003, 166.

Bronze Age chariot warfare in the Near East, infantry 'runners' fought alongside the chariots, playing a crucial role in battle,[78] and I think that their presence in La Tène warfare is also highly plausible. In the initial phase of the engagement, when chariots exchanged projectiles, the third man could fetch javelins to his master (thence the name of spear-bearer?). And once his master descended to fight on foot he could engage in the fighting as well. A third function could be guarding the chariot while his master fought.[79] The readiness to dismount of the Gallic horsemen and the frequent mingling of cavalry and infantry[80] could be a further hint about the presence of 'runners' alongside chariots in fifth and fourth century BC combat.

FROM THE CHARIOT TO THE *TRIMARKISIA*

The mere existence of mounted warriors on the battlefield does not imply the existence of a proper cavalry, which implies a large number of horsemen acting in a concerted way.[81] At the early stages of the La Téne culture, there were aristocratic warriors fighting on horseback (e.g. the ones depicted in the fifth century BC bronze scabbard found at grave 994 in the Hallstatt cemetery),[82] as in the late Hallstatt culture, but in all probability they were not cavalry in the full sense. Their role would be akin to the chariot. Either they clashed heroically with other elite warriors on horseback or dismounted to fight on foot, as did the mounted hoplites of archaic Greece or the Iberian horsemen of sixth and fifth centuries BC.[83] Chariots and mounted warriors were not of course used exclusively. Both types of fighters could be present on the battlefield, as we know for example at Sentinum (Liv. 10.28.6-11), or as Caesar found in Britain (*B Gal.* 4.32; 5.15).

---

[78] Drews 1993, 142-8.
[79] A personal name as Eporedorix might indeed have preserved these kind of 'runners,' if it could be translated as 'King of men who ride after horses' (Kelsey 1897, 43). However, the more accepted translation to Eporedorix is 'king of the running of horses' or 'king of the horsemen' (Dottin *et al.* 1891, 103; Ellis 1967, 90-2; Delamarre 2003, 162). Other authors propose 'king of the trainers of horses' (Belloguet 1872, 413). The name may even disguise a magistracy as the Roman *Magister equitum* (Jullien 1914, 345; Almagro-Gorbea 1995, 253). We know an Eporedorix amongst the Galatians (Plut. *De mul. vir.* 259) and also in Gaul (Caes. *B Gal.* 7.38), and an Eporedirix attested by epigraphy (Delamarre 20007, 96).
[80] Pérez Rubio 2012, 18.
[81] Gordon 1953.
[82] Frey 1976, 176.
[83] Quesada 2005b, 97-98.

However, the importance of chariotry in mainland Europe decreased during the third century BC. This was dictated by the new needs that warfare imposed on migrating 'Celtic' communities and mercenary war bands,[84] reflected both in the archaeological record and in the classical sources, and the reason behind the new developments in the 'Celtic' panoply.[85] The new mobile nature of warfare favored the speed and flexibility that horses could provide. Furthermore, cavalry had several advantages over chariots: it was more suited for broken terrain,[86] it was effective for reconnaissance (an impossible task for a conspicuous and noisy chariot), it was much cheaper - with no need for the high technological craftsmanship needed to build a cart[87] – and it was less vulnerable than chariotry, as a wounded horse in a chariot meant a useless vehicle. Finally, if a chariot needed two horses to move, carrying just a driver and a warrior, but two horsemen meant two warriors, then, with the same number of horses, an army could double its offensive power.

The chariot remained a prominent status symbol, and the dawn of a proper 'Celtic' cavalry did not mean its immediate disappearance. Even the Galatians, credited with the *trimarkisia* by Pausanias, kept using chariots, as documented by the dismantled chariot depicted in the carvings of the temple of Athena *Nikephoros* at Pergamon amongst other Galatian trophies.[88] This ambivalence between the cavalry as the new elite arm, whose importance kept growing in 'Celtic' warfare,[89] and the survival of the chariot as a status symbol (and as such epitomizing the Gaul perceived by the Romans), is reflected in the narrative of the battle of Clastidium in 222 BC by Propertius and Plutarch. According to Propertius (4.10) king Virdomarus of the *Gaesatae* was killed by M. Claudius Marcellus while fighting from his chariot: "He boasted to be sprung from Rhine himself, and nimble was he to hurl the Gallic spear from unswerving chariot. Even as in striped breaches he went forth before his host, the bent torque fell from his severed throat." But Plutarch (*Marc.* 6.4) wrote: "For they [the Gauls] were most excellent fighters on horseback, and were thought to be specially superior as such, and, besides, at this time they far outnumbered Marcellus. Immediately, therefore, they charged upon him with great violence and dreadful threats, thinking to overwhelm him, their king riding

---

[84] Szabó 1991.
[85] Rapin 1991; 1996, 516; 1999, 54-61; Léjars 2013, 315.
[86] Archer 2010, 71.
[87] Furger-Gunti 1991.
[88] Stead 1965, 262.
[89] Pérez-Rubio 2012.

in front of them." Propertius, a poet from the Augustan age, sings about the three occasions when *spolia opima* were dedicated at the temple of Feretrian Jupiter; his description of a Gallic king is surely more indebted to Roman *topoi* (chariot, striped *bracae*, torque) than to reality. On the other hand, although Plutarch's sources for his Roman Lives are difficult to ascertain,[90] he probably is closer to reality and reflects Gallic cavalry in the third century BC.

The *trimarkisia* appeared in this new context. If in Irish literature the heroes were called *eirr* –'chariot man'– as if the ownership of a chariot was their main mark,[91] the 'Celtic' elite warriors were now to express their status in battle by riding three horses, supported by a retinue of two men, as previously they did with a charioteer and a shield/spear-bearer. This transition is somewhat similar to the transition between chariots and cavalry in the Neo-Assyrian Empire. There, when mounted troops began to appear in the ninth century BC they mimicked the charioteer/archer couple:[92] one man, the higher in rank, acted as an archer, while the other, a shield bearer, held both horses' reins. The maintenance of the fighting unit in the Assyrian army was primarily dictated by practical needs, particularly the efficient control of the mount,[93] but it also signals a conservatism in the conception of the new weapon. The displacement of the chariot for the horse in 'Celtic' warfare as the elite vehicle for battle also conveyed this kind of hierarchical conservatism. The maintenance of the number three as an ideal, so pervading in the 'Celtic' mindset, could be considered in the same way. We can speculate that the *trimarkisia* could even have had a mythic equivalent, as in the undead *triar marcach* of *The Destruction of Da Derga's Hostel*, messengers of destruction. Thus the *trimarkisia* prolonged and maintained the social and mental implications of the warrior triads and the chariot fighting, but adapted them to the new realities of warfare. The later corollary of this would be the development of the client-patron relationships and armed retinues, as the *ambacti* (*B Gal.* 6.15) or *soldurii* (*B Gal.* 3.22) mentioned by Caesar.

Of course this pattern cannot be applied to the whole of 'Celtic' Europe, as in some places chariots were probably never used in battle.[94]

---

[90] Mineo 2011, 124.
[91] Greene 1972, 61.
[92] Archer 2010, 71.
[93] Quesada Sanz 2012, 15-6.
[94] Although the distribution of chariot burials (a good map in Koch 2007, 116) may perhaps indicate where in 'Celtic' Europe chariots were used in warfare, we

But some communities would have shared this (or a similar) military institution, probably depending on the development of a proper cavalry as demanded by their needs to wage war. The existence of 'knowledge networks,' with fosterage playing an important part in the exchange of specialist knowledge between elite groups,[95] would explain the diffusion of the *trimarkisia* or similar institutions. James,[96] speaking about the movements between elite groups in the La Tène world, argues for a "trans-ethnic cultural *koine*, marking not common 'Celticness' but a system of interaction between societies which were in other ways culturally diverse". Warfare as a sphere of elite behavior, auto-representation and interaction, was a prime example of that "trans-ethnic cultural *koine*," and in this respect it is remarkable how mutations in the panoply seem to follow quickly the same patterns and chronology throughout all temperate Europe during the third century BC,[97] with the Galatian attack against Delphi in 279 BC as an axis.[98] An attack that according to Pausanias was spearheaded by groups of three horsemen: the *trimarkisia*.

BIBLIOGRAPHY

Almagro-Gorbea, M. (1995) "La moneda hispánica con jinete y cabeza varonil: ¿tradición indígena o creación romana?", *Zephyrvs* XLVIII, 235-266.

Aldhouse-Green, M. (1991) "Triplism and plurality: intensity and symbolism in Celtic religious expression" in P. Garwood, D. Jennings, R. Skeates and J. Toms (eds.) *Sacred and Profane. Proceeding of a Conference on Archaeology, Ritual and Religion*, 100-108, Oxford.

—. (1992a) *Symbol and Image in Celtic Religious Art*. Oxford.

—. (1992b). *Animals in Celtic Life and Myth*. Oxford.

—. (2004) *An Archaeology of Images: Iconology and Cosmology in Iron Age and Roman Europe*. Oxford.

Anthoons, G. and H. Clerinx (eds) (2007) *The Grand 'Celtic' Story? Proceedings of the conference held in Brussels on 19 November 2005*. Brussels.

Anthony, D. W. (2007) *The Horse, the Wheel, and Language: How Bronze-Age Riders from the Eurasian Steppes Shaped the Modern*

---

have to bear in mind the vagaries of archaeological record, the different levels of field work and that not all communities opted for this burial practice.

[95] Karl 2005.
[96] James 2007.
[97] Rapin 1991, 331; Lejars 315-6.
[98] Szabó 1995; Rapin 1996, 517.

World. Princeton.
Archer, R. (2010) "Chariotry to Cavalry: Developments in the Early First Millennium", in G. G. Fagan (ed.), *New Perspectives on Ancient Warfare*, 57-79, Leiden.
Blažek, V. (2008) "Gaulish Language", *Sborník prací Filozofické Fakulty Brněnské Univerzity* 13, 37-65.
Butler, H. E. (1916) *Propertius*. London.
Bradley, C. M. (2009) "The British War Chariot: A Case for Indirect Warfare", *The Journal of Military History* 73, 1073-1089.
Bromwich, R. (1997) "The Triads of the Horses", in S. Davies, N. A. Jones (eds.) *The Horse in Celtic Culture*, 102-120, Cardiff.
Brunaux, J. L. (2004) *Guerre et religion en Gaule. Essai d'anthropologie celtique*, Paris.
Collis, J. R. (1996) "Celts and Politics", in P. Graves-Brown, S. Jones and C. Gamble (eds.) *Cultural Identity and Archaeology. The Construction of European Communities*, 167–78, London.
—. (1997) "Celtic Myths", *Antiquity* 71, 195–201.
—. (2003) *The Celts. Origins, Myths & Inventions*. Stroud.
Crawford, M. H. (1974) *Roman Republican Coinage*. Cambridge.
De Belloguet, D. F. L. (1872) *Ethnogénie Gauloise. Glossaire gauloise*. Paris.
Delamarre, X. (2003) *Dictionnaire de la langue gauloise : Une approche linguistique du vieux-celtique continental*. Paris.
—. (2007) *Noms de personnes celtiques dans l'épigraphie classique*. Paris.
De Witte, J. (1882) "Correspondance", *Bulletin de la Société nationale des antiquaires de France*, 1882, 348.
Desnier, J. L. (1991) "Le Gaulois dans l'imaginaire monétaire de la République romaine. Images plurielles d'une réalité singulière", *Mélanges de l'Ecole française de Rome. Antiquité* Vol. 103, N° 2, 605 – 654.
Dottin, G., E. Ernault and H. d' Arbois de Jubainville (1891) *Les noms gaulois chez César et Hirtius De Bello Gallico*, Paris.
Douglas Olson, S. (ed.) (2006) *Athenaeus. The Learned Banqueters*. London.
Drews, R. (1993) *The End of the Bronze Age: Changes in Warfare and the Catastrophe Ca. 1200 B.C.* Princeton.
—. (2004) *Early Riders. The beginnings of mounted warfare in Asia and Europe*. London.
Ellis Evans, D. (1967) *Gaulish Personal Names. A Study of some Continental Celtic Formations*. Oxford.

Fitzpatrick, A. P. (1996) "'Celtic' Iron Age Europe: the theoretical basis", in P. Graves-Brown, S. Jones and C. Gamble (eds.) *Cultural Identity and Archaeology. The Construction of European Communities*, 238–55, London.

Frey, O. H. (1968) "Eine neue Grabstele aus Padua", *Germania* 46, 317-20

—. (1976) "The Chariot Tomb from Adria: Some Notes on Celtic Horsemansip and Chariotry", in J. V. S. Megaw (ed.) *To illustrate the monuments. Essays on archaeology presented to Stuart Piggot*, 171-80, London.

Furger-Gunti, A. (1991) "Le char de combat: la reconstruction au Schweizerisches Landesmuseum", in S. Moscati (coord.) *Les Celtes*, 356-9, Paris.

Greene, D. (1972) "The chariot as describe in Irish literature", in C. Thomas (ed.) *The Iron Age in the Irish Sea province*, 59-73, London.

Gordon, D. H. (1953) "Swords, rapiers and Horse-riders", *Antiquity* 27, 67-78.

Jackson, K. H. (1964) *The Oldest Irish Tradition: A Window on the Iron Age*. Cambridge.

James, S. (1998) "Celts, politics and motivation in archaeology", *Antiquity* 72, 200–9.

—. (1999) *The Atlantic Celts. Ancient People or Modern Invention?* London.

—. (2007) "Iron Age paradigms and the Celtic metanarrative: a case study in conceptualising the past, and writting histories", in G. Anthoons and H. Clerinx (eds) *The Grand 'Celtic' Story? Proceedings of the conference held in Brussels on 19 November 2005*, 11-31, Brussels.

Jones, W. H. S. (ed) (1918) *Pausanias: Description of Greece, Volume IV, Books 8.22-10: Arcadia, Boeotia, Phocis and Ozolian Locri*. London.

Jullien, C. (1914) *Vercingetorix*. Paris.

Karl, R. (2001) "... on a road to nowhere? Chariotry and the road systems in the Celtic World", *IRQUAS Online Project* Available at: http://homepage.eircom.net/~archaeology/road.htm [Accessed: 13/05/14].

—. (2003) "Iron Age chariots and medieval texts: a step too far in "breaking down boundaries"?", *E-Keltoi* 5, 1-30.

—. (2004) "Celtoscepticism, a convenient excuse for ignoring non-archaeological evidence?", in E. Sauer (ed) *Archaeology and Ancient History – Breaking down Boundaries*, 185-99, London.

—. (2005) "Master and Apprentice, Knight and Squire: Education in the 'Celtic' Iron Age", *Oxford Journal of Archaeology* 24 (3), 255–271.

Karl, R. and D. Stifter (eds) (2007) *The Celtic world: critical concepts in*

historical studies, vol. 1: Theory in Celtic studies, London.
Kelly, P. (1997) "The Earliest Words for 'Horse' in the Celtic Languages", in S. Davies, N. A. Jones (eds) *The Horse in Celtic Culture*, 43-63, Cardiff.
Kelsey, F. W. (2007) *Caesar's Gallic War: With an Introduction, Notes, and Vocabulary*. Eugene. (1st ed. 1897).
Kidd, I. G. (1988) *Posidonius. Vol. 2, Commentary.* Cambridge.
Kispert, R. J. (1971) "Recent Venetic Inscriptions: A Supplement to the Prae-Italic Dialects of Italy, Part One, TheVenetic Inscriptions", *Transactions and Proceedings of the American Philological Association* Vol. 102, 217-263.
Koch, J. T. (2007) *An Atlas for Celtic Studies: Archaeology and Names in Ancient Europe and Early Medieval Ireland, Britain and Brittany.* Oxford.
Lejars, T. (2013) *La Tène: la Collection Schwab (Bienne, Suisse). La Tène, un Site, un Mythe 3. Tome 1.* Lausanne.
Loth, J. (1925) "Notice sur les noms du cheval chez les Celtes en relation avec quelques problèmes archéologiques", *Académie des Inscriptions et Belles-Lettres, Journal des savants, 23e année, Mars-avril 1925*, 95.
—. (1927) "Notice sur les noms du cheval chez les Celtes en relation avec quelques problèmes archéologiques", *Revue Celtique*, 410.
Marszal, J. R. (2001) "Ubiquitous Barbarians. Representations of the Gauls at Pergamon and Elsewhere", in N. T. de Grummond and B. S. Ridgway (eds) *From Pergamon to Sperlonga: Sculpture and Context*, 191-234, Berkeley.
Megaw, M. R. and J. V. S. Megaw (1996) "Ancient Celts and modern ethnicity", *Antiquity* 70, 175–81.
Megaw, M. R. and J. V. S. Megaw (1998) "'The mechanism of (Celtic) dreams': a partial response to our critics", *Antiquity* 72, 276–9.
Mineo, B. (2011) "Principal Literary Sources for the Punic Wars (apart from Polybius)", in D. Hoyos (ed) *A Companion to the Punic Wars.* Oxford.
Mitchell, S. (2003) "The Galatians: Representation and Reality", in A. Erskine (ed) *A Companion to the Hellenistic World*, 280-93, Oxford.
Mikhailova, T. A. (2007) "*Macc, Cailin* and *Ceile*–an Altaic Element in Celtic?" in H. L. C. Tristram (ed) *The Celtic languages in contact: Papers from the workshop within the framework of the XIII International Congress of Celtic Studies, Bonn, 26-27 July 2007*, 4-24, Postdam.
Neill, J. (2009) *The Origins and Role of Same-Sex Relations in Human Societies.* Jefferson.

Nachtergael, G. (1975) *Les Galates en Grèce et les Sôtéria de Delphes. Recherches d'histoire et d'épigraphie hellénistiques.* Bruxelles.
O'Connor, R. (2008) "Prophecy, Storytelling and the Otherworld in *Togail Bruidne Da Derga*", in K. Ritari and A. Bergholm (eds) *Approaches to Religion and Mythology in Celtic Studies*, 55-68, Newcastle.
Ó Cróinín, D. (1998) "Prosopographical Analysis of the *Táin Bó Cuailnge* in a Historical Setting", in H. L. C. Tristram (ed) *New Methods in the Research of Epic*, 153-160, Tübingen.
Oldfather, C. H. (ed) (1939) *Diodorus Siculus: The Library of History, Volume III, Books 4.59-8.* London.
Pare, C. F. E., (1993) *Wagons and Wagons Graves of the Early Iron Age in Central Europe.* Oxford.
Pérez-Rubio, A. (2009) "Putting the Invaders to Use: Mercenary Tribes in Anatolia", *Ancient Warfare* III.1, 36-41.
—. (2012) "Making Epona Proud: Celtic Cavalry at War", *Ancient Warfare* VI.3, 15-19.
Perrin, B. (ed) (1917) *Plutarch's Lives with an English Translation. Vol. 5. Agesilaus and Pompey. Pelopidas and Marcellus.* London.
Piggott, S. (1983) *The Earliest Wheeled Transport. From the Atlantic Coast to the Caspian Sea.* London.
—. (1986) "Horse and chariot: the price of prestige", in D. Ellis Evans and J. G. Griffith (eds) *Proceedings of the Seventh International Congress of Celtic Studies (Oxford, July 1983)*, 25-30, Oxford.
Powell, T. G. E. (1971) "The Introduction of Horse-Riding to Temperate Europe: A Contributory Note," *Proceedings of the Prehistoric Society* 37, 1–14.
Quesada Sanz, F. (2005a) "Carros en el antiguo Mediterráneo: de los orígenes a Roma", in T. Andrada-Wanderwilde Quadras (coord.) *Historia del carruaje en España*, 16-71, Madrid.
—. (2005b) "L'Utilisation du cheval dans le "Far West" méditerranéen: bilan des recherches et étude de cas : le problème de l'apparition de la cavalerie en Ibérie", in A. Gardeisen (ed) *Les Équidés dans le monde méditerranéen antique*, 95-110, Montagnac.
—. (2012) "Del carro a la caballería en Asiria", *Desperta Ferro Antigua y Medieval* 10, 14-9.
Rankin, H. D. (1987) *Celts and the Classical World.* London.
Rapin, A. (1991) "L'armement", in S. Moscati (coord.) *Les Celtes*, 320-31, Paris.
—. (1996) "Les armes des Celtes. Des messages enfouis sous la rouille", *Mélanges de l'Ecole française de Rome. Antiquité T.* 108, N°2, 505-522.

—. (1999) "L'armement celtique en Europe", *Gladius* XIX, 33-67.
Raulwing, P. (2000) *Horses, chariots and Indo-Europeans. Foundations and Methods of Chariotry Research from the Viewpoint of Comparative Indo-European Linguistics*. Budapest.
Renfrew, C. (1998) "All the King's Horses: Assessing Cognitive Maps in Later Prehistoric Europe", in S. Mithen (ed) *Creativity in Human Evolution and Prehistory*, 260-84, New York.
Rolle, R. (1989) *The World of the Scythians*. Berkeley.
Ruggeri, M., (2000) *Posidonio d'Apamea e I celti*. Firenze.
Ruiz Zapatero, G. (2004) "¿Quiénes eran los celtas?: Disipando la niebla: mitología de un" collage" histórico", in M. Almagro-Gorbea, M. Mariné and J. R. Álvarez Sanchís (eds), *Celtas y vettones*, 72-93, Ávila.
—. (2010) "Roma conquistó la Galia... y Astérix y Obelix conquistaron el mundo. Desenmarañando a los celtas", in Mª Cruz Cardete (ed.) *La Antigüedad y sus mitos. Narrativas históricas irreverentes*, 97-114, Madrid.
Speidel, M. P. (2004) *Ancient Germanic Warriors. Warrior Styles from Trajan Column to the Icelandic Sagas*. London.
Stead, I. M. (1965) "The Celtic Chariot", *Antiquity* 49, 259-265.
Stokes, W. (ed.) (1902) *The Destruction of Da Derga's Hostel*. Paris.
Szabó, M. (1991) "Les Celtes et leur movements au IIIe siècle av. J.-C.", in S. Moscati (coord.) *Les Celtes*, 303-19, Paris.
—. (1995) "Guerriers celtiques avant et après Delphes", in J. J. Charpy (ed.) *L'Europe celtique du Ve au IIIe siècle avant J.-C. Contacts, echanges et mouvements de populations*. Sceaux.
Tierney, J. J. (1960) "The Celtic Ethnography of Posidonius", *Proceedings of the Royal Irish Academy. Section C: Archaeology, Celtic Studies, History, Linguistics, Literature* Vol. 60, 189-275
Webster, J. (1999) "At the End of the World: Druidic and Other Revitalization Movements in Post-Conquest Gaul and Britain", *Britannia*, Vol. 30, 1-20.

CHAPTER ELEVEN

THE LATE BRONZE–EARLY IRON AGE TRANSITION: CHANGES IN WARRIORS AND WARFARE AND THE EARLIEST RECORDED NAVAL BATTLES

DR. JEFFREY P. EMANUEL

INTRODUCTION

Seaborne threats were present in the Aegean and Eastern Mediterranean long before the chaotic transition from the Late Bronze Age (LBA) to Iron I, ca. 1200 BC. This can be seen from references in the Amarna Letters,[1] Hittite documents,[2] Ugaritic texts,[3] and Egyptian inscriptions[4] referring to maritime marauders intercepting ships at sea, conducting blockades, and carrying out coastal raids. Military forces were mobilized to defend coastal settlements against these raiders, while merchant ships seem to have taken on an ancient version of private security contractors to defend against encounters with pirates while at sea.[5] However, it was not until the decades leading up to the LBA–Iron I transition that states seem to have sent out fleets against these marauders and taken to the sea to preempt their piratical activities.

---

[1] E.g. EA 38, 105, 113, 126, 155
[2] E.g. KBo XII 38
[3] E.g. RS L.1, 20.18, 20.238, 34.129
[4] E.g. the Aswan and Tanis II Rhetorical Stelai of Ramesses II, and the Medinet Habu inscriptions, Papyrus Harris I, and Deir el–Medineh Stela of Ramesses III
[5] Hafford 2001, 70n27, 199–202; cf., e.g., the possible "mercenaries [or mercenary] from the north who were in the service of the Mycenaeans" aboard the Uluburun ship; Pulak 1998, 219; 2005, 308.

Existential Threats, Palatial Destructions, and Sea Peoples

Evidence from several sources suggests that seaborne threats increased in number and severity as the age of Bronze gave way to that of Iron, perhaps playing a central role in the widespread palatial destructions that marked this watershed period in history.[6] Greater anxiety about maritime threats can be seen in 13th and early 12th century Egyptian inscriptions and reliefs, and in texts from the last years of Ḫatti and Ugarit, while in the Aegean world, signs of growing unease in the Mycenaean palatial system can be detected as early as the Late Helladic (LH) IIIB1–2 transition (ca. 1230 BC). Particular evidence for this may be seen in Linear B tablets from the last days of the palace at Pylos, which was destroyed in LH IIIB2 or LH IIIC Early and abandoned along with the entire Messenian hinterland.[7] Three sets of Linear B tablets, commonly grouped together, have been seen by some scholars as communicating an effort to coordinate a large–scale defensive action or evacuation in response to an existential threat from the coast.[8] The first group, known as the *o–ka* tablets, list the disposition of military personnel (both "watchers" and *e–qe–ta*) assigned to the task of "guarding the coastal areas,"[9] while the second, a single tablet (Jn 829), records the collection of bronze from Pylian temples for the purpose of forging "points for spears and javelins." The third, and perhaps most relevant, of these records is comprised of three tablets (PY An 610, An 1, and An 724) commonly referred to as "Rower Tablets" for their references to *e–re–ta* 'rowers' being called up to man what was most likely a fleet of galleys.[10]

If indeed they do reflect a palatial response to a coastal threat, it is possible that they catalogue efforts to coordinate either a general evacuation or an evacuation of palatial elites who sought to escape as their

---

[6] *Inter alia*, Singer 1983, 217; Baruffi 1998, 10–13, 188; Nowicki 1996, 285, with references.
[7] Shelmerdine 1997, 581 n. 277; Mountjoy 1999, 343–55, figs. 116–20.
[8] For a representative sample of scholarly opinion and its evolution over time, see Chadwick 1976, 141; Palmer 1980, 143–67; Hooker 1982, 209–17; Palaima 1995, 625; Shelmerdine 1997, 583; 1999, 405–10; Dickinson 2006, 43, 46, 55; Tartaron 2013, 64–5.
[9] Deger–Jalkotzy 1978, 14; Hooker 1987, 264.
[10] Palmer 1980, 143–4; Palaima 1991, 286; Wachsmann 1998, 159–61; 1999; Tartaron 2013, 64–5.

situation became precarious late in the LH IIIB.[11] Schilardi and Karageorghis have suggested that Mycenaean elites may have fled to the Cyclades in advance (or in the wake) of the LH IIIB2 destructions, based in part on the appearance of a fortified mansion on an acropolis at Paros on Koukounaries in the transitional LH IIIB2–IIIC Early.[12] A third possible purpose of the Rower Tablets, perhaps more likely in light of contemporary evidence from around the eastern Mediterranean, may have been to call up crew members in preparation for a direct – and ultimately failed – naval action against an existential seaborne threat.

SEA PEOPLES AND NAVAL BATTLES

Somewhere into the events of the LBA–Iron Age transition fit the so–called 'Sea Peoples,' a heterogeneous series of coalition–like groups mentioned primarily in records from Ramesside Egypt (13th and early 12th centuries BC). The most famous representations of these warriors come from Medinet Habu, the well–known mortuary temple of the 20th Dynasty Pharaoh Ramesses III (ca. 1183–1152 BC), where two massive battles with representatives of these groups – one on land and one at sea – are recorded in monumental relief.[13] The naval battle, widely considered the first ever depicted (and perhaps the first ever engaged in), is integral to this study and will be discussed in greater detail below. The land battle relief depicts ox–carts, women, and children of varying age amidst the Sea Peoples warriors,[14] suggesting that the "invasion" may have been part of a migratory movement of people from the Aegean and western Anatolia whose cultural traits begin to appear in the archaeological record of the Cilician and Syro-Canaanite coasts around this time, with particular concentration in Canaan's southern coastal plain.[15]

Though almost always ascribed to Ramesses III's eighth year (ca. 1175 BC), these migratory land and sea invasions were important enough to be mentioned in no fewer than five separate inscriptions at Medinet Habu. Five Sea Peoples groups are named in them: the Peleset (= Philistines), Tjeker or Sikil, Shekelesh, Weshesh, and the Denyen or Danuna (= Δαναοι or Adana?). A later inscription of Ramesses III, on a rhetorical stele in

---

[11] Baumbach 1983; Wachsmann 1999.
[12] Schilardi 1984; 1992; 1999; Karageorghis 2001, 5; Earle 2008, 192.
[13] Epigraphic Survey 1930 (*MH* I) pls. 32–34, 36–41.
[14] Sweeney and Yasur–Landau 1999.
[15] *Inter alia* Birney 2007; Stager 1995; Stone 1995; Sweeney and Yasur–Landau 1999; Yasur–Landau 2010 (with extensive further bibliography).

Chapel C at Deir el–Medineh, also mentions the Peleset and the Teresh among up to 24 groups (22 of which have been lost) as defeated enemies who had "sailed in the midst of t[he s]ea".[16] The slight change in Ramesses' enemies list seen in the Medineh stele – namely, the addition of the Teresh, who are not mentioned in the Medinet Habu inscriptions – can also be seen in the Great Harris Papyrus (P. Harris I), a posthumous *res gestae* of Ramesses III, which replaces the Shekelesh with the Sherden in its narrative of the pharaoh's encounters with the Sea Peoples.

Though he boasts the best known of our available inscriptions and images, Ramesses III was not the first pharaoh to encounter groups associated with the Sea Peoples. Ramesses II, in two stelai from early in his reign a century earlier, claims to have "destroyed the warriors of the Great Green (Sea)" and to have defeated and captured Sherden warriors who "sailed bold–hearted in warships from the midst of the sea."[17] Following the latter defeat, Sherden appear in the Egyptian army, and the threat to Egypt from these and other Sea Peoples groups seems to dissipate (judging from written records) for the remainder of Ramesses the Great's reign, perhaps in part because of Ramesses' establishment of a line of defensive forts along the North African coast.[18]

Only five years into the reign of Merneptah (1213–1203 BC), Ramesses II's successor, the threat to Egypt's borders became immediate once more, as a migratory coalition tens of thousands strong of Libyans and Sea Peoples invaded from the west, and occupied a portion of the western Delta for one month before being routed by the pharaoh's army in the Battle of Perire. The battle is recounted in two inscriptions, the monumental Great Karnak Inscription and the Athribis stele. It is in the latter that the origin of the term "Sea Peoples" can be found: five of these groups are named in Merneptah's records – the Sherden, Ekwesh (= Aḫḫiyawa or Ἀχαιοι?), Shekelesh, Teresh, and Lukka – and all but the latter being referred to as "of the foreign countries of the sea." The Athribis stele omits this designation for all groups save for the Ekwesh, while the other two inscriptions that reference this event, on the Cairo Column and Heliopolis Victory Column, contain between them the mention of only one Sea Peoples group, the Shekelesh, whose naming is followed with "and every foreign country" .

---

[16] Peden 1994, 65.
[17] de Rougé 1877, 253.8; Kitchen 1996, 120, 182.
[18] Habachi 1980; Snape 1997, 23; Yurco 1999, 877.

THREATS TO ḪATTI, UGARIT, AND CYPRUS

The Hittites, who were not historically inclined toward maritime affairs, were also forced to look to the sea with more interest at this time, perhaps as a result of the threat posed by an increase in coastal raiding. Two texts from the early 12th century especially seem to show increased Hittite concern with threats from the Mediterranean coast and beyond, with the latter serving – along with Ramesses III's naval battle inscription – as the earliest literary evidence for a true sea battle. In the first, RS 34.129, the Hittite king writes to the prefect of Ugarit about the *Šikala* "who live on ships," and requests that an Ugaritian who had been taken captive by them be sent to Ḫattuša so that the king can question him about this people and their homeland. The *Šikala* have been connected to two groups of Sea Peoples from the aforementioned records of Merneptah and Ramesses III, discussed above: the Shekelesh[19] and the Sikil (or Tjeker).[20] The second text, attributed to the last Hittite king, Šuppiluliuma II (ca. 1207–1178 BC), mentions "ships of Alašiya" which "met [him] in the sea three times for battle," followed by a land battle presumably against the same foe.[21]

The latter is highly reminiscent of Ramesses III's aforementioned claims to have fought land and sea battles against migratory Sea Peoples, which would have taken place at generally the same time. This similarity in chronology and narrative raises the possibility that Šuppiluliuma may have been facing repeated waves of raiders or migrant warriors (perhaps the same ones mentioned in Egyptian records), while clearly reinforcing the need for the Eastern Mediterranean's Late Bronze Age empires to take to the sea and engage in history's first naval battles in an effort to ward off this growing maritime threat.

NEW WARRIORS FOR A NEW TYPE OF WARFARE?

In addition to an increase in seaborne threats, this period was also marked by the appearance – seemingly *ex nihilo* – of a new type of warrior in Eastern Mediterranean iconography. These warriors, frequently pictured wearing "feathered headdresses," appear in martial scenes on land and at sea across the Aegean and Eastern Mediterranean beginning in transitional LH IIIB2–IIIC Early, and have typically been associated with the 'Sea

---

[19] Yon 1992, 116; Redford 2006, 11.
[20] Wachsmann 1982, 297; 1998, 359 n. 10; Stager 1991, 19 n. 23.
[21] KBo XII 38; Güterbock 1967, 78.

Peoples' who are so well known from the aforementioned records.[22]

Ramesses III's reliefs at Medinet Habu portray these headdresses, and the warriors wearing them, in great detail.[23] The plumed portions are largely identical, but individual groups of warriors seem to be differentiated from each other by the patterns on the headbands beneath the feathers. These include zigzag, circular, and crosshatched patterns, with some headdresses featuring two courses of the same pattern and one or two featuring both circular decoration and crosshatching.[24] Characters painted on Mycenaean vases, on the other hand, are often shown in silhouette, and are always portrayed far more schematically and stylistically, and in less detail, than their companions in Egyptian relief. In the case of the feathered headdresses depicted at Medinet Habu, therefore, the Aegean analogue appears to be a much less detailed set of dark spikes or lines protruding from the head, sometimes set above a checkered or "zigzag" band similar to those seen at Medinet Habu. Most examples of the latter style take the form referred to as the "hedgehog helmet" for its similarity to Aegean portrayals of hedgehogs in similar media, though representations from the Dodecanesian island of Kos provide slightly different portrayals of this headdress.

The best–known example of the "hedgehog"–style headdress, and the most complete picture of warriors in full complementary combat gear, comes from the Warrior Vase, found by Heinrich Schliemann in the "House of the Warrior Vase" at Mycenae.[25] This vessel, which like almost all examples of this motif is dated LH IIIC Middle, features two processions of warriors – one on each side. On the obverse are six bearded soldiers marching "in step" to the right. Each carries a nearly–circular shield, a leather "ration bag, and a single spear with a leaf–shaped point on his right shoulder, and they wear corslets, kilts,"[26] greaves, and horned helmets with plumes flowing from the crest (see further below). The five soldiers on the reverse are identical except for the placement of their spears (they are cocked in each soldier's right arm in preparation for throwing), the absence of the "ration bags," and the composition of their helmets, which are "hedgehog" in style instead of horned. This latter scene

---

[22] Sandars 1985, 134; Vermeule and Karageorghis 1982, 132; Mountjoy 2005, 425; and see now Yasur–Landau 2013.
[23] *MH* I pls. 19, 33–4, 37–9, 41–4, 46.
[24] Oren 1973, 136–7 figs. 7, 9, 18–19.
[25] Vermeule and Karageorghis 1982, 130–32, 222.
[26] Vermeule and Karageorghis 1982, 131.

finds a nearly identical analogue in the aforementioned Warrior Stele, also from Mycenae.[27] Several further comparanda come from Mycenae and elsewhere on the Greek mainland, all dating to LH IIIC Middle,[28] while Cypriot and Levantine examples – which likewise lack precedent in the historical record – can be found from the same period.[29]

Some of the earliest representations of these warriors are found in the earliest known scenes of naval combat. The first representation of this type of headdress from the Aegean and the East Aegean–West Anatolian Interface may be found on an unstratified locally–made krater, from Bademgediği Tepe (ancient Puranda) in southwestern Anatolia, which has been dated to between the transitional LH IIIB2–IIIC and LH IIIC Middle.[30] If the earlier of these dates for the Bademgediği krater is accurate, this would place the earliest representations of "feather–hatted warriors" in southwestern Anatolia and the Dodecanese less than a quarter century (at most) prior to their appearance in Egyptian relief, and well before their appearance on the Greek mainland in LH IIIC Middle.[31] This, in turn, may provide further support for the possibility that at least some of these warriors originated in the area of southwestern Anatolia and the Dodecanese (the eastern edge of the East Aegean–West Anatolian Interface) and spread from there westward to the Aegean and south and eastward to Cyprus and the Levant.

Both the Bademgediği krater and a similarly–decorated LH IIIC vessel from Livanates in east Lokris (Homeric Kynos)[32] appear to depict naval battles between spear–wielding warriors aboard antithetic oared galleys. Interestingly, if the feathered headdresses of the warriors on these vessels do in fact mark them as Sea Peoples, then these first Aegean representations of shipborne combat may not only portray Sea Peoples vessels, but participants in a battle scene *between* ships manned by Sea Peoples – a point that may have historical significance, but which also

---

[27] Tsountas 1886, pls. 1–2.
[28] Kanta 1980, fig. 24.8; Vermeule and Karageorghis 1982, 222–3, pls. XI.1B, 42–3, 45–7, 49, 51, 56–7, 64; Crouwel 1991, figs. 7a–b.
[29] Evans 1900, 210 fig. 6; Murray, Smith and Walters 1900, pl. 1; Oren 1973, 135–42, figs. 1–19; T. Dothan 1982, 4, figs. 11–12; Stager and Mountjoy 2007; Yasur–Landau 2013.
[30] Mountjoy 1998; 2011, 484, 487; Benzi 2013, 521.
[31] Mountjoy 2007, 226 has also tentatively suggested an updating of the rower sherds from Kos into this range.
[32] Dakoronia 1990.

seems to be in keeping with the interesting Mycenaean tradition of largely depicting Aegean warriors in combat against each other rather than against outsiders.[33] The naval battle relief at Medinet Habu is the only representation from this period that includes non–Sea Peoples participants – evidence, perhaps, that only Egypt was able to successfully defend against these foes at sea (though their victory was short–lived, as the events of this period set the Egyptian empire on a course toward inexorable decline).

BOARS' TUSKS, HORSEHAIR CRESTS, AND HORNED HELMETS

Additionally, given the stylistic differences between LH IIIC Mycenaean vase painters and Egyptian artists, it may be that the soldiers in horned helmets on the obverse of the Warrior Vase[34] were intended to represent something akin to the Sherden, who are generally depicted in horned helmets with center–mounted discs in the reliefs of Ramesses II and Ramesses III.[35] Warrior headgear in the Aegean Bronze Age took many different forms, from relatively straightforward bronze helmets to the famous boar's tusk headgear. The most heavily customized zone of these different types of Mycenaean helmet appears to have been the crest, atop which a knob was frequently mounted, to which could be attached a vertical tusk, or crests and plumes of various shape, size, color, and texture. The variety of this helmet adornment even within a single representation is striking; for example, in both the north wall frieze of the miniature fresco at Akrotiri (eight examples) and the silver battle krater from Shaft Grave IV (seven remaining examples), no two boar's tusk helmets feature identically–depicted accoutrements.[36]

The most common accoutrement placed atop these helmets appears to have been a horsehair plume or a large, circular crest with a feathered appearance, both of which are visible in the battle krater scene. With its circular shape, the latter provides an interesting analog to the disc mounted atop the crest of Sherden helmets in Egyptian reliefs. One of the most remarkable Mycenaean–style helmets to have entered the archaeological record to date comes from an inscribed bowl from the Hittite capital at

---

[33] Blakolmer 2013.
[34] Vermeule and Karageorghis 1982, pl. XI.42.
[35] Emanuel 2013, 16.
[36] Morris 1989, 523 fig. 4; Blakolmer 2007, pl. LVI.1.

Boğazköi/Ḫattuša, which has been dated to ca. 1400 BC, and includes both horsehair plume and circular accoutrement – along with, perhaps most interestingly, horns.[37] Expected stylistic differences aside, the warrior represented on this Hittite bowl is strikingly similar to the horn–helmed soldiers depicted on the LH IIIC Middle Warrior Vase from Mycenae – who are, in turn, very similar in appearance to the Sherden seen in the reliefs of Ramesses II and III.

The two and a half centuries that separate the Boğazköi and Warrior Vase depictions are interesting to consider. On the one hand, this seems to demonstrate a striking, long–lived continuity of some aspects of Aegean–style warrior dress and equipment. On the other hand, though, this type of dress – in particular, the horned helmet – is *only* seen in these two periods (the 15th/14th and the 12th centuries), and in both cases an association with Anatolia can be argued. While this is obvious in the case of the Boğazköi bowl due to its provenance, the representation of horn–helmed warriors on the Warrior Vase is connected to Anatolia more indirectly: via the image on the reverse of the vase, the "hedgehog–helmed" warriors whose earliest known appearance is at Bademgediği Tepe (and perhaps Kos), on the eastern edge of the Interface. Rather than a sign of a westward movement by Anatolian warriors, then, this may demonstrate the martial assertion of people from the Interface at the end of the Late Bronze Age. Certainly, as shown above, the "feather–hatted" warriors appear in the Eastern Mediterranean first in the late 13th c. and appear to spread westward across the Aegean through the 12th c., while the horn–helmed warriors on the obverse of the Warrior Vase are both new to LH III imagery, and nearly identical to the "Mycenaean" warrior pictured on the Boğazköi bowl two centuries prior.

THE HELLADIC OARED GALLEY AND THE BRAILED SAIL

Thus far, we have discussed the growing maritime threat that faced the eastern Mediterranean civilizations at the end of the Late Bronze Age, the unprecedented naval engagements that the region's great powers entered into in an effort to stave off this threat, and the new type of warrior that appeared for the first time amidst this chaos. At this point, it is important to consider both the *type* and the *potential capacity* of the ships used in these actions, particularly in light of the new maritime technology introduced in the Aegean and Eastern Mediterranean at this time.

---

[37] Bittel 1976, 9–14; Kelder 2010, 40; cf. Schofield and Parkinson 1994.

Traditional Bronze Age Aegean ship design, typified by Minoan and Egyptian sailing vessels, carried over into the Mycenaean period, with iconography providing evidence for its adoption by mainland polities.[38] Alongside this, though, the LH IIIA2–IIIB period saw the development and introduction of an altogether new type of vessel: the Helladic oared galley. A long, narrow, light craft propelled primarily by rowers and designed specifically for speed, the galley was a vessel best suited for martial purposes, including raiding, piracy, and naval warfare, and its invention has been called "the single most significant advance in the weaponry of the Bronze Age Eastern Mediterranean."[39]

The first depictions of the vessel type most relevant to this discussion appear late in the LH IIIB, and represent a true "break with the preceding development" of sailing vessels, typified by Minoan and Cycladic ships like the craft depicted on the Akrotiri miniature fresco. Unlike these earlier ships, the galley is a vessel built around its human "motor" – a crew of oarsmen – and its development is marked by "the struggle to place as many rowers as possible into as small a hull as practical."[40]

Iconographic evidence from Egypt and the Aegean suggests that, sometime around the LH IIIB–C transition, this vessel type began to be outfitted with the brailed rig and loose–footed sail.[41] This combination, which would become a mainstay of eastern Mediterranean sailing vessels for the next two millennia,[42] was probably developed in the area of the Syro–Palestinian littoral and diffused from there to the south and west via the "raiders and traders" of the LBA, including perhaps members of the Sea Peoples groups.[43] The brailing system consisted of lines attached to the bottom of a sail and run vertically through rings called "brails," which were sewn into the front of the sail. From there, they were run vertically over the yard and aft to the stern, where they were controlled by the steersman. Using this system, sails could be easily raised, lowered, and otherwise manipulated in a manner similar to a set of Venetian blinds.[44]

---

[38] Cosmopoulos 2010, 3–4; Shaw 2001.
[39] Wedde 1999, 465, 470; Tartaron 2013, 63–4.
[40] Wedde 1999, 465–6.
[41] Wedde 2000, no. 6003; *MH* I pls. 37–39; Wachsmann 1998, 156–7
[42] Roberts 1991, 59.
[43] Artzy 1988; Emanuel 2014
[44] Cf. Roberts 1991, pls. XVIIa, XIX–XX; Wachsmann 1998, 251.

If the introduction of the Helladic oared galley was "a strategic inflection point in ship architecture,"[45] the development of the brailed rig was a technological revolution in Mediterranean seafaring. The manipulation of the sail made possible by the addition of brails allowed for far greater maneuverability of sailing vessels than had been the case previously, as well as the ability to sail much closer to the wind, while the removal of the boom allowed warriors to move more freely about the deck when engaged in ship–to–ship combat.[46] Thus, once outfitted with the brailed rig and loose–footed sail, the Helladic oared galley became an ideal vessel for rapid travel, for lightning–fast raids on coastal settlements, and for combat in the open sea.[47]

MARITIME INNOVATION AND MODES OF FIGHTING

Brailed sails are first shown on galleys in the naval battle depiction from Medinet Habu, which was carved no later than Ramesses III's twelfth year, ca. 1171 BC. This relief serves as a monumental "coming out party" for several other new features of maritime technology, as well, including the top–mounted crow's nest and partial decking, from which warriors could engage enemy vessels with spears and grapnels. Remarkably, these attributes – including sail and rigging – are presented identically on both the Sea Peoples' and the Egyptian vessels.

The Egyptian ships depicted in the naval battle were neither Helladic galleys nor traditional Egyptian vessels; instead, they were evidently developed by combining elements of the new Sea Peoples vessels and familiar, old riverine "travelling ships" into a hybrid form of warship.[48] Interestingly, the inspiration for Egypt's adoption of these features might be found one century earlier, in the aforementioned early 13th century naval combat against seaborne Sherden warriors. A noteworthy element of the Tanis II inscription's reference to this event is the fact that the encounter it describes forced the Egyptians to invent a new term for "warship" in order to commemorate it.[49] As seagoing ships had been used for some time in the Egyptian military,[50] the need to coin a new term

---

[45] Wedde 1999, 465.
[46] Sølver 1936, 460; Monroe 1990, 87; Roberts 1991, 57–9; Wachsmann 1998, 330; Wedde 2000, 90.
[47] Roberts 1991, 59.
[48] Landström 1970, 98–115. Emanuel 2014, 42.
[49] Yoyotte 1949; Emanuel 2013, 15.
[50] Jones 1988, 130.5, 131.13.

suggests a certain lack of prior experience either with the *type* of vessel sailed by the Sherden or with the *capabilities* of those vessels. Should this "rebellious–hearted" enemy have been in possession of the brailed rig, crow's nest, and other uniquely–effective technology, appropriating it at this time would have allowed for a "breaking in" period of roughly a century prior to the flawless integration of these components seen in the Egyptian ships whose naval triumph is memorialized at Medinet Habu.

So, how were these earliest naval battles conducted? There is no evidence for the presence of the Iron Age ram, so well known from Classical naval battles, prior to at least the 9th c. BC.[51] Instead, the mode of fighting in these earliest engagements seems nearly identical to that seen on land: standoff weaponry – arrows, slings, and thrown spears – was employed when the warring vessels were still at a distance, and then, when in close enough proximity to board, close combat techniques were employed. The techniques of fighting on the sea, then, were different to those on land only insofar as the method of approach was different: infantry fought as infantry, but with slightly different firing platforms, and with the added risk of a hostile element – the sea – surrounding them.[52] This is clearly seen on the Kynos and Bademgediği kraters and at Medinet Habu, with the chief exception to this being the ingenious employment by the Egyptians of the grapnel, which was used to capsize Sea Peoples' vessels by catching the enemy ship, then swiftly rowing backwards whilst abeam the captured vessel.[53] This way, ship–based soldiers could be defeated without even needing to engage in close combat.

FLEET SIZES AND SHIP CAPACITY

How many warriors, and in how many ships, should we expect to have participated in these earliest naval combats? Our best visual examples consist of just two (Bademgediği), three (Kynos), and nine (Medinet Habu) vessels in total, with only a handful of warriors atop the decks of each. However, as early as transitional LH IIIB2–IIIC Early, we begin to see evidence in the Aegean for the use of *pentekonters,* or galleys rowed by fifty men (twenty–five on each side).[54] A LH IIIC pyxis from Tholos Tomb 1 at Tragana near Pylos features a ship with twenty–four vertical

---

[51] Wachsmann 1998, 157.
[52] Wachsmann 1998, 317; Crouwel 1999.
[53] Wachsmann 1998, 319.
[54] Wachsmann 1998, 132, 138, figs. 7.7, 7.27, 7.30–31; 2013; Wedde 2000, figs. 607–8, 643, 6003

stanchions,[55] thereby separating the rowers' gallery into twenty–five sections. A LM IIIB larnax from Gazi on Crete features a large ship with what appears to be twenty–seven stanchions, which could signify a ship crewed by even more than fifty men; however, as the "horizontal ladder" motif used to represent rowers' galleries on Late Helladic ship depictions also seems to have served to address a certain *horror vacui* on the part of Mycenaean artists,[56] it seems more likely that the Gazi painter intended to portray a *pentekonter* than a ship with fifty–four oarsmen.[57] 'Kynos A,' one of the aforementioned ship representations found at Pyrgos Livanaton, features nineteen oars and schematically–rendered rowers. The odd number of rowers, combined with the need to fit two antithetic vessels onto a single side of a krater, suggests that this vessel was also intended as a *pentekonter* but the artist was forced to abbreviate due to space constraints.

Further evidence for the use of *pentekonters* in the years surrounding the Late Bronze–Early Iron Age transition, and for the employment of such vessels by the Sea Peoples, may be found in a remarkable recently–published model of a Helladic oared galley from Tomb 611 at Gurob in Middle Egypt.[58]

Crews of roughly *pentekonter* size may also be attested in the aforementioned Rower Tablets from Pylos. Tablet An 610 records approximately 600 oarsmen, while An 1 lists thirty "rowers to go to Pleuron" summoned to man what is likely a single ship, a 30–rower *triakonter*.[59] When ship numbers are considered in light of likely crew sizes, the danger that raiding parties made up of small "fleets" could pose to unwary coastal settlements is clear. For example, if the ships crewed by the men of An 610 were *pentekonters*, the 600–man force would be enough to man only twelve ships. Even if they were *triakonters*, like the vessel crewed by the An 1 rowers, there would only be enough to fully man twenty ships. Two late 13th–early 12th c. letters from Ugarit (RS 20.238 and 20.18) mention enemy fleets of seven and twenty ships respectively, thus attesting to the panic small numbers of ships could

---

[55] Stanchions supported the superstructure and partial decking on galleys, while also serving to divide the rower's gallery in ship representations.
[56] Cf. Wachsmann 1998.
[57] Wachsmann 1998, 138.
[58] The model was incorrectly assembled and labeled "Pirate Boat?" by its excavator, Flinders Petrie 1933, 74 fig. 85.
[59] Chadwick 1973, 186–7, 431; 1987, 77; cf. Linder 1970, 321; Killen 1983.

create in the inhabitants of coastal targets. The vessels mentioned in these texts may have contained an aggregate of between 210 and 1000 rowers if the respective fleets were composed of *triakonters, pentekonters*, or some combination thereof – enough combatants to create havoc on an unprepared or lightly defended coastal settlement if allowed to make landfall.

The tumultuous transition from the LBA to the Iron I is noteworthy for many reasons.[60] Significant among these is the rise of seaborne foes that threatened the established polities of the Bronze Age to such a degree that navies were sent out for the first time to engage in battles on the open sea. The evidence for this shift in warfare, found in text and iconography from the western Aegean to the Near East, aids our understanding of the events at the close of the Bronze Age. It also heralds the arrival of the Age of Iron, a period in which the descendants of several of these Bronze Age Groups – the Phoenicians, the Greeks, and eventually the Romans – would themselves engage in maritime activity, including both colonization and warfare, on a much larger scale.

BIBLIOGRAPHY

Artzy, M. (1988) "War/Fighting Boats in the Second Millennium BC in the Eastern Mediterranean", *Reports of the Department of Antiquities, Cyprus* 1988, 181–186.

Baruffi, J. T. (1998) *Naval Warfare Operations in the Bronze Age Eastern Mediterranean*. PhD dissertation, University of Chicago.

Baumbach, L. (1983) "An Examination of the Evidence for a State of Emergency at Pylos c. 1200 B.C. from the Linear B Tablets", in A. Heubeck and G. Neumann (eds) *Res Mycenaeae*, 28–40, Göttingen.

Benzi, M. (2013) "The Southeast Aegean in the Age of the Sea Peoples", in A. E. Killebrew and G. Lehmann (eds) *The Philistines and Other 'Sea Peoples' in Text and Archaeology*, 509–542, Atlanta.

Bittel, K. (1976) "Tonschale mit Ritzzeichnung von Boğazköy", *Revue Archéologique* 1, 9–14.

Blakolmer, F. (2007). "The Silver Battle Krater from Shaft Grave IV at Mycenae: Evidence of Fighting 'Heroes' on Minoan Palace Walls at Knossos?", in S. P. Morris and R. Laffineur (eds) *EPOS: Reconsidering Greek Epic and Aegean Bronze Age Archaeology*, 157–

---

[60] Cf., *inter alia*, Ward & Joukowsky 1992; Gitin, Mazar & Stern 1998; Oren 2000

166, Liège.

—. (2013) "The Missing 'Barbarians': Some Thoughts on Ethnicity and Identity in Aegean Bronze Age Iconography", *Talanta* 45, 53–77.

Chadwick, J. (1976) *The Mycenaean World*. Cambridge.

Cosmopoulos, M. B. (2010) *Iklaina Archaeological Project: 2010 Internet Report*. http://iklaina.files.wordpress.com/2011/11/2010report.pdf.

Crouwel, J. H. (1991) *Mycenaean Pictorial Pottery*. Oxford.

—. (1999) "Fighting on Land and Sea in Late Mycenaean Times", in R. Laffineur (ed) *Polemos: Le Contexte Guerrier en Égée à l'âge du Bronze*, 455–460, Liège.

Dakoronia, F. (1990) "War–Ships on Sherds of LHIIIC Kraters from Kynos", in H. Tzalas (ed) *TROPIS II*, 117–122, Athens.

de Rougé, E. (1877) *Inscriptions Hiéroglyphices Copiées en Égypte Pendant la Mission Scientifique de M. le Vicomte Emmanuel de Rougé*. Paris.

Deger–Jalkotzy, S. (1978) *E–QE–TA. Zur Rolle des Gefolgschaftwesens in der Sozialstructure Mykenischer Reich*. Vienna.

Dickinson, O. T. P. K. (2006) *The Aegean from Bronze Age to Iron Age: Continuity and Change between the Twelfth and Eighth Centuries B.C*. London.

Dothan, T. K. (1982) *Philistine Material Culture*. New Haven.

Earle, J. W. (2008) *Trade and Culture in the Cycladic Islands During the Late Bronze Age*. PhD dissertation, New York University.

Emanuel, J. P. (2012) "Cretan Lie and Historical Truth: Examining Odysseus' Raid on Egypt in its Late Bronze Age Context", in V. Bers, D. Elmer, D. Frame, and L. Muellner (eds) *Donum Natalicium Digitaler Confetium Gregorio Nagy Septuagenario a Discipulis Collegis Familiaribus Oblatum*, 1-41, Washington, DC.

—. (2013) "Šrdn from the Sea: The Arrival, Integration, and Acculturation of a Sea People", *Journal of Ancient Egyptian Interconnections* 5, 14–27.

—. (2014) "The Sea Peoples, Egypt, and the Aegean: Transference of Maritime Technology in the Late Bronze–Early Iron Transition (LH IIIB–C)", *Aegean Studies* 1, 21–56.

Epigraphic Survey (1930) *Medinet Habu I: Earlier Historical Records of Ramses III*. Chicago.

—. (1932) *Medinet Habu II: Later Historical Records of Ramses III*. Chicago.

Evans, A. J. (1900) "Mycenaean Cyprus as Illustrated in the British Museum Excavations", *Journal of the Royal Anthropological Institute* 30, 199–220.

Flinders Petrie, W. M. (1933) "Egyptian Shipping: Outlines and Notes," *Ancient Egypt and the East*, parts 1–4, 4–5.
Gitin, S., A. Mazar & E. Stern (eds) (1998) *Mediterranean Peoples in Transition: Thirteenth to Early Tenth Centuries BC*. Jerusalem.
Güterbock, H. G. (1967) "The Hittite Conquest of Cyprus Reconsidered", *Journal of Near Eastern Studies* 26, 73–81.
Habachi, L. (1980) "The Military Posts of Ramesses II on the Coastal Road and the Western Part of the Delta", *Bulletin de l'Institut Français d'Archéologie Orientale* 80, 13–30.
Hafford, W. B. (2001) *Merchants in the Late Bronze Age Eastern Mediterranean: Tools, Texts, and Trade*. PhD dissertation, University of Pennsylvania.
Hooker, J. T. (1982) "The End of Pylos and the Linear B Evidence", *Studi Miceneied Egeo–Anatolici* 23, 209–227.
—. (1987) "Titles and Functions in the Pylian State", in J. Killen, J. Melena and J. P. Oliver (eds) *Studies in Mycenaean and Classical Greek: Presented to John Chadwick*, 257–268, Salamanca.
Jones, D. (1988) *A Glossary of Ancient Egyptian Nautical Titles and Terms*. London.
Kanta, A. (1980) *The Late Minoan III Period in Crete: A Survey of Sites, Pottery, and Their Distribution*. Göteborg.
Karageorghis, V. (2001) "Patterns of Fortified Settlements in the Aegean and Cyprus c. 1200 B.C", in V. Karageorghis and C. E. Morris (eds) *Defensive Settlements of the Aegean and the Eastern Mediterranean After c. 1200 B.C.*, 1–12, Nicosia.
Kelder, J. M. (2010a) *The Kingdom of Mycenae: A Great Kingdom in the Bronze Age Aegean*. Bethesda.
Killen, J. T. (1983) "PY An 1", *Minos* 18, 71–80.
Kitchen, K. A. (1996) *Ramesside Inscriptions Translated and Annotated: Translations II*. Cambridge, MA.
Landström, B. (1970) *Ships of the Pharaohs: 4000 Years of Egyptian Shipbuilding*. Garden City.
Linder, E. (1973) "Naval Warfare in the El–Amarna Age.", in D. J. Blackman (ed) *Marine Archaeology*, 317–324, Hamden.
Monroe, C. (1990) *The Boatbuilding Industry of New Kingdom Egypt*. MA Thesis, Texas A&M University.
Morris, S. P. (1989) "A Tale of Two Cities: The Miniature Frescoes from Thera and the Origins of Greek Poetry", *American Journal of Archaeology* 93, 511–535.
Mountjoy, P. A. (1998) "The East Aegean–West Anatolian Interface in the Late Bronze Age: Mycenaeans and the Kingdom of Ahhiyawa",

Anatolian Studies 48, 33–67.
—. (1999) *Regional Mycenaean Decorated Pottery* (2 vols). Rahden.
—. (2005) "Mycenaean Connections with the Near east in LH IIIC: Ships and Sea Peoples", in R. Laffineur and E. Greco (eds) *Emporia: Aegeans in the Central Mediterranean,* 423–431, Liège.
—. (2011) "A Bronze Age Ship from Ashkelon with Particular Reference to the Bronze Age Ship from Bademgediği Tepe", *American Journal of Archaeology* 115, 483–488.
Murray, A. S., A. H. Smith and H. B. Walters (1900) *Excavations in Cyprus: Bequest of Miss E. T. Turner to the British Museum.* London.
Nowicki, K. (1996) "Arvi Fortetsa and Loutraki Kandilioro: Two Refuge Settlements in Crete", *Annual of the British School at Athens* 91, 253–285.
Oren, E. D. (1973) *The Northern Cemetery of Beth Shan.* Leiden.
—, (ed) (2000) *The Sea Peoples and Their World: A Reassessment.* Philadephia.
Ormerod, H. A. (1924) *Piracy in the Ancient World.* Baltimore.
Palaima, T. G. (1991) "Maritime Matters in the Linear B Texts", in R. Laffineur and L. Basch (eds) *Thalassa: l'Egée Préhistorique et la Mer,* 273–310, Liège.
—. (1995) "The Last Days of the Pylos Polity", in R. Laffineur and W.-D. Niemeier (eds) *Politeia: Society and State in the Aegean Bronze Age,* 623–633, Liège.
Palmer, L. R. (1980) *Mycenaeans and Minoans: Aegean Prehistory in the Light of the Linear B Tablets.* Westport.
Papadopoulos, A. (2009) "Warriors, Hunters and Ships in the Late Helladic IIIC Aegean", in C. Bachhuber & R. G. Roberts (eds) *Forces of Transformation: The End of the Bronze Age in the Mediterranean,* 69–78, Oxford.
Peden, A. J. (1994) *Egyptian Historical Inscriptions of the Twentieth Dynasty.* Jonsered.
Pulak, C. (1998) "The Uluburun Shipwreck: an Overview", *International Journal of Nautical Archaeology* 27, 188–224.
—. (2005) "Who Were the Mycenaeans Aboard the Uluburun Ship?", in R. Laffineur & E. Greco (eds) *Emporia: Aegeans in the Central Mediterranean,* 295–310, Liège.
Redford, D. B. (2006) "The Tjeker", *Scripta Mediterranea* 27–28, 9–14.
Roberts, O. T. P. (1991) "The Development of the Brail into a Viable Sail Control for Aegean Boats of the Bronze Age", in R. Laffineur and L. Basch (eds) *Thalassa: l'Egée Préhistorique et la Mer,* 55–64, Liège.
Rougé, E. de. 1877. *Inscriptions Hiéroglyphices Copiées en Égypte*

Pendant la Mission Scientifique de M. le Vicomte Emmanuel de Rougé. Paris.

Sandars, N. K. (1985) *The Sea Peoples: Warriors of the Ancient Mediterranean*. London.

Schilardi, D. U. (1984) "The LH IIIC Period at the Koukounaries Acropolis, Paros", in J. A. MacGillivray and R. L. N. Barber (eds) *The Prehistoric Cyclades: Contributions to a Workshop on Cycladic Chronology*, 184–206, Edinburgh.

—. (1992) "Paros and the Cyclades after the Fall of the Mycenaean Palaces", in J. P. Olivier (ed) *Mykenaïka: Actes du IXe Colloque International sur les Textes Mycéniens et Égéens, 621*–693, Paris.

—. (1999) "The Mycenaean Horseman (?) of Koukounaries" in P. Betancourt, V. Karageorghis, R. Laffineur and W–D. Niemeier (eds) *Meletemata: Studies in Aegean Archaeology Presented to Malcolm H. Weiner*, 751–756, Liège.

Schofield, L. and R. B. Parkinson (1994) "Of Helmets and Heretics: A Possible Egyptian Representation of Mycenaean Warriors on a Papyrus from El–Amarna", *Annual of the British School at Athens* 89, 157–170.

Shaw, M. C. (2001) "Symbols of Naval Power at the Palace at Pylos: The Evidence from the Frescoes", in S. Böhm and K–V. von Eickstedt (eds) *Ithakē: Festschrift für Jörg Schäfer*, 37–43, Würzburg.

Shelmerdine, C. W. (1997) "Review of Aegean Prehistory VI: The Palatial Bronze Age of the Southern and Central Greek Mainland", *American Journal of Archaeology* 101, 537–585.

—. (1999) "Pylian Polemics: The Latest Evidence on Military Matters", in R. Laffineur (ed) *Polemos: Le Contexte Guerrier en Égée à l'âge du Bronze,* 403–410, Liège.

Singer, I. (1983) "Western Anatolia in the Thirteenth Century B.C. According to the Hittite Sources", *Anatolian Studies* 33, 205–217.

Sølver, C. V. (1936) "Egyptian Shipping of About 1500 B.C", *Mariner's Mirror* 22, 430–469.

Snape, S. R. (1997) "Ramesses II's Forgotten Frontier", *Egyptian Archaeology* 11, 23–24.

Stager, L. E. (1991) *Ashkelon Discovered: From Canaanites and Philistines to Romans and Moslems*. Washington, DC.

Stager, L. E. and P. A. Mountjoy (2007) "A Pictorial Krater from Philistine Ashkelon", in S. White Crawford, A. Ben–Tor, J. P. Dessel, W. G. Dever, A. Mazar and J. Aviram (eds) *Up to the Gates of Ekron*, 50–61, Jerusalem.

Sweeney, D. and A. Yasur–Landau (1999) "Following the Path of the Sea Persons: The Women in the Medinet Habu Reliefs", *Tel Aviv* 26, 116–

145.
Tartaron, T. F. (2013) *Maritime Networks in the Mycenaean World*. Cambridge.
Taylour, L. W. (1983) *The Mycenaeans*. London.
Tsountas, Ch. (1886) "Graptē Stēlē ek Mykēnōn", *Ephemeris Archaiologikē* 4, 1–22.
Vermeule, E. T. and V. Karageorghis (1982) *Mycenaean Pictorial Vase Painting*. Cambridge, MA.
Wachsmann, S. (1982) "The Ships of the Sea Peoples (*IJNA*, 10.3: 187–220): Additional Notes", *International Journal of Nautical Archaeology* 11, 297–304.
—. (1998) *Seagoing Ships and Seamanship in the Bronze Age Levant*. College Station.
—. (1999) "The Pylos Rower Tablets Reconsidered", in H. Tzalas (ed) *TROPIS V*, 491–504, Athens.
—. (2013) *The Gurob Ship–Cart Model and Its Mediterranean Context*. College Station.
Ward, M. & M. S. Joukowsky (eds) (1992) *The Crisis Years: 1200 BC from Beyond the Danube to the Tigris*. Dubuque.
Wedde, M. (1999) "War at Sea: The Mycenaean and Early Iron Age Oared Galley", in R. Laffineur (ed) *Polemos: Le Contexte Guerrier en Égée à l'âge du Bronze*, 465–476, Liège.
—. (2000) *Toward a Hermeneutics of Aegean Bronze Age Ship Imagery*. Mannheim.
Yasur–Landau, A. (2010) *The Philistines and the Aegean Migration at the End of the Late Bronze Age*. Cambridge.
—. (2013) "The 'Feathered Helmets' of the Sea Peoples: Joining the Iconographic and Archaeological Evidence", *Talanta* 45, 27–40.
Yon, M. (1992) "The End of the Kingdom of Ugarit", in W. A. Ward and M. S. Joukowsky (eds) *The Crisis Years: The 12th Century B.C. from Beyond the Danube to the Tigris,* 111–122, Dubuque.
Yoyotte, P. J. (1949) "Les Stèles de Ramsès II a Tanis: Première Partie", *Kémi* 10, 65–75.
Yurco, F. J. (1999) "Sea Peoples", in K. A. Bard and S. B. Shubert (eds) *Encyclopedia of the Archaeology of Ancient Egypt*, 876–879, London.

CHAPTER TWELVE

THUCYDIDES' NARRATIVE ON NAVAL WARFARE: *EPIBATAI*, MILITARY THEORY, IDEOLOGY[1]

DR. MATTEO ZACCARINI

INTRODUCTION

The Athenian attitude to sea warfare changed dramatically during the first part of the 5th century BC. The tradition credits Themistocles with the construction of a large, modern military fleet of nimble triremes. These, however, lacked a continuous deck (Thuc. 1.14.3) and were replaced, probably in the early 460s, by a more standard design: Cimon, according to Plutarch, rebuilt the Athenian triremes with a continuous deck so that more soldiers could be transported (*Vit. Cim.* 12.2). By the last decades of the century the Athenians, while not removing the full deck, had dropped the idea of regularly filling the ships with soldiers. A light load and excellently trained crews allowed the Athenian "fast trireme" (τριήρης ταχύς) to achieve superior mobility and to rely on the ram as its primary weapon.[2]

Given the vast sea power acquired by Athens during the 5th century, the kind of bias usually referred to as 'Athenocentrism' has also affected sea warfare. A large part of the available data comes from Thucydides or other Athenian sources and reflects personal beliefs, attitudes and narrative aims. The analysis will first deal with the elusive epigraphic and literary

---

[1] All English translations of Greek texts are mine, unless otherwise specified. I am indebted to Hugh Bowden, Alessandro Iannucci, Matthew Trundle and the team of reviewers for their constructive criticisms and suggestions.
[2] On Themistocles' and Cimon's naval reforms see Zaccarini 2013. On ramming and manoeuvring see Morrison *et al.* 2000, 25-46; cf. de Souza 2013, 369.

evidence on the embarked soldiers, then will aim to define 5th century – mainly Thucydidean – recurring keywords and definitions related to sea combat. An analysis of specific literary themes relating to sea combat may reveal how the Athenian approach to maritime warfare reflects significant cultural and ideological aspects besides – and possibly before – actual military, tactical practice.

2. SOLDIERS AND NAVAL BATTLES

2.1. ARCHERS, HOPLITES, *EPIBATAI*

According to the inscription known as the 'Decree of Themistocles', the standard load of Athenian triremes at Salamis was 14 men, of whom 10 were young ἐπιβάται and 4 τοξόται (archers) (ll. 23-6). Plutarch (*Vit. Them.* 14.2) conversely states that there were 18 μαχόμενοι (generic "fighters"), of whom 14 were ὁπλῖται (hoplites) and 4 τοξόται. It is generally assumed that these numbers, although not implausibe, reflect late 5th or 4th century customs.[3]

While the role of archers and their equipment is relatively clear,[4] evidence on the *epibatai* is more ambiguous. The term *epibates* is often translated, in a military context, as "marine",[5] but its literal meaning of "passenger" already suggests a rather vague definition. At the time of the Peloponnesian War, some *epibatai* were, technically speaking, hoplites: in 426 BC, 300 Athenian *epibatai* disembarked from 30 ships (3.95.2; cf. 91.1, 94.1),[6] supported by archers (98.1), and fought and died as hoplites in Aetolia (98.4).[7] Thucydides once reports that some Peloponnesian

---

[3] Morrison *et al.* 2000, 109-10; Trundle 2010, 148-52; cf. Zaccarini 2013, 10; on the debated dating and context of the Decree see Meiggs-Lewis 23.

[4] On archers aboard triremes see Krentz 2007, 123; on the mixed feelings that sources display towards archery see Trundle 2010, 144-8.

[5] On this view of Greek *epibatai* see Jordan 1972, 192; Morrison *et al.* 2000, 109-10 (but one cannot agree with the idea that their main role was disciplinary).

[6] Thucydides' use of νῆες (generic "ships") in these passages is ambiguous, but apparently confirms the standard load of 10 *epibatai* per trireme (thus 300 men on 30 ships). At the same time, the addition of troop-transports (on which see Zaccarini 2013, 23 n. 49) to standard triremes sent to Melos seems implied by the 2000 "hoplites" on 60 ships (Thuc. 3.91.1).

[7] The archers could well be those from the ships, although other allies were present (3.95.2); Thucydides' almost obsessive redundancy in reminding that the Aetolians had javelin-armed *psiloi* ("light infantry": 94.4; 95.3; 97.2; 98.1-2)

nautai (oarsmen or sailors) and *epibatai* were selected for their hoplite equipment which, in turn, implies that others did not employ it (7.1.5).[8] Conversely, an Athenian fleet could embark hoplites from the civic list (ἐκ καταλόγου), 'forcing' them to serve as *epibatai* (Thuc. 8.24.2 εἶχον δ' ἐπιβάτας τῶν ὁπλιτῶν ἐκ καταλόγου ἀναγκαστούς, "having [on board] hoplites from the civic list compelled to serve as *epibatai*") or, if needed, hoplites could even be employed as rowers (cf. 3.18.3-4). Even members from the lowest citizens class (*thetes*) serving as *epibatai* could be counted as hoplites, but it was convenient to do so separately from hoplites ἐκ καταλόγου (6.43).[9] Numbering the ways a "good soldier" (στρατιώτης ἀγαθός) could serve his country, Lysias separates ὁπλίτης from ἐπιβάτης (6.46), a dichotomy which conveniently suits his argument.

Overall, apart from being regularly distinguished from 'archers,' *epibatai* seem to represent a rather vague definition of embarked soldiers, drawing from a peculiar mix of different social and military categories. Even when outfitted as hoplites, *epibatai* were counted separately from the 'standard' hoplites from the civic list; furthermore, the latter were not normally assigned to the navy. Further investigation on their armaments and social role may shed some light on the 'identity' of the *epibatai*.

2.2. PERSONAL EQUIPMENT AND THE TACTICAL ROLE OF THE EPIBATAI

Trying to assess the armament(s) used by the rather broad group of the *epibatai* (Section 2.1) may shed some light on their tactical role. The following overview of relevant literary passages gathers together

---

stresses the critical lack of an Athenian counterpart. See Hornblower 1991, 513 (on Thucydides' interest in light troops) and 514 (on his ambiguous treatment of *epibatai* in these passages).

[8] This practice seems unparalleled: more commonly, *nautai* could be equipped as peltasts (Xen. *Hell*. 1.2.1), or as generic light troops (van Wees 2004, 62-4; Trundle 2010, 154-5).

[9] On these passages, and on limited evidence on *thetes* serving as hoplites see De Ste. Croix 2004, esp. 13-4, 20-2 (on his approach see, however, van Wees 2006, 373, with further sources); on the ambiguity of Thuc. 8.24.2 see Gomme, Andrewes and Dover 1981, 56; cf. Hornblower 2008, 815-6, on Thuc. 3.16.1, usually taken as evidence for *epibatai* normally being *thetes* (although the passage does not exactly says this); van Wees 2004, 16-7, on hoplites ἐκ καταλόγου; note that, on the contrary, there is no convincing evidence that fleet personnel were mustered by tribes: Pritchard 2000, 112-5.

significant 5th century evidence from various contexts.

Aeschylus has the Greek soldiers wear bronze weaponry when disembarking at Psyttalea during the battle of Salamis (*Pers.* 456-7 φράξαντες εὐχάλκοις δέμας ὅπλοισι ναῶν ἐξέθρῳσκον, "fencing their bodies in armour of bronze, they leapt from their ships").[10] The high risk of falling into the water may have induced men to drop the heavier parts of the panoply while at sea.[11] Aeschylus also reports, although vaguely, that Greek naval soldiers employed stones and arrows (*Pers.* 459-61).

Herodotus repeatedly and variously refers to *epibatai* wearing 'Greek weapons' but, as his audience was obviously familiar with such a definition, he provides scant detail. If anything, he confirms that a certain set of weapons and armour was generally shared and recurrent among the Greeks at sea, as well as by many barbarians, much as in land warfare.[12] On the other hand, he provides a reasonable amount of information on peculiar barbarian outfits. Phoenician *epibatai*, for example, were equipped with a linen cuirass, shield and javelins (7.89.1); the Egyptians employed spears specifically designed for sea combat (89.3 δόρατα ναύμαχα), which the Greeks certainly knew of, although there is no proof they used them in the same period.[13]

Taking into account the whole fighting potential of a Greek trireme at

---

[10] Transl. H. W. Smyth, adapted.
[11] But then again, it is difficult to guess where such gear could be stored, given the extremely limited space on board, both for Themistoclean (Section 1) and later triremes, which embarked various provisions (cf. Shear 1995; Krentz 2007, 153-4). On possible echoes of Homeric scenes in the *Persians* see remarks in Zaccarini 2013, 17. On the perils of wearing armour while embarked cf. Section 2.3 on the death of Callicratidas.
[12] Herodotus employs *hellenika hopla* (7.91 Ἑλληνικοῖσι ὅπλοισι ἐσκευασμένοι, "outfitted with Greek weapons"; cf. 74.1 Ἑλληνικῶν ὅπλα, "weapons of the Greeks"), or apparently similar expressions, to define the outfit of a part of Xerxes' naval forces: 7.89.1 (τρόπον τὸν Ἑλληνικόν, "the Greek way"), 90 and 93 (κατά περ Ἕλληνες, "like Greeks"), 94 and 95.1-2 (ἐσκευασμένοι ὡς Ἕλληνες, "outfitted like Greeks"), 95.1 (ὡπλισμένοι ὡς Ἕλληνες, "armed like Greeks").
[13] Such weapons are already in *Il.* 15.389, as noted by Macan 1908, 113. Herodotus elsewhere (9.32) states that Egyptians employed swordsmen (μαχαιροφόροι) as *epibatai*, which may be a stress on the particularly noteworthy (cf. 7.91) μάχαιραι μεγάλαι, "large blades," which are part of their outfit in 7.89.3. It is also worth noting that some barbarian *epibatai* carried bows (e.g. 7.92), unlike their Greek counterparts as described by later sources (Section 2.1).

the sea battle of Syracuse in 413, Thucydides records the use of arrows, stones and javelins by "those on the decks" (Thuc. 7.70.5 οἱ ἀπὸ τῶν καταστρωμάτων), probably a generic reference to both *epibatai* and *toxotai*. The former were tasked also with close combat and boarding once ships came close enough (70.5 ἐπειδὴ δὲ προσμείξειαν, οἱ ἐπιβάται ἐς χεῖρας ἰόντες ἐπειρῶντο ταῖς ἀλλήλων ναυσὶν ἐπιβαίνειν, "once they came close, the *epibatai*, fighting hand to hand, tried to board each other's ship"), attacking the enemy deck and defending their own (cf. 7.63.1). Implicitly involving relevant technical skills, Thucydides has Gylippus state that the Athenians were poor when it came to imitating the 'Peloponnesian way' (7.67.2) by filling up the decks, in contrast to their own custom (παρὰ τὸ καθεστηκὸς), with a number of hoplites (πολλοὶ μὲν ὁπλῖται) and javelin throwers untrained in sea figthing (χερσαῖοι).[14]

These passages suggest yet one more peculiarity of the *epibatai* – their shifting and varied tactical role, reflected by their armament, ranging from melee to thrown weapons. *Epibatai* must have regularly, and possibly primarily, resorted to thrown weapons, such as stones and javelins, addressing an obvious and specific issue of deck to deck fighting: attacking enemies beyond the reach of hand weapons.[15]

It is worth recalling one further task carried out by the *epibatai*, which required timing and skill: operating specific onboard devices. Herodotus (9.98.2) recalls that the Ionians at Lade used ἀποβάθραι, "gangways", to board enemy ships in 494. Apparently, these were the same wooden planks employed to embark and disembark their own ships. The word is extremely rare in classical sources: it is explained by a scholiast to Thucydides as "the way out from the ship to the land" (*schol. ad* Thuc. 4.12.1 ll.3-4 Hude ἡ ἀπὸ τῆς νεὼς ἐπὶ τὴν γῆν ἔξοδος ἀποβάθρα καλεῖται). This device was possibly complemented, since at least the early 420s, by the "iron hand" (Thuc. 4.25.4 χείρ σιδήρεα), the grappling iron notably

---

[14] Cf. below, Section 3. Unskilled movements on the deck could endanger the ship (cf. Morrison *et al.* 2000, 226-7). On the skilled use of javelins see the performance of the Samothracians at Salamis (Hdt. 8.90.2). Plutarch, as elsewhere (Zaccarini 2013, esp. 17-8), occasionally provides reliable technical information on naval warfare: On thrown projectiles see his story on Ariston of Corinth instructing the Syracusans (*Vit. Nic.* 25.2-4).
[15] The intense use of projectiles led to different means to increase protection of the decks: on Phoenician hull side shields see Zaccarini 2013, 12; on leather ·eens, παραρ(ρ)ύματα, employed at least by 4th century Greeks see *IG* II^2 1609 47, 85-6, 113; Xen. *Hell.* 1.6.19; Shear 1995, 201-2.

employed at the battle of Syracuse to immobilise, board and possibly damage a ship. Thucydides explains how its proper use required co-ordinated work from the *epibatai* (7.62.3 ἦν τὰ ἐπὶ τούτοις οἱ ἐπιβάται ὑπουργῶσιν), and the skilled Gylippus and the Syracusans knew how to counter it (7.65.2). Various tasks related to damaging, attacking, and boarding enemy ships were, thus, a job for the *epibatai*.

2.3. INDIVIDUAL GALLANTRY AND *TAXIS*

Additional literary evidence shows the role of the *epibatai* in deck fighting and boarding. Herodotus tells the story of Pytheas of Aegina who, while "serving as *epibates*" or, perhaps more correctly, "while being embarked" (7.181.1 ἐπιβατεύοντος) on a ship captured by Persians before the battle of Artemisium, performed a remarkable last man stand which impressed the enemy *epibatai*. Similar stories of heroic, sometimes almost legendary, 'Homeric' combat deeds, are quite frequent in Herodotus, such as that of Sophanes of Decelea in the Thracian interior (6.92.3; 9.73-4).[16]

This all stated, there are significant examples of e*pibatai* fighting collectively with order and tactics. Thucydides (7.70.3) reports that Athenian and Syracusan *epibatai* rivaled each other in their "skill" (τέχνῃ) with each man being: "there where he had been assigned" (ἐν ᾧ προσετέτακτο) on the deck, trying to excel. The technical verb προστάττω suggests an organised and disciplined combat, as much as τέχνη involves a further layer of skill. This scene somewhat underlines Pytheas' kind of individual gallantry, while clearly implying that *epibatai* had to hold their battle stations, in a similar way to how hoplites had to hold formation. Thucydides elsewhere employs προστάττω in the same meaning (2.87.8) both for *nautai* and *kybernetai* (helmsmen). Xenophon, apparently inheriting Thucydides' views on naval matters, employs the notion of fighting in *taxis* (battle array) for the whole crew of a ship (*Oec.* 8.8).

That of Pytheas was hardly the typical combat performance of an *epibates*.[17] Perhaps, as was theoretically the case with hoplites in land

---

[16] On acts of heroism in Herodotus see Baragwanath 2012, esp. 287-91. Individual feats were rewarded by Xerxes among his own soldiers (Hdt. 8.90.4); on personal deeds at Salamis cf. Plut. *Vit. Them.* 14.4 (a few remarks in Zaccarini 2013, 12). Diodorus' version of the death of Callicratidas at sea (13.99.4-5) is similar to Pytheas' fall, possibly a literary model which Xenophon did not follow at all (cf. *Hell.* 1.6.33).

[17] Rawlings 2000, 236-7, believes *epibatai* regularly engaged in individual

battles, an *epibates* was expected to continue to fight alone after his comrades had fallen. However, in practice, like the rest of a trireme crew, and like each member of a land army, an *epibates* was instructed to fight in his place as part of a single, coherent body; personal initiative was rather discouraged in favour of a formation (*taxis*) as long as the *epibatai* stood together. *Taxis* represents an important, shared value between land warfare and sea warfare. This is also supported by the recurring formulas employed in regard to combat-ready forces[18] and to the appointment of commanders.[19] Furthermore, Athenian culture lacked a specific word for 'admiral': a *strategos* could command in both naval and land warfare, two parts of a discipline every general was supposed to master.[20]

3. SKILL, COURAGE, NUMBERS: THUCYDIDES' CHARACTERISATION THROUGH KEYWORDS

The above analysis of the *epibatai* has highlighted that Athenian sources consciously perceived land battles and sea battles as, to some extent, closely related in the Greek experience (Sections 2.2-3). However, Thucydides in particular seems to put great effort into trying to separate the two contexts, even when they are entwined in amphibious operations. While his narrative is not always consistent in regards to naval matters,[21] the aim of such an approach becomes clear through specific examples: it is therefore worth eploring in more depth relevant passages before going back to the *epibatai*.

3.1. THE PELOPONNESIAN DOCTRINE: COURAGE, NUMBERS AND DILETTANTISM

The battle of the Sybotae is the occasion for Thucydides to describe the

---

combat. While a naval battle was certainly chaotic (cf. Strauss 2008, 233-4), the stress on *taxis* by sources rather suggests that organised group fighting was the rule.
[18] Cf. e.g. again προστάττω, which denotes both ships assigned to a commander (Thuc. 8.26.1) and the land host which Brasidas assigns to Clearidas (5.8.4).
[19] Typically with the form ἄρχοντα προστάξαντας (e.g. Thuc. 8.39.2), "appointing to the command," both on land and water (e.g. 3.16.3 ναύαρχον προσέταξαν, "they appointed as navarch").
[20] The Spartans, on the other hand, reserved naval command for the dedicated office of ναύαρχος: It has been noted that skilled *nauarchoi* significantly affected Spartan naval performances during the Deceleic war (Naiden 2009).
[21] Cf. a few remarks in Lapini 1997, 38.

Peloponnesians' sea fighting technique, little focused on manoeuvres, and heavily reliant on masses of embarked hoplites, archers, and javelin throwers. Thucydides notoriously dismisses this doctrine as "old-fashioned" and "rather inexperienced" (1.49.1 τῷ παλαιῷ τρόπῳ ἀπειρότερον ἔτι παρεσκευασμένοι), amateurish, not complying to his idea of relevant "skill" (49.2 τῇ μὲν τέχνῃ οὐχ ὁμοίως) and "rather similar to a *pezomachia* (infantry battle)" (πεζομαχίᾳ δὲ τὸ πλέον προσφερὴς οὖσα). Thucydides repeatedly underlines these and related themes through both his own words and those attributed to various characters: it is convenient to review a few relevant passages.

A first major difference between the Athenians and some of the Peloponnesians is that of expertise (Thuc. 2.85.2). While the former claim a "long experience" (ἐκ πολλοῦ ἐμπειρίαν), the Spartans are limited by their "recent exercise" (τῆς σφετέρας δι' ὀλίγου μελέτης).[22] On the other hand, the Peloponnesians feature two recurring advantages (2.89.2) – a "great number of ships" (πλῆθος τῶν νεῶν) and a manly, martial courage (ἀνδρεία). Phormio, however, warns the Athenians not to be afraid, as the Peloponnesians' confidence (2.89.2 θαρσοῦσιν κτλ.) comes from their "experience" (ἐμπειρία) with land armies.[23] Elsewhere Thucydides (1.121.2) has the Corinthians say that the Peloponnesians are superior to the Athenians in both "numbers" (πλήθει) and "military experience" (ἐμπειρίᾳ πολεμικῇ), but it is clear that the latter is limited to land warfare.

The same themes emerge in commenting that the attempt of the Peloponnesians to rely on their "numbers" to add "confidence" to their "ignorance" (1.142.8 πλήθει τὴν ἀμαθίαν θρασύνοντες) during the ensuing maritime battles is destined to fail, as seamanship is rather a "skill" (142.9 τέχνη).[24] The Corinthians believe that they could learn to match the Athenians' "understanding" (ἐπιστήμη) through exercise, while the Athenians could never acquire their same innate good spirit and courage

---

[22] On this passage see Strauss 2008, 231-2; below (Section 3.2); also cf. Pericles on the Peloponnesians being "inexperienced" at sea (Thuc. 1.141.1 ἄπειροι), and Archidamos on the Athenians "most experienced at sea" (80.3 θαλάσσης ἐμπειρότατοι).
[23] Hence Phormio claims the Athenians are not inferior in "good spirit," εὐψυχία, but rather superior in confidence (θρασύτεροί) thanks to their own ἐμπειρία (89.3). See below on these keywords.
[24] On θάρσος (confidence, courage, resolve) and related terms in Thucydides see Huart 1968, 423-4, 426-31; on these keywords see de Romilly 1980, esp. 309-10.

(121.4 εὐψυχίᾳ).[25] This attitude certainly reinforced the cliché of the courageous but simple-minded Peloponnesian,[26] and was definitely suited to Thucydides' audience.

The aforementioned passages suggest that Thucydides was particularly concerned with questioning the Peloponnesian 'land-based' approach to naval warfare. This doctrine aimed to turn the naval engagement into a land battle on water (cf. 2.89.8) by employing masses of embarked soldiers on relatively static ships. In line with this approach, the Peloponnesians at sea relied on "numbers" (πλῆθος) and on typical hoplite values, such as "good spirit" (εὐψυχία) and "manly courage" (ἀνδρεία). The latter, especially, was a chief virtue in traditional land battle, as reflected by the famous Aristotelian passages in the *Nicomachean Ethics*.[27] However, Thucydides believed that sporting 'land' virtues at sea ultimately made the Peloponnesians inferior and naive in comparison to the Athenian navy, which relied on mobility and τέχνη, and took pride in representing an utterly different area of expertise from land engagements.[28] Relevant passages show how the 'Athenian way' is described through entirely different themes and perspectives.

3.2. THE ATHENIAN DOCTRINE: BOLDNESS, POWER AND THE MOB

Thucydides also employs the notions of "numbers" and "courage" for the Athenians. However, in certain instances, he chooses specific terms: τόλμα is frequently used to define the Athenian form of courage at sea,

---

[25] On εὐψυχία (a wider form of innate courage) and ἀνδρεία (military courage proper; cf. below) and their relationship in Thucydides, see Huart 1968, 418-25.
[26] A successful Athenian literary commonplace: see a sceptical approach in Powell 1988, ch. 4.
[27] On ἀνδρεία, especially in Thucydides, see Bassi 2003; on Aristotle see Sanford 2010. R. K. Balot has devoted studies to the theme of courage, mainly focusing on ἀνδρεία as distinctively Athenian (e.g. 2010, 89-90). Hence, his approach is rather different from the one I advocate.
[28] Cf. Thuc. 7.70.3, where ἀντιτέχνησις is referred to competing helmsmen (cf. Section 2.3 on this passage). The humiliation suffered by the Athenians at Syracuse was, in the first instance, ideologic, as they were forced to deploy "many archers and javelin throwers, a mob" (Thuc. 7.62.2 καὶ γὰρ τοξόται πολλοὶ καὶ ἀκοντισταὶ ἐπιβήσονται καὶ ὄχλος; on the syntax see Smith 1886, note to Thuc. 7.62.2): the last resort of a *pezomachia* ("infantry battle") over water prevented the (only) skill (ἐπιστήμη) they recognized as such, i.e. fast maneuvering. On ὄχλος ("mob") see Section 3.2.

while their numbers (of sailors) are sometimes expressed with the word ὄχλος. Both are strongly characterizing terms. Focusing on their occurences allows identification of further thematic patterns in Thucydides' narrative.

Although semantically connected to the idea of courage, τόλμα reflects a completely different form of extreme "daring", a "boldness" which goes beyond normal limits and proves dangerous for all parties involved. Unlike ἀνδρεία, τόλμα is not regularly associated with the military, nor was it always viewed as a commendable virtue in Greek literature. Moreover, it is normally used in reference to individuals.[29] Thucydides, on the other hand, tends to employ it in an essentially – or, at least, potentially – positive sense when referring to the Athenian forces as a whole.[30] Pericles declares that their daring (2.40.3 τολμᾶν), as well as their consideration (ἐκλογίζεσθαι), makes the Athenians stand out from other Greeks, to the point that both land and sea have been overcome by the Athenians' "boldness" (41.4 τῇ ἡμετέρᾳ τόλμῃ, "by our *tolma*"). Pericles also reminds us that, at the time of the Persian Wars, the Athenians made up for their lack of "power" (δύναμις) through their τόλμα (1.144.4). The association between Athenian boldness and the defence of Greece recurs several times in Thucydides: it celebrates the rise of a decisive 'Athenian spirit' facing the risk of complete destruction. The Athenians proudly boasted of their "most daring eagerness" against Xerxes' invasion (1.74.2 προθυμίαν δὲ καὶ πολὺ τολμηροτάτην) and even the Peloponnesians acknowledged the τόλμα the Athenians displayed against the Medes (1.90.1).[31] Once Athens gained both δύναμις and τόλμα after the Persian

---

[29] In Homeric poetry, the term usually means reckless courage, with (*Od.* 8.519) or without (9.322; *Il.* 12.50-1) military implications (cf. *Il.* 10.205 and *Od.* 17.284 on Odysseus' τολμήεις θυμός, "daring spirit"). Herodotus praises the τόλμα of Hegesistratus (9.37.3), Sperthias and Boulis (7.135.1). Despite Aristotle's interest in courage in the *Nicomachean Ethics* (Section 3.1), τόλμα and parent forms are rarely found in his *corpus*: one notable case is in *NE* 1117a 1-2, where τολμηρός is employed in an out of context reference to adulterers, as already by Euripides on the τόλμας οὐ καλὰς ("ignoble daring", transl. D. Kovacs) of adulterous women (*Hipp.* 413-4).

[30] See Huart 1968, 431-6; de Romilly 1980, esp. 315-7; cf. Bassi 2003, 31-2 and n. 19. As a personal trait, however, Thucydides does not necessarily employ the term in the same meaning: τόλμα is a (not always positive) typical characteristic of Alcibiades, among others (cf. Carter 1986, 13-4); cf. Harmodius and Aristogeiton's antityrannical attack as an "act of *tolma*" (Thuc. 6.54.1 τόλμημα), an "irrational (ἀλόγιστος) *tolma*" (59.1; cf. 56.3).

[31] This combined use persists in later tradition: Isocrates claims Athenians and Spartans "dared" (ἐτόλμων) to compete against the Persians (4.91; cf. Plut. *Vit.*

Wars, it became a major power and grounded its sovereignty (*arche*), as stated repeatedly through the words of Hermocrates of Syracuse (6.33.4) and of the Corinthians, according to whom the τόλμα of the Athenians was even greater than their δύναμις (1.70.3).

Other Greeks, the Peloponnesians in particular, are usually noted by Thucydides for their lack of τόλμα. As their manly courage is limited by their characteristic prudence, the Spartans, rather: "are used to daring as little as possible" (5.107.1 ἥκιστα ὡς ἐπὶ τὸ πολὺ τολμῶσιν; cf. 8.96.4). In Nicias' words, the Syracusan forces were militarily inferior to the Athenians due to their lack of τόλμα and, to an even greater extent, their lack of ἐπιστήμη (6.68.2). Prudence was a notorious trait of the Spartans, just as the notion of τόλμα aptly represented the Athenian attitude to sea warfare, which was based on hazardous manoeuvres, speed and timing.

Coming to the alternative way to define Athenian numbers, Thucydides occasionally employs ὄχλος, "mob", especially when referring to navy crews. To Archidamos, one of the advantages of the Athenians is their generic ὄχλος (1.80.3), apparently a thematic counterpart of the Peloponnesian πλῆθος, "numbers" (see Section 3.1). The term ὄχλος often defines, in a broad sense, the lower social masses.[32] This mob, the political weight and balance of the democracy, was held in low esteem by Thucydides, due to its typically erratic, irrational and impatient behaviour (cf. 4.28.3; 6.63.2); its tendency to suffer from political instability (6.17.2) and from manipulation (6.89.5; 7.8.2; 8.48.3, 86.5); its poor, virtually non-existent combat skills, which limited its military contribution to trireme crews, rather than to hoplites, archers and javelin throwers (6.20.4). In fact, hoplites are not usually considered ὄχλος, from whom they stand out, socially and militarily, due to their superior battlefield performance.[33] Hoplites and knights were counted separately from the (uncountable) casualties among the ὄχλος during the Athenian pestilence (3.87.3). The significant, circumstantial exception is found when hoplites are part of a

---

Arist. 14.4); he also employs the term to portray a "powerful boldness" required to "deal with the mob" (5.81; cf. below on ὄχλος). To Plutarch, Miltiades' exceptional feature of τόλμα and ἀνδρεία is tied to Themistocles' envy (*Mor.* 84c).

[32] See *LSJ*, s.v. ὄχλος, for its generally negative meaning in various contexts; the term is rare before Thucydides. For remarks on Thucydides' use of ὄχλος and its relation with ὅμιλος ("crowd", "throng", etc.), see Hunter 1988; Karpyuk 2000 for further occurrences; Brock 1991, 165 on ὄχλος as an oligarchic term for the poor.

[33] Thuc. 4.56.1; 4.126.6; 7.78.2 for supply carriers and ὄχλος in the army set apart from hoplites; cf. 6.64.1.

generic, oblivious mass, fooled by charismatic characters. In such cases, Thucydides employs ὄχλος to specifically denigrate some social and political attitudes, in particular during the events related to the Four Hundred: ὁ ὄχλος defines both the 'oligarchic' hoplites (8.92.9-10) manipulated by Theramenes in Athens (92.11) and the 'democratic' Athenian navy crews on Samos deceived by Alcibiades (8.86.5), specifically the ναυτικὸς ὄχλος, the "naval mob" (8.72.2; cf. 48.3).[34]

The lower classes, from which seamen usually came, receive little consideration in ancient sources. Despite their primary, importance to the 'Athenian doctrine' at sea, rowers and helmsmen are often protrayed as unreliable, subject to panic and mutiny, their losses scarcely recorded.[35] In contrast, *epibatai* seem to hold a greater prestige.[36] Hostility towards the 'mob of seamen', and the navy in general, is a notoriously recurring theme in literary sources. The moment when Themistocles "urged the Athenians to become seamen"[37] was seen as the catalyst of many evils in Athenian society. This is underlined by the numerous authoritative attacks prior to Aristotle's, who scornfully blamed the ναυτικὸς ὄχλος for having made

---

[34] See also Xenophon on the attitude of the ὄχλος toward the 'great deceivers': Alcibiades (*Hell.* 1.4.13), Theramenes (2.2.21); cf. Lysander (3.4.7). On the 'naval mob' see Strauss 2000, 275; van Wees 2007, 295-6.

[35] Sources on 'seamen' in Strauss 2000, 274-5, 261-2; Strauss 2008, esp. 227, 234; cf. Tzahos 2001, 578-9; also cf. the fearful chorus of sailors in Sophocles' *Ajax* (Osborne 2010, 247; but cf. Miller 2010, 333 on Aristophanes). On the scarce attention of sources on rower casualties see van Wees 2004, 63-4 (literary); Arrington 2011, esp. 204 (epigraphic); on the paucity of artistic depictions of naval warfare see Meyer 2005; Miller 2010, 326-34; Strauss 2000, esp. 264-6. For a sound reconsideration of the cultural importance of collective tombs of the war dead in Athens see, however, Low 2010, esp. 341-50. The Athenian 'naval catalogue' (*IG* I³ 1032; see Bakewell 2008) lists the *nautai* by name, although in the last hierarchical position of the crew. Obviously, citizen crewmen were still superior to slaves (Thuc. 7.13.2-14.1; cf. Lapini 1997, 36-7).

[36] On departing for Sicily, libations for the whole fleet were carried out by archons and *epibatai* (Thuc. 6.32.1); cf. van Wees 2001, 60 (on Thuc. 3.98.4 praising fallen Athenian *epibatai* hoplites); van Wees 2004, 210-11, 229-31, on the hierarchy of naval personnel and the high status of *epibatai;* van Wees 2007, 295-6 on hoplite-level prestige. On land battle ideals affecting a celebration of naval warfare in Athenian art, see Osborne 2010, 246-8. Perhaps the stele of Demokleides (see Strauss 2000, esp. 262-5) belonged to a regular hoplite who died while embarked.

[37] On Themistocles (cf. Section 1) as the father of the 'classical' Athenian navy see Herodotus (7.144.2 ἀναγκάσας θαλασσίους γενέσθαι Ἀθηναίους); cf. Thucydides' more generic remark (1.18.2); further sources below.

democracy too strong.[38] For example, the 5th century 'Old oligarch' openly contrasts the navy and hoplites:

> It is the demos who man the ships and impart power to the city; the steersmen, the boatswains, the pentekontarchoi, the look-out officers, and the shipwrights – these are the ones who impart power to the city, far more than the hoplites, the high-born, and the good men ([Xen.] *Ath. Pol.* 1.2).[39]

Most interesting is Plato's resentful, nostalgic view:

> Indeed, it would have profited them [the Athenians] to lose many times seven children, rather than, once they had became seamen instead of steadfast land hoplites, getting used to jump ashore frequently and run back at full speed to the ships, believing there is no shame in not dying boldly (τολμῶντας ἀποθνῄσκειν) at their posts when the enemies attack; and offering excuses, and readily throw away their arms and flee, as they say, a 'not dishonorable flight'. These are words usually coming from naval soldiery (ναυτική ὁπλιτεία) etc. (*Lg.* 4.706b-c).[40]

Plato, probably refering to transported troops, also attacks Athenian naval personnel in general by specifically arguing that the "naval soldiery" (ναυτική ὁπλιτεία) is different and inherently worse than the 'land' soldiers (hoplites).[41] Plato also includes the theme of τόλμα through the expression "dying boldly" (τολμῶντας ἀποθνῄσκειν). However, to him, boldness is a virtue only when facing death: his theory of courage in the *Laches*, in fact,

---

[38] *Pol.* 5.1304a; cf. 4.1297b; *Ath.Pol.* 41.2 on the eleventh constitution.
[39] ὅτι ὁ δῆμός ἐστιν ὁ ἐλαύνων τὰς ναῦς καὶ ὁ τὴν δύναμιν περιτιθεὶς τῇ πόλει, καὶ οἱ κυβερνῆται καὶ οἱ κελευσταὶ καὶ οἱ πεντηκόνταρχοι καὶ οἱ πρῳρᾶται καὶ οἱ ναυπηγοί, οὗτοί εἰσιν οἱ τὴν δύναμιν περιτιθέντες τῇ πόλει πολὺ μᾶλλον ἢ οἱ ὁπλῖται καὶ οἱ γενναῖοι καὶ οἱ χρηστοί (transl. E. C. Marchant, adapted). Relevant remarks on social and political points in Lapini 1997, 36-43. On "power" (δύναμις) see above.
[40] ἔτι γὰρ ἂν πλεονάκις ἑπτὰ ἀπολέσαι παῖδας αὐτοῖς συνήνεγκεν, πρὶν ἀντὶ πεζῶν ὁπλιτῶν μονίμων ναυτικοὺς γενομένους ἐθισθῆναι, πυκνὰ ἀποπηδῶντας, δρομικῶς εἰς τὰς ναῦς ταχὺ πάλιν ἀποχωρεῖν, καὶ δοκεῖν μηδὲν αἰσχρὸν ποιεῖν μὴ τολμῶντας ἀποθνῄσκειν μένοντας ἐπιφερομένων πολεμίων, ἀλλ᾽ εἰκυίας αὐτοῖς γίγνεσθαι προφάσεις καὶ σφόδρα ἑτοίμας ὅπλα τε ἀπολλῦσιν καὶ φεύγουσι δή τινας οὐκ αἰσχράς, ὥς φασιν, φυγάς. ταῦτα γὰρ ἐκ ναυτικῆς ὁπλιτείας ῥήματα φιλεῖ συμβαίνειν κτλ. (transl. R. G. Bury, adapted).
[41] Plutarch quotes Plato and adds a further uncredited (the nearby mention of Stesimbrotus, *FGrHist* 107/1002 F 2, is not enough to prove a 5th century source), eloquent accusation to Themistocles: that of having "robbed his fellow-citizens of spear and shield, and degraded the people of Athens to the rowing-pad and the oar" (*Vit. Them.* 4.4).

opposes ἀνδρεία, the true and only courage, to τόλμα and other irrational passions (197b).[42] Whereas Thucydides does consider τόλμα a military virtue overall, to Plato it really has no place in proper combat.

To summarise, Thucydides' vision of the 'Athenian way' at sea, characterised by τόλμα and ὄχλος, shows that his structured treatment of naval warfare is driven by strong ideological features. His criticism of different naval doctrines is part of a significant 5th century literary interest on the matter, generally focused on recurring major themes: reproaching the Athenians for having resorted to the navy at the expense of hoplite warfare, and segregating 'naval' hoplites, as a part of the *epibatai*, from 'land' or 'standard' hoplites. When comparing the two, the common view is that the former are unworthy of the title of hoplite, while the latter, when embarked, seem inherently out of place.

CONCLUSIONS

Two related themes have been analysed: the specific figure of the *epibates* and various aspects of Thucydides' narrative on naval warfare in a wider 5th century context.

Due to the peculiar nature of sea warfare, the 'fluid' figure of the *epibates* reflects a part of the ideological debate which literary tradition has built around naval warfare. While potentially being a 'hoplite' (Section 2.1), trained to fight in formation as in land warfare (Section 2.3), the *epibates* also had to regularly employ both thrown and melee weapons, to rely on mobility, and to play a flexible role (Section 2.2). Sometimes, *epibatai* were defined as peculiar, lower grade hoplites, while hoplites from the list (*ek katalogou*) were sometimes employed as *epibatai* (Sections 2.1, 3.2). When disembarked, these soldiers were generally defined and deployed – and thus, presumably, equipped – as hoplites. When embarked, however, none strictly fought as land hoplites did – or were supposed to do – in terms of outfit and tactical roles.

Such a peculiar status, essentially questioning the very essence and self definition of hoplite combat, could be perceived as disturbing to an ideology in which land hoplite battle was the archetypical conflict. In this

---

[42] Cf. the definition of ἀνδρεῖος (*Lach.* 190e); on the *Laches* as a criticism of the Athenian Sicilian disaster see Foley 2009, esp. 214-19. See de Romilly 1980, esp. 310-15, on Thucydides' and Plato's approaches. On Plato's idea of hoplite warfare cf. Hanson 2000, 219-20.

regard, it must be noted that the notion of the hoplite as a close combat soldier, essentially defined by spear and shield,[43] as well as the separation between hoplites, light troops and missile throwers, from both a military and ideological perspective, may have started as late as the Persian Wars.[44] Hence, the figure of the *epibates* might be more in line with an earlier military doctrine, later perceived as conflicting in comparison to the hoplite model and idea of struggle. The word ὁπλίτης itself, which could be preferably, literally translated as "man at arms", is not found earlier than Pindar; in poetry, at least at the time of the Persian Wars, men fighting with spears on both ships and land could be referred to as αἰχμηταί.[45] The way their military and social identity has been treated by sources shows that *epibatai* represent a significant aspect of Greek warfare, in terms of definition, tactical flexibility, cultural impact. Their apparent secondary role in the Athenian doctrine seems mostly due to the ideological bias of literary sources.

In this regard, Thucydides generally gives a significant literary elaboration on the theme of naval warfare, vigorously relying on thematic keywords. One of his aims is certainly to promote and prove the superiority of the Athenian doctrine to the obsolescence and inadequacy of the Peloponnesian. His position and occasional self-contradictions probably reflect purely narrative purposes.

---

[43] See van Wees 2004, 209-10. Hoplites only circumstantially hurl their spear, especially when holding higher ground: see Xen. *Hell.* 3.5.20; 4.6.11; 5.4.42; 2.4.12-6 (less explicit). Also note that to Callinus "hurling the dart" (ἀκοντίζω, apparently referring to the spear) with one's last breath, i.e. as a last resort, was part of the "manly fighting" (fr. 1 W. ll. 5-6 ἀνδρὶ μάχεσθαι). On missiles as low grade weapons in Greek culture see van Wees 2004, 65. My view on the operational use of *epibatai* agrees, to some extent, with that of Rawlings 2000 on the flexibility of hoplites: both may be cases of Greek literary ideology differing from practice.

[44] On the 'hoplite ideal' see Hanson 2000, esp. 206, 219-20; Krentz 2002, esp. 29-30 (armaments), 36-7 (ideology); van Wees 2001, esp. 49, 51-3 (on the inconsistency of the 'hoplite class'), 56-61 (also on the *thetes* voluntary enrolling in the navy to acquire wealth); De Ste. Croix 2004, *passim*; Hunt 2007, 125-7, on military and cultural hierarchy, incl. 'hoplites' vs. navy. On the general hostility of Athenian sources toward light troops see Trundle 2010, esp. 141-4 (cf. Section 2.1). Also cf. the 'ideological' opposition between Greek spear and Persian bow developed on Greek art after the Persian Wars: Miller 2010, 312-13.

[45] 'Simonides' *FGE* 46 l. 3 *ap. Anth. Pal.* 7.258 (on which see Bravi 2006, 84, dating the poem to the Eurymedon campaign, c. 465); a few remarks in Zaccarini 2013, 16. On the meaning of 'hoplite' see Lazenby and Whitehead 1996; van Wees 2006, 355.

Thucydides reports that Athens acknowledged the naval power of some Peloponnesians, especially Corcyraeans (1.44.2), while elsewhere generally dismissing them as inferior at sea (Section 3.1). Whereas Thucydides himself writes that Athenian maritime expertise and power goes back to the Second Persian War (Section 3.2), elsewhere he claims it was longstanding (Section 3.1). This is a literary overstatement, as Athens, in comparison to many Peloponnesians and other Greeks, was rather a child prodigy in naval warfare, developing a late, strong tradition in a relatively short time.[46] Thucydides builds a strong contrast (Section 3) between the amateurish 'Peloponnesian way' of fighting sea battles by relying on courage and land values, and the opposing, dedicated and professional Athenian doctrine of boldness: the close association between Athenian τόλμα and δύναμις (Section 3.2) is particularly meaningful as the latter is, essentially, a major, long term cause of the war against Sparta (cf. 1.118.2 on ἡ δύναμις τῶν Ἀθηναίων, "the power of the Athenians"). Therefore, in Thucydides' view, the Athenian naval doctrine and supremacy are dramatically tied to native Athenian traits, to the past glorious defence against the Persians, and to the inescapability of the contemporary Peloponnesian War.

Thucydides' narrative on naval warfare is structured on a number of different layers reaching far beyond military history or theory. His use of recurring keywords reflects his view of naval warfare as a literary means to stress further, cross-thematic issues. Ultimately, Thucydides' theory of two opposing philosophies of sea combat seems to address the needs of a strong cultural bias: it should be interpreted, first of all, as a refined representation of irreconcilable cultural enmity between Athenians and Peloponnesians rather than a strictly factual, rigid military dichotomy. Furthermore, by criticising the fleet, its doctrines and its personnel, sources express the ongoing debate on the social, ideological and political developments of 5th century Athens. The figure of the *epibates* embodies the significant contradiction between Athens' reliance on the navy and its cultural idiosyncrasy against the model of war it represents:[47] from a tactical point of view, Athenian culture might have overcome the rules of hoplite engagement, but had not managed to do so from a strictly ideological perspective. The literary reception of naval warfare represents

---

[46] On archaic navies see de Souza 1998; van Wees 2004, 206-7; further studies in Zaccarini 2013, 21 n. 44.

[47] On the Athenian paradox of relying on the navy to ground the empire and, at the same time, maintaining a dominating hoplite ideology, see Cartledge 1998, esp. 55-6, 62-5.

a significant case-study both on Thucydides' narrative technique and on Athenian self-definition, identity, and culture.

BIBLIOGRAPHY

Arrington, N. T. (2011) "Inscribing defeat: the commemorative dynamics of the Athenian casualty lists," *Classical Antiquity* 30.2, 179-212.
Bakewell, G. (2008) "Trierarchs' records and the Athenian naval catalogue (*IG* I^3 1032)," in E. Anne Mackay (ed) *Orality, literacy, memory in the ancient Greek and Roman world,* Leiden and Boston, 143-62.
Balot, R. K. (2010) "Democratizing courage in classical Athens," in Pritchard, D. M., 88-108.
Baragwanath, E. (2012) "Returning to Troy: Herodotus and the mythic discourse of his own time," in E. Baragwanath and M. de Bakker (eds) *Myth, truth, and narrative in Herodotus*, Oxford, 287-313.
Bassi, K. (2003) "The semantics of manliness in ancient Greece," in R. M. Rosen and I. Sluiter (eds) *Studies in manliness and courage in classical antiquity*, Leiden and Boston, 25-56.
Bravi, L. (2006) *Gli epigrammi di Simonide e le vie della tradizione*, Roma.
Brock, R. (1991) "The emergence of democratic ideology," *Historia* 40.2, 160-9.
Carter, L. B. (1986) *The quiet Athenian,* Oxford.
Cartledge, P. (1998) "The *machismo* of the Athenian empire – or the reign of the *phaulus*?," in L. Foxhall and J. Salmon (eds) *When men where men. Masculinity, power and identity in classical antiquity*, London and New York, 54-67
De Romilly, J. (1980) "Réflexions sur le courage chez Thucydide et chez Platon," *Revue des études greques* 93, 307-23.
De Souza, P. (1998) "Towards thalassocracy? Archaic Greek naval developments," in N. Fisher and H. van Wees (eds) *Archaic Greece. New approaches and new evidence*, London and Swansea, 271-93.
—. (2013) "War at sea," in B. Campbell and L. A. Tritle (eds) *The Oxford handbook of warfare in the classical world,* New York, 369-94.
De Ste. Croix, G. E. M. (2004) "The Solonian census classes and the qualifications for cavalry and hoplite service," in G. E. M. De Ste. Croix, *Athenian democratic origins and other essays,* edited by David Harvey and Robert Parker with the assistance of Peter Thonemann, Oxford, 5-72.
Foley, R. (2009) "The better part of valor: the role of wisdom in Plato's

Laches," *History of Philosophy Quarterly* 26.3, 213-33.
Gomme, A. W., Andrewes, A. and Dover, K. J. (1981) *A historical commentary on Thucydides* 5, *Book VIII*, Oxford.
Hanson, V. D. (2000) "Hoplite battle as ancient Greek warfare. When, where and why?," in van Wees, H., 201-32.
Hornblower, S. (1991-96-2008) *A commentary on Thucydides.* 3 vols., Oxford.
Huart, P. (1968) *Le vocabulaire de l'analyse psychologique dans l'oeuvre de Thucydide*, Paris.
Hunt, P. (2007) "Military forces," in Sabin, P. *et al.*, 108-46.
Hunter, V. (1988) "Thucydides and the sociology of the crowd," *Classical Journal* 84.1, 17-30.
Jordan, B. (1972) *The Athenian navy in the classical period. A study on the Athenian naval administration and military organization in the fifth and fourth centuries B.C.*, Berkeley, CA.
Karpyuk, S. (2000) "Crowd in archaic and classical Greece," *Hyperboreus* 6.1, 79-102.
Krentz, P. (2002) "Fighting by the rules. The invention of the hoplite agôn," *Hesperia* 71, 23-39.
—. (2007) "War," in Sabin, P. *et al.*, 147-85.
Lapini, W. (1997) *Commento all'*Athenaion Politeia *dello Pseudo-Senofonte*, Firenze.
Lazenby, J. F. and Whitehead, D. (1996) "The myth of the hoplite's *hoplon*," *Classical Quarterly* 46.1, 27-33.
Low, P. (2010) "Commemoration of the war dead in classical Athens: remembering defeat and victory," in Pritchard, D. M., 341-58.
Macan, R. W. (1908) *Herodotus. The seventh, eighth, & ninth books* 1, Part 1, London.
Meyer, M. (2005) "Bilder und Vorbilder. Zu Sinn und Zweck von Siegesmonumenten Athens in klassischer Zeit," *Jahreshefte des Österreichischen Archäologischen Instituts* 74, 277-312.
Miller, M. C. (2010) "I am Eurymedon: tensions and ambiguities in Athenian war imagery," in Pritchard, D. M., 304-38.
Morrison, J. S., Coates, J. F. and Rankov, N.B. (2000), *The Athenian trireme. The history and reconstruction of an ancient Greek warship*, Cambridge (2nd ed.; 1st ed. 1986).
Naiden, F. (2009) "Spartan naval performance in the Decelean War, 413-404 BCE," *Journal of Military history* 73.3, 729-44.
Osborne, R. (2010) "Democratic ideology, the events of war and the iconography of Attic funerary sculpture," in Pritchard, D. M., 245-65.
Powell, A. (1988) *Athens and Sparta. Constructing Greek political and*

social history from 478 B.C., London.
Pritchard, D. M. (2000) "Tribal participation and solidarity in fifth century Athens: a summary", *Ancient History* 30.2, 104-18.
—. (ed) (2010) *War, democracy and culture in classical Athens*, Cambridge.
Rawlings, L. (2000) "Alternative agonies. Hoplite martial and combat experiences beyond the phalanx," in van Wees, H., 233-59.
Sabin, P., van Wees, H. and Whitby, M. (eds) (2007) *The Cambridge history of Greek and Roman warfare* 1, *Greece, the Hellenistic world and the rise of Rome*, Cambridge.
Shear, J. L. (1995) "Fragments of Naval Inventories from the Athenian Agora," *Hesperia* 64, 179-224.
Sanford, J. J. (2010) "Are you man enough? Aristotle and courage," *International Philosophical Quarterly* 50.4, 200, 431-45.
Smith, C. F. (1886) *Commentary on Thucydides Book 7*, Boston.
Strauss, B. S. (2000) "Perspectives on the death of fifth-century Athenian seamen," in van Wees, H., 261-83.
—. (2008) "Naval battles and sieges," in Sabin, P. *et al.*, 223-36.
Trundle, M. (2010) "Light troops in classical Athens," in Pritchard, D. M., 139-60.
Tzahos, E. E. (2001) "A trireme on a funerary lekythos," in H. Tzalas (ed) *Tropis 6. International Symposium on Ship construction in antiquity, Lamia, 28, 29, 30 August 1996. Proceedings*, Athens, 575-88.
Van Wees, H. (ed) (2000) *War and violence in ancient Greece*, London.
—. (2001) "The myth of the middle-class army: military and social status in ancient Athens," in T. Bekker-Nielsen and L. Hannestad (eds) *War as a cultural and social force. Essays on warfare in antiquity*, Copenhagen, 45-71.
—. (2004) *Greek warfare. Myths and realities*, London.
—. (2006) "Mass and elite in Solon's Athens: the property classes revisited," in J. H. Blok and A. P. M. H. Lardinois (eds) *Solon of Athens. New historical and philological approaches*, Leiden and Boston, 351-89.
—. (2007) "War and society," in Sabin, P. *et al.*, 273-99.
Zaccarini, M. (2013) "Dalla "triere leggera" alla "triere pesante": l'evoluzione della flotta ateniese tra Temistocle e Cimone," *Rivista di Studi militari* 2, 7-27.

Chapter Thirteen

Commemorating War Dead and Inventing Battle Heroes: Heroic Paradigms and Discursive Strategies in Ancient Athens and Phocis[1]

Dr. Elena Franchi and Dr. Giorgia Proietti

Remembering the War: Social Practices of Memory, Identity, and Discourse

Commemoration of the war dead and war in general, in antiquity, is receiving extensive and multifaceted attention in modern scholarship. In recent years, more than ever, it is approached not only as a type of appendix to ancient warfare studies, but it is also investigated as a social act of memory, which can significantly contribute to our understanding of ancient societies.[2] Nonetheless, despite the growing and more sophisticated attention paid by recent research to the nature and functioning of social memory, it is still mostly examined on the basis of a rigid classification of both ancient documentary evidence and modern categories.

---

[1] Sections 1 and 4 are written by Giorgia Proietti and Elena Franchi, section 2 by Giorgia Proietti, section 3 by Elena Franchi. We would like to thank Geoff Lee, the organizer of the International Ancient Warfare Conference (Aberystwyth, 18th-20th September 2013), where this paper was first delivered, and both the editors of the volume and the anonymous referees for their helpful comments on the draft of this essay.
[2] *E.g.* Chaniotis 2005; Beck – Wiemer 2010; Low 2010; 2012; Arrington 2011.

This paper argues instead, that it must be explored in the light of the fluidity which is intrinsic to every social practice of memory: Commemoration of the war dead is a dynamic process, the aims and contents of which change over time, as do the associated social frames and needs for identity.[3] Through two historical examples, different in space and time, this paper shows how the commemorative acts in themselves, and the heroic pattern they express, far from being stable and watertight, are instead embedded in a complex network of discursive practices which give them meaning (only that meaning and only in that given space and time). We refer to the concept proposed by Michel Foucault in his *Archaeology of Knowledge* when we use the term "discursive strategy".[4] According to Foucault a discursive strategy is a consequence of arranging and manipulating concepts, i.e. "of giving them rules for their use, inserting them into regional coherences and thus constituting conceptual architectures".[5]

In other words, "the history of a concept is not wholly and entirely that of its progressive refinement, its continuously increasing rationality, its abstraction gradient, but that of its various fields of constitution and validity, that of its successive rules of use, that of the many theoretical contexts in which it developed and matured".[6]

As such, a discursive strategy intrinsically depends on the time and space in which it is built up, and is inherently affected by contingent needs for identity. In this paper, both 5th century Athenians and 4th century Phocians are seen as social networks creating new meanings through discursive strategies. A social network here is meant in the sense of 'network sociology', therefore as a set of nodes, linked by ties, where the changing of the ties (which are usually multiple from the very beginning) determines the changing of the configuration of the whole network.[7] As the sociologist Harrison White, has underlined, "a central claim of the

---

[3] On the concepts of social memory and related social practices, see Connerton 1989; Assmann 2011; on the concept of social frames, as a determining factor for collective memories and identities, see Halbwachs 1925; 1950, discussed by Giangiulio 2010; Proietti 2012a, 13-19.
[4] Foucault 1972, 64, and elsewhere.
[5] Foucault 1972, 70.
[6] Foucault 1972, 4.
[7] For a basic introduction to the concept of network see the introduction, by the same authors, in Malkin, Constantakopoulou and Panagopoulou 2009, 1-11, which includes a select bibliography.

theory [the network theory] is that identities are triggered by contingency".[8] Esther Eidinow, drawing on White's work, has recently emphasized the relationship between networks, knowledge and identity: "networks are not only social but 'cognitive', and participation in a network helps to create meaning. Through this process of creating meaning, networks offer a way of constructing individual and group identities and vice versa."[9] Identities, therefore, always emerge in response to contingency, and from interactions with other identities: both the identities themselves and the new meanings they create are elastic, and likely to change over time. In this sense, exploring through the prism of discursive practices and social networks the commemoration of war dead, and war in general, in a given space and time, may shed some light on the mentality behind them in *that* space and *that* time.

COMMEMORATING WAR DEAD IN 5TH CENTURY ATHENS: THE *POLIS* DISCOURSE ON CIVIC HEROISM[10]

The space and time I will focus on is 5th century Athens, and the war dead I will refer to are those who fell both in the Persian Wars and in the following decades. Modern scholarship has always tried to fit them into the traditional binary model which distinguishes between heroes of cult and heroes of epic. Some scholars say that they were the object of a heroic cult, while others say they were not worshipped on a cultic level but shared the same privileged status as the Homeric heroes.[11] On the basis of an overall re-examination of the ancient evidence I will call this dichotomic view into question. I will argue, on the one hand, that the definition of heroes in cult is not supported by contemporary evidence, on the other hand, that the definition of heroes of epic is not sufficiently appropriate either. A new pattern of heroism was established for the war dead in 5th century Athens, both those who fell in the Persian Wars and

---

[8] White 2008, 5.
[9] Eidinow 2011, 12-13. On the application of the network theory in ancient studies see also Collar 2007; Malkin 2003; 2011.
[10] All English translations of Greek texts are by the author, unless otherwise specified.
[11] The binary model opposing 'heroes of cult' and 'heroes of epic' was first formulated by West 1978, 370-73; Nagy 1979, 114-17, 151-73. Today the distinction between cultic practices and heroic narratives is taken as a starting point for a more fluid and variegated appreciation of the types and levels of heroism in ancient Greece. For this perspective see Whitley 1995; Stevanovic 2008; Jones 2010. For the heroisation of historical people see in general Boheringer 1996.

those who died in the following decades, which can only be fully appreciated through the prism of the discursive paradigm.

'Hero cult' is a complex phenomenon. Neither 'hero' nor 'cult' can, of course, be intended metaphorically: hero-cult in the strictest sense points to a religious activity regularly carried out by a community towards special mortals who had died but continued to affect the living.[12]

The hypothesis of a heroic cult of the war dead in 5th century Athens is based on the following ancient evidence:

a) Concerning the Athenians fallen at Marathon, the *Marathonomachoi*
- some ephebic inscriptions dating to the late Hellenistic age, according to which the ephebes crowned the funerary monument of the *Marathonomachoi* (both the one on the battlefield and the one in Athens), competed in athletic games and offered sacrifices;[13]
- the literary definition of the *Marathonomachoi* as heroes given by 2nd century AD sources: according to Pausanias they were worshipped as heroes by the local inhabitants.[14]

b) Concerning all the Greeks fallen at Plataea
- 5th and 4th century sources recording the customary honors performed every year by the Plataeans at the tombs of those who were buried on their land;[15]

---

[12] Modern bibliography on hero-cult is certainly expansive. For a recent *status quaestionis* see Ekroth 2007; 2009; Bravo 2009.
[13] *IG* II-III³ 1.5, 1313, 15-18 (176/5 BC): "παραγενόμενοι δὲ καὶ εἰς Μα[ραθῶ]να [τό τε] πολυανδρεῖον ἐστεφάνωσαν καὶ ἐπιτάφιον ἀγῶνα ἐποίησαν, καθάπερ ἐ[πὶ νν] [τοῦ] πρὸς τῶι ἄστει πολυανδρείου γίνεσθαι νόμιμόν ἐστιν, καλὸν εἶναι κρίνον[τες ἀξίως τ]ιμᾶν τοὺς ἠγωνισμένους ἐνδοξότατα περὶ τῆς ἐλευθερίας." ("The (ephebes) also visited Ma[ratho]n and (there) crowned [the p]olyandreion and performed a funeral contest, according to what is customarily done [in front] of the city polyandreion, since they judged it a fine thing to pay [due] honour to those who fought most brilliantly for freedom." (transl. by Matthaiou 2003, 197). Compare also *IG* II² 1006, ll. 26-27; 69-70 (122/1 BC).
[14] Paus. 1.32.3: "σέβονται δὲ οἱ Μαραθώνιοι τούτους τε οἳ παρὰ τὴν μάχην ἀπέθανον ἥρωας ὀνομάζοντες" (The Marathonians worship those who died in the fighting, calling them heroes). For the fallen at Marathon as heroes during the Second Sophistic see also Ael. Arist. *Defence of the Four* [3] 188 Lenz-Behr.
[15] Thuc. 3.58.4 specifically refers to *aparchai*, i.e. first-fruit offerings, among the customary honours due to the fallen: "ἀποβλέψατε γὰρ ἐς πατέρων τῶν ὑμετέρων θήκας, οὓς ἀποθανόντας ὑπὸ Μήδων καὶ ταφέντας ἐν τῇ ἡμετέρᾳ ἐτιμῶμεν κατὰ

- a mid-3rd century Plataean inscription (the so called 'decree of Glaukon', ca. 261-246 BC), which records commemorative games for the fallen;[16]
- the different types of sacrifices which, according to Plutarch, were offered to the fallen during the pan-Hellenic festival of the *Eleutheria*.[17]

c) Concerning the Athenians who fell all throughout the 5th century, during the nearly permanent status of war following the Persian wars:
- 5th century literary evidence about a public funeral oration, which was given every year for the fallen of that year (the well-known *logos epitaphios*);[18]
- some 5th century prize-vases, which define themselves as "Athenians prizes for those who fell in war",[19] and 4th century literary evidence recording the annual funeral game for the fallen (the so-called *agon epitaphios*);[20]

ἔτος ἕκαστον δημοσίᾳ ἐσθήμασί τε καὶ τοῖς ἄλλοις νομίμοις, ὅσα τε ἡ γῆ ἡμῶν ἀνεδίδου ὡραῖα, πάντων ἀπαρχὰς ἐπιφέροντες, εὖνοι μὲν ἐκ φιλίας χώρας, ξύμμαχοι δὲ ὁμαίχμοις ποτὲ γενομένοις" (Look at the tombs of your fathers, slain by the Medes and buried in our country, whom year by year we have publicly honored with garments and all other dues, and the first fruits of all that our land produced in their season, as friends from a friendly country and once allies to our old companions in arms); see also Isocr. 14.61.

[16] "[...] καὶ τὸν ἀγῶνα ὅν τιθέσσιν οἱ Ἕλληνες ἐπὶ τοῖς ἀνδράσιν τοῖς ἀγαθοῖς καὶ ἀγωνισαμένοις πρὸς τοὺς βαρβάρους ὑπὲρ τῆς τῶν Ἑλλήνων ἐλευθερίας" (the contest which the Greeks celebrate on the tomb of the heroes who fought against the barbarians for the freedom of the Greeks). See *SEG* 1977, 65; Étienne and Piérart 1975.

[17] Plut. *De Mal. Her.* 42 872f, where he speaks of the most common form of sacrifices, the *enagismata* (i.e. the destruction sacrifices, or holocausts); *Arist.* 21.1.5, where he extensively describes a less common, typically Boeotian form, that of the *haimakouria* (on which see Ekroth 2002, 171-72*)*.

[18] Thuc. 2.34.1-6; Stesimbr. *FGrHist* 107 F 9 (*apud* Aristot. *Rhet.* 1365a 32-33; see also Plut. *Vit. Per.* 8.9; 29.4-5); Gorg. fr. 6 D.-K., ll. 7-32. The *logos epitaphios* is thought to have been introduced soon after the Persian Wars: among many others, see Thomas 1989, 208; Parker 1996, 134-35.

[19] *IG* I³ 523; 524; 525, which bear around their rim the inscription "Ἀθεναῖοι ἆθλα ἐπὶ τοῖς ἐν τοῖ πολέμοι", and equivalent expressions. These vases (dating from c. 480 to 450 BC) were found in different areas of Athens and Attica: see Vanderpool 1966; Amandry 1971.

[20] Lys. 2.80 speaks about contests of strength and knowledge and wealth ("ἀγῶνες [...] ῥώμης καὶ σοφίας καὶ πλούτου"); Plat. *Menex.* 249b-c speaks about contests in athletics and horse-racing and music of every kind ("ἀγῶνας γυμνικοὺς

- Demosthenes' isolated record of public sacrifices to the war dead.[21]

Let us try to put all of this in some order. What are the problems with inferring from this framework proof of a hero-cult of the war dead since the immediate post-war period? If we consider the evidence concerning the Persian War dead, the first obvious problem lies in its chronology: it is mostly late, Hellenistic at the earliest. The ephebic inscriptions about the *Marathonomachoi*, the account of the *Eleutheria* by Plutarch, and the veneration of the *Marathonomachoi* as heroes as attested by Pausanias, belong therefore to another 'discourse' of commemoration. Starting from Hellenistic times, Persian War dead came, in fact, to be included in a complex network of memories, symbols, values, and images of the past which were provided with a founding relevance for the present:[22] It is this new role as 'founding heroes' within Greek cultural memory which in turn determines the commemorative acts they received. In other words, we are dealing with a web of meanings which has an inherent tie with contingency, and hence works and makes sense only in that specific context, and cannot be automatically moved back over the centuries. Once Hellenistic and

---

καὶ ἱππικοὺς [...] καὶ μουσικῆς πάσης"). According to Demosth. 60.36.6, the fallen were judged worthy of honours such as sacrifices and games for all future time ("σεμνὸν δέ γ' ἀγήρως τιμὰς καὶ μνήμην ἀρετῆς δημοσίᾳ κτησαμένους ἐπιδεῖν, καὶ θυσιῶν καὶ ἀγώνων ἠξιωμένους ἀθανάτων").

[21] Demosth. 60.36.6: see *supra*, n. 20. I am intentionally not considering the sacrifices cited in Aristot. *Ath. Pol.* 58.1, regarding the public honors performed by the polemarch to both the war dead and the tyrannicides: "ὁ δὲ πολέμαρχος θύει μὲν θυσίας τῇ τε Ἀρτέμιδι τῇ ἀγροτέρᾳ καὶ τῷ Ἐνυαλίῳ, διατίθησι δ' ἀγῶνα τὸν ἐπιτάφιον {καὶ} τοῖς τετελευτηκόσιν ἐν τῷ πολέμῳ καὶ Ἁρμοδίῳ καὶ Ἀριστογείτονι ἐναγίσματα ποιεῖ" (The polemarch offers sacrifices to Artemis the Huntress and to Enyalius, and arranges the funeral games in honor of those who have fallen in war, and offers sacrifices to Harmodius and Aristogeiton). Starting from Canyon's edition in 1891, the second *kai* in the text clearly needs, in fact, to be expunged: the result is that the *enagismata* are linked with the tyrannicides only, and not with the fallen. Compare Pollux 8.91: "ὁ δὲ πολέμαρχος θύει μὲν Ἀρτέμιδι ἀγροτέρᾳ καὶ τῷ Ἐνυαλίῳ, διατίθησι δὲ τὸν ἐπιτάφιον ἀγῶνα τῶν ἐν πολέμῳ ἀποθανόντων, καὶ τοῖς περὶ Ἁρμόδιον ἐναγίζει", where the polemarch arranges the funeral games in honor of those who died in war and offers sacrifices to Harmodios. More comments and bibliographical references on Aristoteles' passage are provided by Ekroth 2002, 83-85; Shear 2012, 108-109.

[22] On the memory of the Persian Wars in Hellenistic and Roman times there is a vast bibliography: see most recently Spawforth 1994; Oudot 2010; Chaniotis 2012; Proietti 2012b, 108ff. More specifically on the ephebic honours to the war dead see Newby 2005; on *enagismata* as the distinctive feature of war dead cult in Roman times see Ekroth 2002, 81-82.

Roman sources are put aside, what evidence is left to highlight the status of the war dead in 5th century Athens? Is there any contemporary evidence from which we can infer that they were cultic heroes? The answer, in my opinion, is no.

First, the war dead were indeed the focus of some cults, but not as heroes: they just received the same customary honours, inclusive of offerings and sacrifices, which were due to the ordinary dead.[23] It is in this perspective that we must view the offerings brought to the fallen by the Plataeans on behalf of all the Greeks: the burial of the war dead at Plataea, though organized according to their belonging to the different *poleis*,[24] was conceived as a sort of national cemetery; given this supranational character the Plataeans were appointed, as local inhabitants, to offer to the war dead the funerary honors which were due by custom.

Second, war dead received some special honors, but these were not cultic. Despite the arguments adduced by Loraux, neither the funeral oration nor the funeral games implied, in fact, a cult: they were not celebrated every year for the same group of fallen, but every year for those who had fallen in that year.[25] They were honorific activities carried out just once by the *polis* to its fallen citizens.[26]

Further considerations lead towards this very perspective focused on civic honorific practice. First, as Polly Low has recently pointed out, war dead were buried in the outer *Kerameikos*, together with lawgivers, the tyrannicides, and other civic benefactors: as were theirs, the tombs of the war dead were not heroic burials (*heroa*), but honorific burials.[27] Second,

---

[23] On the importance of the collective commemoration of the ordinary dead within the *polis*, and the rituals implicated, see Georgoudi 1988. On the contiguity of the ritual practices, such as holocaustic sacrifices offered to both the ordinary and the war dead, see Welwei 1991; Ekroth 2002, 74ff.; Parker 2005.
[24] As Herodotus (9.85.1) records.
[25] Loraux 1986, 39-42. She herself admits that funeral orations never define war dead as heroes, nor give any hints to ritual activities, but she ascribes this feature to the alleged intentional suppression of the religious in favour of a thoroughly civic perspective.
[26] As were their private aristocratic precedents: see Roller 1982; Kyle 1987. In this perspective see most recently Mari 2012.
[27] Low 2010. Incidentally, the fact itself that they were buried outside the city gates, on an ontological level means that they were impure, a source of *miasma* (i.e. pollution), and therefore not heroes. On the concept of *miasma* see Parker 1983.

ancient sources themselves insist on speaking about civic honour (*timé*): *timé*, not cult, was the universal acknowledgement of the war dead.[28] Third, the 'immortality' which is often associated with the war dead,[29] in no way points to a concrete *post-mortem* existence:[30] the immortality is clearly that of renown, in other words the Homeric *athanatos kleos*, i.e. everlasting fame.[31]

This last consideration leads us to approach the other side of the question mentioned at the beginning: if war dead were not heroes of cult, shall we say that they were instead heroes of epic?[32] No, I do not think the metaphor of epic heroism is in itself a sufficient definition. On the one hand, it is clear that war dead were honored in ways that could make them resemble Homeric heroes. Fifth century Athenian civic discourse about the war dead indeed rested on epic-aristocratic patterns. Incineration on the battlefield, funeral games, language and style of the epitaphs, and iconographic representations of *monomachiai* were all deliberate references to the world of the Homeric heroes.[33] On the other hand, however, this manifold epic legacy was systematically re-shaped, re-semantized and coalesced around a new pattern of civic heroism, where individual aristocratic performance in search for personal glory was replaced by the collective action of the citizens towards the common good.[34] In other words, the epic pattern of heroism, which in archaic times stood in a relationship of continuity and contiguity with individual warrior aristocrats, in post-Cleisthenic times instead comes to be embedded within a new honorific and commemorative discourse of civic heroism.

---

[28] See for instance: Lys. 2.80; Demosth. 18.208; Plat. *Leg.* 947b-e; Plat. *Menex.* 249b-c; *IG* II-III[3] 1.5, 1313, 15-18, where public *timai* always go together with the war dead as *agathoi andres*, not heroes.
[29] Simon. fr. 11 W^2, 27-28; Thuc. 2.43.2; Lys. 2.79-81; Hyper. 6.24; 42.
[30] As some have instead argued: Boedecker 1998; Currie 2005, 89-119.
[31] On this point see Steiner 1999; Bremmer 2006.
[32] As some have proposed: see above all Whitley 1994 on the *Maratonomachoi*.
[33] For Homeric burials in Classical Athens see Guggisberg 2008; for funeral games as nostalgic reminiscences of epic practice see Shapiro 1991, 639 ff.; for the tendency to ideally reduce battles to epic-flavour *monomachiai* see Lendon 2005, 61-65.
[34] In this perspective see also Georgoulaki 1996; Prandi 2003. Also in favour of a new *status* of the war dead are Welwei 1991; Parker 1996, 135-37.

To conclude, we can recognize in the status of the war dead in 5th century Athens a new pattern of heroism, which does not fit the traditional dichotomic model of cultic/epic heroism. When dealing with ancient documentary evidence stretching so far in time, we must remember that not only the facts changed, but also the ideas behind them; in this case, not only the rituals and narratives concerning the war dead, but also the very pattern of war heroism. War dead in classical Athens came to be at the core of a complex web of discursive strategies carried out by the *polis* in order to fulfill new needs for identity, to commemorate war and to honor its new civic benefactors: therefore, according to the new historical situation, its social frames and cognitive networks, a new pattern of civic heroism was shaped.

COMMEMORATING WAR AND WAR DEAD IN 4TH CENTURY PHOCIS: INVENTING NEW HEROES FOR OLD BATTLES

The aim of the second part of this paper is to show how 4th century Phocians built up a discursive strategy which turned an archaic tradition about an archaic war into an 'identity-founding' war, which is referred to as the war fought by Phocians against the Thessalians at the end of the 6th century. In the 4th century, during or shortly after the so-called Third Sacred War, the Phocians transformed the archaic tradition of this war into an identity-founding event for the Phocian *ethnos*: the result of this re-shaping of tradition was a complex discursive strategy.

This discursive strategy made use of the initiation pattern, and invented new heroes and new forms of commemoration. This was expressed through a) storytelling: An oral tradition-story; b) monumentalisation: a monument plus an inscription; c) ritual performance: a burning stake resembling an holocaust rite perhaps recalled in the festival of the Elaphebolia.

That storytelling can express, and be part of, a discursive strategy is not a foregone conclusion. As White emphasised, storytelling is part of the process of creating identity and of the formation of networks. In fact, stories create and transmit meaning, that is, they are shared with others about the immediacy of events and are continually reshaped.[35] I take for

---

[35] White 2008, 30; Eidinow 2011, 16. See also Somers 1994, 620 ff. with literature.

granted that White's assumptions also apply to *ethne* seen as a whole.[36] Indeed, their national identity too, is created and shared also through stories that are continually reshaped to accommodate different events. This joint and continuous activity of story creation, embedded in a network, is a key part of how the Phocians make sense of and shape their national identity. Such a discursive approach also brings to light the identity implications of the commemoration of war.

Herodotus (8.27-29.1) records two battles between the Phocians and Thessalians: the first occurring on the Parnassos; the second in the pass by Hyampolis. Pausanias (10.1.3-11) adds other episodes, as, for example, the massacre of three hundred Phocians led by the general Gelon. This disaster led to a desperate decision by the Phocians, who were determined either to win or to die; They placed their wives, children, and all their property on a pyre which would be lit if they lost the battle: this is, according to Pausanias, the Φωκική ἀπόνοια, the "Phocian desperation" (10.1.7). Pausanias (10.1.8-10) also records some offerings, e.g. the statues of the heroes and of the generals in the battle, among others Daiphantus of Hyampolis. According to Plutarch (Plut. *De mul. vir.* 244A-D), it was by this very Daiphantos that the desperate decision was taken. However, Plutarch adds that the Phocian victory was still celebrated at his time with the festival of the Elaphebolia at Hyampolis.

What about these sources? 1) Herodotus reflects a tradition which is mixed up with a Phocian tradition and a Thessalian one; 2) Plutarch and Pausanias used a common source; 3) the decree of the Phocians, i.e. the Phocian desperation, belongs at least to the fourth century, as a passage of Aeschines proves.[37] Moreover, there is some evidence about the

---

[36] The Ancient Greeks called *ethne* (the plural of *ethnos*, which means "tribe" or "people") 1) the regions dotted with small villages that lacked a central town which could serve as a political and economic capital; 2) more generally, marginal, frontier tribes; 3) communities that resided in *poleis*; 4) in poetry, also groups and bands. The modern scholars studying ancient Greek *ethne* assume that an *ethnos* has an identity not tied to a specific set of institutions: members of an *ethnos* are tied by a common cultural background and *ethne* therefore comprise a group that identifies itself as a people. See Malkin 2001 with further literature, and, with reference to the Phocians, McInerney 1999, 21 ff. (with ancient sources).

[37] In the tradition reflected in Herodotus' account details about how Phocians win twice and the one about the offerings in Abai and in Delphi are clearly coming from a Phocian tradition; the siege on the Parnassos and the ruse of the chalk, which symbolizes the Thessalian expansion (see Demon *FGrHist* 327 F 7) are in fact details coming from a Thessalian tradition. The stories told by Pausanias and

desperation of the Phocians, the central focus of Pausanias and Plutarch, in the narratives of the "Third" Sacred War, where the fate of the Phocians is often recounted following the paradigm of the desperation.[38] In other words, it is highly probable that the story of Daiphantos dates to the 4th century.

In the 4th century, therefore, the Phocians reinvented the archaic war narrated by an archaic Phocian tradition, which was reflected in Herodotus. At that time, the Phocians were involved in the "Third" Sacred War and occupied the sanctuary of Delphi.[39] That was the golden age of the Phocians within the 4th century central Greece balance of power. They needed a founding myth which could represent their emergence as an *ethnos*. The archaic battle won against the Thessalians, one of their

---

by Plutarch are similar, that is, they use a common source: the second is an excerpt from the larger story which he has told in detail in the *Life of Daiphantus* and both authors refer to Phocian desperation. The decree of the Phocians, *i.e.* the Phocian desperation, belongs at least to the 4th century: Aeschines (2.140-41), reminding the Athenians of the enmity towards the Phocians which the Thessalians has developed since ancient times when the Phocians take their hostages and flog them to death, uses the words "ὁμήρους" and "κατηλόησαν", which are probably echoed by Plutarch's "ὁμήρους κατηλόησαν" (see Stadter 1965, 37, and, more generally, Lehmann 1983).

[38] Dem. de f.leg. 51: "ἀλλ' ἵνα, ἃ ἐβούλεσθ' οἰόμενοι πράξειν αὐτόν, μηδὲν ἐναντίον ψηφίσησθ' αὐτῷ, μηδ' ἀμύναιντο μηδ' ἀντέχοιεν οἱ Φωκεῖς ἐπὶ ταῖς παρ' ὑμῶν ὑπέχοντες ἐλπίσιν, ἀλλ' ἀπογνόντες ἅπανθ' αὑτοὺς ἐγχειρίσαιεν" (see also 5.19; 18.33; 19.30; 19.44; 19.56; 19.63-4; 19.74; 19.220): according to Demosthenes, Philip's objective was that the Athenians, in the belief that he would do all that they wanted, were to make no decree prejudicial to him, and "the Phocians might not stand their ground and hold out in reliance upon hopes afforded by you, but might make unconditional surrender to him in sheer desperation" (transl. by C. A. Vince, - J. H. Vince). "ἀπογνόντες" comes from "ἀπογιγνώσκω", "despair", "give up as hopeless"; the meaning is similar to that of the verb "νοέω", "perceive", "observe", "consider", which is part of the verb "ἀπονοέομαι", "to be desperate", and has the same stem as "ἀπόνοια" (TGL, *sv.*). Demosthenes does not use the term *aponoia* because it does not always denote "desperation", actually often it denotes "ignorance of the right way to behave", "lack of sense", in contrast to "πρόνοια" ("foresight", "forethought": see 25.32 ff; and, in other sources: Isocr. *Pac.* 93; Theophr. *Char.* 6; Polyb. 1.70.5; 82.1; 4.3.1; 18.54.8-11; see Dover 1974, 149; MacDowell 2009, 302; and Ellinger 1993, 275 ff); moreover, the negative connotation is related to insolence (*hybris*) and impiety (*asebeia*), a detail which must not be underestimated.

[39] Diod. 16.23.4-6, 29.4, 31.5; Paus. 10.2.2-3; Justin. 8.1.8; see Buckler 1989, 22; and Beck-Buckler 2008, 21, 51, 222-23 with sources and literature.

opponents during the "Third" Sacred War, was an ideal candidate for this role: it represented, in fact, a victory against the greatest enemy of the Phocians in archaic times, the expanding Thessalians. New heroes, such as the deviser of the desperate decision, Daiphantus, or Gelon, the general who died together with his 300 soldiers, were invented; new forms were introduced to commemorate this war and these heroes (the statues mentioned by Pausanias); and the battle itself was represented as an "initiation battle",[40] in order to symbolize the initiation of the Phocian *ethnos*. Indeed, there are many clues that the archaic was represented mostly from then on as an "initiation battle": 1) the three hundred soldiers under Gelon are likely to be interpreted as initiation candidates: the number 300 remembers age-classes;[41] 2) their mission and their death are likely to be interpreted as the second stage of the three-staged rite of passage, i.e. the liminal phase, during which the candidates have to experience endurance tests and a symbolic death (the third and final phase usually provides a symbolic rebirth: i.e. the Phocian victory);[42] 3) the same applies to the fire and the desperate decision, and the ensuing Phocian victory; 4) the five-hundred chosen soldiers marked by chalk and the night attack by full moon are likely to be interpreted as an age-class: candidates in an initiatic ritual were typically represented as ghosts or sacred beings during the liminal phase of the ritual; and an initiatic endurance test was typically carried out by full-moon.[43] None of these "initiatic" details are initiatic *per se*. They work as initiatic elements only in the light of the other details, that is, every detail becomes initiatic only within the framework of that discourse. This discursive strategy, meant as a new system of meanings, built up by the Phocians in the 4th century, was also monumentalized.

In fact, the offerings recorded by Pausanias (10.1.8-10), i.e. the statues of the heroes and of the generals in the battle, among others Daiphantus, were identified by G. Daux with some remains including the base with the

---

[40] I.e. a battle functioning as an endurance test to enter manhood: see Brelich 1961.
[41] See Van Gennep 1909 with literature; Brelich 1969, chap. 5; Jeanmaire 1939, 354-56; Vidal-Naquet 1983, 170, 173; Snoek 1987, 13, 64, 72 with literature; Vidal-Naquet 1988, 270 ff., 299.
[42] See Van Gennep 1909 with literature; Frobenius 1898, 374, 381; Eliade 1958, 15, 17 ff., 370 ff., 384; 1957, 200; Volpini 1978, 166 ff.; Buxton 1987, 69, 71; Snoek 1987, 104 ff. with literature; Nazionale 1999.
[43] See e.g. Weniger 1906; Orde-Browne 1915, 68; Jensen 1933, 428; Lanternari 1976, 123; Jeanmaire 1939, 354-56; Snoek 1987, 69, 71, 164 with literature.

marks of the statues' feet and a fragmentary dedication (*Inv.* 4553α–ζ= Jacquemin 2000, N. 397= *Syll.*³ 202B)[44]:

Φωκε[ῖς Ἀ]πόλλωνι [ἀνέθ]ηκαν δ[εκάταν ἀπὸ Θεσσαλῶν[45]

The base can be dated to between the second half of the 4th century and the first half of the 3rd century BC on a palaeographical basis.[46] This is exactly the time during which the tradition about the archaic battle was reshaped in an initiatic discursive strategy.

Furthermore, the monument must be interpreted in the light of the spatial politics in Delphi. It is probable that Pausanias' offerings were originally placed between a Theban and a Thessalian 4th century dedication[47] since both the Thebans and Thessalians were in fact the most

---

[44] The base is *in situ*, on the southwest side of the terrace of the temple; the slabs are of marble and rabbeted and 12.61 inches high.
[45] "The Phocians dedicated a tithe from the spoils of the Thessalians to Apollo".
[46] See also Keramopoullos 1907; Bourguet 1912; 1914, 153; Jacquemin 2000, *ad l.*
[47] See Scott 2010, fig. 5.10, 141. The Boeotian monument (Bommelaer nr. 211= Jacquemin nr. 99=Scott nr. 250) is a limestone base in gamma with statues, dating back to the middle of the 4th century. It features, among numerous proxeny decrees, a dedication: an inscribed list of contributors to the wars against the Phocians, who are addressed as *asebantes* (inv. 390; Daux-Salač, *FD* III 3, 77; Roesch 1982, 447-62; *Id.* 1984, 177-195). The text is fragmentary, but can be understood by comparing it with a similar inscribed dedication found in Thebes which also refers to the so-called Sacred War (*IG* VII 2418). According to scholars, the monument was erected after 346, i.e. after the end of and the victory in the Sacred War (Bommelaer 1991, nr. 211; Jacquemin 1999, 59). The Thessalian monument (inv. 4673+6325= Scott nr. 65=Jacquemin nr. 411) is instead archaic and consists of a marble base dating back to a period between the end of the 6th and the beginning of the 5th century. It is possible that it was placed in this area (Rougemont *CID* I 9-10; Scott 2010, 83). The monument features an inscription stating that it was commissioned by the *Pieres*: they dedicated a *pelanos* of the value of 15 drachmai. It could be identified with an offering of the city of Dion described at Pausanias 10.13.5 which is a statue of Apollo (Amandry 1939, 183-21, esp. 216-19, pl. 2-4; *Id.* 1950, 99 n. 1; Daux 1936, 141; De La Coste Messelière 1950, 145-59, esp. 156 n. 1; Rougemont *CID* I 9-10; Jacquemin 1999, 65), but the evidence is not unfailing. What is relevant for us, however, is that the Pieres are the inhabitants of Pieria, a Thessalian region which was conquered by Philip in the 4th century. We can, thus, expect that in the 4th century the monument was perceived as both Thessalian and Macedonian. Moreover, it is likely to have represented the Thessalian-Macedonian alliance: it was the Thessalian league that called Philip for help against the Phocians during the Sacred War.

important opponents of the Phocians during the "Third" Sacred War. The three monuments performed, therefore, a sort of "war between monuments".[48] The Phocians dedicated an anathema to the heroes of their national saga against Thebans and Thessalians. This national saga was elaborated during the fourth century; it is quite evident that the saga was reshaped also later on.

We catch some glimpses of this further reshaping activity by virtue of Plutarch, who describes the festival of the Elaphebolia which celebrates the Phocian desperation episode. No other details about this festival are known to us, as Plutarch is our only source. But Plutarch is from Chaironea, which is near Hyampolis, where the festival was celebrated during his times, and is likely to have known of it personally.[49] He explicitly says that the festival commemorates the victory after the desperate decision. There is a Greek inscription, which dates to Roman times, citing the Elaphebolia among other festivals:

ἐκ τῶν ἰδίων ἀνέθηκεν καὶ τῇ πόλει, ἀγωνοθ[ε]
τήσας αὐτοῦ τῶν μεγάλων Καισαρήων καὶ τῶν μεγά
λων Ἐλαφηβολίων τε καὶ Λαφρίων δίς, ὃς ἀγῶνας
μόνος καὶ πρῶτος εἰσηγήσατο καὶ ἐτέλεσεν ἐκ τῶν ἰδί[ων].[50]

According to Yorke, Nilsson, Ellinger and Sève, the grammar of the inscription seems to imply that the Elaphebolia and Laphria were one and the same festival, i.e. the Elaphebolia was also called the Laphria.[51] Moreover, Nilsson[52] wonders if the Phocian Laphria-Elaphebolia commemorating the Phocian *aponoia* resembles another festival called Laphria, the one of Patras described by Pausanias (7.18.8-13). In fact, according to Pausanias, the Laphria was founded by a Phocian and animals were burned on a stake. Did the Phocian Elaphebolia consider a similar stake and was that stake commemorating the desperate decision? This sounds attractive, but hard to prove. Pritchett and Pirenne-Delforge

---

[48] Scott 2010, 141 ff.
[49] Plut. *Mor.* 660d; 1099e-f; Boulogne 2002, 31.
[50] *IG* IX 1, 90: "(X, son of X...) has consecrated at his own expense to (…) and to the city, having been twice agonothetes of the Great Kaisareia and of the Great Elaphebolia and Laphria, games of which the one and the first he introduced and celebrated at his own expense." (transl. by Pirenne Delforge 2006).
[51] Yorke 1896, 309; Nilsson 1906, 221-22; Ellinger 1993, 243-45; Sève, 345-46, who notes the position of "*μεγάλων*" and the use of different verbs ("*εἰσηγήσατο καὶ ἐτέλεσεν*").
[52] Nilsson 1906, 221-22.

choose, as the first editor Dittenberger, the *lectio facilior*, i.e. the more easy reading, assuming that the Laphria and Elaphebolia were two distinct festivals both celebrated at Hyampolis.[53] Pritchett goes further by supposing that they were both previously celebrated in Kalapodi-Abai and then shifted to Hyampolis as Sulla razed Kalapodi to the ground. There may be a lack of consistency in this thought, however, a strong connection between (Phocian) Elaphebolia and (Phocian) Laphria is nevertheless impossible to rule out.[54] What is more significant is that the desperate decision and the stake are, in fact, described by the sources as a holocaust rite,[55] which resembles other holocaust rites described e.g. by Pausanias.[56] In other words, it is likely that when inventing the tradition about the desperate decision the Phocians imagined a fully-fledged ritual performance. By imagining such a ritual, perhaps also performed during the Elaphebolia, they built up the above mentioned discursive strategy.

The imagined holocaust seems to work in the same discursive strategy built up through storytelling and monumentalizing: the Phocian story about the desperation and the monument of the generals put into effect an initiatic representation of Phocian history, which was likely to be periodically renewed by the Elaphebolia through ritual repetition. The new heroes of an old war, who suggested the desperate decision (as Daiphantos did), or died with their soldiers (as Gelon did), were commemorated through ever-changing stories and cults.

---

[53] Pritchett 1996, 105 ff.; Pirenne-Delforge 2006, 116 ff. See in particular Pritchett's analysis of the use of μεγάλα referring to a festival and of other cases in which more than one festival is mentioned and the second festival is anathrous in the "τε καί" construction.

[54] See *e.g.* the Laphria in Patras: Paus.7.18.8-13 (founded by the Phocian Laphrios?: 7.18.9); the Laphria in Delphi: *CdD* 9 face D line 8; *FdD* 3.3 (1943) 214 with *SEG* 18.245; see also Hesych. *s.v.* Laphriadai; the Aetolian Laphria: Strab. 10.2.21.459; Paus.4.31.7; *SEG* 25.261; Poulsen 1948; the Elaphebolia in Attica: Anecd. Bekk. 1.249 *s.v.* Elaphebolion; Athen.14.646e. Cfr. Yorke 1896, 309 Nr. 6; Nilsson 1906, 224: "plutarch bezeichnet als das phokische fest mit dem attischen parallelnamen, die inschrift fuegt den heimischen namen hinzu"; see also Fraenkel 1894, 1384; Kroll 1925, 767; Deubner 1932, 205; Wilamowitz 1932, 381-87, and, more recently, Boulogne 2002, 283.

[55] See Nilsson, 221-222; Pirenne Delforge 2006. The holocaust is a religious animal sacrifice in which the animal is completely consumed by fire.

[56] See Nilsson 1906 and Piccaluga 1980 with literature; and compare Paus. 10.1.7: „ὡς ἱερεῖα ἀναθέντας ταῦτά τε καὶ τὰ χρήματα ἐπὶ τὴν πυρὰν"; with Paus. 7.18.12: „ἐπὶ ἐλάφων; and *ibidem* "ἔτι δὲ ὗς ἀγρίους καὶ ἐλάφους τε καὶ δορκάδας".

CONCLUSIONS: ANCIENT HISTORY AS A HISTORY OF DISCURSIVE OBJECTS

The two case studies of our paper - 5th century Athenians and 4th century Phocians - represent both paradigmatic examples of how: 1) commemoration of war dead, and more generally of war, is a social act of memory, i.e. it has strong identity implications and is therefore influenced by the social frameworks of memory; 2) such implications determine the continuous reshaping of the old forms of commemoration and the invention of new forms of commemoration; 3) therefore, they determine the continuous change or the invention of various details, so as to change the heroic paradigms and to invent new heroes to commemorate; 4) this reshaping activity concerns the discursive strategy in which the above mentioned elements work; 5) consequently, it is worthwhile to go beyond a rigid classification of both ancient documentary evidence and modern categories and to analyze the question of the commemoration of war dead, and of war itself, from the point of view of the discursive strategies that lie behind them.[57] Groups representing social networks, such as the Athenians and the Phocians, created new meaning through discursive strategies.

The ancient evidence, on which the hypothesis of a hero cult of the war dead in 5th century Athens is based, is mostly late, dating to Hellenistic or even Roman times. However, it is exactly starting from Hellenistic times that the Persian War dead were included in a complex network of memories and values of the past which provided a new found relevance for the present, and conversely determined the commemorative acts that they received, for both the rituals (*enagismata*) and their performers (in most cases the ephebes). A new web of meanings, which has an inherent tie with contingency, works and makes sense only in that specific context. Within the framework of the Second Sophistic, the heroic pattern was once again embedded in a further different network of functions and meanings, and it is in this perspective that the intended worship of the *Marathonomachoi* by the inhabitants of the deme of Marathon should be considered. Similarly, the Persian War dead can be considered epic heroes only within the network of meanings and practices created by the post-Cleisthenic *polis*, i.e. within the discursive strategies of commemoration centered on specific civic honors.

A similar fluidity of the forms of commemoration of war and war dead is to be found in Phocis. In this case as well, the acts of commemorating

---

[57] Foucault 1972, 5.

an archaic war are part of a dynamic process, which changes in time depending on the corresponding social framework and needs for identity.

During the 4th century the Phocians transformed the archaic tradition about an archaic war against the Thessalians into an identity-founding event for the Phocian *ethnos*, putting into effect a complex discursive strategy. This discursive strategy made use of the initiation pattern, and invented new heroes and new forms of commemoration. Glimpses of that strategy can be caught through stories, monuments and a festival, the Elaphebolia. Stories were reshaped, monuments were built and a holocaust was performed to commemorate new heroes of an old war, heroes who devised an important decision or died during combat. All this reshaping activity started in the 4th century, during or shortly after the "Third" Sacred War: that was the golden age of the Phocians and they needed a founding myth which could represent their emergence - their initiation - as *ethnos*. Reshaping activity did not stop because that golden age was supposed to be commemorated also when it was over.

To sum up, the two case studies are paradigmatic of how ancient history can benefit from being studied as a history of discursive objects. In fact, the forms of commemoration of the war and the war dead of the Athenians and of the Phocians use discursive strategies. In this sense, they can be described as relations between objects - battles, heroes, rituals, festivals - that exist under the positive conditions of a complex group of relations. These relations are regulated by rules that are immanent in practice and define the group in its specificity in time and place: Athens in the 5th century/Hellenistic/Imperial times, as Phocis in the 4th century/Hellenistic/Imperial times. Studying ancient history as a history of discursive objects implies not to plunge them into the common depth of a primal soil, but to deploy the nexus of regularities that govern their dispersion: "a task that consists of no longer-treating discourses as groups of signs [...] but as practices that systematically form the objects of which they speak."[58]

---

[58] Foucault 1972, 49.

BIBLIOGRAPHY

Albersmeier, S. (ed) (2009) *Heroes: Mortals and myths in ancient Greece*, Baltimore.
Amandry, P. (1939) "Convention religieuse conclue entre Delphes et Skiathos", *BCH* 63, 183-219
—. (1950) *La mantique Apollinienne a Delphes: Essai sur le fonctionnement de l'oracle*, Paris.
—. (1971) "Collection Paul Canellopoulos: armes et lébès de bronze", *BCH* 95, 585-626.
Arrington, N. T. (2011) "Inscribing Defeat: the Commemorative Dynamics of the Athenian Casualty Lists", *ClAnt* 30,179-212.
Assmann, J. (2011) *Cultural Memory and Early Civilization: Writing, Remembrance, and Political Imagination*, Cambridge [München 1992].
Beck, H. and J. Buckler (2008) *Central Greece and the Politics of Power in the Fourth Century BC*, Cambridge.
Beck, H. and H. U. Wiemer (2010) "Feiern und Erinnern – eine Einleitung", in H. Beck, and H. U. Wiemer (eds) *Feiern und Erinnern: Geschichtsbilder im Spiegel antiker Feste*, Berlin, 9-54.
Boedecker, D. (1998) "The New Simonides and Heroization at Plataia", in N. Fisher and H. van Wees (eds), *Archaic Greece: New Approaches and New Evidence*, London, 231-49.
Boehringer, D. (1996) "Zur Heroisierung Persönlichkeiten bei den Griechen", in M. Flashar, H.-J. Gehrke and E. Heinrich (eds) *Retrospektive. Konzepte von Vergangenheit in der griechisch-römischen Antike*, München, 37-61.
Bommelaer, F. (1991) *Guide de Delphes Le site*, Paris.
Boulogne, J. (2002) *Plutarque Oeuvres morales: Mulierum virtutes*, Paris.
Bourguet, E. (1912) "Rapport sur une mission a Delphes (1911)", *REG* 111, 12-23.
—. (1914) *Les ruines de Delphes*, Paris.
Bravo, J. J. (2009) "Recovering the Past: the Origins of Greek Heroes and Hero Cult", in Albersmeier 2009, 10–29.
Brelich, A. (1961) *Guerre, agoni e culti nella Grecia arcaica*, Bonn.
—. (1969) *Paides e parthenoi*, Roma.
Bremmer, J. N. (2006) "The Rise of the Hero Cult and the New Simonides", *ZPE* 158, 15-26.
Buckler, J. (1989) *Philip II and the Sacred War*, Leiden.
Buxton, R. (1987) "Wolves and Werewolves in Greek Thought", in J. Bremmer (ed) *Interpretations of Greek Mythology*, London and

Sydney, 70-89.
Chaniotis, A. (2005) "The Memory of War", in *Id. War in the Hellenistic World. A Social and Cultural History*, Oxford, 214-44.
—. (2012) "The Ritualized Commemoration of War in the Hellenistic City: Memory, Identity, Emotion", in Low, Oliver and Rhodes 2012, 41-62.
Collar, A. (2007) "Network Theory and Religious Innovation", *MHR* 22, 149-62.
Connerton, P. (1989) *How Societies Remember,* Cambridge.
Currie, B. (2005) *Pindar and the Cult of Heroes*, Oxford.
Daux, G. (1936) *Pausanias à Delphes*, Paris.
De La Coste Messelière, P. (1950) "L'oracle de Delphes [P. Amandry. La mantique apollinienne à Delphes. Essai sur le fonctionnement de l'Oracle [compte rendu]", *JS*, 145-59.
Dover, K. J. (1974) *Greek Popular Morality in the Time of Plato and Aristotle*, Oxford.
Eidinow, E. (2011) "Networks and Narratives. A Model for the Study of Ancient Greek Religion", *Kernos* 24, 9-38.
Ekroth, G. (2002) *The Sacrificial Rituals of Greek Hero-Cults*, Liège.
—. (2007) "Heroes and Hero-Cults", in D. Ogden (ed) *Greek Companion to Greek Religion*, Oxford, 100-14.
—. (2009) "The Cult of the Heroes", in Albersmeier 2009, 120-43.
Eliade, M. (1958) *Rites and Symbols of Initiation (Birth and Rebirth)*, London.
Ellinger, P. (1993) *La légende nationale phocidienne*, Paris.
Étienne, R. and Piérart, M. (1975) "Un décret du 'koinon' des Hellènes à Platées en l'honneur de Glaucon, fils d'Etéocles, d'Athènes", *BCH* 99, 51-75.
Foucault, M. (1972) *The Archaeology of Knowledge*, London [Paris 1962].
Fraenkel, S. (1894) s.v. Artemis (Elaphia), in *RE* II, 1384.
Frobenius, L. (1898) *Die Masken und Geheimbünde Afrikas*, Halle.
Georgoudi, S. (1988) "Commémoration et célébration des morts dans les cités grecques: les rites annuels", in P. Gignoux (ed) *La Commémoration. Colloque du Centenaire de la Section des Sciences Religieuses de l'École Pratique des Hautes Etudes*, Louvain – Paris, 73-89.
Georgoulaki, E. (1996) "Religious and Socio-Political Implications of Mortuary Evidence", *Kernos* 9, 95-120.
Giangiulio, M. (2010) "Le società ricordano? Paradigmi e problemi della 'memoria collettiva' (a partire da Maurice Halbwachs)", in *Id. Memorie coloniali*, Roma, 29-43.

Guggisberg, M. A. (2008) "Gräber von Bürgern und Heroen: 'Homerische' Bestattungen im klassischen Athen", in C. Kümmel, B. Schweizer and U. Veit (eds) *Körperinszenierung – Objectsammlung – Monumentalisierung: Totenritual und Grabkult in frühen Gesellschaften. Archäologische Quellen in kulturwissenschaftlicher Perspektive*, Münster, New York, München, Berlin, 287-317.
Halbwachs, M. (1925) *Les cadres sociaux de la mémoire*, Paris
—. (1950) *La mémoire collective*, Paris.
Hammond, N. G. L. and G. T. Griffith, (1979) *A History of Macedonia*, II, Oxford.
Harris, E. M. (1995) *Aeschines and Athenian Politics*, New York.
Hiller von Gaertringen, F. (1901) s.v. Daiphantos, in *RE* IV 2, 2012-13.
Jacquemin, A. (1999) *Offrandes Monumentales à Delphes*, Paris.
Jeanmaire, H. (1939) *Couroi et Courètes*, Lille.
Jensen, A.E. (1933) *Beschneidung und Reifezeremonien bei Naturvölkern*, Stuttgart.
Jones, C. P. (2010) *New Heroes in Antiquity, from Achilles to Antinoos*, Cambridge MA and London.
Keramopoullos, E. (1907) "Φωκικὸν ἀνάθημα ἐν Δελφοῖς", *EphArch*, 91-104.
Kroll, W. (1925) s.v. Laphria, in *RE* XII 1, 766-68.
Kyle, D. G. (1987) "Athenian Civic Athletics: Festivals and Activities", in Id. *Athletic in Ancient Athens*, Leiden, 32-55.
Lanternari, V. (1976) *La grande festa. Vita rituale e sistemi di produzione nelle società tradizionali*, Bari.
Lehmann, G.A. (1983) "Thessaliens Hegemonie über Mittelgriechenland im 6. Ih. V. Chr." in *Boreas* 6, 35-43.
Lendon J. E. (2005) *Soldiers and Ghosts: A History of Battle in Classical Antiquity*, New Haven.
Loraux, N. (1986) *The Invention of Athens. The Funeral Oration in the Classical City*, Cambridge MA and London [Paris 1981].
Low, P. (2010) "Commemoration of the War Dead in Classical Athens: Remembering Defeat and Victory", in D. Pritchard (ed) *War, Democracy and Culture in Classical Athens*, Cambridge, 341-58.
—. (2012) "The Monuments to the War Dead in Classical Athens: Forms, Contexts, Meanings," in Low, Oliver and Rhodes 2012, 13-39.
Low, P., G. Oliver, and J. P. Rhodes (eds) (2012) *Cultures of Commemoration: War Memorials, Ancient and Modern*, Oxford.
MacDowell, D. M. (1990) *Demosthenes: Against Meidias*, Oxford.
—. (2009) *Demosthenes the Orator*, Oxford.
Malkin, I. (2001), *Ancient Perceptions of Greek Ethnicity*, Harvard.

—. (2003) "Networks and the Emergence of Greek Identity", *MHR* 18, 56–75.

—. (2011) *A Small Greek World: Networks in the Ancient Mediterranean*, Oxford and NY.

Malkin, I., C. Constantakopoulou, and K. Panagopoulou (eds) (2009) *Greek and Roman Networks in the Mediterranean*, London.

Mari, M. (2012) "La morte, il tempo, la memoria. Funerali pubblici e calendario civico nella Grecia antica", in V. Nizzo and L. La Rocca (eds) *Antropologia e archeologia a confronto, Atti dell'Incontro Internazionale di studi, Roma 20-21/5/2011*, Roma, 167-87.

McInerney, J. (1999) *The Folds of Parnassos: Land and Ethnicity in Ancient Phokis*, Austin.

Nagy, G. (1979) *The Best of the Achaeans*, Baltimore.

Nazionale, I. (1999) "Andro-poiesi samburu. Marginalità del moranato e sospensione dell'umanità", in F. Remotti (ed) *Forme di umanità. Progetti incompleti e cantieri sempre aperti*, Torino, 72-94.

Newby, Z. (2005) "The Athenian Ephebeia: Performing the Past", in Z. Newby, *Greek Athletics in the Roman World. Victory and Virtue*, Oxford, 168-201.

Nilsson, M. P. (1906) *Griechische Feste von religiöser Bedeutung, mit Ausschluss der attischen*, Leipzig.

Orde-Browne, G. St. J (1913) "The Circumcision Ceremony in Chuka", *Man* 39, 65-68.

Oudot, E. (2010) "Marathon, l'Eurymédon, Platées, laissons-les aux écoles des sophistes!'. Les guerres médiques au second siècle de notre ère", in P.-L. Malosse, M.-P. Noël and B. Schouler (eds) *Clio sous le regard d'Hermès. L'utilisation de l'histoire dans la rhétorique ancienne de l'époque hellénistique à l'Antiquité Tardive*, Alessandria, 143-57.

Parker, R. (1983) *Miasma. Pollution and Purification in Early Greek Religion*, Oxford.

—. (1996) *Athenian Religion. A History*, Oxford.

—. (2005) "ὡς ἥρωι ἐναγίζειν", in R. Hägg and B. Alroth (eds) *Greek Sacrificial Ritual, Olympian and Chthonian. Proceedings of the Sixth International Seminar on Ancient Greek Hero Cult organized by the Department of Classical Archaeology and Ancient History, Goteborg University, 25-27 April 1997*, Stockholm, 37-45.

Piccaluga, G. (1980) "L'olocausto di Patrai", in J.-P. Vernant (ed) *Le sacrifice dans l'antiquité Fondation Hardt. Entretiens* 27, Vandœuvres-Genève, 243-87.

Pirenne-Delforge, V. (2006) "Ritual Dynamics in Pausanias: The Laphria", in E. Stavrianopoulou (ed) Ritual and Communication in the Graeco-

Roman World, Liège, 111-29.
Poulsen, F. (1948) "Das Laphrion" in E. Dyggve (ed) *Der Tempelbezirk von Kalydon*, Copenhagen.
Prandi, L. (2003) "I caduti in guerra. Eroi necessari della cultura greca", in A. Barzanò (ed) *Modelli eroici dall'antichità alla cultura europea*, Roma, 99-114.
Pritchett, W. K. (1996) *Greek Archives, Cults and Topography,* Amsterdam.
Proietti, G. (2012a) "Memoria collettiva e identità etnica. Nuovi paradigmi teorico-metodologici della ricerca storica", in E. Franchi and G. Proietti (eds) *Forme della memoria e dinamiche identitarie nell'antichità greco-romana*, Trento, 13-41.
—. (2012b) "La memoria delle Guerre Persiane in età imperiale. Il classicismo di Erode Attico e la 'stele dei Maratonomachi'", *ASAA* 90, s. III 12, 97-117.
Roesch, P. (1984) *Études Béotiennes*, Paris
—. (1982) "La base des Béotiens à Delphe", *CRAI*, 128, 1, 177-195
Roller, L. E. (1982) "Funeral Games for Historical Persons", *Stadion* 7, 1-18.
Sánchez, P. (2001) *L'Amphictionie des Pyles et de Delphes*, Stuttgart.
Scott, M. (2010), *Delphi and Olympia: The Spatial Politics of Panhellenism in the Archaic and Classical Periods*, Cambridge and New York.
Sève, M. (1993) "Note sur l'inscription d'Hyampolis *IG* IX 1, 90" in Ellinger 1993, 345-46.
Shapiro, H. A. (1991) "The Iconography of Mourning in Greek Art", *AJA* 95, 629-56
Shear, J. L. (2012) "The Tyrannnicides, their Cult and the Panathenaia: A Note", *JHS* 132, 107-119.
Snoek, J. A. M. (1987) *Initiations. A Methodological Approach to the Application of Classification and Definition Theory in the Study of Rituals*, Diss. Leiden.
Somers, M. R. (1994) "The narrative constitution of identity: A Relational and Network Approach", *Theory and Society* 23 (5), 605-49.
Sordi, M. (1953) "La guerra tessalo-focese del V secolo", *RFIC* 31, 235-58.
Spawforth, J. S. (1994) "Symbol of Unity? The Persian-Wars Tradition in the Roman Empire", in S. Hornblower (ed) *Greek Historiography*, Oxford, 233-47.
Stadter, Ph. A. (1965) *Plutarch's Historical Methods. An Analysis of the mulierum virtutes*, Cambridge (Mass.).

Steiner, D. (1999) "To Praise, not to Bury: Simonides fr. 531P", *CQ* 49, 383-95.
Stevanovic, L. (2008) "Human or Superhuman: the Concept of Hero in Ancient Greek Religion and/in Politics", *Bulletin of the Institute of Ethnography SASA* LVI (2), 7-20.
Thomas, R. (1989) *Oral Tradition and Written Record in Classical Athens*, Cambridge
Vanderpool, E. (1969) "Three Prize Vases", *ArchDelt* 24 A', 1-5.
Van Gennep, A. (1909) *Les rites de passage*, Paris.
Vidal-Naquet, P. (1983) *Le Chasseur noir. Formes de pensée et formes de société dans le monde grec*, Paris.
Vince, C. A. and Vince, J. H. (1926) *Demosthenes*, London.
Volpini, D. (1978) *Il seme del ricino. Iniziazione tribale e mutamento culturale fra I Tharaka del Kenya*, Roma.
Welwei, K.-W. (1991) "Heroenkult und Gefallenenehrung im antiken Griechenland", in G. Binder and B. Effe (eds) *Tod und Jenseits im Altertum*, Bochumer, 50-70.
Weniger, L. (1906) "Feralis exercitus", *ARW*, 9, 201-47.
Wilamowitz, U. v. (1959) *Der Glaube der Hellenen I³*, Basel-Stuttgart.
West, M. L. (1978) *Hesiod's Works and Days*, Oxford.
White, H. (2008) *Identity and Control: A Structural Theory of Social Action*, Princeton.
Whitley, J. (1994) "The Monument That Stood before Marathon: Tomb Cult and Hero Cult in Archaic Attica", *AJA* 98, 213-30.
—. (1995) "Tomb Cult and Hero Cult. The Uses of the Past in Archaic Greece", in N. Spencer (ed) *Time, Tradition and Society in Greek Archaeology*, London, 43-63.
Yorke, V. W. (1896) "Excavations at Abae and Hyampolis in Phocis", *JHS* 16, 291-312.

Chapter Fourteen

Ajax, Cassandra and Athena: Retaliatory Warfare and Gender Violence at the Sack of Troy[1]

Dr. Susan Deacy and Dr. Fiona McHardy

This chapter builds on recent work arguing for the centrality of violence against women to ancient warfare. It uses Gaca's model of retaliatory warfare[2] to frame a discussion of how, in representations of the sack of Troy, the actions of the Greeks fit ancient patterns of violent behaviour and may reflect evolutionary dispositions, too. We show that this is even – perhaps especially – true of the actions of Locrian Ajax. His behaviour has previously been interpreted as flying in the face of acceptable behaviour. However, we show that his ill-treatment of Cassandra displays expected, even required, warrior behaviour towards enemy females. We consider how it also offens a goddess, Athena, because of where the actions take place, and because the goddess is the recipient of his aggression in two respects – as a rival warrior and as a female whose vulnerability to gender violence is consonant with that of Cassandra.

The subject of this paper is one that, until recently, might have appeared of marginal significance for inclusion in a volume about the

---

[1] Our paper at the 2013 warfare colloquium marked the start of a lively journey from conference paper to completed chapter. We are grateful for the penetrating post-paper questions at the conference. In post-conference discussions, Hans van Wees encouraged us to sharpen the case we made at the conference for the typicality of the behaviour of Ajax and made insightful comments on a subsequent version of the paper for which we are deeply grateful. We are indebted to Jason Crowley, Mike Edwards and Nick Fisher for their astute comments on the penultimate draft of the chapter. All translations are our own unless otherwise stated.
[2] Gaca 2011.

history of warfare. It concerns a topic once regarded as a by-product of war rather than an integral feature of what motivates it and shapes the behaviour of combatants. However, its topic has now become timely – thus, it is fitting for a volume not just on ancient warfare *per se*, but one that is specifically concerned with introducing new research. Research in a range of areas is converging in a common aim to show the central role of sexually violent acts carried out against females to how and why warfare is conducted, including the following, that focus largely on explaining the phenomenon in modern warzones: human rights, international relations, peace studies, political sociology and security studies.[3] From the perspective of some of the research conducted from a further disciplinary area, evolutionary psychology, the wartime subjugation of women might even be traced as far back as the Pleistocene Era, when the human brain was evolving.[4] From this perspective, the wartime abuse of women is more than solely a weapon of war or "an exultant postconquest celebration" as some have argued,[5] but a motivation for warfare in the first place. It is likewise more than a "dramatic demonstration of [masculine] dominance";[6] rather, it is what induces such dominance.

We opt for "gender violence" rather than "sexual violence" or "rape" in our title because it is the term that best captures the various issues we explore. "Rape" is too narrow because, although Cassandra has been described as nothing short of "the archetypal mythic victim of violent rape,"[7] we question the assumption that Ajax rapes Cassandra. Indeed, we argue that a more profitable question to ask of Ajax's act is not "does he or doesn't he rape Cassandra?", but – instead – "why did the Greeks depict the encounter in ways that frustrate any straightforward answer?" "Sexual violence" is better, as this term can include rape, but also other violent or

---

[3] See e.g. Askin 1997; Bergoffen 2009; Buss 2009; Card 1996; Kirby 2012; Skjelsbæk 2001; Leatherman 2011; Wood 2009. The International Campaign to Stop Rape and Gender Violence in Conflict expresses the issue in clear-cut terms: "[r]ape in conflict is not a new phenomenon". StopRapeInConflict.org, 2012.
[4] According to Gat (2000, 10), ancestral warfare "regularly involved stealing of women, who were then subjected to multiple rapes, or taken for marriage, or both". Potts and Hayden (2010) posit that team aggression may have given reproductive advantages to violent ancestral men. Evolutionary theories of warfare are evaluated in Livingston Smith 2012.
[5] Gaca 2011, 73, summarising Brownmiller 1975. Other assessments of Browmiller include Skjelsbæk 2001, 215–18; Kirby 2012, 4–5.
[6] Merry 2009, 16.
[7] Blondell 2013, 7.

aggressive actions.[8] But best for our present purposes is "gender violence", which, defined by Merry, constitutes "[v]iolence whose meaning depends on the gendered identities of the parties".[9]

Research on a range of historical warzones has sought to establish how, in numerous periods, gender violence has been key to warfare – including ancient warfare.[10] The following studies into ancient warfare bear particularly on our chapter. According to Gottschall, who applies evolutionary theory to ancient evidence, the story of the Trojan War was generated out of an historical shortage of women of reproductive age caused by polygyny among powerful men.[11] McHardy, again informed by evolutionary approaches, has argued that the Homeric epics, with their focus on violent retaliation in response to the theft or attempted theft of women, reflect upon and symbolise the vital male struggle over female reproductive resources.[12] Gaca argues that the current "social justice concern" over "the practice of armed men at war…seizing, traumatizing, and subjugating foreign or enemy girls and women"[13] needs to take account of ancient as well as modern conflicts. Gaca identifies several modes of ancient warfare, all of which were motivated by a desire to subjugate enemy women, including predatory warfare, parasitic warfare, and retaliatory warfare.[14] She argues that, while ancient conflicts concern the kind of man-on-man battlefield violence exemplified in the description at *Il.* 8.64-5 of "both the wailing and the exultation of men killing and being killed" ("*οἰμωγή τε καὶ εὐχωλή…ἀνδρῶν ὀλλύντων τε καὶ ὀλλυμένων*"), this is only the first phase of warfare. What happens next is a second phase which involves the killing of any remaining adult males who have survived their defeat and the subjugation of the non-combat population: "once the attacking males kill most of the grown males among the opposition, they then consider it their right and even their obligation to exact additional punishment by sexually mauling the women".[15]

---

[8] Heineman 2011, 2.
[9] Merry 2009, 3.
[10] See esp. Heineman 2011.
[11] Gottschall 2008.
[12] McHardy 2008a, esp. 61. On the potential of evolutionary psychology to inform classical research, see also Deacy and McHardy 2013, esp. 994-5; Scheidel 2009.
[13] Gaca 2011, 73.
[14] Gaca 2008; 2010; 2011.
[15] Gaca 2011, 85. On the killing of adult males, see Rosivach 1999.

A variety of sources have been used to discuss the prevalence of wartime sexual violence, including modern imaginative sources such as novels,[16] and ancient imaginative evidence, notably the Homeric poems.[17] Our focus is likewise on imaginative sources: a range of representations for a specific episode of the Trojan War – when, as the city is being attacked after the ten-year siege, one of the Greek warriors, Locrian Ajax, tries, with different degrees of violence depending on the source in question, to drag the Trojan princess Cassandra away from her place of refuge, the statue of Athena. We examine how representations of this episode reflect on and fit the kill men-subjugate women mode of warfare by considering the episode in relation to one of the forms of ancient warfare identified by Gaca, that of retaliatory warfare, which was "motivated by an ostensible or genuine grievance against another group,"[18] and which could involve especially aggravated sexual violence.

The Trojan War is represented in ancient sources as retaliatory in terms of its cause – the theft of Helen by Paris – and in terms of how it is conducted and concluded. For example, at Herodotus 1.1.3-1.4.4, this theft is said to mark the latest in a series of reciprocal abductions between Asia and Europe.[19] When Nestor urges the Greeks to stay and fight in *Iliad* 2, he uses the vocabulary of payment to intimate that no Greek should leave Troy until he has slept with the wife of a Trojan man and taken revenge (τίσασθαι) for what happened to Helen.[20] The decision to end the war with a duel between Helen's offended husband and her abductor is accompanied by an oath and accompanying prayer that further demonstrates the double requirement of killing men and subjugating females.[21] Both sides pray that should either side break the oath, first, the

---

[16] Heineman 2011, 103-69.
[17] On two of these – Gottschall 2008, McHardy 2008 – see above. Gaca argues that a metaphor used by Achilles at *Il.* 16.7-11, which previous commentators have regarded as an "image of peaceful maternity," (2008, 161) actually describes a mother and her daughter fleeing their home pursued by enemy warriors. Thus, according to Gaca, it depicts the kind of action typically carried out by Achilles against the communities around Troy (see *Il.* 9.325-9, 20.193-4; 2.354-6, 3.301, 22.59-65).
[18] Gaca 2011, 84.
[19] Cf. Eur. *Med.* 256.
[20] Hom. *Il.* 2.354-6. The "collective guilt" of the Trojans over the theft by Paris of Helen, made worse by their refusal to return Helen, is explored in Castriota 1992, 87. See also Lloyd-Jones 1983, 74-5.
[21] Cf. the connection between the killing of the men and the subjugation of the women expressed by Phoenix at *Il.* 9. 593-4: ἄνδρας μὲν κτείνουσι, πόλιν δέ τε πῦρ

offending warriors will die, along with their sons, and second, their wives will be subjugated: "*σφ' ἐγκέφαλος χαμάδις ῥέοι ὡς ὅδε οἶνος αὐτῶν καὶ τεκέων, ἄλοχοι δ' ἄλλοισι δαμεῖεν*" ("may their brains pour to the ground as does this wine, and also the brains of their children, and may their wives be subdued").[22] We explore Ajax's action in relation to this retaliatory ethos by considering how it shows the same "obligation" to participate in the "sexual mauling" of enemy women that, according to Gaca, is evident in many instances of wartime rape.[23]

We outline what is represented as taking place between Ajax, Cassandra and Athena and what the aftermath is. We then survey how it has tended to be read by classical scholars. Then we interpret the conflict as an instance of the gender violence that was integral to retaliatory warfare.

VICTIMS WITH NAMES AND FACES

According to Gaca, "heterosexual practices of sexual violence in ancient warfare hardly register in our historical consciousness, just like the countless victims themselves, who are mainly nameless and faceless to us".[24] Our concern here is with the key exception, the mythological evidence, which abounds with female victims, including the pair who figure in the specific myth we are exploring – one mortal, one immortal – both of whom are subjected to gender violence in the context of retaliatory warfare.

We are wary of running through what "the myth" is as if there is some clear-cut macromyth that the various authors and artists who represented the episode were somehow drawing on. Myth did not work like this – contrast the neatly-packaged, but simplified, accounts that mythological dictionaries provide. However, there is a recurrence of certain features

---

ἀμαθύνει, τέκνα δέ τ' ἄλλοι ἄγουσι βαθυζώνους τε γυναῖκας ("they kill the men, use fire to level the city, and other men take away the children and the deep-girded women"). Gaca tr. adapted. Van Wees 1992, 252 explores the concept of a "war of annihilation" as described here.
[22] *Il.* 3.300-301 tr. Kitts. The escalated violence that could follow the breaking of an oath is discussed in Gaca 2011, 85. On the reciprocal violence in retaliatory conflict, see McHardy 2008a, 60. See also Daly and Wilson 1988, 128; van Wees 1992, 88.
[23] Gaca 2011, 85.
[24] Gaca 2011, 76.

across a range of sources.[25] Ajax enters the sanctuary of Athena in pursuit of Cassandra, the most eligible of the Trojan women. Cassandra manages to seek asylum at the image of the goddess; Ajax tries and fails to pull her away – because she is clutching it so tightly (περιπεπλεγμένην "embracing" it at Apollod. *Epit.* 5.22; cf. also Alcaeus fr. 298.10) and, potentially, because the goddess is keeping Cassandra fixed to her own body. Such a reading might be supported by the description at Pausanias 10.26.3 of how Polygnotus depicted the captured Cassandra still clutching the image of Athena in his painting of the Iliupersis. It could be that we are to see Cassandra as falling under the protection of the goddess, who has a particular association with asylum and whose divine image is especially invested with her own embodied presence – on which, more later. What Ajax manages to do is to dislodge the *pair* of them: Ajax never pulls Cassandra away from the statue, despite what some commentators have assumed. Instead, he dislodges the statue from its base with the suppliant still clutching it. The episode shows the protective power that the goddess/image of the goddess offers, but also her/its vulnerability. One of the conditions for the taking of Troy was the taking of the Palladion, which gives talismanlike protection to the city but only as long as it is in its set place in the sanctuary of the goddess.[26] What happens to Cassandra at the statue of Athena fits the associations between the security of women and the security of the state, which has been scrutinised from several disciplinary perspectives, including evolutionary psychology and political sociology.[27] The violence perpetrated by Ajax shows up the vulnerability of Troy as symbolised by its highest-status mortal woman and also by Athena, the highest-status divine female of the city. The deposing of

---

[25] The earliest known work to represent the episode is Arctinus' *Iliupersis*, which as summarised in Procl. *Chrestomathy* 3, described an offence committed by Ajax in the sanctuary of Athena, after which Ajax took refuge at altar of Athena. On the possibility that Arctinus' account inspired the next extant account, Alc. fr. 298 Voigt, see Connelly 1993, 88. On other early literary depictions, see Mazzoldi 1997, 7-8 n. 3. Soph. *Locrian Ajax* conceivably centred on Ajax's actions in the sanctuary of Athena (Sutton 1984, 7-9). The episode may also have featured in the same poet's *Lacaenae*, *Teucer* and *Antenoridae* (Sutton 1984, 21-23). Later versions include Lycoph. *Alex.* 5.357; Prop. 4(5) c. I, 118; Ov. *Ars am.* 1.7.17; *Met.* 14.468; Tryphiodorus, *Sack of Troy* 647; Quint. Symrn. *Posthomerica* 13.422. Surveys of the artistic evidence include Carpenter 1991, 209; Castriota 1992, 268-7 n.3; Connelly 1993; Anderson 1997, 199-202. On the relationship between artistic and literary representations, see Gantz 1993, 650-5; Mazzoldi 1997.
[26] Apollod. *Epit.* 5.8-10.
[27] Hudson and den Boer 2012, 306.

Athena's statue is itself an image of wartime gender violence.[28]

By dislodging the statue, Ajax opens up a new conflict, where Athena turns against the Greeks, her erstwhile favourites. The behaviour of the goddess continues to conform to the same premise of "help friends, harm enemies" that she followed during the siege, and then the taking, of Troy, the difference being that, in the wake of Ajax's actions, whom the enemy is shifts to Ajax and the other Greeks. The action that causes the turnaround could be any of the following: what Ajax does at/to Cassandra/the statue of Athena; the failure of the Greeks to punish Ajax; or what Ajax does next, namely to seek refuge at the altar of Athena and thereby put himself in the same role of the suppliant as his victim, Cassandra.

THE IGNOMINY OF AJAX

The behaviour of Ajax is interpreted by some commentors as the most excessively abhorrent and outrageous of the acts perpetrated by the Greeks as they storm Troy. For example, Mazzoldi describes Ajax's act as: "*un sacrilegio, una vera e propria ἀσέβεια*" ("a sacrilege, an out-and-out impiety").[29] According to Castriota it stands alongside wider acts of violence and sacrilege from the sack of Troy in representations from the Orientalising period onwards as: "[a]n ignominious and savage event ending in the slaughter of old men and children, and in the violation of women and temples".[30] The popularity of depictions of Ajax, Cassandra and Athena/the Palladion in late archaic Attic vase painting has been connected to the Athenians' preoccupation with concepts of *asebeia* ("impiety") and asylum, not least in the wake of the Alcmeonid violation of Cylon's asylum.[31] The popularity of the episode in fifth-century Athenian art and literature has been explained in relation to Athenian appraisals of the brutality of war, including the destruction of Acropolis sanctuaries by the Persians in 480.[32]

---

[28] Cf. *Il.* 16.100, where Achilles wishes that he and Patroclus alone were left to sack Troy by tearing off its veil. We are grateful to Hans van Wees for suggesting this parallel.
[29] Mazzoldi 1997, 8.
[30] Castriota 1992, 97.
[31] See Connelly 1993, 108.
[32] E.g. Boardman 1975, 94; Castriota 1992, esp. 98, 108; Connelly 1993, 89, 120-1.

One does not have to look far to find ancient evidence to support these readings. The popularity of the myth appears to be predicated on its potential as a model for how to behave/not behave. This is how Alcaeus uses it, in relation to his treatment at the hands of Pittacus (fr. 298 Campbell). Its popularity in Athenian art in the late archaic period comes at a time of particular interest in the ethics of asylum and *asebeia* in the wake of the Cylon episode, when Cylon took refuge at the temple of Athena, and his rights as a suppliant were violated. Then, in the classical period, its popularity comes at a time of reflection on the brutality of warfare, including in relation to the Persian sack of the city. Who each character stands for appears to be determined by the particular motivating circumstance. In Alcaeus, Ajax stands for Pittacus, while Cassandra stands for Alcaeus, and so too does Athena. In archaic Attic art, Ajax is possibly standing for Cylon as an asylum claimant but also for Cassandra when he makes his own claim to asylum. In classical artistic representations, Ajax and the Greeks would appear to stand for the Persians who sack the Acropolis in 480.

The terminology used for Ajax's actions further shows how far his behaviour appears to have been regarded in criminal terms. For example, what Ajax does is described as a τόλμημα ("offence," "outrage") by Pausanias in his description of Polygnotus' painting of the Iliupersis in the Cnidians's Lesche at Delphi.[33] The episode is also described as involving *bia* (e.g. βιάζεται - Apollod. *Epit.* 5.22), a term which may encapsulate physical or sexual violence. *Bia* is the word used by Poseidon in connection with the dragging of Cassandra from Athena's sanctuary in Euripides' *Troades* (70), while Athena refers to what is done to herself and to her sanctuary as *hybris* (69),[34] another term that could denote either physically or sexually violent behaviour. *Hybris* is the likeliest missing word in Alcaeus' fragmentary poem describing Ajax's actions and Athena's response.[35] It seems likely that the longest surviving fragment of Sophocles' *Locrian Ajax* also described the deeds of Ajax in relation to both *hybris* and *bia* when, musing on the nature of the offence, Athena asks, "what sort of man can I guess was author of these deeds, the man who in his insolence [ὑβρίζων] wrenched headlong from its base my

---

[33] Paus. 10.26.3. On the possibility that Pausanias is applying post-classical concepts of victimage, see Mazzoldi 1997, 12-13. Cf. Anderson 1997, 202: "The concern of the Greek warriors, of course, lies not with the maiden, but with the offended deity and her offender".
[34] See Rabinowitz 2011, 14.
[35] Cf. Mazzoldi 1997, 8.

image, not fastened there, and dragged the prophetic maiden from the altar in defiance [*βίᾳ*] of the gods.[36] This incident, compounded with subsequent acts, leads Athena and/or Poseidon to cause the death of Ajax by drowning,[37] a punishment that was considered suitable for perpetrators of acts of *hybris*.[38]

However, what does it mean to call the behaviour of Ajax offensive? Against whom is it an offence? We argue that it is not the offence in itself that is the problem, but whom it is an offence against – and we argue that it is offensive in the context of the logic of retaliatory warfare, which involved one individual or group seeking redress for a perceived offence through actions that could then breed further grievances. It is not enough to say, then, that what Ajax did was wrong. Rather, it is necessary to establish whom he was wronging, and what was driving his behaviour in the first place.

AJAX AS RETALIATORY WARRIOR

That retaliatory behaviour can be regarded as the fitting redress to a perceived grievance may be exemplified by the assessment by Isocrates that the Greeks' response to the theft of Helen is an appropriate recourse against those who carry off their women.[39] The actions of Ajax counterbalance the abduction of Helen, whom Paris "carried away" (e.g. *ἀνῆγες* – *Il.* 3.48) by a two-stage reciprocal act. First, Ajax seeks to carry off Helen's Trojan counterpart, Cassandra, and second, he enables the goddess herself to be carried off. This retaliatory behaviour changes him from a respondent to the perpetrator of an act that needs, in turn, to be redressed.

The theft of the most beautiful and highest-status Greek woman is countered with Ajax's attempt to abduct the "most beautiful" (*Πριάμοιο θυγατρῶν εἶδος ἀρίστην* - *Il.* 13.365) and eligible of Priam's daughters, whose appearance evokes that of "golden Aphrodite" (*ἰκέλη χρυσῇ*

---

[36] Fr. 10c. 7-10 tr. Lloyd-Jones.
[37] E.g. at Alcaeus fr. 298, it is Athena's fury that generates a storm at sea. In Euripides' *Troades*, Athena asks Poseidon to help her achieve revenge (73) by giving the Greeks a bitter homecoming (66, 75). In the *Odyssey*, Poseidon drowns Ajax because of his boasting (*Od.* 4.499-511).
[38] On drowning at sea as a suitable punishment for insults against gods, see McHardy 2008b, 6-7.
[39] Isoc. 4.181, 12.80, 12.83.

Ἀφροδίτῃ - 24.699), and who attracted high-status suitors, among them, a god: Apollo.[40] The repeated motif, seen as early as shield straps dating to the first quarter of the sixth century from Olympia and Delphi, showing Ajax grabbing Cassandra by the arm, bears comparison with representations of Helen and Menelaus, and South Italian vases juxtapose Ajax grabbing Cassandra with Menelaus making a similar gesture towards Helen.[41] There is also a fit between the representations of Ajax grabbing Cassandra with the abduction of Helen that sparked the conflict in the first place, including depictions of Paris making the same grabbing gesture made by Ajax.[42] The eligibility of both women in relation to retaliatory ethics is repeated at Eur. *Tro.* 353-8 by Cassandra, as the prospective bride of Agamemnon, whose marriage to the king will bring about deadly retaliation in the same way as Paris' marriage to Helen destroyed Cassandra's family.

In addition to helping in the quest to seek redress for the abduction of Helen, the actions of Ajax conform to the terms of the broken oath between the Greeks and the Trojans which, as outlined above, required the subjugation of the womenfolk of the enemy and the killing of their sons. This might explain why Ajax's attempt to abduct Cassandra is counterpoised with the killing of Astyanax on a fragmentary belly amphora of c. 560-40 by Lydos, where with a drawn sword, Ajax looks down on a crouching Cassandra, whose hand is raised in supplication. Behind Ajax, the tiny figure of Astyanax is held upside down by one of his feet by another warrior, possibly Neoptolemus. The arm of the warrior is reaching back, suggesting that he is about the hurl the child, or use the child's body to batter that of Priam, which is lying on an altar.[43]

AJAX AS WARTIME RAPIST?

Artistic depictions of Ajax match the behaviour of victorious warriors assembled by Gaca, including pulling hair and stripping off clothing, in order to remove them from their place of refuge or hiding place and take them to the place where they will be temporarily held before being divided

---

[40] Othryoneus (*Il.* 13. 361-9) and Coroebos (Ver. *Aeneid* 2. 341-4) fight at Troy to win her hand. On Cassandra's suitors, see Gantz 1993, 650 n. 88.
[41] Connelly 1993, 107, 115, with n. 69, 70, 102.
[42] See Connelly 1993, 107, with n. 69. Redfield argues that the north metopes of the Parthenon paired Cassandra and Ajax with Helen and Paris (2003, 35).
[43] Paris F 29=*LIMC 1.1 Aias II* no. 50 (Touchefeu 1981). Connelly (1993, 91) compares and contrasts this vase with other black-figure representations.

as spoils of warfare.[44] For example, on bronze shield straps from Olympia (c. 590-80) and Delphi (c. 560), Ajax is grabbing Cassandra's elbow.[45] On a black-figure Siana cup (c. 575-50), Ajax is holding her by the upper arm,[46] while on a Honolulu-class olpe, he grabs her by the wrist.[47] In Attic red-figure vases, he grabs her variously by the wrist, the hair, and the head.[48]

What takes place at Athena's statue is a violent encounter between a rampaging warrior and a resisting woman. It is a sexually aggravated action, with the often-naked body of Cassandra put on show. Cassandra's nakedness has been interpreted either in relation to the erotic context,[49] or as indicating her vulnerability,[50] or as "perhaps a bit of both".[51] Much attention has been devoted to the question of whether or not Ajax rapes Cassandra. We argue that, in fact, the sources are consistently ambiguous, including in ways not previously explored. We show how this ambiguity is typical of the ambiguity surrounding classical representations of sexual violence in general,[52] and of other representations of both Cassandra and of Athena. This ambiguity even allows for, while never articulating, the possibility that Athena – in one respect the masculine protector of Cassandra – is the victim of an assault that includes possible intimations of rape.

Some, like Jackson, have argued that there is no explicit reference to rape.[53] Others, including Sourvinou-Inwood, understand that what Ajax does is to rape Cassandra.[54] Lloyd-Jones, summarising Arctinus' *Iliupersis*,

---

[44] See esp. Gaca 2010.
[45] Olympia B 1801=*LIMC* 1.1 "Aias II" no. 48 (Touchefeu 1981), Olympia B 975, Delphi 4479= *LIMC* 1.1 "Aias II" no. 49.
[46] London B 379=*LIMC* 1.1 "Aias II" no. 16 (Touchefeu 1981).
[47] Paris, Cabinet des Médailles 181= *LIMC* 1.1 "Aias II" no. 36 (Touchefeu 1981).
On the motif of hair grabbing, see Moret 1975, 193-225, 234-40.
[48] Connelly 1993, esp. 116.
[49] Furtwängler and Reichhold 1904, 85; Davreux 1942, 141.
[50] Bonfante 1989, 560.
[51] Connelly 1993, 103.
[52] On the challenges faced in relation to defining specific ancient Greek acts as rape, see Stewart 1995; Omitowoju 2002; Harris 2004; Rabinowitz 2011, esp. 6; Deacy 2013.
[53] Jackson 1996/7.
[54] Sourvinou-Inwood 2010; Lissarrague 2001, 106; Mitchell-Boyask 2006, 273. Rabinowitz cautiously interprets Ajax's behaviour as rape (2011, 14, with n. 64).

writes that "during the sack of Troy Ajax the son of Oileus violated Cassandra in the temple of Athena, pulling down the image of the goddess as he did so."[55] Woodford reads it as an insinuation of Cassandra's impending rape.[56] We have already adduced Blondell's description of Cassandra as the "archetypal" rape victim of classical mythology.[57] Others are more circumspect, including Connelly, who argues that the attack fits the schemata for attack rather than erotic pursuit established by Sourvinou-Inwood by showing Ajax moving from left to right, brandishing a sword and, typically, dressed as a warrior.[58] Thus by applying Sourvinou-Inwood's methodology, Connelly reads the episode differently from the author herself.[59] Another approach has been to argue that, in archaic Greece, either the rape was not a feature of the myth, or the Greeks were simply not bothered one way or the other, or they regarded the violation of the sanctuary as more serious than the rape of a suppliant. The oath sworn by Ajax, as depicted by Polygnotus and as described at Paus. 10.26.3, has been interpreted as consisting of an admission of an offence against Athena and a denial of rape.[60] Then, it has been suggested, during the classical period the experiences of Cassandra became increasingly foregrounded in response to a developing interest in human suffering and the brutality of warfare. Finally, according to this interpretation, in the Hellenistic period, this focus on Cassandra's terrified response to Ajax's violent advances developed into the transformation of Cassandra into an unambiguous rape victim.[61]

In fact, every representation of the encounter is clouded in ambiguity – and matches the ambiguity over whether or not Paris' theft of Helen involved force, or consent, or some blending of the two possibilities.[62] For

---

[55] Lloyd-Jones 1996, 12.
[56] Woodford 1993, 110.
[57] Blondell 2013, 7.
[58] Connelly 1993, 127 n. 53, citing Sourvinou-Inwood 1987.
[59] Cf. Gantz's observation that, since, "on some examples the tip of the sword is dangerously close to Kassandra's neck…did we not know better we would surely assume that she was executed on the spot" (1993, 655).
[60] For scholarship, see Castriota 1992, 272-3 n. 43.
[61] Connelly 1993 explores differences between archaic and classical depictions; Mazzoldi 1997 traces a development across archaic, classical and subsequent depictions and explains this in relation to changing religious and ethical values. On the rape as unknown in earlier sources and subsequently invented in Alexandria, see Mason 1959, 82.
[62] The ambiguities surrounding the abduction of Helen are surveyed most recently in Blondell 2013.

instance, Proclus' summary of Arctinus' *Iliuspersis*, which Lloyd-Jones describes as involving the rape of Cassandra,[63] says only that Ajax pulled Cassandra from the altar along with the statue of Athena, for which offence the Greeks wanted to stone him. The verb used here, ἕλκω, could denote rape, or simply dragging.[64] Other terms used to describe the actions of Ajax likewise need not specifically denote rape. For instance, the range of possible meanings of *hybris* could denote forced sex, but the term could also be used of an offence against the honour of another.[65] When Athena describes what Ajax did to her as *hybris* at *Tro.* 70, it seems likely that the goddess is referring to how his actions have sought to compromise her honour, which now needs to be restored through retaliatory action on her part. This slight to her honour could be due to the violation of her sanctuary, or because, now in the role of the protector – and thus, perhaps the *kyrios* ("guardian") – of Cassandra, she is considering the behaviour by Ajax as an offence against her own honour. Such an interpretation is consistent with Greek understandings of rape as an offence principally against a woman's *kyrios* rather than against a woman herself.[66] This possibility, that Athena could be in the role of the *kyrios* of Cassandra who has sought her protection, may help explain why it is that archaic visual sources depict the encounter as a standoff between two warriors, while Cassandra crouches between them, as on an Attic black-figure amphora from Vulci, now in Munich.[67] On this reading, the principal offended party is Athena, whose honour has been compromised by the attack on someone under her protection.

As in any discussion of *hybris* or any other Greek terms that could have connotations of sexual violence, it is vital to consider the context in which it was used. But when used in relation to Cassandra, the context is racked with ambiguity. Depictions of the relationship of Cassandra with Apollo interweave imagery of rape and resistance to rape, while Agamemnon is variously her violator, husband, and would-be bridegroom.[68]

---

[63] Lloyd-Jones 1996, 12.
[64] On ἕλκω in early sources, see Mazzoldi 1997, 7-8, with n. 2-3.
[65] See Omitowoju 1997; 2002, 29-50.
[66] See Omitowoju 1997, 6. Rabinowitz (2011, 14, n. 64) allows for the possibility that "despite the lack of specific reference to the rape...the ὕβρις can be taken to refer to it".
[67] Attic black-figure amphora, c. 540 from Vulci. Staatliche Antikensammlungen, Munich 1380.
[68] On Cassandra's sexual relations/lack of such, with Apollo and Agamemnon, see Mitchell-Boyask 2006.

Previous scholars have noted incongruities between the sources.[69] In contrast, we understand Cassandra's relationship with both men as part of a recurring ambiguity surrounding her virginity and violability. At the same time, the ambiguity surrounding Cassandra matches the vulnerability of Athena, the other recipient of the violent behaviour of Ajax. Cassandra thus places herself in the protection of a goddess who, likewise, varies between resisting and encountering unwanted sex.[70] Indeed, one way to read Ajax's attack is as one made directly against the goddess, and which succeeds insofar as he manages to uproot the statue from its base. Just as Cassandra will be taken to the place where spoils of war will be divided, the goddess can now be carried off.[71]

ATHENA, AJAX AND RETALIATORY CONFLICT

When Ajax follows Cassandra into the sanctuary of Athena, he performs an act of violence against Cassandra as an enemy female, as befits the retaliatory context of his actions. But, by directing his violence towards Athena, he performs a fresh act of gender violence that itself requires restitution. Thus, although Ajax's behaviour conforms to acts associated with retaliatory warfare, it precipitates his own downfall and also the difficult homecomings of the Greeks. The behaviour of Ajax is intended to compromise the honour of a deity insofar as he acts without the restraint deemed fitting before a god, and he might be attacking the deity directly as well. Athena is variously a living person responding to an act of violence, and a supernatural agent who will ensure that the impiety of Ajax will be followed by disaster. There is a further possibility, namely that Athena is in the role of the victim of gender violence. For all that modern understandings of Athena are premised on an assumption that the virginity of the goddess was key to her nature, such a conception does not

---

[69] Mason 1959, 82; Gantz 1993, 665.
[70] See Deacy 1997.
[71] The ambiguity over whether Ajax is trying to drag Cassandra away to be given later as a spear prize, or whether she is raped at the point of capture, is consistent with ambiguity in the oath sworn by the Greeks and Trojans over the necessity that the womenfolk of the oath-breakers should be "subjugated" ($δαμεῖεν$ - $Il.$ 3.301). $Δαμεῖεν$ could refer to rape – either at the point of capture, or subsequently – or to the humiliation of being captured or forced into concubinage. On the interplay between force and consent surrounding the Trojan women's submission to their new sexual partners, see Scodel 1998, who interprets their behaviour in relation to Stockholm Syndrome.

always fit the ancient evidence for this deity.[72]

It is Athena who creates the conditions that enable the Greeks to take the city through the creation of the wooden horse.[73] Up to this point, the interests of the Greeks and the interests of Athena have been consistent. Like Ajax, Athena has been following the precepts of retaliatory warfare, including the kill men–subjugate women style of conflict. For example, the goddess engineers the breaking of the truce in the *Iliad* by appearing to Pandarus disguised as Laodocus and persuading him to fire at Menelaus, telling him that Paris will be pleased with him should he fire the shot that breaks the truce (*Il.* 4.85-105). The decision of the goddess to bring about the end of the truce depicts her as desiring the annihilation of the Trojan fighters and the subjugation of their wives. Athena's friendship turns to enmity when Ajax enters the sanctuary of the goddess to dislodge Cassandra. The cause of the conflict is the perennial one of the ownership of women,[74] with Ajax trying to carry Cassandra off and Athena trying to protect the mortal woman, because Cassandra is a suppliant, and potentially because Athena is now, as we propose above, performing the role of *kyrios*.

In attacking Cassandra, Ajax abuses Athena too, such that the goddess also comes to be treated as an enemy female. It is not only the case that the behaviour of Ajax towards Cassandra is consistent with expected behaviour of a warrior capturing a city, so too is his behaviour towards the image of Athena, which was depicted both as a representation of the goddess, and as invested with the presence of the goddess. There has been a divide in scholarship over whether to interpret Athena as a statue or as a living goddess.[75] However, seeking an either/or explanation runs counter to Greek notions of statues, especially *xoana*, as representations of anthropomorphised gods.[76] The episode constructs female subjectivity by representing Athena and Cassandra as variously vulnerable and inviolable.

---

[72] See Deacy 2008, 82-4.
[73] Hom. *Od.* 8.492-3. See Deacy 2008, 68-70.
[74] Cf. the depictions of the episode across black-figure vase-painting as a clash between two warriors, where Ajax rushes at Athena and Athena storms towards him. Meanwhile, Cassandra, often smaller in stature, and at times seemingly incidental to the violent encounter, crouches or kneels between them. See Jackson 1996/7; Connelly 1993, 90-109; Anderson 1997, 200-1.
[75] See Matheson 1986, 105-6; Shapiro 1989, 27-36; Connelly 1993, esp. 90, 101.
[76] See here Schnapp 1988, 568-74; Gantz 1993, 655. On the encounter as an attack at once on the image and on the goddess herself, see Connelly 1993, 100-3, 114-6; Anderson 1997, 201.

The wartime gender violence that Ajax is displaying is conducted not only against Cassandra, but also against Athena, who was venerated in numerous ancient cities, but who was also conceived as the local tutelary maiden of many communities, Troy included.[77]

The connotations of *asebeia* include thinking oneself superior to the gods, dishonouring the gods, going so far as to do violence to the gods, and risking the wrath of these gods. According to Burkert, "[a]sebeia brings the wrath of the gods on the whole community…the real danger begins when man tries to place himself above the gods…clear, actionable asebeia is found when there is active violation of cult or sanctuary, priests or consecrated persons…then catastrophe may strike from the gods."[78] There is a fit between these implications and what Ajax does, including to violate a sanctuary, and perhaps also to violate Cassandra as a consecrated person (the priestess of Apollo). At Alcaeus fr. 298.5, Ajax is "he who did violence to the gods" (αἰ τὸν θεοβλάβεντα κατέκτανον).[79] His actions incur divine wrath upon himself and upon his community (of warriors wanting to return home). The "active violation," to quote Burkert, of the sanctuary by Ajax also includes violence against the image of the goddess, which is invested with the presence of the goddess, and also *is* the goddess. Ajax attacks a mortal woman, Cassandra, and the statue at which she has taken refuge; equally, he attacks two persons, the young woman Cassandra and a goddess who is both a warrior and a woman.

Ajax's actions parallel those of Paris that instigated the war, but with a difference: Paris successfully carries off Helen, but Ajax does not manage to carry off Cassandra. However, by dislodging the statue of Athena, he enables a female, Athena, to be carried away from Troy, offending the very deity that enabled the victory. This act concludes the retaliatory war but creates a new offence that requires punitive action, this time to punish Ajax and the other Greeks by hampering their homecomings.

Conclusion

We have provided a new way to interpret the much-discussed behaviour of Ajax during the taking of Troy by showing how it constitutes the expected and typical behaviour of a victorious Greek warrior during a

---

[77] E.g. Athena is the "Zeus-born Trojan girl" (Ἰλιάδι Διογενεῖ κόρᾳ) at Eur. *Tro.* 526). On the numerous poliad Athens, see Deacy 2008, 122-37.
[78] Burkert 1985, 274.
[79] Tr. Campbell.

conflict with a retaliatory basis. When Ajax tries forcibly to pull Cassandra away from the statue of Athena, his behaviour epitomises the acts performed against enemy women as part of the process of subjugating the surviving non-combat population, and of taking revenge for a perceived insult through gender violence. As well as conforming to expected behaviour of an ancient Greek warrior, the behaviour of Ajax resonates with male wartime behaviour across cultures and which has potential evolutionary roots.

However, ambiguity remains over whether Ajax is seeking to rape Cassandra, and if so, whether or not he succeeds – an ambiguity which is central to the depiction of Ajax's attack across the various sources. Thus, while the episode demonstrates the centrality of gender violence in retaliatory warfare, and the significant role played by women in the competition for dominance and status between enemy warriors, it also shows the care that needs to be taken over assuming that when Greek warriors subjugated enemy women, they necessarily raped them at the point of capture.

Ajax's attack on Cassandra also draws in Athena. As is typical of the goddess, her role and gender are complicated in ancient depictions of the episode. The goddess is simultaneously an aggressor driving on the Greek warriors to kill the Trojan men and subjugate their women, and the last bastion of the Trojans' defence. Like Ajax, the goddess is represented as a warrior keen to gain revenge for the slight of Paris and the *hybris* of Ajax. She is also the unwilling victim of Ajax's attack in her sanctuary. Athena is a *kyrios* figure protecting a vulnerable young woman in her care, but is also, herself, embodied as an enemy female whose capture is an integral part of the conflict. Athena is a power that spurs men to victory, and that shares the vulnerability of the defeated population. The same deity that favours the kill men-subjugate women style of warfare can, herself, become an exemplar of the subjugated woman – such is the far-reaching significance of her role as a war deity.

This, then, is our contribution to the call from policy initiators, action groups and scholars across several disciplines to understand how gender violence has played a role in conflicts across cultures and throughout history. We have found that, by reading an episode from a mythological conflict in relation to the ethics of a particular style of warfare, it emerges in a fresh light – as one that is more than an instance of what happens when appropriate warrior behaviour is suspended. Rather, it presents elements of the characteristic gender violence perpetuated on enemy females by conquering warriors.

BIBLIOGRAPHY

Anderson, M. J. (1997) *The Fall of Troy in Early Greek Poetry and Art*, Oxford.
Askin, K. D. (1997) *War Crimes Against Women*, The Hague.
Bergoffen, D. (2009) "Exploiting the Dignity of the Vulnerable Body: Rape as a Weapon of War," *Philosophical Papers* 38, 307–25.
Blondell, R. (2013) *Helen of Troy: Beauty, Myth, Devastation*, Oxford.
Boardman, J. (1975) *Athenian Red Figure Vases: The Archaic Period*, Oxford.
Bonfante L. (1989) "Nudity as Costume in Classical Art," *American Journal of Archaeology* 93, 543-70.
Brownmiller, S. (1975) *Against Our Will: Men, Women, and Rape*, London.
Burkert, W. (1985) *Greek Religion: Archaic and Classical*, Oxford.
Buss, D. E. (2009) "Rethinking Rape as a Weapon of War," *Feminist Legal Studies* 17, 145-63.
Card, C. (1996) "Rape as a Weapon of War," *Hypatia* 11, 5–18.
Carpenter, T. (1991) *Art and Myth in Ancient Greece*, London.
Castriota, D. (1992) *Myth, Ethos, and Actuality: Official Art in Fifth-Century B.C. Athens*, Madison.
Connelly, J. B. (1993) "Narrative and Image in Attic Vase Painting: Ajax and Kassandra at the Trojan Palladion," in P. J. Holliday (ed.) *Narrative and Event in Ancient Art*, 88-129, Cambridge.
Daly, M. and M. Wilson (1988) *Homicide*, New Brunswick.
Davreux, J. (1942) *La legend de la prophetesse Cassandre*, Liège.
Deacy, S. (1997) "The Vulnerability of Athena: *Parthenoi* and Rape in Greek Myth," in S. Deacy and K. Pierce (ed.), *Rape in Antiquity*, 43-63, London.
—. (2008) *Athena*, London.
—. (2013) "From 'Flowery Tales' to 'Heroic Rapes': Virginal Subjectivity in the Mythological Meadow," *Arethusa* 46.3, 395-413
Deacy, S and F. McHardy (2013) "Uxoricide in Pregnancy: Ancient Greek Domestic Violence in Evolutionary Perspective," *Evolutionary Psychology* 11.5, 994-1010.
Furtwängler, A. and C, Reichhold (1904) *Griechischen Vasenmalerei*, Munich.
Gaca, K. (2008) "The Little Girl and Her Mother: *Iliad* 16.7-11 and

Ancient Greek Warfare," *American Journal of Philology* 129, 145-71.
—. (2010) "The Andrapodizing of War Captives in Greek Historical Memory," *Transactions of the American Philological Association* 140, 117-61.
—. (2011) "Girls, Women, and the Significance of Sexual Violence in Ancient Warfare," in E. Heineman (ed.) *Sexual Violence in Conflict Zones*, 73-88, Philadelphia.
Gantz, T. (1993) *Early Greek Myth: A Guide to Literary and Artistic Sources*, Baltimore.
Gat, A. (2000) "The Human Motivational Complex: Evolutionary Theory and the Causes of Hunter-Gatherer Fighting," *Anthropological Quarterly* 73.2, 74–88.
Gottschall, J. (2008) *The Rape of Troy: Evolution, Violence and the World of Homer*, Cambridge.
Harris E. M. (2004) "Did Rape Exist in Classical Athens? Further Thoughts on the Laws about Sexual Violence," *Dike* 7, 41–83.
Heineman, E. D. (ed.) (2011) *Sexual Conflict in Conflict Zones: From the Ancient World to the Era of Human Rights*, Philadelphia.
Hudson, V. M. and den Boer, A.M. (2012) "A Feminist Evolutionary Analysis of the Relationship Between Violence Against Women and Inequitable Treatment of Women, and Conflict Within and Between Human Collectives," in Shackelford, T. K. and V. A. Shackelford-Weekes (ed.) *The Oxford Handbook of Evolutionary Perspectives on Violence, Homicide, and War*, 301-323, Oxford.
Jackson, H. (1996/7) "A Black-Figure Neck Amphora in Melbourne: the Nudity of Kassandra," *Mediterranean Archaeology* 9, 53-75.
Kitts, M. (2005) *Sanctified Violence in Homeric Society*, Cambridge.
Kirby, P. (2012) "How is Rape a Weapon of War? Feminist International Relations, Modes of Critical Explanation and the Study of Wartime Sexual Violence," *European Journal of International Relations.*
Leatherman, J. L. (2011) *Sexual Violence and Armed Conflict*, Cambridge.
Livingstone Smith, D. (2012) "War, Evolution and the Nature of Human Nature," in Shackelford, T. K. and V. A. Shackelford-Weekes (ed.), *The Oxford Handbook of Evolutionary Perspectives on Violence, Homicide, and War*, 339-50, Oxford.
Lissarrague, F. (2001) *Greek Vases: The Athenians and their Images*, New York.
Lloyd-Jones, H. (1983) *The Justice of Zeus*, Berkeley, Los Angeles and London.
—. (1996) *Sophocles: Vol. 3. Fragments*, Cambridge, Mass.
McHardy, F. (2008a) *Revenge in Athenian culture*, London.

—. (2008b) "The 'Trial By Water' in Greek Myth and Literature," *Leeds International Classical Studies* 7.1.
Mason, P.G. (1959) "Kassandra," *Journal of Hellenic Studies* 79, 80-93.
Matheson, S. B. (1986) "Polygnotos: An Iliupersis Scene at the Getty Museum," in *Greek Vases in the J. Paul Getty Museum*, 101-14, Malibu.
Mazzoldi, S. (1997) "Cassandra, Aiace e lo ξόανον di Atena," *Quaderni Urbinati di Cultura Classica* n.s. 55.1. 7-21.
Merry, S. (2009) *Gender Violence: A Cultural Perspective*, London.
Mitchell-Boyask, R. (2006) "The Marriage of Cassandra and the *Oresteia*: Text, Image, Performance," *Transactions of the American Philological Association* 136.2, 269-97.
Moret, J. M. (1975) *L'Ilioupersis dans la ceramique italiote*, Rome.
Omitowoju, R. (1997) "Regulating Rape: Soap Operas and Self-Interest in the Athenian Courts," in S. Deacy and K. Pierce (ed.) *Rape in Antiquity*, 1-24, London.
Omitowoju, R. (2002). *Rape and the Politics of Consent in Classical Athens*, Cambridge.
Potts, M. and T. Hayden (2010) *Sex and War: How Biology Explains Warfare and Terrorism and Offers a Path to a Safer World*, Dallas.
Rabinowitz, N. S. (2011) "Greek Tragedy: A Rape Culture," *EuGeStA* 1, 1-21.
Redfield, J. (2003) *The Locrian Maidens: Love and Death in Greek Italy*, Princeton.
Rosivach, V. (1999) "Enslaving "*Barbaroi*" and the Athenian Ideology of Slavery," *Historia* 48, 129-157.
Scheidel, W. (2009) "Sex and Empire: a Darwinian perspective," in I. Morris and W. Scheidel (eds) *The Dynamics of Ancient Empires: State Power from Assyria to Byzantium*, 255-324, Oxford.
Schnapp, A. (1988) "Why Did the Greeks Need Images," in J. Christiansen and T. Melander (ed.) *International Vase Symposium: Proceedings of the Third Symposium on Ancient Greek Art and Related Poetry, August 31-Septembe r 4, 1987*, 568-74, Copenhagen.
Scodel, R. (1998) "The Captive's Dilemma: Sexual Acquiescence in Euripides' *Hecuba* and *Troades*," *Harvard Studies in Classical Philology* 98, 137-54.
Shapiro, H. A. (1989) *Art and Cult under the Tyrants in Athens*, Mainz.
Skjelsbæk, I. (2001) "Sexual Violence and War: Mapping Out a Complex Relationship," *European Journal of International Relations* 7, 211-37.
Sourvinou-Inwood, C. (1987) "Menace and Pursuit: Differentiation and the Creation of Meaning," in C. Bérard et. al (ed.) *Images et société in*

Grèce ancienne, 41-58, Lausanne.
—. (2011) *Athenian Myths and Festivals*: *Aglauros, Erechtheus, Plynteria, Panathenaia, Dionysia*, Oxford.
Stansbury-O'Donnell, M. (1989) "Polygnotos's *Iliupersis*: A New Reconstruction," *American Journal of Archaeology* 93, 203-15.
Stewart, A. (1995) "Rape?," in E. D. Reeder (ed.) *Pandora: Women in Classical Greece*, 74–90, Princeton.
StopRapeinConflict.org (2012) "Stop Rape in Conflict", *The International Campaign to Stop Rape & Gender Violence in Conflict.* Available at: http://www.stoprapeinconflict.org/ [Accessed: 29.08.14].
Sutton, D. F. (1984) *The Lost Sophocles*, Lanham.
Touchefeu, O. (1981) "Aias II," in *Lexicon Iconographium Mythologiae Classicae* 1, 336-51, Zurich and Munich.
Wees, H. van (1992) *Status Warriors: War, Violence and Society in Homer and History*, Amsterdam.
Wood, E. J. (2009) "Armed Groups and Sexual Violence: When Is Wartime Rape Rare?," *Politics & Society* 39, 131–61.
Woodford, S. (1993) *The Trojan War in Ancient Art*, London.

CHAPTER FIFTEEN

TREATING HEMORRHAGE IN GREEK AND ROMAN MILITARIES[1]

DR. JULIE LASKARIS

The treatment of wounds in Greek and Roman militaries is the subject of Christine Salazar's highly useful book,[2] but even it does not devote much attention to the aspect of trauma care that is of the greatest initial concern: Hemostasis, the arrest of bleeding. This paper discusses some of the methods for treating hemorrhage that were available to the doctors who travelled with Greek and Roman militaries, and argues that doctors' skills were honed through their regular use of therapeutic bloodletting (venesection) and, for those who had started out with a civilian practice, their frequent treatment of uterine hemorrhage.

We do not have a great deal of direct evidence for the details of medical practice in Greek and Roman militaries or, on the Greek side, even for the presence of doctors in the military. Salazar discusses the available textual evidence from the classical and Hellenistic periods and draws the reasonable conclusion that, because doctors are referred to casually by Greek historiographers, poets, and other writers, with no apparent need for elaboration, most Greeks would have expected them to accompany armies or at least to be available to the wounded.[3] This is not

---

[1] I wish to thank Geoff Lee for organizing a stimulating conference. This paper has benefitted greatly from the remarks of the conference participants and, especially, by the careful editing of Geoff Lee, Hélène Whittaker, Graham Wrightson, and the anonymous referees. All remaining errors are my own.
[2] Salazar 2000.
[3] Salazar 2000, 68-74. Salazar notes that our sources tend to focus on the wounding of commanders and kings more than of the ordinary soldier; she discusses the mention of doctors (generally more than one) in these passages, among them the woundings of Alexander (Arr. *Anab.* V.11.1) and of Epaminondas (D. S. 15.87.5). She points also to inscriptions that allude to expert care of the

to say that fellow soldiers did not attempt to help their wounded comrades,[4] but the need for expertise is recognized as far back as the *Iliad*, where the doctor (*iētēr*) was highly valued. In Book 11, Idomeneus becomes alarmed at the wounding of Machaon, a son of Asclepius, who, with his brother Podalirius, serves a dual role as doctor and warrior. Idomeneus urges Nestor to get Machaon out of harm's way swiftly on the grounds that a doctor's skills in treating wounds makes him worth many men (Hom. *Il*. 11.510-5). Achilles and Patroclus have the same dual role, with Achilles having been taught medicine by Cheiron and having passed his knowledge on to Patroclus. The wounded Eurypolus asks Patroclus to cut the arrow from his thigh, wash the wound, and apply soothing medicine to it, because Machaon is himself in need of a doctor, and Podalirius is still in the thick of the fighting (Hom. *Il*. 11.828-36).

Our earliest textual evidence for the existence of medical specialists in Greece comes, however, from the Bronze Age: A Linear B text granting land to a physician, using the same agent-noun (*i-ja-te*) as is found in Homeric and later texts (*PY Eq* 146).[5] Earlier still are the eleven finely-made doctor's tools found in a Bronze Age burial (1450-1400 BCE) at Nauplia; they are strikingly similar to medical instruments found in the classical period, and some of them are appropriate for wound treatment.[6] This evidence indicates that medicine was a recognized and valued craft already in the Bronze Age, and the similarity of the instruments' form suggests continuity in the transmission of techniques and skills.

For the classical period, an important text is Xenophon's report that eight doctors (*iatroi*) were appointed to care for those wounded in a skirmish with the Persians (ἰατροὺς κατέστησαν ὀκτώ *Anab*. 3.4.30-1). There is some debate concerning whether '*iatroi*' here indicates trained doctors, or merely orderlies hastily assigned to take on the duties of a doctor as best they could.[7] With regard to who would be considered a

---

wounded by civilian doctors, one of whom was sent for from another city (*I. Cret.* 4.168; Solmsen 19304). The medical texts mentioned by Salazar will be discussed below.

[4] Sternberg 2006, 104-45 discusses the emotional, moral, ethical, and logistical aspects of the care of sick and wounded soldiers; her focus is on their transport and not on their medical care.

[5] Chadwick 1958, 116-7; Ventris and Chadwick 1973 (2nd ed.), 547; Palmer 1963, 422.

[6] Protonotariou-Deilaki 1973, 92 with plates.

[7] Anderson 1970, 70, for example, holds that: "The eight 'doctors' appointed by the Ten Thousand to deal with their numerous wounded during the retreat through

qualified doctor, I think we would do well to bear in mind Vivian Nutton's observations regarding the "informality and improvisation" of Greek and Roman medical education, which seldom involved medical schools, but rather apprenticeships that could begin at an early age; Nutton notes that with the prominence of "experience and success" as criteria, it was likely that a twenty-year old who enlisted in the army would be seen as a legitimate doctor.[8]

In any event, I doubt that Xenophon would have used *iatros* of an attendant with little or no training. This passage, stating as it does the precise number of *iatroi* and noting that they were appointed, seems aimed at underscoring that the wounded were being cared for in a competent and well-organized manner.[9] In the *Constitution of the Lacedaimonians*, Xenophon uses *iatros* when he lists the members of the support staff of the battalions (*morai*) led by the Spartan king; among the number were "diviners, doctors, aulos-players, and commanders" – all experts in their fields (μάντεις καὶ ἰατροὶ καὶ αὐληταὶ <καὶ> οἱ τοῦ στρατοῦ ἄρχοντες, *Lac.* 13.7). Xenophon takes up care of the wounded (and preservation of the health of all troops) in the idealized world of the *Cyropaedia* (1.6.15-16); Cyrus the Great tells his father that he has learned from military experts that generals bring doctors (*iatroi*) with them for the sake of their soldiers and that he, now himself in command of troops, intends to have with him men well-versed in the art of medicine (...οἶμαι...πάνυ ἱκανοὺς τὴν ἰατρικὴν τέχνην ἕξειν μετ' ἐμαυτοῦ ἄνδρας 1.6.15.4-9). Xenophon's use in this passage of *iatrikē technē* (art of medicine) demonstrates clearly that he is among those who believed that medicine was a true art that functioned on the basis of reliable axioms that produced reliable results. This conception

---

Mesopotamia were presumably only orderlies, who did what they could in the way of bandaging." Salazar 2000, 68-9 thinks that since these *iatroi* were appointed because of the large number of casualties, that their work was limited to wound treatment; she also suggests that the criteria for accepting someone as a *iatros* may have been lowered, particularly because the army was in retreat, though she suggests that diminished expectations regarding the calibre of military doctors may have been typical during any time of war. Waterfield 2005, 73 (with note) translates as "doctors," then notes that they were "probably slaves" (the two categories were by no means mutually exclusive). Lee 2007, 244 believes the *iatroi* were veterans with "some practical surgical knowledge" but possessed of "neither formal training nor proper equipment." Ambler 2008, 116 translates simply as "doctors" without further comment.

[8] Nutton 1969, 264. See also Scarborough 2007 / 1968.
[9] Sternberg 2006, 144 observes (though not with regard to this passage) that in the *Anabasis* Xenophon is at pains to show that he cares for his troops.

of medicine was by no means uncontested: Medicine's frequent failures made it easy for its detractors to claim that it was a lowly skill that could be performed by anyone.[10] Holding that medicine was a true *technē* may have been to take a somewhat loftier view of it than the one articulated above by Nutton – and was perhaps more suited to the ideal state of the *Cyropaedia* than to the harsh realities of the *Anabasis*; nevertheless, with his use of *iatrikē technē*, Xenophon situates himself clearly in the contemporay debates over medicine's technical status, and I therefore find it highly unlikely that he would have used *iatros* of a semi-skilled attendant in the *Anabasis* passage under discussion.

A second piece of textual evidence for the presence of doctors in Greek militaries is found in *Physician*, a text of the Hippocratic *Corpus* that is most likely dated to the Hellenistic period. The author mentions how very rarely doctors in civilian life were required to extract missiles when treating wounds, and advises that a doctor desiring this sort of experience should accompany an army serving abroad – a topic that he takes up, he tells us "in other writings" (Hippoc. *Medic*. 9.218-20 L). As so often, these writings have not survived. Our passage, written not long after the *Anabasis*, makes it apparent that at least some doctors in Hellenistic armies were likely to have practiced first as civilians and to have gained some part of their medical education from texts. This was sometimes the case in the Roman army, where doctors might come from relatively high-status and well-educated families, and have had earlier civilian careers to which they may have planned to return.[11] It is possible, then, that the *iatroi*

---

[10] The Hippocratic treatises *On the Art* and *On Breaths* offer particularly good examples of such arguments; see Laskaris 2002, 73-82.

[11] Nutton 2013, 185-6 (with notes) offers examples: Marcus Valerius Longinus, who had served as a doctor in the Seventh Legion, returned to his home in Drobeta (Turnu Severin, Romania), where he had been a member of the city council (*CIL* 3.14216.9); Marcus Ulpius Telesporus became the town physician of Ferentrium (Italy) after his military service with auxiliary cavalry units in Africa and Germany (*CIL* 11.3007 = *ILS* 2542); Numisius, who served as a doctor with the Second Adiutrix Legion, was clearly a wealthy man with a civilian practice to which he intended to return, since he wrote to the Emperor Caracalla regarding the potential loss during his military service of the tax immunity he had enjoyed as a civilian doctor (Justinian, *Code* 10.53.1); wealth is also evidenced in the elegance of the grave of Caius Papirius Aelianus, *medicus ordinarius* of the Third Legion in North Africa (*CIL* 8.18314); a high level of education is revealed by the ornate dedication in Greek to Asclepius, Hygieia, and Panacea set up by a doctor named Antiochus serving in Chester (England) and by the figure of Calliomorphus, a military doctor who wrote of the Parthian wars of the 160s.

of whom Xenophon spoke were at least literate and perhaps even reasonably well-educated, though this is necessarily speculative.

The paucity of direct textual evidence for military medical practices exists despite the fact that warfare was all too common, and that texts on medicine and biology constitute a large portion of the extant works from Greek and Roman antiquity and are found in every period from the Classical through to Late Antiquity. The earliest medical works, dated to about 450 BCE, are among the oldest extensive Greek prose texts that we have. They are part of the Hippocratic *Corpus*, a collection of 60-70 anonymous texts, most of them composed or compiled between 420 and 350 BCE, with a few arising in the first and second centuries CE. At one time, the collection appears to have included one (or possibly two) treatises on wounds and arrows, but these are now lost to us.[12] A late and valuable Greek source is Paul of Aegina, a seventh-century CE practicing physician and surgeon, famous in his own day as a gynecologist and obstetrician,[13] and the author of a highly influential medical encyclopedia that includes a lengthy description of extracting arrowheads.

Several works of the Hippocratic *Corpus* discuss wound treatment, and in some passages it is certain, or likely, that the patient suffered the wound while in the military. We hear, for instance, of a man struck by a catapult during the siege of Datum, of another wounded in the back, of several whose injuries result in bones being laid bare and eventually rotting (πελιαινομένων τῶν ὀστέων), of a man with an arrow wound to the upper abdomen, and of another whose head was struck by a stone (Hippoc. *Epid.* 5, 5.254-7 L). We do not, however, often learn how doctors treated the blood loss that surely resulted from wounds such as these. A doctor using a medical text was probably expected to know what the usual methods were for treating hemorrhage, so descriptions did not need to be spelled out each time. While it is risky to make an argument from silence, we see this sort of omission in medical texts frequently. Later authors do take up the task – we will come to one of them below – but it would not have been practical to bring lengthy written instructions to any real-life setting, and especially not to a battlefield.

There are texts of the *Corpus* that give some information on the treatment of hemorrhage in a military setting. For example, the man mentioned above who was wounded in the back (perhaps the lungs),

---

[12] Salazar 2000, 3.
[13] Salazar 1998, 170.

hemorrhages; his wound is bound with a bandage containing styptics, and he is said to have recovered (Hippoc. *Epid.* 5, 5.256 L). Another case involves a man struck through the eyelid by an arrow, its point penetrating to some degree, though with the barb sticking out. The arrowhead was successfully removed and the eye recovered quickly after there was a vigorous flow of blood of "a sufficient amount" (Hippoc. *Epid.* 5, 5.236 L).

This last remark reflects the belief common among most Greek and Roman doctors that some blood loss was beneficial on the grounds that it reduced inflammation, which was thought to produce pus (*e.g.*, Hippoc. *Ulc.* 6.400-2 L).[14] Celsus, the early first-century CE author of a medical encyclopedia, offers essentially the same view, saying that the doctor must balance the risks of the patient's dying either from hemorrhage or inflammation (*Med.* 5.26.21).

Such natural bloodletting could obviate the need for venesection, which was practiced regularly by Greek and Roman doctors in treating many conditions. So common a therapeutic method was it that many doctors were very likely causing – and eventually stopping – blood loss as a regular, perhaps even daily, part of their practice. According to Celsus, the practice grew in favour over time, so that in his own day it was even being used on children, the elderly, and pregnant women, and for nearly every illness (*Med.* 2.10.1). Celsus remarks at some length on the difficulties for the inexperienced in performing venesection correctly, though he claims that it is easy for the experienced. The vein is to be cut only half-way through, and the color and nature of the blood noted as it streams out. If the blood is thick and dark, rather than thinner and red, it is defective (*vitiosus*) and the venesection will probably have to be repeated the next day (*Med.* 2.10.18-19). After each session, the doctor soaks a bandage in cold water, then squeezes it out and applies it to the site. The following day, he gets the blood flowing again simply by flicking the coalesced ends with the tip of his middle finger (*Med.* 2.10.18). While it is beneficial to let the thick, dark defective blood, the letting of thinner red blood is actually harmful and should be stopped immediately (*Med.* 2.10.18). The confident expectation with which this directive is given is

---

[14] Medical opinion concerning suppuration (pus formation) varied among authors, with some holding that certain types of it were good, or were beneficial in certain conditions or in certain amounts, while others believed it should generally be avoided. Several authors distinguish between "good" and "bad" pus. Salazar 2000, 24-8 has a good discussion of this.

striking. The rest of the section gives us a sense of just how frequently a doctor was likely to perform this procedure, which in turn helps us to understand Celsus' assumption that a skilled doctor could achieve immediate hemostasis. While letting blood until he reaches the redder, thinner blood is the goal, the doctor should stop the procedure if "enough has been let," and he must certainly do so before the patient faints (*Med.* 2.10.18), although other medical authors state that loss of consciousness is beneficial in that it halts bleeding.[15] When the goal of the desirable red blood has been reached, the arm is to be kept bandaged until the scar that forms is firm and strong – something that Celsus claims happens very quickly (*Med.* 2.10.19).

Celsus' text goes into unusual detail, but it is not the only one to describe venesection or refer to its effects. The Hippocratic *Ulcers* states that blood should be made to flow abundantly in all wounds but those in the abdomen; even old wounds should be bled, because it is the superfluity of blood that is preventing them from drying up and healing (Hippoc. *Ulc.* 6.402 L). *Ulcers* and several other Hippocratic texts provide details of where and how to perform venesection so that blood flow will be controllable and they give instruction on stopping the flow, both from the initial cut and from a vessel that has re-opened. Though the details vary from text to text, the general assessment is that the cut area must be raised and pressure applied with a dry bandage; cold water, wine, or vinegar should be daubed around the wound, though not directly onto it. In some cases, a bandage is impregnated with plaster, or with oil (to keep it from sticking), or with a compound that might include styptics and/or substances we now know to be antibacterial; if the blood flow does not stop from the application of pressure, the wound might then be cauterised (*Ulc.* 6.410-8; 430-2 L; *Epid.* 2 5.114-6 L; *Medic.* 9.210-4 L, *Loc.* 6.330-2 L).

Galen describes virtually the same steps for the control of traumatic hemorrhage, though for this he recommends gentle pressure with a finger on the vessel, at least if the vessel is close to the surface; if it is not, the vessel should be pierced with a hook, pulled up, and gently twisted. If that does not suffice, then a styptic compound should be sprinkled on while the vessel is compressed and, once the blood has coagulated, an eschar should be made to form by the use of either caustics or cautery (2.1-7 K).[16] If these methods all fail, Galen advocates tying the vein or artery with two

---

[15] Salazar 2000, 44.
[16] Salazar 2000, 43.

ligatures, then cutting between them, which would cause the ends of the vessel to pull back and close.[17] In the Hippocratic *Epidemics* 2, there is the recognition that in venesection, an external ligature that is loose will cause the blood to flow more quickly and that a tight one will make it stop (Hippoc. *Epid* 2, 5.114-5 L), but the risk of gangrene from bandaging or ligatures that are too tight is also recognized (Hippoc. *Art*. 4.283 L), and it may be for this reason that we do not see tourniquets advocated in our texts, though Scribonius Largus (ca. 1-50 CE) does allude disparagingly to doctors who use them.[18]

Some elements of these scenarios are basic to hemostasis techniques today (e.g., elevation of the wounded area, the application of pressure, and cautery).[19] Therefore, given the similarities between the hemostasis techniques used in venesection and those described by Galen for trauma care, it is safe to conclude that Greek and Roman doctors very likely gained a great deal of valuable experience in trauma care by regularly causing trauma themselves, and that they thereby became fairly adept at stopping all but the most serious hemorrhages in their wounded patients.

While venesection may have improved doctors' skill in treating hemorrhage, it had its obvious down side – and perhaps for patients suffering trauma more than for any others. A belief that appears to have gone uncontested until the anatomist Erasistratus came along in the first half of the third century BCE was that blood loss from a wound could be checked by diverting blood away from the wound through bloodletting either near the wound or distant from it.[20] This was sometimes done in conjunction with cupping, which enhanced the drawing of the blood by creating a vacuum. The doctor placed a piece of burning lint into a small cup, often bronze, and inverted the cup over the bloodletting incision.

---

[17] Salazar 2000, 44

[18] *Comp.* 84. I imagine that, just as tourniquets are coming back into favor today, with the risk of gangrene weighed against the risk of imminent death from blood loss, so, too, some ancient doctors made use of tourniquets in extreme circumstances - they simply do not happen to be our authors. For fuller discussion of the relationship between the use of tourniquets, the development of gangrene, and the ability to amputate a gangrenous limb (which required controlling hemorrhaging with arterial ligatures), see Majno 1975, 152-3, 205, 403-5; Salazar 2000, 44-5.

[19] Pressure and elevation: Henderson 2006, 534. Cauterization (now achieved through electrosurgery or chemical agents): Vaezy and Zderic 2007, 203-11; Karia 2011, 228.

[20] Opinions varied (see Celsus 2.10.12-15).

Once the oxygen had been used up, the draw of the resulting vacuum was believed to aid in diverting the blood away from the wound. The objections of Erasistratus, his followers, and of some later doctors to this and other forms of venesection did not even put a dent in the practice, perhaps because the highly influential Galen was a strong advocate for venesection and convinced the Erasistrateans that they had misinterpreted the anatomist.[21] It is highly likely, then, that soldiers wounded in battle suffered additional loss of blood at the hands of their doctors, either while still bleeding freely from their wounds, or later, if their wounds became inflamed or infected.

The negative consequences of venesection for patients are obvious, but its regular practice did confer valuable hemostatic skills to doctors for treating many sorts of wounds. There were, however, limitations to the skills doctors acquired since, done properly, venesection was highly controlled bleeding. Because they took care that the cut be made in certain areas only and with scalpels small enough to cause only moderate bleeding (Hippoc. *Medic.* 6.210-2 L), doctors would not have got practice in stopping severe hemorrhaging by their practice of venesection.

The skills developed by the regular performing of venesection would not have been sufficient for treating some of the wounds most likely to be fatal in any period of Greek or Roman history: Deep wounds to the abdomen and chest.[22] With these wounds, in addition to the obvious danger that a major organ was pierced, there was the possible complicating factor that the site of the wound was so deep within the body that it could not easily be found. If the wound was the result of an arrow or other missile, problems in locating and extracting it were likely to have been very common; indeed, Paul of Aegina stated that arrows were intentionally constructed to hold together until they hit their target, at which point the shafts were designed to fall off, making extraction of the arrowheads far more difficult (6.88.2). Paul describes two other types of arrowhead: One has barbs that would unfold on hinges if someone attempted to extract them, and so cause further damage as they were being extracted; the other had grooves containing small pieces of metal that would slide out and remain behind in the wound when the main part of the arrowhead was

---

[21] Nutton 2013, 246.
[22] The head, throat, and groin were also major targets in close-quarter combat, and wounds in those sites could very well be lethal. Since, however, those wound sites were likely to be obvious, they are not relevant to the present discussion.

pulled out (6.88.2; cf. D. C. 36.5).[23] In addition, lead balls, pebbles, and any other missiles hurled by slingers might penetrate just as deeply as arrows and be harder to locate.[24] In such cases, the doctor would have been working blind to find the missile and would have had to resort to palpation or to the use of a probe – the surgical tool mentioned most often in medical texts and the one found most frequently in archaeological excavations.[25] Salazar notes the great expertise doctors developed with the probe, their only diagnostic tool for the examination of wounds, and calls attention to the detailed description of the varied sensations conveyed by the probe as described in a passage of Celsus.[26] She observes, too, that this work required true expertise and special tools, and could not safely have been left to fellow soldiers or inexperienced doctors.[27] A great risk was run if the wounded soldier followed his first impulse, and either attempted to yank the shaft out himself, or got a fellow soldier to do it for him, thus causing further tearing and hemorrhage.[28] Equally dangerous was if the shaft was pulled out but the arrowhead still lodged in the body where, thoroughly concealed, it would be difficult for even an experienced doctor to find.[29]

If some military doctors got at least some portion of their education in a civilian setting, how might they have learned to treat abdominal or chest wounds – especially those with a hidden site? Galen gained experience with abdominal and other serious wounds during his early years tending to the gladiators in Pergamon; he describes repositioning intestines that had fallen out through the wound (10.410-23 K), and discusses wounds to the diaphragm (10.345 K). In treating gladiators, Galen had the ideal educational background to become a military doctor – something he rather adroitly managed to avoid – but such experience was not open to all and, obviously, not to Greek doctors in the Classical period. Nevertheless, we do see from the Classical period onward that even grave chest and abdominal wounds, though often fatal, were sometimes healed by medical intervention (*e.g.*, Hippoc. *Morb.* 1, 6.180 L).

---

[23] Salazar 2000, 18-9.
[24] Salazar 2000, 17.
[25] Salazar 2000, 19.
[26] Salazar 2000, 19-20 with n. 36, 47-8.
[27] Salazar 2000, 47; cf. Hippoc. *Medic.* 9.220 L.
[28] Salazar 2000, 47-8.
[29] Salazar 2000, 48.

Civilian doctors who did not have opportunities like Galen's had to learn how to treat serious chest and abdominal wounds, and particularly how to control their bleeding when the site of the wound could not be determined immediately. They surely could have learned, and no doubt many did learn, simply by experience once in the military.[30] I suggest, however, that they also could very well have gained such experience by treating uterine hemorrhage, which was one of the most dangerous and severe forms of hemorrhage ancient doctors faced, and probably the most frequent and the most difficult to treat. The Hippocratic *Corpus* contains several references to uterine hemorrhage (*e.g.*, *Epid*. 5, 5.210-2 L and, possibly, *Epid* 7.394-8 L); in a passage that discusses which conditions are sure to be fatal and which are not, the text of *Diseases* 1 says that hemorrhage in a woman is "necessarily long" and is of uncertain outcome - which does imply that she might live (Hippoc. *Morb*. 1, 6.144 L).[31] Soranus provides us with an extensive passage on the treatment of uterine hemorrhage (*Gyn*. 3.40-2); he remarks how difficult a condition it is, though obvious "from the sudden and measureless flow of blood" (*Gyn*. 3.40). He says that pressure, plugs, hooks (a hemostatic tool), ligatures, and stitching are all useless (*Gyn*. 3.40). The origin of the bleeding, he says, is difficult to determine, and it can best be done by probing with a speculum (*Gyn*. 3.40), a tool designed to dilate an orifice or cavity to permit inspection and not unlike the one used in modern gynecology.[32] Soranus then goes into great detail concerning the treatment that followed the discovery of the source of the bleeding; this could entail cold baths, the application of pressure, and injections into the uterus via pipes or syringes of various medicinal washes, whose ingredients sometimes included astringents or styptics (*Gyn*. 3.41). Soranus ends the section with a statement on the treatment of hemorrhage in general, again clearly considering uterine hemorrhage akin to wound treatment. The treatment of hemorrhage, he says, requires not venesection, which relaxes, but rather constriction and contraction: The blood must be stopped, not diverted (*Gyn*. 3.42). Thus, a doctor who treated uterine hemorrhage with any regularity was likely to learn how to probe with a speculum to find the site of a deep and gushing wound, apply pressure to that wound, and wash it

---

[30] Nutton 1969, 264-5.
[31] Gorgias's wife, the subject of *Epid* 5.210-2 L, survives a 40-day long siege of hemorrhage and fever.
[32] See Jackson 1991 on the suitability of the speculum for wound treatment and of its particular use as an aid in extracting weapons. Jackson argues convincingly that, in his section on extracting arrowheads, Celsus is referring to a speculum when he describes an instrument "shaped like a Greek letter" (7.5.2).

with medicinal remedies. Experience with uterine hemorrhage would have given civilian doctors the opportunity to develop skills for which they otherwise would seldom have had the need and which would be highly useful to them if they became military doctors.[33]

This argument will be valid only if civilian doctors in fact encountered uterine hemorrhage with some frequency. In the absence of records from antiquity, it will be worthwhile to make cautious use of modern data. We know today that while uterine hemorrhage can be the result of such underlying conditions as uterine fibroids, it occurs most often in relation to childbirth and miscarriage, when it is termed obstetric hemorrhage. Obstetric hemorrhage causes 25% of the more than 500,000 pregnancy-related deaths that are estimated to occur yearly world-wide (99% of them in low to middle-income countries,[34] and 67% of them in just thirteen countries).[35]

Post-partum hemorrhage is severe blood loss that occurs as the result of childbirth. It is the most frequently occurring type of obstetric hemorrhage, and is an important factor in maternal mortality, even in developed countries. More relevant for our purposes, however, is the incidence of post-partum hemorrhage, not the mortality rate from it, since girls and women today, even those with very little chance of receiving such life-saving treatments as blood transfusions or emergency hysterectomies, still obviously have a better chance than did even the most fortunate of their counterparts in antiquity. While precise figures are hard to come by, an estimate for the year 2000 puts the incidence of severe post-partum hemorrhage, defined as a loss of one litre or more of blood up to forty-two weeks following delivery, at 10.5% of all live births worldwide.[36] For the year 2000, the estimate is that nearly 14 million women suffered severe post-partum hemorrhage and that 1% of them died from it; another 12% survived, but with severe anemia. If, instead of considering only severe post-partum hemorrhage, the normal baseline definition of post-partum hemorrhage had been used, where half a litre of blood is lost up to 42 weeks following delivery, the figure would have

---

[33] With respect to this, it is worth recalling that Paul of Aegina, a major source on techniques for extracting arrowheads, was most famous in his own day as a gynecologist and obstetrician; Salazar 1998, 170.
[34] Goldenberg and McClure 2011, 294.
[35] AbouZhar 2003, 13.
[36] AbouZahr 2003, 6.

been significantly higher.[37] The baseline definition was not used in the report, which is concerned with maternal mortality, because death and the more serious clinical repercussions generally result only from severe hemorrhaging, but for the purposes of the present discussion, concerned as it is with doctors' facility in treating blood flowing freely from an obscure site, the great likelihood of an even higher rate of occurrence should be borne in mind.

Due caution is required in applying modern data to ancient conditions. Greek and Roman mothers shared some of the major risk factors for post-partum hemorrhage that mothers in present-day developing nations do, such as giving birth before the age of eighteen (the younger the girl, the higher the risk), multiple births, and giving birth past the age of thirty-five. But they did not share them all; they were not, for instance, routinely subjected to infibulation, the most severe form of genital mutilation, as are so many young girls and women today.[38] On the other hand, as mentioned above, they had no hope of benefitting from the life-saving medical treatments that women in developing countries today do sometimes receive. Taken all together, it is reasonable, perhaps conservative, to suggest that roughly 10-15% of live births in Greek and Roman antiquity were complicated by moderate to severe post-partum hemorrhage; it is hard to imagine how the figure could have been significantly less.

From regularly encountering post-partum hemorrhage, Greek and Roman civilian doctors ought to have had ample opportunity to learn how to treat any serious hemorrhage arising from an obscure site. Indeed, it seems likely that not only was post-partum hemorrhage a familiar condition for a civilian doctor, but it was probably by far the most familiar form of serious hemorrhage that he met. Moreover, a civilian doctor treating a post-partum hemorrhage would have had a better chance of developing his technical skills than with any other type of hemorrhage since, at least if he had been called in during the earlier stages of labour, he would have been present before the hemorrhage began. This would have

---

[37] AbouZahr 2003, 6.
[38] For a survey of the Greek and Roman sources concerning the "lighter" forms of female genital cutting, see Knight 2001; she concludes that Greeks and Romans carried out such procedures only when the clitoris was considered excessively large and that they did not perform them routinely or for ritual purposes. According to Knight, the Egyptians did regularly perform genital cutting on their daughters, and Greeks and Romans living in Egypt may have been influenced by this custom to do the same, though the evidence is ambiguous.

permitted him to approach the situation more methodically than in a non-obstetric emergency, where the patient would have been injured for some time before he even arrived.

Among the remedies available to doctors for the treatment of hemorrhage were medicines with styptic properties, some of them derived from metals, often silver and copper. These are of particular interest because of what we now know are their antimicrobial properties. The Hippocratic *Diseases* 2 tells us that flower of silver was used in a compound to treat head ulcers (Hippoc. *Morb* 2, 7.22 L), and Pliny the Elder suggests use of silver slag as a styptic that is highly effective in treating wounds and sores (*HN* 33.105-6). Silver's long history as an effective antimicrobial agent is recognised by modern science and industry. Silver is used today, as it has been for many years, as a component in several prescription drugs, including some used to treat burns, and conjunctivitis in newborns. More relevant to this discussion is a recent study that advocates the use of silver dressings over topical antibiotics in the treatment of poorly healing wounds that show signs of secondary infection.[39]

Copper, however, is found far more frequently in our texts than is silver. Recent studies have demonstrated that copper and copper compounds are highly effective antimicrobial agents against strains of tuberculosis (including one strain that is resistant to antibiotics), pneumonia, and other pathogens.[40] The results have led researchers to believe that the extensive use of copper in door and faucet handles and other "touch surfaces" in hospitals, and on textiles, will prove useful in combatting the infections that sweep through hospitals, killing approximately 100,000 people annually in the United States alone.[41]

Copper is found in Greek medical texts in remedies for many conditions where its antibacterial properties would have been beneficial: It is used in various forms in the treatment of, for instance, tonsillitis (Hippoc. *Morb.* 2, 7.48 L), and lesions and sites where surgery had been performed (*e.g.*, where a hemorrhoid (Hippoc. *Hem.* 6.438-40 L) or nose polyp had been cut off (Hippoc. *Morb.* 2, 7.50-3 L) or where the eyelid

---

[39] Lipsky and Hoey 2009, 1541.
[40] Mehtar, Wiid, Todorov 2008, 45. See Majno 1975, 111-5 for early testing of the antimicrobial efficacy of some ancient medicaments containing copper compounds.
[41] Wheeldon 2008, 522.

had been operated on (Hippoc. *Vid. Ac.* 4-5)). With regard to the eyelids, one of the passages states that "one of the moist remedies with flower of copper" should be used – a remark that speaks at once to the frequency with which this ingredient was used and to the recognition of its effectiveness. Copper in various forms is also among the ingredients called for to impregnate bandages for moist applications (Hippoc. *Ulc.* 6.419-22).

Copper's styptic properties were also recognised: It is often among the ingredients in the styptic compounds with which bandages were steeped prior to being used on bleeding wounds, and it is a component of one of the more drastic treatments Soranus recommended for uterine hemorrhage (*Gyn*. 3.43). In the Hippocratic *Fistulas*, a plaster to stop rectal hemorrhage includes copper ore (Hippoc. 6.458-60 L). *Ulcers*, in a section devoted to styptics and the prevention of suppuration, calls for copper in various forms along with a host of ingredients with either styptic or antibacterial properties (*e.g.*, alum, sulphur, natron, vinegar, myrrh, frankincense); one passage notes that a recipe containing flower of copper cleans better than the one preceding it (Hippoc. *Ulc.* 6.412-28 L).

Pliny the Elder, too, wrote extensively about the medicinal uses of copper. He notes that copper and several minerals containing copper saw wide use in wound treatment and in eye salves, and he remarks on how very quickly sores are healed by copper (*HN* 34.100). According to him, copper scale and flower were frequently used for treating edemas and swellings in any part of the body (*HN* 34.105-109), and copper pyrites for stopping hemorrhages (*HN* 34.117- 122).

Medicines derived from metals were hardly the sole type used for wound treatment in Greek and Roman medicine. Plant-based medicines were by far the more common – and are far too numerous to be treated here.[42] Some botanical medicines had styptic and antimicrobial properties, too, but they were generally not as powerful in those respects as the metals, nor were they likely to have been as practical. Metal-based medicines would not have lost their effectiveness while in storage and would have been easier to transport and, possibly, less easy to fake or adulterate – common problems in ancient pharmacology.

We can see from the discussion above that Greek and Roman doctors did have to hand techniques for treating hemorrhage that may have been successful when wounds were not especially severe or if only the arms and

---

[42] See Salazar 2000, 54-67 for an overview.

legs were struck. Wounds to the chest or abdomen, on the other hand, were likely to have been fatal, but were not so necessarily. Doctors were able to save some patients with grievous injuries, using some methods and substances that are accepted as valid treatments today. Assuming that some military doctors received their medical education while civilians, we can conjecture that the regular use of venesection and frequent encounters with uterine hemorrhage provided opportunities to develop valuable hemostatic techniques.

BIBLIOGRAPHY

AbouZahr, C. (2003) "Global burden of maternal death and disability", *British Medical Bulletin* 67, 1–11.
Ambler, W. (trans.) (2008) *Xenophon – The Anabasis of Cyrus*. Ithaca and London.
Anderson, J. K. (1970) *Military Theory and Practice in the Age of Xenophon*. Berkeley and Los Angeles.
Chadwick, J. (1958) *The Decipherment of Linear B*. Cambridge.
Craik, E. M. (ed. and trans.) (2006) *Two Hippocratic Treatises – On Sight and On Anatomy*. Leiden and Boston.
Goldenberg, R. L. and E. M. McClure (2011) "Maternal Mortality", *American Journal of Obstetrics and Gynecology*, 205(4), 293–5.
Heiberg, J. L. (ed) (1921-4) *Paulus Aegineta*, CMG 9.1-2. Leipzig and Berlin.
Ilberg, I. (ed) (1927) *Soranus of Ephesus. Gynaeciorum libri IV / De signis fracturarum / De fasciis / Vita Hippocratis secundum Soranum*. CMG IV. Leipzig and Berlin.
Henderson, S. (2006) *Emergency Medicine*, Georgetown, TX.
Jackson, R. (1991) "Roman bivalve dilators and Celsus' 'instrument like a Greek letter'...(*De med*. VII, 5, 2, b)", in G. Sabbah (ed) *Le Latin médical. La Constitution d'un langage scientifique*, 101-9, St. Étienne.
Jouanna, J., (ed., trans., and notes) (1988) *Hippocrate* V, 1 - *Des Vents, De L'Art*. Paris.
Karia, R. A. (2011), "Hemostasis and Tourniquet", *Operative Techniques in Sports Medicine* 19, 224-30.
Knight, M. (2001) "Curing Cut or Ritual Mutilation?: Some Remarks on the Practice of Female and Male Circumcision in Graeco-Roman Egypt", *Isis* 92(2), 317-38.
Kühn C. G. (ed) (1821-30) *Claudii Galeni Opera Omnia*. Leipzig.
Laskaris, J. (2002) *The Art is Long: On the Sacred Disease and the Scientific Tradition*. Leiden, Boston, and Köln.

Lee, J. W. I. (2007) *A Greek Army on the March: Soldiers and Survival in Xenophon's Anabasis.* Cambridge.
Lipsky, B. A. and C. Hoey (2009) "Topical Antimicrobial Therapy for Treating Chronic Wounds", *Clinical Infectious Diseases* 49, 1541–9.
Littré, E. (ed. and trans.) (1839-1861) *Œuvres Complètes d'Hippocrate.* Paris.
Majno, G. (1975) *The Healing Hand: Man and Wound in the Ancient World.* Cambridge, MA and London.
Marchant, E. C. (ed) (1904-20) *Xenophontis Opera Omnia*, Vols. 3-5. Oxford.
Mehtar S., I. Wiid, and S. D. Todorov (2008) "The antimicrobial activity of copper and copper alloys against nosocomial pathogens and Mycobacterium tuberculosis isolated from healthcare facilities in the Western Cape: in in-vitro study", *Journal of Hospital Infection* 68(1), 45-51.
Monro, D. B. and T. W. Allen (eds) (1920) *Homer- Opera*, Vol. 1. Oxford.
Mukherjee, S., and S. Arulkumaran (2009) "Post-partum haemorrhage", *Obstetrics, Gynaecology & Reproductive Medicine*, 19(5), 121–6.
Nutton, V. (1969) "Medicine and the Roman Army: A Further Reconsideration", *Medical History* 13, 260-70.
—. (2013 / 2004) *Ancient Medicine.* Oxford and New York.
Palmer, L. R. (1973 / 1963) *The Interpretation of Mycenean Greek Texts.* Oxford.
Protonarious-Deilaki, E. (1973) "Ανασκαφκαὶ Ερευναι εις Περιοχὴν Ναυπλίας", *Archaiologikon Deltion* 28, 91-5.
Rackham, H. (1952) *Pliny – Natural History, Books XXXIII-XXXV.* Cambridge, MA and London.
Salazar, C. F. (1998) "Getting the Point; Paul of Aegina on Arrow Wounds", *Sudhoffs Archiv* 82(2), 170-87.
—. (2000) *The Treatment of War Wounds in Graeco-Roman Antiquity.* Leiden.
Scarborough, J. (2007 / 1968), "Roman Medicine and the Legions", in R. L. Anderson (ed) in *Sources in the History of Medicine: the Impact of Disease and Trauma*, 98-101, Upper Saddle River (New Jersey).
Sconocchia, S. (ed) (1983) *Scribonii Largi Compositiones.* Leipzig.
Smith, W. D. (ed. and trans.) (1994) *Hippocrates - Epidemics* 2, 4-7. Cambridge, MA.
Spencer, W. G. (ed) (1960/1) *Celsus. De Medicina.* London and Cambridge, MA.
Sternberg, R. H. (2006) *Tragedy Offstage.* Austin, TX.
Vaezy, S. and V. Zderic (2007) "Hemorrhage control using high intensity

focused ultrasound", *International Journal of Hyperthermia* 23(2), 203-11.

Ventris, M. and J. Chadwick (1973 / 1956) *Documents in Mycenean Greek*. Cambridge.

Waterfield, R. (2005) *Xenophon – The Expedition of Cyrus*. Oxford.

Wheeldon, L. J., et al. (2008) "Antimicrobial efficacy of copper surfaces against spores and vegetative cells of *Clostridium difficile*: the germination theory", *Journal of Antimicrobial Chemotherapy* 62(3), 522-5.

CHAPTER SIXTEEN

ARE YOU (RO)MAN ENOUGH? NON-ROMAN *VIRTUS* IN THE ROMAN ARMY

DR. ADAM ANDERS

With the professionalization of the Roman army, the tactical delegation of light tactics from lightly armed infantry (such as *velites*) to more heavily armed infantry such as the imperial *auxilia* ensued.[1] As a result, imperial light infantry is designated as such in our sources by their function, rather than their equipment.[2] In what follows, I will examine the possibility that the light infantry of the cohortal legions were tactically versatile, and further, that they were often trusted with the difficult and dangerous assignments in Roman warfare.[3] The following paper will describe in detail the various tactical uses of light-armed troops in the cohortal legions. It will begin with a short review of the historiography on the subject, followed by a discussion of the tactical uses of light infantry on campaign, particularly in reconnaissance and swift offensives, as well as their use in difficult terrain and other special deployments.

HISTORIOGRAPHY

Much of the scholarship on cohortal 'light' troops focuses on the *auxilia* and the important issues of the *auxilia*'s historical and geographical

---

[1] See e.g. Vegetius' description of extensive missile training for line infantry (1.14-17); cf. also Parker 1928, 259-60; Wheeler 1979, 304.
[2] See Anders 2012, esp. Ch. 5.
[3] NB. The type of light infantry that will be the focus of the arguments herein are the line infantry (e.g. the *auxilia* of the professional Roman army), rather than light missile troops (e.g. archers, slingers) or foreign light infantry (e.g. *numeri*)

origins.[4] There is relatively little on the other light troops associated with cohortal legions such as the *antesignani*, and other *expediti*. Cheesman's seminal work on the *auxilia*, although written in 1914, still stands as one of the most useful scholarly works on the subject.[5] However, a wealth of new archaeological evidence on the *auxilia* has come to light since its publication. In regards to its usefulness for the present work, Cheesman gives nominal attention to tactics, but he does mention the *auxilia*'s employment on the flanks in pitched battle, as well as their defensive use on the frontier as 'police'.[6] Parker, writing in 1928, added little to Cheesman's research on the tactical role of the *auxilia*. He implied that they fought in loose order – which made them stronger mêlée combatants than their legionary counterparts.[7] Research on the *auxilia* advanced slowly over the century; Rainbird, for example, had little to add other than noting that the increase in number of auxiliary units could mean the increase in their strategic and tactical use, an occurrence observable throughout Tacitus.[8]

In 1982, Saddington expanded on his earlier article regarding the development of auxiliary forces in the Principate, with the publication of a good improvement on Cheesman's work. Yet, as its antecedent from 1914, it is also limited in its scope, focusing mostly on the historical and geographical origins and movements of auxiliary units. To his credit, Saddington gathers and cites the many references to auxiliaries (in various capacities) in our ancient sources throughout his work, and does occasionally reflect on the strategic functions of the *auxilia*.[9] More recently, there has been a greater volume of research on the nature of the *auxilia*'s roles in various types of combat, including discussions on their tactical uses, especially in pitched battle. Gilliver's article on the *auxilia*'s role at Mons Graupius convincingly argues for the tactical importance of these units in battle, and she has elsewhere suggested that the *auxilia* could bear the brunt of battle.[10]

---

[4] E.g. Cheesman 1914, 21-102, 107, 113, 116-17; Watson 1969, 15; Hassall 1970, 135; Dobson & Mann 1973, 191-93, 196; Saddington 1975 & 1982; Webster 1980, 144; Gilliver 1999, 23, 2007, 193; Rankov 2007, 50.
[5] Saddington 1982, expands on much of Cheesman's work, but is also limited in its analysis (see below).
[6] Cheesman 1914, 103-111.
[7] Parker 1928, 259-60, cf. Bishop & Coulston 2006, 257.
[8] Rainbird 1969, 11-12.
[9] Saddington 1982, for material especially relevant to the present assessment, see 183-6.
[10] Gilliver 1996: tactical importance: *throughout*, bear the brunt: 1999, 26.

Deployment and use in pitched battle is the focus of Goldsworthy's references to *auxilia*, and specific discussions of combat are grouped with those of the legions seemingly on the basis that both groups of infantry 'were primarily swordsmen' or otherwise similarly equipped. As with Gilliver's argument, he says that it was normal practice to place the *auxilia* in tactically decisive positions in battles.[11] Lendon has stressed the importance of the auxiliaries in battle as well, emphasizing competition, *virtus* and the pursuit of glory amongst these troops.[12] He has further pointed out that the auxiliaries are often seen doing most of the fighting, while their legionary counterparts are assigned to non-combat duties such as foraging: an idea brought up in earlier scholarship by Richmond, and then Lepper and Frere.[13] This can be especially observed in the iconographic evidence on Trajan's column, and the idea that the *auxilia* excelled at combat over the legionaries will be examined below.[14] In a recent chapter on tactics, Thorne had little to add about the *auxilia* or other light units, noting only that the *auxilia* were used when the army needed rapid mobility.[15] Gilliver's recent discussion on low-intensity warfare stands as a respectable introduction to the tactical use of light units, a longer discourse on the subject is warranted by the current state of scholarship.[16] Finally, Haynes, in his very recent monograph, provides us with the most complete volume on the *auxilia* since Saddington. While he explores the *auxilia*'s various roles with admirable thoroughness, it is the aim of this paper to explore one topic Haynes glosses over. He acknowledges that auxiliary units were more adaptable than their legionary counterparts but as to possible reasons why this was, he only goes so far as to engage in a thorough discussion of whether equipment differences existed and the importance (or lack thereof) of the possibilities therein.[17]

---

[11] Goldsworthy 1996, similarly equipped: 177, 181. Gilliver as well as Bishop and Coulston have also discussed the general deployment of auxiliary forces in pitched battle: deployment: 1999, 113-114; 2007b, 128. Bishop & Coulston 2006, 257, esp. n. 13.

[12] The role that the display of *virtus* played in the Roman army will be explored in some detail below.

[13] Richmond 1982, 19; Lepper & Frere 1988, 110; Lendon 2005, 242-247. This idea can also be drawn from the ancient historiography, see Lendon 2005, esp. n. 21.

[14] Lepper & Frere 1988; excelled at combat, see 'Fighting Capability', below.

[15] Thorne 2007, 221.

[16] Gilliver 2007, 141-143.

[17] Haynes 2013, ch. 16.

This paper then, seeks to explore the different roles of the *auxilia*, and to highlight their tactical flexibility, particularly with regards to their legionary counterparts.

ON THE CAMPAIGN TRAIL

While on campaign, light troops were used in various tactical capacities, including guarding the marching column, scouting and gathering intelligence while the army was on the march or in camp, and both foraging and protecting foragers.

GUARDING THE MARCHING COLUMN

Some of the most devastating ambushes befell the Romans when marching through enemy territory, the most famous probably being the Varian disaster. Our sources often state the existence of guards in these cases, but the security of the column could be affected by many factors, such as lack of discipline and/or training, low morale, and poor intelligence.[18] Since the marching column was vulnerable, the Romans had several methods of deploying their column depending on the perceived level of threat. In many of these deployments, the light infantry had a significant role to play, as noted in numerous examples from our sources, throughout the history of the cohortal legion. Sallust for example, points out that Metellus marched through Numidia "with some light-armed cohorts, and a select handful of slingers and archers, was always at the front" (*'cum expeditis cohortibus, item funditorum et sagittariorum delecta manu apud primos'*); even when the level of threat seemed low. Later in the Jugurthine war, Marius similarly marched with light infantry guarding both the front and rear of his column.[19] Using auxiliaries in the dangerous position of the advance guard was a regular feature of the Roman marching column and was a tradition that stretched back through the Republic. As Gilliver has pointed out, the recommendations of Vegetius (as well as Onasander, although his suggestions lack detail on the placement of specific troops) are similar to those of Polybius.[20] Polybius describes the marching column headed by the *ektraordinarioi* or, 'the select' who "[out of] the whole force of allies assembled the horsemen and footmen [were deemed] most fitted for actual service" (Polyb. 6.26.6).

---

[18] Existence of guards: Sall. *Iug.* 46, 100; Caes. *B Gal.* 2.19; Tac. *Ann.* 1.51, 2.16; Jos. *BJ* 3.97, 3.115, 5.39; cf. Gilliver 1999, 38-45, security factors: 51-53.
[19] Sall. *Iug.* 46, 100.
[20] Gilliver 1999, 40.

These Republican predecessors of imperial *auxilia* were placed at the head or at the rear of the column, depending on from where the Romans thought the enemy might attack (Polyb. 6.40.6-9).[21]

Roman military theory also reiterates that caution be taken on the march, Vegetius for example, warns that:

> The general should take steps with all caution and prudence to ensure that the army suffer no attack on the march, or may easily repel a raid without loss.[22]

He goes on to say that light infantry (*levi armatura*) should reinforce the vulnerable areas of the column, particularly the side(s) where intelligence says the enemy is expected (Veg. 3.6). In the same way, when Germanicus expected an ambush while marching through Germany, he too placed auxiliary infantry and cavalry at the head of his column, and used the rest of his auxiliaries to guard the rear (Tac. *Ann.* 1.50-51). The Batavian and Transrhenane auxiliaries proved their worth in the face of danger against enemy reconnoitres during the civil upheavals throughout AD 69. Zealously crossing the river Po in full armour they seized some of Otho's scouts and by the rapidity of their attack terrified the rest into fleeing and announcing that the whole army of Caecina was at hand (Tac. *Hist.* 2.17). Josephus notes that when Vespasian marched out of Ptolemais, he:

> put his army into that order wherein the Romans used to march [that included] auxiliaries which were lightly armed (*psilous ton epikuron*), and the archers, to march first, that they might prevent any sudden insults from the enemy, and might search out the woods that looked suspiciously, and were capable of ambuscades.[23]

Josephus also mentions Titus using this formation (*BJ* 5.2.1). Yet, the tactic of putting the light troops in the front or rear of the column was not only to guard against sudden attacks. The other benefit of this formation was that the column could wheel directly into a line of battle, with the traditional deployment of the *auxilia* on the wings and the legions in the centre. This tactic is expressly stated by Tacitus when describing the prelude to the battle of the Weser River in AD 16.[24]

---

[21] As to why the task should be given to non-Romans, see 'Fighting Capability', below.
[22] Veg. 3.6.
[23] Jos. *BJ* 3.6.2.
[24] Tac. *Ann.* 2.16-18; cf. Gilliver 1996a, 58, especially n. 28.

These cases of light troops' positions on the march are just a few examples of one of their more hazardous roles within the Roman army. This role of being trusted to bear the brunt of a front or rear attack against the vulnerable marching column is evidence for what may be greater skill in hand-to-hand combat capability or simply a greater desire for such combat; either of which could be due to specific skill sets or regional specializations, exploited by Roman commanders. This idea will be explored further below.

TACTICAL INTELLIGENCE

Intelligence gathering and reconnaissance was another task commonly delegated to light troops and auxiliaries that was performed either on the march or from a base such as a marching camp or frontier fort by units known as *exploratores* (or 'scouts').[25] During our period, cavalry were commonly assigned with the task of scouting;[26] however, during the Empire, foot soldiers from the *auxilia* are found being used for reconnaissance as well, perhaps as a mixed unit.[27] As Southern points out "it is expected that such units would be mobile, but they were not necessarily all mounted"; *Cohors IX Batavorum* and *Cohors XX Palmyrenorum* are examples of such mixed units. The former was made up of mostly *pedites*, and in the latter, the unit roster from AD 219 notes that there were five infantry with ten cavalry in the *exploratores* unit, and in

---

[25] Arr. *Ektaxis* 1.1, Ps.-Hyginus 24, 30; cf. Speidel 1970, 148. NB.: These units appear most frequently in our sources after the first century AD, e.g. Veg. 3.6; Onas. 6.7; cf. Austin & Rankov 1995, 40, 42, 52, 101.
[26] e.g. Caes. *B Gal.* 7.56, *BC* 3.38; Tac. *Hist.* 3.52; Sall. *Iug.* 53; Arr. *Ektaxis* 1. It must be noted that when the literary sources do not mention cavalry as scouts, they are often inexplicit about exactly what type of troops are functioning as *exploratores* (e.g. Caes. *B Gal.* 2.17, 7.44; Vell. 2.112.5). When we have specific references to the distances at which *exploratores* function, we can assume that further distances (e.g. 24 *milia passuum* - approx. 35kms - in Caes. *B Gal.* 1.41) suggest cavalry are doing the scouting. Thus, for our purposes, when light infantry is explicitly described as being assigned to scouting, the troop type is auxiliaries, as shall be shown below. Whether or not other types of troops (i.e. legionaries/heavy infantry) functioned as scouts, is not made explicit by our sources.
[27] *P.Dura* 100, *CIL* VIII 21516, cf. Speidel 1970, 148, esp n. 69; Southern 1989, 110; Austin & Rankov 1995, 244. On both cavalry and infantry reconnoitering together, see also Austin & Rankov 1995, 190, 194-5.

AD 222, there were four infantry combined with five cavalry.[28] Austin and Rankov have suggested that this combination of infantry and cavalry is indicative of the possibility that these men were intended to operate individually rather than as a standing patrol, a method that could be well suited to keeping watch on a frontier.[29] If this were indeed the case on campaign, the individual soldiers would be easy targets for the enemy: either simply to kill the wandering scout as a spy or an unwelcome enemy, or capture him as a prisoner-of-war (a possibility more viable for those on foot who might find it harder to escape such a situation compared to those on horseback). Based on the Roman army's previously noted use of the combat tactic of placing light infantry with cavalry, I would suggest that these small units of *exploratores* worked together in scouting.[30] In either case, whether operating individually or as a small detachment, scouting was a dangerous task, and, furthermore, a vital one for keeping a vulnerable marching column safe in enemy territory, highlighting the tactical value Roman commanders put in the light infantry.[31]

The use of allies as scouts could have also been a result of the fact that when scouting in their own homeland, they would know the terrain best. As Austin and Rankov have noted:

> the availability of allies for the collection of tactical intelligence was one of the factors which enabled commanders to proceed even when their sources of strategic intelligence had dried up.[32]

Yet it was not until the establishment of the frontiers in the second century AD that specialized bodies of troops known as *exploratores* became standing units.[33] Up until that time, as mentioned above, Speidel has suggested that "in every operational unit of the Roman army, some men…were assigned the job of reconnoitering", and this important task

---

[28] *cohors IX Batavorum*, *CIL* III 11918 = *ILS* 9152, cf.. *CIL* III 12480; *cohors XX Palmyrenorum*, *P.Dura* 100, *CIL* VIII 21516; also Southern 1989, 114.
[29] Austin & Rankov 1995, 195.
[30] Breeze 1969, has argued that legionary infantry fought separately from the legionary cavalry (despite being administered in the same books), but this seems not to be the case with auxiliary infantry and cavalry, e.g. Tac. *Ann.* 4.73.
[31] A dangerous task: e.g. see Speidel 1992, 100, where *cohors IX Batavorum* were assigned to watch "over the distant but dangerous Macromanni", and other examples of dangerous assignments for *exploratores*.
[32] Austin & Rankov 1995, 102; see also Southern 1989, 113.
[33] Speidel 1992, 89 ff.

was regularly given to the auxiliaries.[34] Evidence for this can be found for example in Tacitus, who mentions the frequent skirmishes of auxiliary scouts in passing, unfortunately brushing them off as "not worth relating".[35] Another example is the career of T. Porcius Cornelianus, recorded in a Greek inscription from the third century, which notes his time in several auxiliary command posts prior to his position as "commander of the scouts of Germany".[36] Much of our evidence that specifically designates the auxiliaries as *exploratores* is like this one. This evidence is epigraphic in nature, and includes Roman military tombstones, many of which Speidel has detailed in his article on the auxiliary scouts of Roman Germany.[37] Because these auxiliaries function as *exploratores*, we may identify them as light infantry.

Intelligence gathering occurred not only on the march or from stationary forts, but evidence from Ammianus (19.3.3) suggests it occurred during sieges as well. Although his account of the siege of Amida is well after our period, the auxiliary units he describes gathering tactical intelligence are classified as *exploratores*, and it is likely that these late-Roman units retained not only the name, but also the function of their namesakes from the Principate. During the siege, the Roman commanders unsuccessfully attempted to get *exploratores* into the town on several occasions, to give and receive information. This incident has been pointed out by Austin and Rankov as evidence that *exploratores* were trained in security of movement, a possibility that may be further supported by other covert political operations performed by these units, which Ammianus also mentions.[38] Yet, clandestine operations may simply have been a later development of the function of the *exploratores*. Austin and Rankov point out, however, that Dio (68.23.2) mentions scouts (*proskopoi*) circulating false reports, as directed by Trajan, who was attempting to keep his army and officers on their toes. Yet it seems to me, that the reporting of intelligence – whether real or false by the commander's order – should be a regular part of scouting, and is unlike the more clandestine activities of

---

[34] See Speidel 1992, *throughout*.
[35] Tac. *Hist.* 2.24: *crebra magis quam digna memoratu proelia inferior.*
[36] *ILS* 8852: πραιφεκτὸς ἐξπλωρατόρων Γερμανίας, i.e. a specially raised unit from German allies, who later became a regular part of the garrison in the province in which they had been operating, cf. Austin & Rankov 1995, 191.
[37] Speidel 1992, e.g. cf. *CIL* VIII 21668 = *ILS* 9107, *CIL* VIII 9060 = *ILS* 2627, *CIL* VIII 9798, *CIL* VIII 9059 = *ILS* 2628, *CIL* III 728 = 7237, all of which are light auxiliaries; see also Southern 1989, 111.
[38] Political Ops: 17.9.7, 21.7.2; cf. Austin & Rankov 1995, 49.

spying on imperial staff members (as noted above, Amm. 17.9.7; 21.7.2). What we should take from Ammianus' example then, is the likelihood that there were varying methods and situations in which tactical intelligence was gathered and distributed.

Scouting and intelligence gathering, then, was a task that may have confided in scouts delicate information regarding where the army was headed, and what paths through enemy territory its leaders planned to take. The scouts were entrusted to keep this information safe, when out of sight of their comrades and out of reach of immediate assistance in a desperate situation. It provided soldiers with the possibility of betraying their army. Despite this risk, it has been shown that auxiliaries were regularly assigned to function in a light capacity as scouts, thus underlining both their combat skill and overall trustworthiness.

FORAGING

The *auxilia* were also available for the task of protecting fellow soldiers (along with other troop types) during foraging, and the danger of this task is highlighted in several examples from the cohortal period.[39] The vulnerability of foraging soldiers could be especially high if working without the protection of their shields or helmets. Onasander (10.8) suggests a solution to this, stating:

> When the general himself sends out foraging parties, he should send with the light-armed men (*psilois*) and unarmed men (*anoplois*), guards (*makhimous*), both horse and foot, who shall have nothing to do with the booty, but are to remain in formation and guard the foragers, that their return to camp may be safely accomplished.

Roth has suggested that this should be interpreted as legionaries guarding the auxiliaries who are foraging, but this suggestion is based on an unrelated passage in Josephus.[40] Rather, *makhimoi* refers to warriors or warlike men in our sources, and these references seem to refer consistently to non-Romans.[41] Furthermore, although our sources mention legionaries

---

[39] e.g. Plut. *Vit. Sert.* 7.3; Caes. *B Gal.* 5.17, 7.16, 7.20, 8.10, 8.16 *BAfr.* 24 *BHisp.*21; Dio 49.26.3, 65.4.5; Tac. *Ann.* 12.38. cf. Roth 1999, 286-287.

[40] Roth 1999, 290, claims Josephus uses *makhimous* at *BJ* 5.43 to describe legionaries, but Roth must be mistaken, as this word is not used in said passage. At *BJ* 3.155, *makhimoterois* is used to describe Romans fighting desperately, and this is the only usage of the word related to Romans in the work.

[41] e.g. Strab. 7.3 (referring to light-armed troops), 11.3; App. *Gal.* 2; *Hisp.* 66, 72;

being assigned the task of guarding foragers, there are several examples of auxiliaries being put in this position as well. Caesar had his German and Gallic auxiliaries skirmish with the enemy while the Roman troops were foraging, and an earlier attack on his foragers was warded off by the combined force of three legions and all the auxiliaries.[42] In another example, Q. Fabius Maximus had his legionaries forage for grain or water, while legionary cavalry and auxiliary soldiers stood on guard close by – a similar method to that of Caesar.[43] What these examples make clear is the importance of the role of protecting Roman foragers, which was regularly designated to auxiliaries.

SPECIAL DEPLOYMENT

USAGE IN DIFFICULT TERRAIN

> The Roman soldier is heavily armed and afraid to swim, while the German, who is accustomed to rivers, is favoured by the lightness of his equipment and the height of his stature.[44]

Although this is probably just narrative rhetoric on Tacitus' behalf, the theme of auxiliaries being used in difficult terrain is a consistent one in our sources. Indeed, Onasander advises generals to use light infantry in these situations:

> If the battle should happen to be in country that is level in some places but hilly in others, then the light-armed troops (*psiloi*) should by all means be stationed in the uneven section, and then, if the general himself should have seized the plain and some part of the enemy's phalanx should possess the heights, he should send against them the light-armed troops (*psiloi*); for from the uneven ground they can more easily hurl their weapons and retreat, or they can very easily charge up the slopes, if they are agile.[45]

Other examples include the battle at the Axona in 57 BC, which was

---

Ill. 15, 25; Polyb. 1.2, 15.3.
[42] Caes. *B Gal.* 5.17, cf. also 8.10, 8.17.
[43] Livy 22.12.8-9. Cf. Scenes 107 and 109 on Trajan's column which depict the same practice. Also, in a different but related scene on the column (Scenes 126-127), legionaries are seen constructing fortifications, having laid aside their shields, and some even their helmets, and are being guarded by a group of auxiliary infantry.
[44] Tac. *Hist.* 5.14.
[45] Onas. 18, trans. Illinois Greek Club.

fought in and around the banks of the river (probably the modern Aisne), a mode of attack that disordered the enemy but not Caesar's auxiliaries. According to Caesar, the auxiliaries showed even greater zeal in such difficult terrain, for when they had already killed a great part of the enemy, they continued to chase those who managed to cross the river, having to climb over the bodies of their fallen foes (Caes. *B Gal.* 2.10). Indeed, such heroic displays of courage, *virtus*, and as Caesar puts it in this case, *audacia*, in difficult terrain are common to the auxiliary forces in our sources. With the establishment of the professional *auxilia*, the Roman army was equipped with units of 'light' infantrymen who were very capable of executing difficult manoeuvres in unfavourable terrain.

There are numerous examples in the sources of the *auxilia* being sent in (or charging in on their own accord) when the terrain was unfavourable to the legionaries and their close-order, large-scale combat tactics.[46] One of the most notable instances of this happening was the battle of Mons Graupius during Agricola's campaigns. In this particular battle, Agricola kept his legions in reserve and sent the whole of his auxiliary forces against the large congregation of Caledonians in what was literally an uphill battle. Tacitus claims the Roman commander deployed his units in that way because "victory would be more glorious if achieved without the loss of Roman blood."[47] However, as Gilliver convincingly argues, this is far from the truth; that being that the auxiliaries were simply the best suited for the job, since the legionaries preferred static fighting on level ground in pitched battle.[48] But the use of auxiliaries in difficult terrain often spread into the domain of non-pitched battle combat. In the early first century AD, P. Vellaeus sent light auxiliaries into the Balkan Mountains to quell plundering tribes, who were also recruiting followers.[49] Mountainous terrain also brought non-pitched battle combat to Corbulo's troops on his march towards Tigranocerta. His army was plagued by the men of the Mardi tribe who were "trained in brigandage, and defended by mountains against an invader," and he sent Iberian auxiliaries to counter them, who then "ravaged their country and punished the enemy's daring".[50] There were also many actions taking place in and around water.

---

[46] Charging in on own accord: see Tac. *Hist.* 2.17.
[47] Tac. *Agr.* 35: "*ingens victoriae decus citra Romanum sanguinem bellandi*"
[48] Gilliver 1996, 62, *throughout*.
[49] Tac. *Ann.* 3.38-39
[50] Tac. *Ann.* 14.23: '*latrociniis exerciti contraque inrumpentem monitbus defense; quos Corbulo immissis HHisp.is vastavit hostilemque audaciam externo sanguine ultus est*'

Tacitus describes how in AD 68, German auxiliaries fighting for Vitellius took the battle to the difficult terrain of boat decks and the Po River on which they floated. They attacked the Othonian gladiators manning the boats after diving into the river and out-swimming the boats (in full armour), pulling the vessels into the shallows, then climbed onto the decks, and "sank them in hand-to-hand combat" (Tac. *Hist.* 2.35). During Agricola's campaigning in Britain, a group of Batavian auxiliaries braved the waters of the Menai Straits, swimming over to the island of Mona (modern Anglesey), and took the inhabitants by surprise, as the latter expected an assault by a naval fleet. Astonished by the audacity of the auxiliaries, the inhabitants gave up the island, worried that "to such assailants nothing could be formidable or invincible."[51]

The question remains as to why the auxiliaries in particular were used in difficult conditions. Gilliver suggests that they were physically and tactically best suited for the job, a conclusion based on their armament.[52] Bishop and Coulston's assessment of the differences between traditional legionary and auxiliary equipment comes to the same conclusion.[53] To me, however, solely attributing their armament as the reason for such deployments, while prudent, seems limited, especially during the Principate. Rather, I think there are further historical grounds for this development.

As indicated in the introduction, it is significant that the tactical delegation of 'light' tactics changed from lightly armed infantry (e.g. *velites*) to more heavily armed infantry (for example the *antesignani*), most of which were performed by the *auxilia* during the Principate. This could have been a result of a trend that began with the manipular legion. During the wars of the mid-Republic, where the versatility of the *velites* was not enough, specialist foreign infantry was hired, referred to as *auxilia* in our Republican sources. This tradition was not uncommon even before the Roman republican period; for example, fifth-century Athens recruited specialist foreign infantry where and when required as well.[54] Indeed, Best

---

[51] Tac. *Agr.* 18; cf. Hassall 1970, 135. See also Tac. *Ann.* 14.29: an attack on Anglesey by a group of what was like Batavian cavalry auxiliaries under Suetonius Paullinus in AD 60, cf. Hassall 1970, 132.
[52] Gilliver 1996, 56-7, 61-2. For a discussion on how auxiliaries' armament affected their fighting capability, see 'Fighting Capability', below.
[53] Bishop & Coulston 2006, 257.
[54] See Trundle 2010, 157, 159, light troops were used historically in Greek armies to adapt to changing combat circumstances, and they fulfilled a variety of

points out that hoplites suffered severe losses without the help of peltasts.[55] So, regarding the Romans, the establishment of the professional army and the long service and the professionalism of the army allowed the legionaries (the *antesignani* in particular) to take over some of the roles previously assigned to the *velites*.[56] Yet the first few decades of the cohortal system still saw the recruitment of specialist foreign *auxilia*. Under the Empire, these were absorbed into the Roman military system, and became the 'specialist' imperial *auxilia*; many of these cohorts having been recruited from particularly skilled warrior societies. Furthermore, these foreign specialties and the training of the Roman imperial army resulted in the establishment of its most tactically versatile corps. These foreign specialties rested chiefly in their fighting capability.

FIGHTING CAPABILITY

As noted briefly above, I suggest that the auxiliary line infantry forces were perhaps more zealous fighters than their legionary counterparts were. This arises from the suggestion that line infantry auxiliary (*auxilia, psiloi*) and 'light' (*leves cohortes, leves armaturae, legiones expeditae, antesignani, psiloi*) armament, was not necessarily that much 'lighter' than legionary equipment, and thus armament cannot be the only explanation for the preferred usage of these units in special deployments.

The armament of the professional *auxilia* and the *antesignani* reflected that of the legionaries: that the mail they wore could have been/was also worn by some legionaries, depending on personal preference.[57] Moreover, the segmented armour traditionally attributed to legionaries was in fact

---

combat roles. This is probably the reason specialist foreign troops were hired by Rome as well, and Trundle's argument (157) may be correlated to Roman forces: "Best rightly claims that "the majority of mercenaries who fought in Spartan and Athenian armies in Greece proper in the fourth century were peltasts" (1969: 134). The Greek cities of the mainland, whose need for specialist troops to augment their hoplite (heavy infantry) armies always remained critical, hired them prolifically. That they hired from outside so commonly demonstrates that they had no full time specialist light troops ready for service from within their own communities. Peltasts (light infantry) provided very useful support to hoplite armies in reconnaissance, van and rearguard actions, actions on irregular terrain and provisioning, and especially to mercenary armies, in plundering regions of enemy territory, which was often essential for paying mercenary soldiers."
[55] Best 1969, 78, cf. Xen. *Anab.* 3.4.25-30, 4.1.17-19, 6.3.7-8.
[56] Bell 1965, 421, cf. Anders 2012, 134.
[57] Gilliver 2007, 5; see also Anders 2012, 32ff.

lighter than the mail attributed to the *auxilia*.[58] Regardless of this, differentiation between sets of armour between the infantry classes is a vexed question and can still at times be difficult.[59] The only difference between their equipment in the imperial period that we can be most sure of was the shield and the spear, and this has been the evidence for the traditional argument discussed earlier, that the *auxilia* were used in various capacities because of their more suitable equipment.[60] Yet, the evidence remains that it was unlikely that *auxilia* were really 'lighter' troops.[61]

Furthermore, I find Bishop and Coulston's argument regarding auxiliary shields to be better suited to open-order (i.e. non-pitched) combat, to be unconvincing. They provide no concrete proof that the flat oval shield was in fact a better shield to be used in hand-to-hand combat than the rectangular curved shield of the legionaries.[62] Rather, recent studies suggested that the curved shield was more effective as a defensive weapon in hand-to-hand combat.[63] Besides, our examples demonstrating the *auxilia*'s (and other light units') skill, aggression and success as hand-to-hand fighters cannot be attributed to equipment alone.[64] Thus, there must be more to using the *auxilia* and light units in special deployments such as those discussed above.[65]

Outstanding courage or bravery is one possibility for such use of auxiliary and light units. Rawlings has drawn attention to Caesar's appreciation for courage (*virtus, audacia*) as a key to victory in battle. Interestingly, in *De Bello Gallico*, Caesar applies the term to non-Romans

---

[58] Bishop & Coulston 2006, 258.
[59] Bishop & Coulston 2006, 258-259.
[60] Cf. Bishop & Coulston 2006, 257.
[61] Cf. Haynes 2013, 274.
[62] Bishop & Coulston 2006, 254-259.
[63] Goldsworthy 1996, 210; Lee 1996, 200.
[64] As for the late Republican period, Sallust (Sall. *Iug.* 105), for example, notes how even though Sulla equipped an auxiliary cohort with 'light arms' (*velitaribus armis*) in the Jugurthine War, they were still able to stand their ground against the enemy.
[65] As far as training may have been a factor in this, little is known of the training of the *auxilia* and light troops, although it is assumed that by the time of the Empire they had the same training as legionaries, cf. Cheesman 1914, 70; Goldsworthy 1996, 20. During the Republic it seems allies were also trained in Roman discipline, e.g. App. *Hisp.* 11.65. Some auxiliaries who were not trained in Roman discipline were known to get out of control, e.g. Caes. *B Gal.* 2.24, 3.12, 5.16, cf. Goldsworthy 1996.

more often than he does to Romans, with *audacia* being "a mainly Gallic attribute...with a more dynamic resonance [than *virtus* or *fortis*]".[66] This notion that non-Romans show outstanding courage in battle is one that has been picked up by other scholars as well. While Lendon suggests that auxiliary troops were naturally more eager, spurred on by military decorations, and advancement in rank, he also believes their performance was driven by inherent *virtus*.[67] Though he draws on Tacitus' interesting comment that the Batavians are the foremost in *virtus*; that they are "set apart for fighting purposes, like a magazine of arms, [reserved] for [Roman] wars", I would rather focus the argument on their social status.[68]

I believe it would not be erroneous to say that auxiliaries and allied light-troops, as non-Romans – that is, as people without the full citizen rights of their fellow legionary soldiers – may have wanted to validate their equality as Roman soldiers by showing the highest possible levels of *audacia* or *virtus* in battle. When they did, their pride remains as evidence for the struggle they overcame. A funerary inscription from the Danube area, dated to the second century AD has a Batavian solider boasting of his fame for swimming across the Danube fully armed, and being the best javelin thrower and archer amongst his fellow auxiliaries and legionaries.[69] This pride was also seen during the Civil Wars of AD 69-70, when Batavian cohorts boasted of their victories against legionaries to other Romans, claiming "that the whole destiny of the war lay in their hands," starting brawls and quarrels with the other soldiers. Yet, even the legionaries supposedly admitted that the auxiliaries taken from them during the Civil Wars were the "bravest of men."[70] Whether it was *virtus*, advancement, or pride, there seems to have been more to the auxiliary forces than just a difference in armament that allowed for their tactical usage in difficult terrain. Our sources also seem to stress excellent fighting capability and the zeal of the auxiliaries. For example, Plutarch relates how "Against Otho's gladiators, too, who were supposed to have

---

[66] Rawlings 1998, 179-180, esp. n. 30: *virtus* used for Roman individuals or groups 33 times, for Gauls and Germans combined, 36. *Audacia* used 7 times for Gauls, once for Britons, once for Romans. This could of course, be a result of Caesar trying to make his enemies sound more intimidating and thus his victories seem more glorious. As for light troops, *fortissimos* is used to describe *antesignani* at Caes. *B Civ.* 1.57.
[67] Lendon 2005, 247-248.
[68] Tac. *Ger.* 29, cf. Lendon 2005, 247.
[69] *ILS* 2558.
[70] Tac. *Hist.* 2.27; 2.28; this could of course, just be rhetoric from Tacitus.

experience and courage in close fighting, Alfenus Varus led up the troops called Batavians", who then swiftly eliminated the gladiator unit (Plut. *Vit. Otho* 12.4). Another passage, already mentioned above (Tac. *Hist.* 2.35), where German auxiliaries out-swam enemy boats (whilst in full-armour), and in the following water-borne fight with Othonian gladiators "leapt into the shallows, laid hold of the boats, climbed over the gunwales, or sank them with their hands," provides similar evidence supporting their zeal for combat. In another example (Tac. *Ann.* 12.35), Tacitus explains how the auxiliaries helped lead Ostorius' forces to a glorious victory against Caractacus' army. Josephus claims that in the Jewish War, some freshly recruited auxiliaries from free cities, made up for their lack of experience with "their alacrity (*prothumia*) and in their hatred for the Jews".[71] A scene from Trajan's column appears to reflect this understanding in the literary sources of the fighting capability and zeal of the auxiliaries. In scene 24, an auxiliary is seen fighting with a severed head held by the hair in his teeth. Not only was fighting in such a manner likely more difficult than fighting without the burden of a severed head (thus requiring notable skill), but the zeal and alacrity displayed by the auxiliary in this scene is plainly evident.

Thus, it seems that our sources present a bias towards the *virtus/audacia* of the auxiliaries. Because of this bias, we should not assume that legionaries lacked *virtus* or *audacia*. Rather, I would argue that if auxiliaries were especially keen on proving themselves (possibly due to their inferior social status), then commanders may have wanted to exploit this enthusiasm by using them instead of the legionaries in the most demanding tactical assignments, as argued throughout this paper.

Conclusions

With the gradual disappearance of the *velites* and the emergence of the cohortal legion, one of Rome's most tactically versatile units needed to be replaced. The auxiliary units of the Roman army took up the mantle, and with the establishment of the professional *auxilia* during the imperial period, they also came to replace the foreign allied units (*socii*) to an extent as well. Although these new auxiliaries differed in equipment, organization and role from their predecessors, they were no less tactically versatile. This can be seen in their usage in scouting, guarding the marching column and foragers, reconnaissance, and as combatants in

---

[71] Joseph. *BJ* 2.18.9.

difficult terrain. Their fighting capability, whether a result of natural aggressiveness, alacrity, or desire to prove themselves as worthy of Roman citizenship, resulted in their noticeable displays of *virtus* and pride. Their commanders seem to have recognized this, and so deployed them accordingly in situations where they bore the brunt of combat, including pitched battle scenarios.

BIBLIOGRAPHY

Anders, A.O. (2012) *Roman Light Infantry and the Art of Combat* (unpublished doctoral thesis, Cardiff University).

Austin, N. J. E. and Rankov, N. B. (1995) *Exploratio: Military and political intelligence in the Roman world from the Second Punic War to the battle of Adrianople*. London.

Bell, M. J. V. (1965) "Tactical reform in the Roman republican army," *Historia* 14, 404-422.

Best, J. G. P. (1969) *Thracian Peltasts and their Influence on Greek Warfare*. Groningen.

Bishop, M. C., and J. C. Coulston. (2006) *Roman military equipment*. 2nd Edition. Oxford.

Breeze, D. J. (1969) "The Organization of the Legion: The First Cohort and the Equites Legionis," *JRS* 59, 50-55.

Cheesman, G. L. (1914) *The Auxilia of the Roman Imperial Army*. Chicago.

Dobson, B. and Mann, J. C. (1973) "The Roman Army in Britain and Britons in the Roman Army," *Britannia* 4, 191-205.

Gilliver, K. (1996) "Mons Graupius and the role of auxiliaries in battle," *Greece and Rome* 43, 54-67.

—. (1999) *The Roman art of war*. Stroud.

—. (2007) "The Augustan Reform and the Imperial Army," in P. Erdkamp (ed), *A Companion to the Roman Army*. Oxford, 183-200.

Goldsworthy, A. K. (1996) *The Roman army at war 100 BC-200 AD*. Oxford.

Hassall, M. W. C. (1970) "Batavians and the Roman conquest of Britain," *Britannia* 1, 131-136.

Haynes, I. (2013) *Blood of the Provinces*. Oxford.

Lee, A. D. (1996) "Morale and the Roman Experience of Battle," in A. Lloyd (ed), *Battle in Antiquity* London, 199-217.

Lendon, J. E. (2005) *Soldiers and ghosts. A history of battle in Classical Antiquity*. New Haven.

Lepper, F., and F. Sheppard. (1988) *Trajan's Column*. Gloucester.

Parker, H. M. D. (1928) *The Roman Legions.* Oxford.
Rainbird, J. S. (1969) "Tactics at Mons Graupius," *The Classical Review* New Ser., 19, No. 1, 11-12.
Rankov, B. (2007) "Military Forces," in P. Sabin, H. Van Wees, M. Whitby (eds) *The Cambridge History of Greek and Roman Warfare. Vol. II.*, 30-75.
Rawlings, L. (1998) "Caesar's portrayal of Gauls as warriors," in K. Welch and A. Powell (eds), *Julius Caesar as Artful Reporter.* Swansea, 171-92.
Roth, J. (1999) *The Logistics of the Roman Army at War.* New York.
Saddington, D. B. (1975) "The development of the Roman auxiliary forces from Augustus to Trajan," *ANRW* II-3, 176-201.
Southern, P. (1989) "The numeri of the Roman imperial army," *Britannia* 20, 81-140.
Speidel, M. (1992) "Exploratores. Mobile Elite Units of Roman Germany," *Roman Army Studies, vol. 2*, 89-104. Stuttgart.
Thorne, J. (2007) "Battle, Tactics, and the *Limites* in the West," in P. Erdkamp (ed) *A Companion to the Roman Army*, 218-234, Chichester.
Trundle, M. (2010) "Light troops at Classical Athens," in D. M. Pritchard (ed) *War, Democracy and Culture in Classical Athens* Cambridge, 139-160.
Watson, G. R. (1969) *The Roman Soldier.* Bristol.
Webster, G. (1980) *The Roman Invasion of Britain.* . London.
Wheeler, E. L. (1979) "The Legion as Phalanx," *Chiron* 9, 303-318.

CHAPTER SEVENTEEN

TO THE VICTOR THE SPOILS? POST-BATTLE LOOTING IN THE ROMAN WORLD

JOANNE BALL

INTRODUCTION

Graham Webster, when discussing the possibility of archaeologically locating the first battle fought between Romans and Britons in the invasion of AD 43, expressed doubt that a substantial artefact assemblage would survive on the battlefield. "All the valuable equipment would have been carefully collected after the fighting, and the bodies removed for proper burial".[1] Roman battlefield research has therefore tended to focus on the identification of features mentioned in battle narratives rather than artefact scatters, from natural topographic features to constructed mass graves and entrenchments.[2] The indiscriminate recovery of metal equipment by the Roman army, itself a form of looting, would serve to leave little behind to be taken by subsequent looters. It certainly is the case that the majority of Roman military sites were subjected to clearance of metal artefacts when the army departed, as metal was a particularly valuable resource in the ancient world and would not have been abandoned lightly. As Bishop and Coulston point out, the effort required to mine, process and manufacture metal artefacts to replace abandoned examples was substantial, particularly where the sources of certain metals were limited, and they conclude that "it does not take long to work out that the Romans took most

---

[1] Webster 1993, 100.
[2] This is particularly notable in Greek battlefield studies, which have almost exclusively surveyed for and excavated features documented by the literary accounts, see e.g. Pritchett 1965-1992.

of their metal with them when they left a site".[3] Much of the equipment used by the Roman army was probably produced by reprocessing the metal from damaged kit and other metal artefacts.[4] Hoards recovered from Colchester, Essex,[5] Corbridge, Northumberland,[6] and Grad near Šmihel in Slovenia[7] all contain damaged military equipment evidently awaiting reprocessing.

That on the abandonment or closure of a site, the Roman army removed the majority of metal artefacts is not particularly questioned. On some occasions it was evidently not possible to remove everything, which could result in substantial assemblages being left behind, such as the nail hoard from Inchtuthil in Perth and Kinross[8] and the military equipment and scrap hoard from Newstead in the Scottish borders.[9] In such cases, the hoards were deeply buried, perhaps to minimise the chance of the raw materials within being recovered by local populations.[10] Why they were left is less certain. Manning suggested that what was left behind was the surplus and least functional equipment, abandoned because logistical considerations made transport impractical.[11] However, while military sites appear to have been stripped of large caches of military equipment and other metal upon abandonment or closure, other installations suggest that non-weaponry small finds could easily be misplaced and forgotten upon departure, as occurred at many of the turrets on Hadrian's Wall.[12]

However, is it reasonable to suggest that the same processes of site clearance could have been conducted with the same efficiency on Roman battlefields? Certainly, there is no real doubt that these sites were looted, though the details of the process were not detailed by the historical record. As a result, the mechanics of the process are poorly understood, as is the onward transmission of the artefacts which were recovered. There have been, and remain, doubts that battlefield archaeology can be successfully

---

[3] Bishop and Couslton 2006, 27 (see 27-30 for full details).
[4] Bishop 1985a.
[5] Hakes and Hull 1947, 335-40.
[6] Allason-Jones and Bishop 1988.
[7] Horvat 2002.
[8] Pitts and St Joseph 1985.
[9] Curle 1911.
[10] Curle 1911, 347.
[11] Manning 1972, 246. The hoards at Inchtuthil, Newstead and Bar Hill and a number of continental sites have all been linked with ritual deposition, see Hingley 2006, 228-9.
[12] Allason-Jones 1988.

conducted on sites of ancient battle, compared to more modern counterparts.[13] However, the discovery of substantial assemblages on three Roman battlefields in the last two decades has suggested that battlefield clearance or looting did not serve to strip sites of all metal artefacts. This paper examines the historical and archaeological evidence for battlefield looting in the Roman world alongside wider sociological looting theory, and explores the impact of the process and priorities on the site formation of Roman battlefields.

BATTLEFIELD LOOTING

The political theorist Roger Mac Ginty identified four prerequisites to looting in any violent context: the availability of (potential) looters, the availability of 'lootable' goods, the absence of restraint, and a permissible socio-cultural environment.[14] These prerequisites cover a range of diverse behaviours. Looting is predominantly characterised as a process of predatory economic appropriation and acquisition of material resources for individual, rather than state, gain.[15] Additional motivations for looting can be celebratory,[16] symbolic/ritualistic,[17] or aimed at terrorising civilians for tactical reasons, predominantly resource denial and reduction of opposition.[18] Resource denial is rarely mentioned as a factor in looting, though attempts to use this as an exonerating excuse have been advanced on some occasions, such as in the case of British soldiers during the Second Boer War.[19] Looted resources may also supplement meagre official military supplies in under-supplied campaigns, and can provide the only means by which rebel or guerrilla forces can continue to fight. This can lead to problems for military authorities in regulating the process, as the British army found in the Second Boer War when looting of civilian property could only be controlled late in the conflict by the imposition of strict disciplinary measures.[20] Nevertheless, this illustrates that once Mac Ginty's third prerequisite- an absence of restraint- ceased to apply, looting could no longer continue unhindered.

---

[13] E.g. Sabin 2007, 400.
[14] Mac Ginty 2004, 861-66.
[15] Azam and Hoeffler 2002; for a summary of the 'greed thesis' see Mac Ginty 2004, 857-59.
[16] Mac Ginty 2004, 866-68.
[17] Harrison 2008, 777-78.
[18] Azam and Hoeffler 2002.
[19] Miller 2010, 326.
[20] Miller 2010, 325-7.

From the nineteenth century on, the individual manifestation of these characteristics can be seen in the personal archives of soldiers and official documentation of battles. In this period battle left many 'lootable' artefacts, from high value items such as weaponry and jewellery to clothing and shoes. Records of soldiers looting during this period state that in some cases soldiers looted for the 'sheer fun of destruction', but more commonly for profit.[21] Looted kit might replace damaged or poor quality kit. At Waterloo, soldiers replaced clothing and effects with those recovered from casualties and sold by Lord Edward Somerset shortly after the battle.[22] Less formally, many soldiers during the First World War replaced elements of their kit from casualties in No Man's Land, while the bodies were cursorily buried or abandoned.[23] The greatest profit, however, was through the sale of artefacts on the open market. As a result, every artefact, however low its innate worth, was of value to someone. Looters stood to make significant material gains from the battlefield - at Gettysburg, one visitor in the aftermath noted military supplies worth thousands of dollars being carried off daily from the battlefield by enterprising looters.[24] If a battle became of public interest, even the smallest artefacts could become marketable as relics of battle. While it had previously not been uncommon for soldiers to take such items as souvenirs, keeping them or sending them home to family or even selling them to rear-posted troops,[25] the nineteenth century saw a growth in interest for owning such objects among the general population. This could extend the period of looting far beyond the immediate post-battle period in which looting would usually occur. It was most common for munitions to be traded, not least because they remained in the greatest numbers on the field, but the more esoteric collector had access to a wide range of battle souvenirs, perhaps most grimly exemplified at Waterloo where relic hawkers were said to offer thumbs and teeth of the dead preserved in gin.[26] Such was the demand for battlefield relics among the European and American elites that faked artefacts flooded the collectables market, particularly from Waterloo[27] and Gettysburg, where locals, particularly children, were recruited by relic hawkers to search the site for munitions to

---

[21] March Phillips 1902, 130-131.
[22] Mercer 1870, 62.
[23] Fraser and Brown 2007.
[24] *New York Evening Post*, July 10th, 1863.
[25] Harrison 2008, 777-78.
[26] Semmel 2000, 12.
[27] Seaton 1999, 137-8.

sell.[28] Relic hunting served to severely impact the surviving archaeology, and is an ongoing problem even today. The market for battlefield relics did not remain restricted to contemporary warfare, and most notably arrowheads from Marathon (and their faked counterparts) also became of commercial interest during the nineteenth and early twentieth centuries.[29] Such processes ensured that sites were largely stripped of metal artefacts, but the resources frequently did not stay within the military economy, but instead passed into private, often civilian, ownership.

Battlefield archaeology has served to illustrate that these processes on modern battlefields did not serve to strip the battlefield entirely of artefacts, but they did have a significant impact on the content of assemblages. Weapons are almost entirely absent from the industrial (post-medieval/blackpowder) battlefield record. A small number of sites, including Culloden[30] and the Little Bighorn,[31] have firearm fragments, but no complete weaponry. Far higher quantities of munitions survive, with hundreds or even thousands of individual artefacts recovered from battlefields from this period.[32] Personal effects are almost entirely absent, represented by small numbers of buckles, buttons, insignia and coins often associated with areas of hand-to-hand fighting towards the periphery of the battlefield.[33] Archaeological projects to date have struggled to locate significant artefact scatters on most pre-industrial battlefields. Though a large number of arrowheads and personal items have been recovered from Towton,[34] other near-contemporary battlefields such as Flodden and Bosworth have produced few projectiles[35] and little military kit.[36] However, these absences may not reflect looting alone, but also the negative conditions for the survival of ferrous material at these sites[37] and the impact of subsequent land-use.

---

[28] Reardon and Vossler 2013, 753.
[29] Forsdyke 1927, 147.
[30] Pollard 2009a.
[31] Scott *et al* 1989, 186.
[32] Foard and Morris 2012, 66-77.
[33] Pollard 2009a.
[34] Sutherland 2000.
[35] Foard and Morris 2012, 23.
[36] Pollard and Oliver 2002, 118-83.
[37] Pollard and Oliver 2002, 52.

ROMAN LOOTING

Looting is well attested in the Roman documentary record, and was described by Livy as a normal part of warfare (Livy 31.30.2-4). It occurred during territorial raiding, after capturing enemy cities, camps or baggage-trains, and on the battlefield, and involved the taking of human captives and chattel (*Caes. B Gal.* 6.3; Livy 31.30; Plut. *Vit. Luc.* 14.1), gold and currency (Plut. *Vit. Luc.* 17.6-7; Tac. *Hist.* 3.33), grain (Caes. *B Civ.* 3.42), and household items such as books and hunting nets (Plut. *Vit. Pomp.* 4.1). These items might be directly distributed to soldiers (Caes. *B Gal.* 7.89; Polyb. 9.27.11; Dio Cass. 11.11) or centrally sold and the profit shared (Polyb. 10.16.4-6). Soldiers under both the Republic and Empire were strongly motivated by the promise of booty (Polyb. 10.17.1; Sall. *Iug.* 54.1; Tac. *Hist.* 3.26),[38] and campaigning to gain booty for soldiers was a proven way to buy their loyalty (Plut. *Vit. Caes.* 23.4). As a result, soldiers could become discontented when they were not able to engage in looting (Dio Cass. 41.26.1; 74.8.1; Plut. *Vit. Luc.* 14.2), and though it sometimes happened, it was considered a poor decision for military commanders to keep booty for themselves and their friends (App. *Ib.* 60; Cato *De Sumptu Suo* 51.169; Sall. *Iug.* 41.7). Territorial looting and the confiscation of supplies served to subdue populations (Sall. *Iug.* 54.5)[39] and compel opponent forces to seek battle (App. *Hann.* 3.17; Polyb. 3.111.3-5; 5.51.10-11). The historical sources describe non-Roman forces as equally motivated by the acquisition of booty (*Caes. B Gal.* 5.34; 6.8; 6.34; Polyb. 3.78.5; Plut. *Vit. Ant.* 45.1), and their greed is often used as a factor in their tactical inferiority (Tac. *Ann.* 1.65; 14.33). Both Roman and non-Roman looters were said to destroy, most often through burning, any booty which they could not transport (Flor. 2.24.9; Livy 23.46.6; Plut. *Vit. Mar.* 22.1; Polyb. 5.8.8-9; Tac. *Ann.* 14.32).

The mechanics of Roman battlefield looting are not often mentioned in the historical record, and it is difficult to extrapolate accurately from the disparate references. The actual process of battlefield looting, rather than the resulting booty, is rarely described. Livy documents the central collection of booty after a battle against the Sabines by the last legendary Roman king Tarquinius Superbus (1.37.5), though his source for this is unclear, and looting on the battlefield of Numistro while soldiers disposed

---

[38] Though Roth 1999, 301-05 suggests that the lure of booty was unlikely to be the sole reason for the long-term commitment to the army required under the Empire.
[39] Roth 1999, 305.

of the dead (27.2.9). Plutarch describes the battlefield booty from the battlefield of Vercellae being collected and removed to the camp of Catulus, where it was used to prove the decisive involvement of Catulus' men at the expense of those of Marius (Plut. *Vit. Marius* 27.4). The process is described as one of total site clearance, conducted by individual soldiers who may or may not have been under institutional direction or supervision. There is no mention in our sources of items deliberately left behind, though there are references to the later emergence of fragmented weaponry and armour at Chaeronea (Plut. *Vit. Sulla* 21.4) and Philippi (Verg. *G.* 1.493-97). No particular time-frame is attributed by these sources to military battlefield looting, though it would have been limited to the often brief period of time between the end of fighting and the departure of the army from the battlefield. This varied by exigency, though the three days Caesar remained on the battlefield at Bibracte (Caes. *B Gal.* 1.26) may represent an upper limit in the context of onward campaigning. Looting the battlefield appears to have been less desirable than looting the enemy camp and baggage, which is more frequently mentioned in post-battle activity narratives (Caes. *B Gal.* 1.26; Livy 27.19.2; Polyb. 15.15.2). After the battle of Cynoscephalae (197 BC), the majority of Roman soldiers rushed to loot the defeated Greek camp, with only a few remaining on the battlefield to strip the dead. When access to camp-looting was barred, the Roman soldiers returned to the battlefield to loot what they could from what had been unclaimed (Polyb. 18.27.3-5).

The historical record refers to the material recovered from a battlefield as *spolia*, in contrast to wider campaign booty, *praeda* or *manubiae*. While the latter referred to anything, from human captives to furniture, taken during the course of a campaign, *spolia* referred exclusively to "weapons and armor [sic] taken from enemy soldiers" on the battlefield.[40] Non-weaponry military ephemera, such as standards or trumpets, recovered at the same time are mentioned in addition to *spolia* rather than as part of it (App. *Civ.* 1.41; Sall. *Iug.* 74.3; Plut. *Vit. Marius* 27.4). Booty acquired from a baggage-train during an attack/ambush was not considered to be *spolia* (e.g. Tac. *Ann.* 1.57; 1.65), nor were arms surrendered by a defeated enemy. There is no mention, as *spolia* or otherwise, of the vast range of non-weaponry objects which archaeology has now demonstrated to have been deposited on Roman battlefields during battle.

The purpose of collecting the *spolia* is not clear from the historical record. There is no record that it was officially distributed to soldiers to

---

[40] Bradford Churchill 1999, 87 n. 9.

supplement or replace their kit, or as a material reward, though authorities were evidently aware of a proclivity for theft of soldiers in such contexts (Polyb. 10.17.1-2; Plut. *Vit. Marius* 21.2; Dio 27.90). Nor was it frequently used in celebrations of victory, judging from the limited number of references to the use of *spolia* in triumphs (Plut. *Vit. Marius* 22.1) and as trophies (e.g. Tac. *Ann.* 2.18; 2.22; Flor. 2.30.23). The majority of (surplus) *spolia* was evidently destroyed, particularly by burning, a practice also used in wider warfare for surplus *praeda* (e.g. Livy 45.33.1; Polyb. 5.8.8-9), serving as a votive offering for victory (Livy 1.37.5; 23.46.5; Plut. *Vit. Mar.* 22.1). This burning may have been limited to the wooden structure of equipment, such as the shield base or *pilum* shaft, after the metal elements had been removed.[41] Florus added that while burning was the usual method, surplus arms were thrown in rivers during the Pannonian War (Florus 2.24.9). *Spolia* do not appear to have been used to rearm Roman soldiers except in times of necessity. During the Second Punic War, the Roman army used armour captured from the Gallic territories to equip new recruits from among the condemned criminals (Livy 23.14.4), and, during battle, projectiles could be gathered for re-use within the same engagement (Caes. *B Gal.* 2.27; Livy 38.22.6). Weaponry and armour captured *from* the Romans was used to equip non-Roman forces. Hannibal is particularly associated with this, arming his Numidian soldiers with Roman arms captured throughout Italy (Polyb. 3.87.3) and using them in battle to devastating effect at Cannae (Polyb. 3.114.1). Hamilcar (Polyb. 1.78.13) and later Arminius (Tac. *Ann.* 2.25) were also documented as arming their soldiers with captured Roman kit.

ROMAN BATTLEFIELD ASSEMBLAGES

The narrative descriptions of Roman battlefield looting suggest a process of total site clearance of the weaponry and armour deposited by battle. As mentioned previously, this has led to pessimism regarding Roman battlefield archaeology and the survival of diagnostically relevant military equipment. The substantial assemblage recovered from Kalkriese was initially dismissed as an aberration resulting from a unique historical event, though it was acknowledged by some that comparable assemblages would be more probable on battlefields of comprehensive Roman defeat.[42] This position is increasingly obsolete in the wake of battlefield excavations at sites of Roman victory. While in some ways the pessimists were not

---

[41] Bishop and Coulston 2006, 25.
[42] Coulston 2001, 44.

incorrect - military equipment has not been found in any great quantity - both the ancient historical record and the finds on medieval battlefields have led to a vast underestimation of the non-weaponry ephemera of battle which survives on these sites.

The most extensively explored battlefield is Kalkriese in north-west Germany near Osnabrück, which has been under intermittent archaeological exploration since 1987. Explorations of the battlefield, which is probably associated with the AD 9 Varian disaster, have surveyed and excavated an area of over 30km², though the most fruitful work has been at the Oberesch, in the western area of the conflict zone.[43] The diversity and range of the extant assemblage from the Oberesch suggests that this area saw conflict late in the engagement, after the Roman force had been pursued through the landscape to the east for three or four days. There is a large amount of material from the baggage train. The archaeology survives particularly well at the Oberesch due to the collapse of a battle-period rampart which protected the artefacts underneath from disturbance.[44] The whole landscape benefitted from the deposition of a layer of fertiliser in the late Medieval period which protected the assemblage from significant agricultural disturbance. Over 5500 metal pieces have been recovered from the battlefield excavations, c. 5000 from the Oberesch and c. 500 from the surrounding conflict landscape.[45] Many are highly fragmented and were significantly damaged either in battle or during the subsequent looting.[46]

Since the discovery of Kalkriese, two more Roman battlefields have been excavated, the site of the battle of Baecula in Spain, and the site of a previously undocumented engagement at Harzhorn in Germany. The Romans were victorious at Baecula and this was probably also the case in the battle that took place at Harzhorn. Baecula has been under exploration since 2002, when a heritage management project identified the battlefield at Santo Tomé near Jaén in southern Spain. Whilst a catalogue of finds has not yet been published, the recovery of over 6000 artefacts has been reported, including projectiles, military kit fragments, coinage and pottery.[47] The Harzhorn battlefield in north-west Germany was identified

---

[43] Wilbers-Rost 2007; see Wilbers-Rost 2012/13 for an overview of the more recent work.
[44] See Wilbers-Rost 2007, 3-7 for details.
[45] Harnecker 2008; 2011.
[46] Rost and Wilbers-Rost 2010, 123.
[47] Bellón Ruiz *et al* 2012.

in 2008 and has subsequently been surveyed and excavated. As yet it has not been possible to provide an exact historical context for the battle, although the coinage and pottery date it to the first half of the third century AD. Consequently, the battle has been tentatively identified with the campaigning of Maximinus Thrax described in the *Historia Augusta* (*Duo Max.* 12.2), though this is still under debate.[48] The nature of the assemblage initially suggested a victory by a Roman force, but there have been subsequent suggestions that the battle may instead have involved Germanic ex-auxiliaries in Roman kit, rather than a Roman army.[49] Excavations have uncovered more than 3000 metal pieces from the site, of which 1740 are from the Roman period.[50]

Very few artefacts recovered from these sites can be categorised as weaponry and armour. Of the extant weaponry, projectiles, particularly long-range, are best represented, while armour is particularly poorly represented. Arrowheads, 27 lead *glandes* and over 200 *plumbatae* were recovered from the lower slopes at Baecula, along the likely route of Roman assault. Towards the summit of the Carthaginian position a smaller quantity of shorter-range projectiles were recovered, particularly *pila* heads, ten of which were recovered from the highest point.[51] No identifiable armour pieces have yet been recovered at Baecula. At Harzhorn, the assemblage also contains a number of projectiles, 214 in total, including arrowheads, *pila*, and *glandes*. The most numerous single weaponry category is catapult bolts, of which 131 have thus far been recovered, primarily along the lower slopes.[52] Only 28 fragments of '*am Körper getragene Ausrüstung*' (body-worn equipment) have been recovered from Harzhorn. They include iron chain mail and bronze armour fragments, and a small number of iron belt fittings and buckles.[53]

Kalkriese presents a significant contrast. Very few projectiles were recovered, with a predominance of shorter-range *pila* (37) and lance/spear (26) elements over arrowheads (3), *glandes* (3) and miscellaneous projectiles (17). The majority of *pila* finds are socket elements, although

---

[48] Berger *et al* 2013.
[49] Meyer and Moosbauer 2013.
[50] Berger *et al* 2010/13, 334. Excavation has recovered a further (c.) 950 pieces which are as-yet undated; many of these may also belong to the Roman assemblage.
[51] Atwood 2014, 34-35.
[52] Berger *et al* 2010/13, 334-5.
[53] Berger *et al* 2010/13, 334-37.

among the lance/spear elements there are complete and almost-complete examples, including one lance-head with a partial fragment of wooden shaft *in situ* measuring 31.6cm in total (24.3cm lance-head alone).[54] The only surviving non-projectile weapon is a single *gladius* tip fragment measuring 14.6cm by 3.8cm.[55] The Oberesch assemblage is dominated by a high quantity of fragmented armour elements. Eighty individual shield pieces have been identified, totalling 363 individual fragments.[56] There are also fragments of ring-mail (9) and *lorica* (36), and a number of helmet fragments (23), predominantly joint fittings but also a substantial iron cheek-piece and the famous Kalkriese cavalry mask.[57]

Unlike battlefields from later periods, a significant assemblage of non-weaponry artefacts also survived on these sites. The non-weaponry small finds assemblage is dominated by clothing and footwear fittings. Excavations at Baecula and Harzhorn recovered hundreds of *caligae* nails. Just under 700 have been found at Baecula, currently making up almost a third of the total surviving assemblage, which have allowed the reconstruction of Roman manoeuvres before and during the battle.[58] Over 1400 *caligae* nails have been recovered from Harzhorn, with over 80% of the assemblage securely identified as Roman.[59] Thirty-six individual shoe-related artefacts were recovered from Kalkriese comprising 64 individual finds, including one partially-preserved leather sole with 3 nails still in place.[60] At Baecula and Harzhorn the *caligae* are concentrated in areas of hard terrain or where large-scale manoeuvres took place, which may partially account for their relative absence at Kalkriese, which lacked the former, and due to the circumstances of battle, potentially also the latter.

A range of other non-weaponry small finds have been found at these sites. Clothing fittings and jewellery are most common at Kalkriese. A number of clothing fittings, many fragmented, survive from Kalkriese including different *fibulae* types (81), belt buckles and fittings (76), decorative plates (9) and nails (33).[61] A small number of amulets, buckles,

---

[54] Harnecker 2008, 4, cat. no. 7.
[55] Harnecker 2008, 5, cat. no. 35.
[56] Harnecker 2008, 5-8, cat. no. 36-91; 2011, 24-5, cat. no. 2078-2101.
[57] Harnecker 2008, 8-10, cat. no. 92-117; Harnecker 2011, 25-6, cat. no. 2102-2138.
[58] Bellón Ruiz *et al* 2012, 366-71.
[59] Berger *et al* 2010/13, 334.
[60] Harnecker 2008, 12, cat. no. 172.
[61] Harnecker 2008, 14-16, 26-36; 2011, 7-9, 14-17.

brooches and jewellery have been reported from Baecula.[62] At Harzhorn, a small quantity of jewellery has been recovered, including a Taunus-Wetterau-type *fibula*, and two bronze finger-rings.[63] No cavalry or mule equipment has been reported from Baecula, but 124 fittings fragments have been recovered from Kalkriese, many from a mule skeleton buried by the collapsed rampart,[64] and 16 from Harzhorn, including wagon fittings and iron horse-shoes.[65] *Dolabra* (pickaxe) heads were recovered from both Kalkriese and Harzhorn; the example from the latter site had the inscription *LEG IIII S A*.[66] Kalkriese has an additional range of artefacts which are not matched at the other two battlefields, including tent-pegs, surveying equipment, *styli*, seals, medical instruments, strongboxes, furniture, and sculpture.[67] This range is thus far exceptional, and the most probable explanation is the presence and destruction of a Roman baggage train in the vicinity.[68] Few non-Roman artefact types have been recovered. A number of arrowheads, coins and pottery fragments from Baecula are of Carthaginian type, and are primarily distributed in the Carthaginian position in the north of the battlefield.[69] As mentioned previously, the historical record claims that Carthaginian troops during the Second Punic War were equipped with captured Roman arms, although the question of 'Roman' military equipment in this period is itself problematic.[70] Few artefacts from Kalkriese have been identified as Germanic in origin, which may indicate the use of Roman-style equipment by the German combatants, some of whom may have been serving or ex-auxiliary soldiers.[71] A small number of artefacts from Harzhorn have been identified as Germanic, including spear and lance heads,[72] but this is uncertain. As at Kalkriese, it has been suggested that many of the combatants at Harzhorn may have been ex-auxiliaries fighting in Roman kit, reducing the quantity of identifiable 'non-Roman' artefacts.[73]

---

[62] Atwood 2014, 34.
[63] Berger *et al* 2010/13, 335.
[64] Harnecker 2008, 17-19, in particular cat. no. 249-252.
[65] Berger *et al* 2010/13, 343-47.
[66] Wiegels *et al* 2011.
[67] See Harnecker 2008; 2011
[68] Rost and Wilbers-Rost 2010, 123.
[69] Bellón Ruiz *et al* 2012, 366-69; Atwood 2014, 35.
[70] Bishop and Coulston 2006, 48-50.
[71] Rost and Wilbers-Rost 2010, 134.
[72] Berger *et al* 2010/13, 349-53.
[73] Meyer and Moosbauer 2013.

THE ASSEMBLAGES AND BATTLEFIELD LOOTING

Returning to Mac Ginty's four requisites of looting, the question can be asked about whether these artefact assemblages were left behind deliberately because they were not considered 'lootable' material, or for a less tangible reason. This requires consideration, firstly, about who was conducting the looting. Certainly Roman soldiers engaged in the process, whether under institutional or individual supervision, but their involvement would have been limited to whatever period of time the army remained in the vicinity of the battlefield. Civilian involvement, either by camp-followers or native populations, is more difficult to assess. There is some emerging archaeological support for the involvement of civilian populations in the Roman world. Recent excavations in the conflict landscape around Kalkriese have recovered Roman military equipment from contemporary Germanic settlements, suggesting a civilian involvement in the recovery of artefacts from the battlefield area.[74] A similar phenomenon is seen in the conflict landscape around the battlefield of Abritus in Bulgaria, another engagement where the Roman army suffered a catastrophic reverse in AD 251. This site has not been discussed in the rest of this paper because the battlefield itself has not been subjected to archaeological research, but the artefact diffusion in the nearby native settlements, currently being excavated, is relevant to and assists in the interpretation of the Kalkriese landscape. Many of the native settlements around Abritus contained a large quantity of contemporary Roman military equipment, including swords, shields, and armour, as well as *pila* and other projectiles. Excavators working on the landscape have suggested that this is indicative of civilian involvement in the looting process.[75] In both cases, however, it is acknowledged that the military equipment might have been deposited by the conflict itself extending to the settlements or by the abandonment of the artefacts within the settlement confines by soldiers.

Elements of the assemblage may have been left behind because it was not feasible to transport them. These artefacts would have become non-lootable because of the logistical issues of moving bulk metalwork, as at Inchtuthil, rather than because they were regarded as not being of sufficient value. This may explain the abandonment of large artefacts on the battlefield, of which a wagon abandoned at Harzhorn is perhaps the most obvious example.[76] The question of transportation away from the

---

[74] Rost and Wilbers-Rost 2014.
[75] Radoslavova 2011.
[76] Berger *et al* 2010/13, 343-47.

battlefield would have been a significant issue. An individual soldier in the Roman army would have been responsible for carrying an estimated weight of up to 43kg,[77] to which any additional items would have proved somewhat of a burden. The baggage-train may have been able to transport some of the more valuable surplus, but as pointed out by Manning in the context of Newstead, over-loading of the baggage was a severe tactical risk when moving through hostile territory.[78] Abandoning or destroying substantial quantities of metal, particularly military equipment, on the battlefield may have had severe consequences on both immediate and long-term military supply of equipment and metal resources. This may also have provided the enemy with access to resources, but may have been the only choice. Unlike at the military installations, there is no significant evidence that abandoned material was successfully hoarded through *en masse* burial after a Roman victory. However, two sites of Roman defeat show some evidence of deliberate hoarding of high value artefacts. At Kalkriese, weaponry pieces, including a scabbard with silver fittings, and caches of high denomination coinage were deposited in the outlying area of the site, almost 2km north from the Oberesch. The concentration of many high value artefacts within a small area away from the battlefield suggests that there were deliberate attempts by individual Roman soldiers to hide valuables from the Germanic looters.[79] Similar hoards of high denomination coinage were recovered from the Roman camp near the battlefield of Abritus. A number of smaller hoards were identified in the wider landscape.[80] Whether or not this was an official Roman military 'policy' when facing a defeat, evidently the obscuration of material by burying it was in some cases a successful way to prevent it being looted- though any less successful examples of the activity would not, of course, be apparent from the archaeological record.

In the historical record, surplus equipment was usually burned, though there is no extant archaeological evidence for this. If Bishop and Coulston are correct that the burning was restricted to the wooden elements of equipment (see n. 40), the question would still remain as to the transportation or obscuration of the remaining metals. At Kalkriese, it is evident that the Germanic looters were faced with the problem of how to carry the material away. Many fragments of shield binding were found at the site, resulting from stripping the metal elements from the wooden

---

[77] Junkelmann 1986, 199.
[78] Manning 1972, 246.
[79] Rost and Wilbers-Rost 2010, 133.
[80] Radoslavova 2011.

shield. Several pieces of binding had been subsequently crumpled into compact balls of metal, which has been interpreted as a crude form of battlefield reprocessing aimed at facilitating easier transportation by decreasing the bulk.[81]

However, the extant assemblages are unlikely to be solely the result of transportation problems. The majority of the extant assemblages are comprised of low value small finds, with little immediate functional use. As discussed previously, high-value large pieces of weaponry and armour were entirely removed from the battlefield by the looting process. These artefacts, no doubt, were targeted first at the expense of the artefact-types which constitute the surviving assemblages. Non-Roman forces were, according to the historical record, keen to supplement their own equipment with the higher-quality Roman work where possible - if indeed, they were not already using Roman kit, as seems increasingly plausible for auxiliary-type non-Roman units. Non-Roman looting of weaponry and armour may therefore have been a process of wealth acquisition, either for supplementation of basic resources or onward sale. By contrast, the Roman recovery of weaponry may have been, as with installation site clearance, a process of resource denial, where surplus weaponry and armour was collected by the Roman army not because they needed or wanted it, but because it was vital that it not fall into the hands of the enemy. Individual Roman soldiers may have taken odd pieces to replace damaged or poor quality items in their own kit, but this would have had little impact on the overall surplus quantity. The assemblages would suggest that the Roman army, knowing there was a limited period of time for collection and a limit to the surplus which could be taken away, targeted the weaponry and armour at the expense of the non-weaponry small finds. Though the latter may not have been individually rejected as such, the Roman army is likely to have been aware that the de-prioritisation of the recovery of these artefact types would result in a number being left behind on the battlefield.

However, due to natural obscuration, subsequent non-Roman looters may not have had much ready access to the metal objects left behind by the Roman army. While the Roman army may not have deliberately buried the surviving assemblages, many may already have been obscured by surface vegetation or within the topsoil by the time that looting began. The impact of obscuration on artefact recovery can be seen at the Oberesch at Kalkriese. A Germanic turf rampart, constructed in the weeks before the

---

[81] Rost 2012/13, 103.

battle to entrap a Roman force, partially collapsed soon after the end of the battle. Comparison between the assemblage from below the collapsed section, where looting was stopped at an early stage, and those from the rest of the Oberesch, provides an insight into the material impact of obscuration and inaccessibility. The presence of weaponry fragments and armour reprocessing fragments suggests that looting had commenced before the collapse, with a wider range of finds recovered from below the rampart in comparison with the immediate vicinity, including an articulated mule skeleton with many fittings.[82] As well as a greater diversity of finds, the collapsed rampart area has a much higher artefact density. The assemblages on either side of the rampart suggest that the looting at Kalkriese took place in several phases. The first is likely to have been a hurried affair, conducted quickly before the evacuation of the battlefield in anticipation of the arrival of an expected Roman reprisal force. When such a force failed to emerge, looters returned to the battlefield for a second, more leisurely and thorough period of looting, to find the rampart partially collapsed and some artefacts therefore inaccessible.[83] Prioritisation was evidently given in the first phase to artefacts of highest value. The famous Kalkriese cavalry mask was found under the collapsed rampart. The silver plating with which it had originally been covered had been removed but the iron base had not been taken at the same time, and was covered under the collapsed rampart. The artefacts rejected in the initial phase of looting were not as highly prized as weaponry and armour, but where accessible were recovered from the rest of the site in the secondary phase of looting. Nonetheless, attempts were not made to disinter the artefacts from below the collapse, which cannot as yet be explained

Natural obscuration would account in part for why a reasonable quantity of projectiles would be left behind by the looting process, rather than deliberate rejection. Many retained functionality, even the *pila* heads which in many cases would only have required the wooden shaft be replaced for them to be used again. What proportion of the original deposition was left behind is impossible to estimate, though when discussing projectile use the literary record numbers missiles in the thousands and tens of thousands, rather than the hundreds recovered from battlefields (e.g. Caes. *B Civ.* 3.53). The projectiles are likely to have been distributed across the battlefield, particularly in the peripheral areas which

---

[82] Rost and Wilbers-Rost 2010, 121.
[83] Rost 2007.

are likely to have been less thoroughly looted than the central areas.[84] As with munitions on modern sites, Roman projectiles were small and could be easily obscured, particularly if they were ground into the terrain during battle and post-battle activity. No doubt many of the projectiles would have been recovered had they been seen, particularly *pila*, if not by the Roman army then by any subsequent civilian looting. A number of projectiles were discovered in the settlements around Abritus, suggesting they were considered items of value by local populations.

Natural obscuration may also have played a role in the deposition of non-weaponry small finds, albeit that they also had a far lower innate value and immediate functionality than the projectiles. As yet the process whereby large quantities of non-weaponry artefacts are left on the battlefield is poorly understood, as the Roman period is somewhat unique in producing so many artefacts of this type within battlefield assemblages. The predominance of military kit elements may partly result from the nature of battle, with the force of close-quarter battle causing increased damage to military kit. On modern sites, military kit is almost exclusively associated with the bodies of casualties[85] or areas of hand-to-hand conflict,[86] and is not a universal battlefield deposition. By contrast, Roman battlefield assemblages are dominated by military kit, as well as clothing fittings, cavalry and mule fittings, tools, and coinage. In the case of larger non-weaponry small finds, such as the *dolabra* from Harzhorn which was 44.5cm in length,[87] natural obscuration would have been more difficult, though this is not to say that this could not be the process whereby the artefact entered the record.

CONCLUSION

Roman battlefield looting was a complex process which, like site clearance in other military contexts, served a number of purposes. Recovery of metal artefacts served to minimise supply demands on the Roman army, while denying resource supplementation to non-Roman populations. On the battlefield, the process prioritised the recovery of weaponry and armour and no complete examples survive on any Roman site, though what was done with the surplus is unclear. By contrast, projectiles and non-weaponry small finds could be left behind by the

---

[84] Rost 2008.
[85] E.g. Little Bighorn, Scott *et al* 1989, 191.
[86] E.g. Culloden, Pollard 2009, 151.
[87] Wiegels *et al* 2011, 562.

process, though it is likely that natural obscuration played a significant role in the abandonment of these artefacts. While each extant artefact may not have been individually rejected, that some metal would be left on the battlefield was an inevitable consequence of the looting process. It may have been hoped that in preventing civilian recovery of the metal resources, the incidental obscuration of these artefacts would prove as effective as the deliberate hoarding at closed installations.

As a result, Roman battlefield looting did not serve to entirely strip battlefields of their assemblages, making the consequent artefact scatters a valuable source of evidence for the identification and exploration of these sites, equal to that of topographic and constructed features. The expectation that it would do so in part results from incorrect assumptions about the nature of the assemblages formed largely before any had actually been found. These assumptions were not entirely incorrect, in that they rightly identified the minimal chances of weaponry and armour surviving on battlefield sites, and this has so far been borne out archaeologically. However, the additional range of military ephemera, entirely undocumented by the written record, had not been factored in. The prioritisation of weaponry and the natural obscuration of projectiles and other small finds resulted in substantial, if predominantly non-martial, assemblages being left behind at Baecula, Kalkriese, and Harzhorn. This would presumably also have been the case at other battlefields. At the time, these artefacts may not have been considered to be of particular value and were therefore not subject to recovery, but they now hold the key to locating, identifying, and exploring Roman battlefields.

BIBLIOGRAPHY

Allason-Jones, L. (1988) "Small Finds from the Turrets on Hadrian's Wall", in Coulston 1988, 197-233.
Allason-Jones, L. and M. Bishop (1988) *Excavations at Roman Corbridge: the Hoard.* London.
Atwood, R. (2014) "An Epic Conflict", *Archaeology* 67.1, 31-36.
Azam, J., and A, Hoeffler (2002) "Violence against Civilians in Civil Wars: Looting or Terror?", *Journal of Peace Research* 39.4, 461-85.
Bellón Ruiz, J. P., F. Goméz Cabeza, A. Ruiz Rodrígue, I. Cárdenas Anguita, M. Molinos Molinos, and C. Rueda Galán (2012) "Un escenario bélico de la Segunda Guerra Púnica: *Baecula*", in Remedios *et al*, 345-378.
Berger, F., F. Bittman, M. Geschwind, P. Lönne, M. Meyer, and G.

Moosbauer (2010/13) "Die römisch-germanische Auseinandersetzung am Harzhorn, Lkr. Northeim, Niedersachsen", *Germania* 88, 313-402.

Berger F., M. Geschwinde, M Meyer, and Moosbauer, G. (2013) "Die Datierung des Fundmaterials. Ist es wirklich der Feldzug des Maximinus Thrax 235.236 n. Chr.?", in Pöppelmann *et al*, 66-70.

Bishop, M. C. (1985a) "The military fabrica and the production of arms in the early principate", in Bishop, 1-42.

Bishop, M. C. (ed) (1985b) *The Production and Distribution of Roman Military Equipment. Proceedings of the Second Roman Military Equipment Research Seminar*. BAR Int. Ser. 275. Oxford.

Bishop, M. C., and J. C. N. Coulston (2006) *Roman Military Equipment from the Punic Wars to the Fall of Rome*. Oxford. 2nd Edition.

Bradford Churchill, J. (1999) "Ex qua quod vellent facerent: Roman Magistrates' Authority over Praeda and Manubiae", *Transactions of the American Philological Association* 129, 86-116.

Coulston, J. C. N. (ed) (1988) *Military Equipment and the Identity of Roman Soldiers*. BAR Int. Ser. 394. Oxford.

Coulston, J. C. N. (2001) "The archaeology of Roman conflict", in Freeman and Pollard, 23-49.

Curle, J. (1911) *A Roman Frontier Post and its People: the fort of Newstead in the parish of Melrose*. Glasgow.

Fiorato, V., A. Boylston, and C. Knüsel (eds) (2000) *Blood Red Roses: The Archaeology of a Mass Grave from the Battle of Towton AD 1461*. Oxford.

Foard, G., and R. Morris (2012) *The Archaeology of English Battlefields: Conflict in the pre-industrial landscape*. York.

Fraser, A. H., and M. Brown (2007) "Mud, Blood and Missing Men: Excavations at Serre, Somme, France", *Journal of Conflict Archaeology* 3, 147-171.

Freeman, P., and A. Pollard (eds) (2001), *Fields of Conflict: progress and prospect in battlefield archaeology*. BAR Int. Ser. 958. Oxford.

Forsdyke, E. J. (1919-1920) "Some Arrow-heads from the Battle of Marathon", *Proceedings of the Society of Antiquaries of London* 32, 146-157.

Harbeck, M., K. Von Heyking, and H. Schwarzberg (eds) (2012/13) *Sickness, Hunger, War and Religion. Multidisciplinary Perspectives*. Munich.Harnecker, J. (2008) *Kalkriese 4. Katalogue Der Römischen Funde Vom Oberesch. Die Schnitte 1 Bis 22*. Mainz.

Harnecker, J. (2011) *Kalkriese 5. Katalogue Der Römischen Funde Vom Oberesch. Die Schnitte 23 Bis 39*. Mainz.

Harrison, S. (2008) "War Mementos and the Souls of Missing Soldiers:

Returning Effects of the Battlefield Dead", *The Journal of the Royal Anthropological Institute* 14.4, 774-790.
Hawkes, C. F. C., and M. R. Hull (1947) *Camulodunum. First Report on the Excavations at Colchester 1930-1939*. Oxford.
Hingley, R. (2006) "The Deposition of Iron Objects in Britain during the Later Prehistoric and Roman Periods: Contextual Analysis and the Significance of Iron", *Britannia* 37, 213-57.
Horvat, J. (2002) "The Hoard of Roman Republican Weapons from Grad near Šmihel", *Arheološki vestnik* 53, 117–192.
Junkelmann, M. (1986), *Die Legionen des Augustus: Der römische Soldat im archäologischen Experiment*. Mainz.
Mac Ginty, R. (2005) "Looting in the Context of Violent Conflict: A Conceptualisation and Typology", *Third World Quarterly* 25.5, 857-70.
Manning, W. H. (1972) "Ironwork hoards in Iron Age and Roman Britain", *Britannia* 3, 224-50.
March Phillips, L. (1902) *With Rimington*. London.
Mercer, C. (1870) *Journal of the Waterloo Campaign: kept through the campaign of 1815*. Edinburgh.
Meyer, M., G. Moosbauer (2013) "Römisch oder germanisch? Wer kämpfte am Harzhorn?", in Pöppelmann *et al*, 71-75.
Miller, S. M. (2010) "Duty or Crime? Defining Acceptable Behavior in the British Army in South Africa, 1899-1902", *Journal of British Studies* 49.2, 311-331.
Pitts, L. F., and J. K. S. St. Joseph (1985), *Inchtuthil. The Roman legionary fortress excavations 1952-65*. Gloucester.
Pollard, T. (2009a) "Capturing the Moment: the archaeology of Culloden battlefield", in Pollard, 130-62.
Pollard, T. (ed) (2009b) *Culloden: The History and Archaeology of the Last Clan Battle*. Barnsley.
Pollard, T., and N. Oliver (2002) *Two Men in a Trench. Battlefield Archaeology: the key to unlocking the past*. London.
Pöppelmann, H., K. Deppmeyer and W-D. Steinmetz (eds) (2013) *Roms Vergessener Feldzug. Die Schlacht am Harzhorn*. Stuttgart.
Pritchett, W. K. (1965-1992) *Studies in Ancient Greek Topography*. Berkeley. 8 volumes.
Radoslavova, G., G. Dzanev, and N. Nikolov (2011) "The Battle at Abritus in AD 251: Written Sources, Archaeological and Numismatic Data", *Archaeologia Bulgarica* 15.3, 23-49.
Reardon, C., and W. T. Vossler (2013) *A Field Guide to Gettysburg: Experiencing the Battlefield through Its History, Places and People*. Chapel Hill, NC.

Reddé, M., and S. Von Schurbein (eds) (2008) *Alésia et la bataille de Teutoburg. Un parallèle critique des sources*. Beihefte der Francia 66. Ostfildern.

Remedios, S., F. Prados, and J. Bermejo (eds) (2012) *Aníbal de Cartago. Historia y Mito*. Madrid.

Rost, A. (2008) "Quellenkritische Überlegungen zur archäologischen Untersuchung von Schlachtfeldern am Beispiel von Kalkriese", in Reddé and von Schurbein, 303-14.

—. (2009) "Characteristics of Ancient Battlefields: Battle of Varus (9 AD)", in Scott *et al*, 50-57.

—. (2012/13) "Methods in Battlefield Archaeology: A Critical Analysis of the Distributional Pattern", in Harbeck, 92–111.

Rost, A., and S. Wilbers-Rost (2010) "Weapons at the Battlefield of Kalkriese", *Gladius* 30, 117-136.

Rost, A., and S. Wilbers-Rost (2014) "The ancient battlefield at Kalkriese: Recent results", Unpublished poster presentation at the Eighth International Fields of Conflict Conference, Columbia, South Carolina, March 2014.

Roth, J. P. (1999) *The logistics of the Roman army at war (264 B.C.-A.D. 235*. Leiden.

Sabin, P. (2007) "Battle", In Sabin *et al*, 399-433.

Sabin, P., H. van Wees and M. Whitby (eds) (2007) *The Cambridge History of Greek and Roman Warfare. Volume I: Greece, the Hellenistic World and the Rise of Rome*. Cambridge.

Scott, D. D., R. A. Fox, M. A. Connor, and D. Harmon (1989) *Archaeological Perspectives on the Battle of the Little Bighorn*. Norman, OK.

Scott, D., L. Babits, and C. Haecker (eds) (2009) *Fields of Conflict: Battlefield Archaeology from the Roman Empire to the Korean War*. Westport.

Seaton, R. (1999) "War and Thanatourism: Waterloo 1815-1914", *Annals of Tourism Research* 26.1, 130-58.

Semmel, S. (2000) "Reading the Tangible Past: British Tourism, Collecting, and Memory after Waterloo", *Representations* 69, pp. 9-37.

Sutherland, T. (2000) "The archaeological investigation of the Towton battlefield", in Fiorato *et al*, 155-68.

Webster, G. (1993) *The Roman Invasion of Britain*. London. Revised edition.

Wiegels, R., G. Moosbauer, M. Meyer, P. Lönne, and M. Geschwinde, (2011) "Ein römisches Dolabra mit Inschrift aus dem Umfeld des

Schlachtfeldes am Harzhorn (Lkr. Northeim) in Niedersachen", *Archäologisches Korrespondenzblatt* 41.4, 561-70.

Wilbers-Rost, S. (2007) "Die archäologischen Befunde", in Wilbers-Rost *et al*, 1-107.

Wilbers-Rost, S., H-P. Uerpmann, M. Upermann, B. Grosskopf and E. Tolksdorf-Lienemann (eds) (2007) *Kalkriese 3. Interdisziplinäre Untersuchungen auf dem Oberesch in Kalkriese. Archäologische Befunde und naturwissenschaftliche Begleituntersuchungen*. Mainz.

Chapter Eighteen

The Role of the Peace-Makers (*Caduceatores*) in Roman Attitudes to War and Peace

Dr. Hannah Cornwell

> This is the account of this staff. Mercury is called the god of oratory and the mediator of the gods. The staff divides the snakes, that is to say, the poison; for that reason the snakes have their heads looking inwards, so that they signify the need for *legati* to come together and talk amongst themselves, because those at war are soothed by the speeches of mediators. That is why, according to Livy, the envoys of peace are called *caduceatores* (heralds): for just as wars are declared through the *fetiales*, by a treaty, so peace is made through the *caduceatores*. (Serv. *Aen.* 4.242)

> *Huius autem virgae haec ratio est. Mercurius et orationis deus dicitur et interpres deorum: unde virga serpentes dividit, id est venena: nam serpentes ideo introrsum spectantia capita habent, ut significet inter se legatos colloqui et convenire debere, quia bellantes interpretum oratione sedantur: unde secundum Livium legati pacis caduceatores dicuntur: sicut enim per fetiales, a foedere, bella indicebantur, ita pax per caduceatores fiebat.*

Servius, the late fourth or early fifth-century grammarian, here explains the origins and purpose of the *caduceus*, the herald's wand, and records the historian Livy as his source for the *legati pacis* (envoys of peace) being named *caduceatores*.[1] Servius understands there to be two separate offices for dealing with the bookends of war: the declaration of war, and

---

[1] See also Serv. *Aen.* 1.297: "Because peace is usually made through the *caduceatores*, that is to say mediators" (*quia per caduceatores, id est internuntios, pax solet fieri*); 4.265: "and it denotes him as performing the office not so much as a messenger, but rather as a *caduceator*, the is to say an orator" (*notandum non eum tantum nuntii, sed etiam caduceatoris, id est oratoris, officio fungi*).

the making of peace. However, quite a different picture is presented in the works of the late Republican authors, where we do not find such a clear articulation of distinct officials responsible for war and for peace.

Varro, in his *de Lingua Latina*, states that the role of the *fetiales* was to ensure not only that war was justly taken up and set aside, but also that the *fides* of peace was established by a treaty:

> The *fetiales* (are so named) because they were responsible for public trust (*fides*) amongst the people: for it was through them that just war was devised, and then ended, so that the trust of peace was established by a treaty (*foedus*). Before war was struck the *fetiales* sent out men to seek restitution. Even now they are responsible for making a treaty (*foedus*), which Ennius writes was pronounced *fidus* (Varro, *de Ling. Lat.* 5.15)
>
> *Fetiales, quod fidei publicae inter populous praeerant: nam per hos fiebat ut iustum conciperetur bellum, et inde desitum, ut foedere fides pacis constitueretur. Ex his mittebantur, ante quam conciperetur, qui res repeterent, et per hos etiam nunc fit foedus, quod fidus Ennius scribit dictum.*

Whilst Varro's silence on the *caduceatores* in respect to the establishment of peace can plausibly be explained by the fact that in this section of his work he is focused on the religious office of the state (*fetiales* being priests), it is noteworthy that he does mark out the *fetiales* as the ones responsible for the establishment of peace. Indeed, the idea that it is the *fetiales* who are, at least conceptually, responsible for *both* war and peace is found in Cicero's *de Legibus* 2.21.7 ("let the *fetiales* be the judges and messengers of treaties, peace, war, armistice and embassies").[2] Whilst this is a highly corrupted passage, Cicero is here associating the *fetiales'* activities with the sphere of treaties, peace, war, truces and embassies.[3] These late Republican passages, then, link the *fetiales* to not just war, but also peace. This, however, still leaves the relationship between the *fetiales* and *caduceatores* unclear, and indeed calls into question the actual role of the *caduceatores*.

This paper examines the ways in which the roles and possible relationships between the *fetiales* and the *caduceatores* can be used to

---

[2] *foederum pacis belli indotiarum <o>ratorum fetiales iudices, nontii sunto, bella disceptanto.*

[3] For the issues of corruption and readings of the passage see Nenci 1958; Rawson 1973, 346-347; Dyck 2004, 309-310; Rich 2011, 190.

understand some aspects of how the Romans conceptualised the making and breaking of war and peace and aims to locate the *caduceatores* within a picture of Roman diplomatic practices and war-mongering. The focus of the paper is not on the historical authenticity of the roles and rituals of the *fetiales, legati,* and *caduceatores* – the issue of historicity and routine, standardised procedures (or the lack thereof) for the declaration of war has already been extensively dealt with by Rich[4] – but rather the ways in which writers from the Late Republic onwards used the formalised ritual for the instigation and cessation of war in order to present and interpret Roman sanctions of warfare and peace. Indeed, what matters for our understanding of Roman attitudes and conceptualisations of the dichotomy between war and peace are the models and ideals expressed in their writings.[5]

In this paper I first present a brief review of the position of the *fetiales* and the *legati*, who fulfilled, in many respects, similar diplomatic functions, and focus on how they are presented in the literary sources from the Late Republic onwards, in order to assess Roman viewpoints on the instigation and cessation of war. I then turn to an examination of who the *caduceatores* were and how they fit into a picture of Roman diplomacy and war. The role of the *caduceator* in Roman literary accounts of the making of peace serves to highlight the actions of Roman enemies, who send such envoys of peace, as acquiescent to the power of Rome, who imposes it.

WAGING WAR AND PEACE: THE ROLE OF THE *FETIALES* AND *LEGATI*

Roman fetial priests (*fetiales*) appear in the literary sources as religious officials responsible for the formal activities prior to war, including the declaration of war, as well as the establishment of treaties. As has been clearly emphasised in work on the military and imperial aspects of the mid-Republic, particularly in the studies of Rich, Harris and Wiedemann,[6] historically the role and importance of the *fetiales* becomes obscure during the period of transmarine expansion. In this period, *legati* are increasingly used in the declaration of war, although the *fetiales* continue to be

---
[4] Rich 1976, 2011.
[5] Woolf 1993, 174. See also Brunt 1990, 288, who proposed to draw on "actual statements by Romans, as the clearest indications of what was most explicit in their own consciousness".
[6] Rich 1976, 2011; Harris 1979; Wiedemann 1986.

consulted as to the formalities of declaring war and other aspects of diplomatic relations and treaties. This is clear, for example, in Livy's account of the declaration of war in 200 BC on Philip V King of Macedon, when the *fetiales* are consulted as authorities regarding the procedures of declaring war, whilst a *legatus* is chosen "from those, who were not in the senate" (31.8.2: *ex iis qui extra senatum*). Furthermore, Livy's account of the fetial rites prior to war (1.32) involves a *legatus* sent to the enemy as a *nuntius* to demand redress,[7] whilst the *fetialis* appears for the spear-throwing rite.[8] In contrast, Varro recorded that four *fetiales legati* were sent to demand redress (Non. 529M). Ogilvie[9] explains Livy's substitution of the traditional role of the *fetialis* with a *legatus* as a result of developments to the procedure of war declaration in the third and second centuries, which saw senatorial *legati* taking of roles previously undertaken by the *fetiales*.[10] Certainly, in his account Livy implies that the rituals for formally declaring war were still maintained in the present (1.32.5: "wars were announced with certain ritual…which now the *fetiales* still use").[11] He emphasises this through the use of the present tense to describe the actions of the *legatus* demanding restitution (1.32.6-10), in contrast to the imperfect tense used to describe the throwing of the spear and the further demands to restitution of the *legatus* (1.32.11-14). This may suggest a historic practice.[12]

Whilst it is necessary to realise that the *fetiales* were not necessarily active in performing ritual declarations of war in the mid-Republic

---

[7] Compare to the words of the *fetialis* in Livy 1.24.5: "King, do you appoint me as the royal messenger of the Roman people, and sanction my instruments and comrades?" ("*Rex, facisne me tu regium nuntium populi Romani Quiritium, vasa comitesque meos?*").

[8] Rich 2011, 208 interprets the spear-throwing as an "initiatory ritual at the start of war" rather than part of the ritual declaration on war.

[9] Ogilvie 1965, 130.

[10] Both the *fetialis* and *legatus* could take on the role of *nuntius populi Romani*: Livy 1.24.5; 1.32.6. For the most recent and detailed discussion on complexities regarding the responsibilities and duties of the *fetiales* see Rich 2011, particularly 199-235 for the ritual preliminaries of war. For the role, position and duties of *legati* see Thomasson 1991. See also Phillipson 1911, i. 304-308, 326, 346 (*legati*) and ii. 315-348 (*fetiales*).

[11] *indicerentur bella aliquo ritu … quod nunc fetiales habent.*

[12] Rich 2011, 202 for Livy's conflation of different ritual narratives in his account of 1.32. For the revival of the spear-throwing ritual by Octavian, see Cass. Dio 50.4.4-5, 72.33.3; Wiedemann 1986; Rich 2011, 204-209.

onwards and that *legati* appear to have fulfilled this role,[13] what is more pertinent to the present discussion is that writers such as Cicero and Varro understood a need for war to be declared formally, through specific officials, which they linked to the *fetiales,* even if only in a theoretical and idealised sense.[14] The sources indicate that the terms *fetiales* and *legati* can inhabit similar aspects of diplomatic practices, which suggests a certain amount of flexibility and fluidity in the terms used for those serving in an ambassadorial role: Varro refers to *fetiales legati* sent before the declaration of war to seek restitution, who were called *oratores,* (Non. 529M); Cato the Elder uses the term *oratores* rather than *legati* (Paul. Fest. 196L) for those sent at the start of war; and Marcinus (*Dig.* 1.8.8.1) and Naevius (Paul. Fest. 424.34-426.5 L) refer to *legati,* but in the context of the *sagmina,* the sacred clumps of grass and earth that were specific implements of the *fetiales.*[15]

There is, however, one clear dimension in which the *fetiales* are distinguished from senatorial *legati,* which is that they are priests (Cic. *Rep.* 2.31; Livy 1.24.4-9; Dion. Hal. 2.72). As priests, the *fetiales* oversaw divinely sanctioned declarations of war and the making of treaties, which would, at least by Cicero's time, become associated with the concept of the *iustum bellum.*[16]

The formal structure of the *ius fetiale,* as presented in sources from the late Republic onwards, suggests not only that formality and ritual were important as a means to ensure and impose divine sanction for any action, but also that the status Rome claimed through these structures (that is, a justified position) was already fixed and confirmed.[17] Although the sources conceptualise this confirmation of Rome's justified position in

---

[13] See n. 10.
[14] Rich 2011, 232. Varro (*de Ling. Lat.* 5.15) uses the imperfect to describe the functions and activities of the *fetiales*, though does emphasise with the present tense that 'even now' in his day they were responsible for treaties.
[15] See Rich 2011, 213-14.
[16] Cic. *Rep.* 2.31: "He (Tullius Hostilius) established the rule (*ius*), by which wars were declared, which, once he himself had created it most justly, he sanctioned by the fetial rites, so that all war, which had not been announced and declared, was judged to be unjust and impious" (*constituitque ius quo bella indicerentur, quod per se iustissime inventum sanxit fetiali religione, ut omne bellum quod denuntiatum indictumque non esset, id iniustum esse atque inpium iudicaretur*). See also Cic. *De Off.* 1.11.36; 3.30.107-108; *Rep.* 2.17; 3.23; Livy 1.32.12; 42.47.8; Dion. Hal. 2.72.4. See Ager 2009, 19-20, esp. n. 10 and 11.
[17] Ager 2009, 17-24.

relation to the *ius fetiale*, aspects of her certainty in *iustum bellum* are also found in accounts of senatorial embassies. Livy records the embassy sent to Carthage in 218 BC to declare war:

> When these preparations were completed, so that everything would be carried out properly before war, they sent envoys distinguished by birth, Q. Fabius, M. Livius, L. Aemilius, C. Licinius and Q. Baebius, to Africa to inquire of the Carthaginians whether Hannibal had attacked Saguntum under instructions of a public sanction, and if, which seems like it was going to be the case, they confessed to this and defended what was done by public sanction, they were to declare war on the Carthaginian people. (Livy 21.18)

> *His ita comparatis, ut omnia iusta ante bellum fierent, legatos maiores natu, Q. Fabium M. Livium L. Aemilium C. Licinium, Q. Baebium in Africam mittunt ad percunctandos Carthaginienses publicone consilio Hannibal Saguntum oppugnasset; et si, id quod facturi videbantur, faterentur ac defenderent publico consilio factum, ut indicerent populo Cathaginiensi bellum.*

Although a choice between war and peace is ostensibly offered to the Carthaginians, the Romans clearly view themselves as wronged by Hannibal and the Carthaginians and believe that their decision to go to war was a justified and necessary one. Polybius' account likewise presents Rome's decision to go to war as an obvious and certain one (Polyb. 3.20).

Prior to the declaration of war on the Carthaginians, the Roman people had voted on war, and a *supplicatio* had been voted in order to assure the favourable outcome (Livy 1.21.27.4). Whether by fetial or senatorial envoy, the declaration of war was a divinely sanctioned activity, and positioned Rome with authority over her enemies, allowing no or little opportunity to negotiate on the decision. Nevertheless, whilst the senatorial embassy to Carthage appears intent on declaring war (Livy 21.19), it is still understood as having at least the capacity to offer peace. Livy records Fabius' act of gathering up his toga in the fold, declaring that Rome brought Carthage war and peace, and that Carthage must choose which to accept. This specious act of offering an 'option' to Carthage is also recorded by Polybius who emphasises the negative aspects of either option for the Carthaginians,[18] and by Varro and Gellius:

---

[18] Polyb. 3.20-6-8: "The Romans…at once appointed ambassadors and sent them straight away to Carthage, giving the Carthaginians the option of two alternatives, the one of which, if they accepted it, entailed disgrace and damage (τὸ μὲν

Q. Fabius, the Roman general, gave a letter to the Carthaginians. In it was written that the Roman people sent to them a spear (*hasta*) and a herald's staff (*caduceus*), the two symbols of war and peace. They might choose, whichever they wanted; whichever they chose, they should consider as sent by the Romans. The Carthaginians replied that they would not choose, but that the Romans could leave whichever one they wanted; whichever they left, the Carthaginians would accept, as if they had chosen it themselves. But Marcus Varro says that it was not an actual spear and herald's staff that were sent, but two tiles, incised with the image of a herald's staff and a spear respectively. (Gellius 10.27)

Q. Fabius, imperator Romanus, dedit ad Carthaginienses epistulam. Ibi scriptum fuit populum Romanum misisse ad eos hastam et caduceum, signa duo belli aut pacis, ex quis, utrum vellent eligerent; quod elegissent, id unum ut esse missum existimarent. Cathaginienses responderunt neutrum sese eligere, sed posse, qui adtulissent, utrum mallent, relinquere; quod relinquissent, id sibi pro electo futurum. M. autem Varro non hastam ipsam neque ipsum caduceum missa dicit, sed duas tesserulas, in quarum altera caducei, in altera hastae simulacra fuerunt incisa.

As with Livy's description of the *ius fetiale* (1.32) the *hasta* is here used to evoke and declare war.[19] The *caduceus*, as a Greco-Roman symbol of peace, in actuality here implies the Carthaginians' acceptance of their violation of treaties with Rome.[20]

The function and capacity for such envoys to deal in both war and peace is likewise apparent in accounts of the *fetiales*. Cicero in his *de Legibus* 2.21.7 associates them with various aspects and procedures surrounding war: *foedera, indutiae* and *pax*; likewise, Varro ties to the establishment of peace through treaties (*foedera*) the ability of the *fetiales* to begin and end war. The connection between the *fetiales* and a *foedus* was clearly strong in Roman thought. This cultural association can be seen in Varro's etymological explanation together with an association with *fides,* whereas modern philologists would rather see the word derived from the Indo-European root *dhe, from which we get the Latin *facio* and *fas*, which suggests a legal force. The ancient cultural association between *fetiales* and *foedus* is also apparent in the manuscript tradition of Servius'

αἰσχύνην ἅμα καὶ βλάβην), while the other would give rise to extreme trouble and peril (τὸ δ'ἕτερον πραγμάτων καὶ κινδύνων ἀρχὴν μεγάλων)."

[19] Moore 2008, 2.

[20] See Moore 2008 for the complications of this episode in terms of *caduceus* as a Punic symbol, where it appears not to have represented peace, but divine protection and presence.

commentary on *Aeneid* 4.242: the phrase *a foedere* has been identified as a later interpolation in the manuscript, suggesting that an expected association existed, even at a later stage.[21] This cultural pseudo-etymological link between *fetiales* and *foedus* emphasises that the *fetiales* were defined by their task.[22] In Livy 30.48.8, the *fetiales* are told to demand of the praetor their *sagmina* (as symbols of their office as envoys) in order to strike the treaty (*ut foedus ferirent illi praetorem sagmina poscerent*). It is their task of the formalisation and examination of treaties that associates them with not just war, when treaties were understood as breached, but also peace. The association with peace is also articulated by the Greek authors Dionysius of Halicarnssus and Appian, who translate *fetiales* as *eirenodikai* (arbiters of peace), and Plutarch, who translates the term as *eirenopoioi* (peace-makers), and *eirenophylakes* (peace-keepers).[23]

If the *fetiales*, and likewise *legati*, have the capacity not only to end war, but also to make peace through *foedera*, what is the precise nature and relationship of the *caduceator* to them?

FITTING THE CADUCEATORES IN TO THE PICTURE

Briscoe, in his commentary on Livy, states that *caduceator* is: "Livy's regular word for a herald seeking a truce or peace, but outside Livy [is] rarely used".[24] Besides Livy, the term is used four times by Curtius Rufus in his history of Alexander the Great, once by Petronius, twice by Festus (once as a quotation of Cato the Elder), twice by Ammianus Marcellanus, twice by Arbonius, and four times by Servius in his commentary on Virgil's *Aeneid* (Servius himself cites Livy as his reference for the definition of the term). Table 17.1 sets out these references to *caduceatores*. The term *caduceator* clearly derives from the word *caduceus*,[25] itself an alteration of the Doric Greek *karykeion* (herald's staff) from *karyx* (or *keryx* in Attic Greek).[26] In its most basic terms, the

---

[21] Sgarbi 1992, 77-78.
[22] Rüpke 1990, 103.
[23] Dio. Hal. 2.72.1; App. *Sam.* 4.5; Plut. *Vit. Num.* 12.5, *Mor.* 279B.
[24] Briscoe 1973, 143. See also Phillipson 1911, i. 306.
[25] Gloss. V 550.8: "The *caduceus* is the staff of the envoy, from which the *caduceatores* are named" (*caduceum virga legatarri, a quo caduceatores dicuntur*).
[26] See *LSJ* s.v. *caduceum*; *RE* XI 340 for the derivation of *caduceus* from *kerykeion*. Gloss. 2.349.14: "the herald, who is sent for the sake of peace, carries the herald's staff" (κῆρυξ ὁ ὑπὲρ εἰρήνης ἀποστελλόμενος τὸ κηρύκιον φέρων). The

word implies a bearer of the staff, and it has certainly been used in modern scholarship to designate anyone coming with a *caduceus* to negotiate a possible peace.[27] However, a closer examination of how and when the term is used in ancient literature will show that the term is only deployed in certain circumstances. Indeed, although certain Roman officials might use the *caduceus* as a symbol of purpose this does not appear to necessarily designate them as a *caduceator*.

Table 18.1 illustrating the occurrences of the term caduceator in Latin authors.

Cato (*ex Fest.* 41)	*Cato: 'caduceatori', inquit, 'nemo homo nocet.'*
Livy 26.17.15	(211 BC) Hasdrubal sends a *caduceator* to the Roman propraetor Nero to seek permission to remove himself from his position, and promised to remove his army from Spain.
Livy 31.38.9-10	(200 BC) Philip sends a *caduceator* to the Roman consul, Sulpicius to ask for *indutiae*, in order that Philip in the meanwhile can escape.
Livy 31.39. 1 & 3	Sulpicius receives Philip's *caduceator* and grants *indutiae*.
Livy 32.32.4	(198 BC) *caduceator* sent by Philip to seek a meeting with Flamininus.
Livy 33.11.3	(197 BC) *caduceator* sent by Philip to ostensibly ask for *indutiae*, but in reality to ask permission for an embassy to be received.
Livy 34.30.1-3	(195 BC) Nabis sends a *caduceator* to ask permission for an embassy to be received.
Livy 35.38.8	(192 BC) The Greeks send a *caduceator* and then *legati* to the Aetolians.
Livy 37.18.10	(190 BC) Antiochus sends a *caduceator* to Aemilius Regullus to treat for peace.
Livy 44.46.1	(168 BC) Paullus retains the *caduceatores* sent by Perseus.
Curtius Rufus 3.1.6.	Alexander sends a *caduceator* to the city of Claenae.
Curtius Rufus 3.1.7	Alexander's *caduceator* appears in the city of Claenae.
Curtius Rufus 4.2.15	The Tyrians kill the *caduceatores*.
Curtius Rufus 4.2.17	The murder of the *caduceatores*.

caduceus/kerykeion was a staff with two serpents entwined around it, and also was often depicted with a pair of wings.
[27] See Moore 2008 for this application of *caduceator*.

Petronius *Sat.* 108.12	Tryphaena acts as a *caduceator* to secure *indutiae*.
Ex *Fest.* 41	*Caduceatores* as *legati pacis*.
Ammianus 20.7.3	The Persian king, Sapor, sends *caduceatores*.
Ammianus 31.12.14	Fritigenus, the Gothic leader, sends one of his normal soldiers as a *caduceator*.
Arnobius *nat.* 3.32	*Caduceator* (i.e. the one carrying the *caduceus*) *ille Cyllenius* (as opposed to Mercury).
Arnobius *nat.* 5.25	The *Eumolpidae* are described as *caduceatores*, *hierophantes et praecones*.
Servius *Aen.* 1.297	Peace is made through *caduceatores*, who are *internuntii*.
Servius *Aen.* 4.242 (x2)	*Caduceatores* referred to as *legati pacis*; peace is made through the *caduceatores*.
Servius *Aen.* 4.265	The *caduceator* as an *orator*.

The earliest reference to the *caduceatores* is a fragment of Cato the Elder, recorded by the second century grammarian Festus (Paul. *Fest.* 41: *Cato: "Caduceatori", inquit, "nemo homo nocet"*), and suggests that *caduceatores*, like *legati* and *fetiales*, were inviolable. Varro appears to have compared the *caduceus* with the *verbena* (the grass of the *sagmina*), used by the *fetiales*:

> Varro declared that the *caduceus* was the symbol of peace in his *de Vita populi Romani* book 2: "the *Verbenatus* carried the *verbena*; so the *caduceus* was the sign of peace, which we equate with the staff of Mercury". (Non. 528M)

> *CADVCEVM pacis signum Varro pronuntiat de Vita populi Romani lib. II: Werbenatus ferebat verbenam; id erat caduceus, pacis signum; quam Mercurii virgam possumus aestimare*

Cicero also implies that the *caduceus* was a symbol of inviolability: "who can turn unharmed even amongst the enemy's weapons, adorned with the name of *orator* rather than with the *caduceus*" (Cic. *De Orat.* 1.202).

Servius' definitions of *caduceatores* display a comparable flexibility in terminology as the language used for ambassadorial roles discussed above: he uses *internuntii* (*Aen.* 1.297), *oratores* (*Aen.* 4.265)[28] and *legati pacis* (4.242) to explain the role of the *caduceatores*.[29] However, although

---

[28] Servius distinguishes the *caduceatores* as *oratores* from mere *nuntii*.
[29] Festus also refers to *caduceatores* as *legati pacis*: Fest. 41.

Servius cites Livy as his source for *caduceatores* being the name for *legati pacis,* Livy refers to the sending of *caduceatores* first, followed by *legati,* suggesting that in Livy's view their function and purpose was somehow separate:

> The king's herald came to him, ostensibly so that there would be a cessation of hostilities until those who had fallen in battle were removed for burial, though in reality to seek permission for envoys to be sent. (Livy 33.11.3)
>
> *Caduceator eo regius venit, specie ut indutiae essent donec tollerentur ad sepulturam qui in acie cecidissent, re vera ad petendam veniam legatis mittendis.*

Livy's account of Philip's embassy to Flamininus in 197 BC is a useful episode to examine in order to determine the distinction between a *caduceator* and *legatus*.[30] The herald is sent ostensibly (*specie*) to secure a cessation of hostilities (*indutiae*) for the burial of the fallen, but in actuality (*re vera*) to organise for the embassy of *legati*. Holleaux argued that for Livy the purpose of the herald's mission was to prepare for the actual embassy of *legati* (the *presbutai* named in Polyb. 18.27), and that Livy's later statement (33.12.1) concerning the granting of 15 days *indutiae* as well as the organisation of a meeting with Philip are both to be understood as the outcome of the conference Flamininus held with the *legati*.[31] Certainly, Livy's later accounts of Nabis' and Antiochus' heralds would suggest that the purpose of the *caduceator* was to pave the way for the actual negotiators.[32] However, from Livy's account of Philip's attempt to trick the Romans with the request of a truce (*indutiae*) in order to escape (Livy 31.38.9-10), it would seem that the request for *indutiae* was within the *caduceator*'s remit. Indeed, the herald sent in 197 BC to Flaminius on the pretext of requiring *indutiae* indicates that this was the expected purpose of the herald. This also appears to be suggested by Petronius'

---

[30] For other embassies involving *caduceatores* see also Livy 26.17.5 (211 BC); 34.30.3 (195 BC); 35.38.8 (192 BC); 37.45.4 (190 BC).
[31] Holleaux 1931, 196.
[32] Livy 34.30.3: "He first sent a *caduceator* into the camp to seeing whether they would allow him to send them envoys" (*caduceatorem primum in castra misit ad explorandum si paterentur legatos ad se mitti*); 37.45.4: "At about the same time, a *caduceator* from Antiochus sought out the consul through the agency of P. Scipio and asked that the king be allowed to send mediators" (*sub idem fere tempus caduceator ab Antiocho per P. Scipionem a consule petit impetravitque ut oratores mittere liceret regi*).

reference to a *caduceator* (*Satyricon* 107-109) In my view, this passage offers further insight into not only the purpose of the *caduceator*, but also how Roman writers conceptualised the office.

Encolpius, the protagonist of Petronius' *Satyricon,* Giton, and the poet Eumolpus, find themselves on board a ship captained by Lichas and carrying Tryphaena – both of whom wish to exact punishments on Encolpius and Giton for past wrongs. Eumolpus takes on the role of *legatus* (107: *Me, ut puto, hominem non ignotum, elegerunt ad hoc officium [legatum]… Deinde, si gratiam a legato moliebantur*),[33] and offers a *decrepatio* (107) on behalf of Encolpius and Giton, which is rejected by Lichas, and despite Eumolpus' cries that Lichas and Tryphaena are acting "against what is right and the law" (*contra fas legemque*), battle-lines are formed and fighting breaks out (108: *stante ergo utraque acie, cum appareret futurum non tralaticium bellum*).[34] At the high point of the battle (with Giton and Encolpius threatening to do themselves injury with the barber's razors), the helmsman calls on Tryphaena to make a truce (*indutiae*) *caduceatoris more* ("in the manner of a *caduceator*"). Whereupon *fides* is given and received, with Tryphaena holding out an olive-branch while she gives a speech extolling the cessation of hostilities (108: *data ergo acceptaque ex more patrio fide praetendit ramum oleae*).[35] With Tryphaena having acted as *caduceator,* it is Eumolpus, depicted as the *dux* of the opposing side, who lays out the terms of the treaty (*foedera*), which hold Lichas and Tryphaena to account, and binds them to restitution should they violate the terms of the treaty (109: *In haec verba foederibus compositis arma deponimus*).[36]

Petronius has Tryphaena responsible for requesting *indutiae* and in the role of the *caduceator*, separate from Eumolpus, who is labelled as both the *legatus* and *dux* and who sets out the terms of the treaty. Notably, the *caduceator* is on the opposite side of the *legatus/dux,* who sets out terms entirely favourable to the side not treating for peace. Whilst this episode in Petronius' poem is comic and carries a mock-tragic tone (particularly in Tryphaena's speech), it does reflect a certain amount of the terminology

---

[33] "I think that they chose me, as a known quantity, for this office [of envoy (*legatus*)] … Then, if they seek forgiveness through an envoy (*legatus*)…"
[34] "Therefore, with both battle-lines drawn up, it seemed that it was not going to be an ordinary war".
[35] "And so when loyalty was given and received in traditional fashion, she held out an olive branch".
[36] "With these words the treaties were made and we set aside our arms".

found in accounts of actual diplomatic negotiations.[37] As with the passages of Livy, the passage of Petronius seems to indicate that the *caduceatores* served the function of requesting from the opposite side the cessation of hostilities (*indutiae*), in order to allow both sides to come to terms and make a *foedus* – the actual process of striking the *foedus* was the responsibility of the *legatus* and *dux*.

Notably, Livy's *caduceatores* only appear in the context of Hellenistic wars, as heralds of the Hellenistic kings and Greek states, and once during the Punic wars, as a herald of Hasdrubal. The use of the term outside Livy may also suggest that the *caduceator* expressed a Hellenistic, rather than Roman office: Curtius Rufus obviously uses the term in the context of Alexander's conquest (Curt. 3.1.6; 3.1.7; 4.2.15; 4.2.17); Arnobius uses the term as a profession of the Attic people, the *Eumolpidae* (Arnob. 5.25); Ammianus uses the term more extensively for the heralds of the Persian King, and the Goths (Amm. 20.7.3; 31.12.14). This is a striking feature of the use of *caduceatores* in our written sources: the term appears to be only used for non-Roman messengers. The Romans do not, it seems, send *caduceatores*. This is not to say that Rome does not use or send messengers or heralds in the context of war: it is clear from Livy's accounts of the *ius fetiale* in 1.24 and 1.32 that both the *fetialis* and the *legatus* represented himself as a *nuntius*. Furthermore, other passages of Livy indicate that *praecones* (criers employed both by the state as a sub category of *apparitores* and in a private capacity, often as auctioneers)[38] could attend a general and army (Livy 6.3.8; 27.19.4). Moreover, the senatorial *legati* of 218 BC, at least according to the accounts of Varro and Gellius, carry a form of *caduceus* as a symbol of peace, yet they are not defined as *caduceatores*, though no doubt because their formal position as *legati* is far more important as well as the fact that their principal function is to declare war.

If, on the basis of the limited evidence from the literary sources, the Romans did not send *caduceatores*, but merely received those sent by kings, how 'Roman' is the concept of the *caduceator*? The term itself appears to refer to a specific type of herald, or perhaps, rather, to the specific task of a herald, deployed during conflict to engage the enemy in cessation of hostilities, rather than the generic term of messenger (*nuntius*) or the more specific Roman term of *praeco*.[39] As discussed above, the

---

[37] Habermehl 2006, 423-464.
[38] See Rauh 1989; Purcell 1983, esp. 147-148; Hinard 1976.
[39] Arnob. 5.25 states that the *Eumolpidae* were *caduceatores, hierophantes* and

herald's wand, the *kerykeion,* derives from the Greek word for herald, *keryx*. *Keryx* is used extensively to refer to all types of messengers in the Greek world, both public messengers of the state and private ones. The second century jurist Marcianus equates the *sagmina* of the *fetiales* (or rather, in his account, the *legati*) carried as symbols of their inviolability, with the emblem of the Greek envoys: "*sagmina* are certain herbs, which the envoys (*legati*) of the Roman people were accustomed to carry, so that no one would do violence to them, just as the envoys of the Greeks carry those, which are *cerycia*" (*Dig.* 1.8.8.1: *Sanctum autem dictum est a sagminibus: sunt autem sagmina quaedam herbae, quas legati populi romani ferre solent, ne quis eos violaret, sicut legati graecorum ferunt ea quae vocantur cerycia*). Rüpke, in his discussion of the purpose and function of the *sagmina* and *verbena,* characterises the *caduceus* as "die sicher griechischer beeinflusste Anglichung" of the older (at least, amongst the Romans) use of the sacred herbs as emblems of envoys.[40] Indeed, whilst in Greek the wand derives its name from the herald, in Latin the *caduceator* clearly derives from *caduceus*, and at least in Livy's histories, only appears in use when Rome interacts with the Greek and Punic world. The earliest attestation of a *caduceus* on Roman coinage is the mid-third century BC (both bronze ingots and *aes grave*). The *caduceus*, then, might be understood as a Greek element introduced into Roman ideology and diplomatic practices, and became, as Varro's testimony suggests, comparable to the *verbena*, but in the specific context of peace.

The use of the *caduceus* as an emblem of peace and as a staff of a protected office was clearly understood and even used by the Romans (cf. Cicero. *De Orat.* 1.202); by the late Republic it appeared on coins as a signifier of peace (*pax*). Its presence on such coins was often accompanied by other iconography, such as the *fasces*, rudders, trophies and victories, placing the Roman idea of peace within a clearly militaristic and victorious context.[41] In 48 BC, L. Hostilius Saserna minted coins celebrating Caesar's victories in Gaul, depicting a Victory holding a trophy and *caduceus*.[42] An earlier coin minted by Sulla on the move in 82 BC (*RRC* 367), depicting him as an *imperator* driving a *quadriga* and holding a *caduceus* whilst being crowned by Victory, suggests that the

---

praecones, implying a possible core skill set for all three professions; see Hinard 1976, 732-734 for the necessary requirements for a *praeco*.
[40] Rüpke 1990, 102.
[41] *RRC* 357/1; 367; 403/1; 440/1; 448/1; 460/3; 460/4.
[42] *RRC* 448/1a.

caduceus as an attribute of victory was in use at least in the second quarter of the first century BC. Crawford[43] has argued that this *caduceus* "may be taken to indicate that victory is hoped for rather than achieved." This is perhaps also the case with coins minted by Caecilius Metellus Pius Scipio in Africa in 47-46 BC during his campaign against Caesar, which depict a *caduceus* carried by Victory on one coin,[44] and associated with a trophy on another.[45]

Since the *caduceus* came to symbolise the Roman concept of peace, it is worth briefly outlining how the Romans conceptualised the term, particularly as it is quite distinctive from the Greek concept of *eirēnē*. The root of *pax* is *pak - ('to fix by a convention; to resolve by an agreement'), from which the verb *pacere* ('to come to an agreement') also derives. Yet its root is also associated with **pag-,* designating a physical act,[46] from which the verb *pango* ('to fix; fasten; secure') derives.[47] Milani has defined *pax* as designating the act of stipulating a convention between two (warring) parties.[48] In this respect, *pax* was part of the ritual practice of concluding conflict and brought Rome's enemies and allies into a relationship and contract with Rome.[49] The verb *pacare* ("to come to an agreement"), which also derives from the root *pak-/pag-* and as a transitive verb means "to bring into a state of peace"[50] or "to impose a settlement upon",[51] articulates the agency involved in defining the relationship. Peace was a state imposed by the Romans upon their enemies from a position of

---

[43] Crawford 1974, 387.
[44] *RRC* 460/3.
[45] *RRC* 460/4.
[46] Milani 1985, 25 argues that because of the concrete meaning of the root (**pak-/*pag-*) it is possible that in origin *pax* indicated something concrete; Sordi 1985, 146-7 associates *pax* struck with the gods with the physical act of striking a nail into a door (cf. Livy *Epit.* 7.2-3); *contra* Santangelo 2011.
[47] Ernout-Meillet 1939, 720 describes *pax* as 'un nom d'action'. See also Fuchs 1926, 182-183; Milani 1985, 24-25; *Neue Pauly* vol. 9. 454; *OLD* s.v. *pacere, pax; LSJ* s.v. *pax.*
[48] Milani 1985, 25.
[49] Milani 1985, 25 argues that because of the concrete meaning of the root (*pak-/pag-*) it is possible that in origin *pax* indicated something concrete; Sordi 1985, 146-7 associates *pax* struck with the gods with the physical act of striking a nail into a door; cf. Livy 7.2-3; see also Fuchs 1926, 184; Sordi 1985, 13; Woolf 1993, 176; Rosenstein 2007, 227; Barton 2007, 246-251; Rich 2008; Parchami 2009, 15-16.
[50] *LSJ* s.v. *pacare.*
[51] *OLD* s.v. *pacare.*

superiority, and bound the defeated in a contractual relationship with Rome.[52] The embassy of 218 BC illustrates that even when peace was ostensibly offered instead of war, Rome was still the one offering and imposing it.

This Roman conceptualisation of peace may help explain why we have no explicit accounts of Roman *caduceatores*: not only did Romans expect their opponents to be the ones to treat for peace – by the Augustan period foreign chieftains and princes were expected to present themselves at the temple of Mars Ultor, amongst a display of Roman victory, to ask for the *fides et pax* from the Roman people (Suet. *Aug.* 21) – but they also looked unfavourably on the concept of surrender and of asking their opponents for peace, as Livy's account of Rome's response to the disaster of Cannae demonstrates:

> Yet, in spite of all their disasters and the revolt of their allies, no one anywhere in Rome mentioned the word 'peace', either before the consul's return or after his arrival when the memories of their losses were renewed. (Livy 22.61.13).
>
> *Nec tamen eae clades defectionesque sociorum moverunt ut pacis usquam mentio apud Romanos fieret neque ante consulis Romam adventum nec postquam is rediit renovavitque memoriam acceptae cladis.*

Likewise, in Livy's presentation of the Roman response to Perseus' offer of a peace treaty on very generous terms after they had lost the battle of Callicinus in 171 BC, the Romans attempt to turn the offer of peace on its head and demand from Perseus that he subject himself completely to the will of the senate (Livy 42.62). Even in the case of the *sponsio* reportedly made after the disaster of the Caudine Forks in 321 BC, Rome, according to Livy's account, dismissed the agreement and the peace made, and forced the Samnites to re-enter the conflict, in order to ensure a Roman victory, and to force the Samnites to send *legati de pace* to Rome (Livy 9.45).[53]

---

[52] Fuchs 1926, 184-186, 193-205; Raaflaub 2007, 13; Rosenstein 2007, 236-240; Rich 2008. As a comparative study to this unequal relationship expressed by *pax*, Liv Yarrow, in an unpublished paper, has emphasized that *Concordia* expresses social hierarchy among the orders, and that the concept implies an unequal partnership.
[53] See Crawford 1973 for a discussion of whether a *sponsio* or *foedus* was made in 321 BC.

The *caduceatores* can, thus, plausibly be understood as a Greek element of diplomatic interaction, or more specifically a Roman conceptualisation of non-Roman diplomacy, which they received but did not conceptualise themselves as sending. Even so, the Romans did employ the emblem of the *caduceus* to promote a discourse on peace, but from a distinctly Roman perspective, as something to be imposed.

BIBLIOGRAPHY

Ager, S. L. (2008) "Roman Perspectives on Greek Diplomacy", in C. Eilers (ed) *Diplomats and Diplomacy in the Roman World,* 14-43, Leiden.

Barton, C. A. (2007) "The Price of Peace in Ancient Rome", in K. A. Raaflaub (ed) *War and Peace in the Ancient World,* 245-255, Oxford.

Briscoe, J. (1973) *A Commentary on Livy, books XXXI-XXXIII.* Oxford.

Brunt, P. (1990) *Roman Imperial Themes.* Oxford.

Crawford, M. H. (1973) "Sponsio and Foedus", *Papers of the British School at Rome* 41, 1-7.

Crawford, M. H. (1974) *Roman Republican Coinage.* London.

Dyck, A. R. (2004) *A Commentary on Cicero, de Legibus.* Ann Abor.

Fuchs, H. (1926) *Augustin und der antike Friedensgedanke.* Berlin.

Habermehl, P. (2006) *Petronius, Satyrica 79-141: Ein philologisch-literarischer Kommentar.* Vol. 1: *Sat.* 79-110. Berlin.

Harris, W. V. (1979) *War and Imperialism in Republican Rome 327-70 BC.* Oxford.

Hinard, F. (1976) "Remarques sur les praecones et praconium dans la Rome de la fin de la Republique", *Latomus* 35, 730-746.

Holleaux, M. (1931) "Notes Sur Tite Live II. Le *caduceator* envoyé par Philippe V", *Revue de Philologie de Littérature et d'Historie Anciennes* 5, 193-208.

Milani, C. (1985) "Terminologia della pace nel mondo antico", in M. Sordi (ed) *La pace nel mondo antico,* 17-29. Milano.

Moore, J. (2011) "The Caduceus in the Second Punic War", in L. Ben Abid Saadallah (ed) *conographie et religions dans le Maghreb antique et médiéval. Actes du Ier colloque international organisé par l'Institut Supérieur des Métiers du Patrimoine, Tunis 21-23 févier 2008.* Tunis.

Nenci, G. (1958) "Feziali ed aruscipi in Cicerone (*de Leg.* II.9.21)", *La Parola del Passato* 13, 134-143.

Ogilvie, M. R. (1965) *Commentary of Livy: books 1-5.* Oxford.

Parchami, A. (2009) *Hegemonic Peace and Empire: The Pax Romana, Britannica and Americana.* London.

Phillipson, C. (1911) *International Law and Custom in Ancient Greece and Rome*. London.
Purcell, N. (1983) "The Apparitores: A Study in Social Mobility", *Papers of the British School at Rome* 51, 125-173.
Raaflaub, K. A. (2007) "Introduction: Searching for Peace in the Ancient World", in K. A. Raaflaub (ed) *War and Peace in the Ancient World*, 1-33.
Rauh, N. K. (1989) "Auctioneers and the Roman Economy", *Historia* 38.4, 451-471.
Rawson, E. (1973) "The Interpretation of Cicero's De Legibus", *ANRW* 1.4, 334-356.
Rich, J. W. (1976) *Declaring War in the Roman Republic in the Period of Transmarine Expansion*. Bruxelles.
—. (2008) "Treaties, allies and the Roman conquest of Italy", in P. Souza and J. France (eds) *War and Peace in Ancient and Medieval History*, 51-75, Cambridge.
—. (2011) "The *Fetiales* and Roman International Relations", in J. H. Richardson and F. Santangelo (eds) *Priests and State in the Roman World*, 187-242, Stuttgart.
Rosenstein, N. (2007) "War and Peace, Fear and Reconciliation at Rome", in K. A. Raaflaub (ed) *War and Peace in the Ancient World*, 226-244. Oxford.
Rüpke, J. (1990) *Domi Militiae: Die religiose Konstruktion des Krieges in Rom*. Stuttgart.
Santangelo, F. (2011) "Pontiffs and pax deorum", in J. H. Richardson, and F. Santangelo (eds) *Priests and State in the Roman World*, 161-186. Stuttgart.
Sgarbi, R. (1992) "A proposito del lessema lation "Fetiales"", *Aevum* 66, 71-78.
Sordi, M. (1985) "Introduzione: dalla 'koinè eirene' alla 'pax Romana'", in M. Sordi (ed) *La pace nel mondo antico*, 3-16. Milano.
—. (1985) "'Pax deorum' e libertà religosa nella storia di Roma", in M. Sordi (ed) *La pace nel mondo antico*, 146-154. Milano.
Thomasson, B. E. (1991) *Legatus: Beiträge zur römischen Verwaltungsgeschichte*. Stockholm.
Weinstock, S. (1960) "Pax and the 'Ara Pacis'", *Journal of Roman Studies* 50, 44-58.
Wiedemann, T. (1986) "The *Fetiales:* A Reconsideration", *Classical Quarterly* 36, 478-490.
Woolf, G. (1993) "Roman Peace", in J. W. Rich and G. Shipley (eds) *War and Society in the Roman World*, 171-195, London.

Contributors

Dr. Adam Anders is a History lecturer at the British International School at the University of Lodz. His PhD was an evaluation of Roman Light Infantry and their experience of combat. He is currently looking at the transmission of commands in battle, and preparing to write a manuscript on the Rise of the Field Army for Nick Sekunda's series "Armies of the Ancient World" with Cambridge University Press.

Dr. Nick Barley is a lecturer in Classics and Ancient History at Gower College, as well as teaching as part of the adult education department at Swansea University. He is currently co-editing a book about Aeneas Tacticus and is researching and writing about light infantry and generalship in the Classical Greek world.

Dr. Borja Antela-Bernárdez is a lecturer in Ancient History at the Autonomous University of Barcelona. He is a researcher in Hellenistic History, especially in the Asian campaign of Alexander the Great. He is also researching the 1st Mithridatic War in Athens and the impact it had on civilians. He is an experienced editor and author whose latest work is the co-edited volume: "Central Asia in Antiquity: Interdisciplinary Approaches", *British Archaeological Reports, Int. Series*, 2014.

Joanne Ball is currently a final-year PhD student in Archaeology at the University of Liverpool. Her research explores methodological approaches to battlefield archaeology in antiquity, particularly post-battle activity and conflict assemblages.

Dr. Anna Busetto got her PhD in Classics at University of Rome "Roma Tre" (Italy) in June 2013. Her research mainly pertains to Greek and Byzantine philology and palaeography, with a special interest toward ancient military manuals. Currently she is also actively involved in the organization of scientific events concerning classical antiquity.

Dr. Hannah Cornwell received her doctorate in Ancient History from the University of Oxford, where she works as a College Lecturer (Trinity College), as well as a postdoctoral researcher for the Ashmolean Latin

Inscription Project (AshLI), a collaborative AHRC funded project between the University of Warwick, the Asholmean Museum, and the Centre for the Study of Ancient Documents, University of Oxford. She is currently working on a monograph on the role of *pax* ('peace') as part of the language of Roman imperialism.

Dr. Susan Deacy and **Dr. Fiona McHardy** are principal lecturers at the University of Roehampton, London, who have worked separately and collaboratively on aspects of violence, war, gender and sexuality in ancient Greece. Their publications to date include *Rape in Antiquity* (ed. Deacy and K. Pierce, 1997, 2002), *Revenge in Athenian Culture* (McHardy 2008) and a jointly-authored article, "Uxoricide in Pregnancy: Ancient Greek Domestic Violence in Evolutionary Perspective" (*Evolutionary Psychology* 2013. 11(5): 994-1010). They are currently writing a book on gender violence in ancient Greece for Bloomsbury.

Dr. Jeffrey P. Emanuel is CHS Fellow in Aegean Archaeology and Prehistory at Harvard University's Center for Hellenic Studies. His academic research and publications focus on maritime affairs in the Aegean and Eastern Mediterranean during the transition from the Late Bronze to the Early Iron Age, with particular emphasis on naval warfare and the development and spread of maritime technology in this key transitional period, as well as its connections to ancient Greek epic. Additionally, he is the inaugural Senior Fellow at "HarvardX," an initiative in digital teaching, learning, and research at Harvard.

Dr. Elena Franchi is Assistant Director of the LabSA (Laboratorio di Storia Antica-Dipartimento di Lettere e di Filosofia) at the University of Trento and member of the International Network Historiai. Her PhD Thesis was on "Frontier Wars between Sparta and Argos beyond the mirage" (forthcoming). She was awarded a fellowship at the Alexander Von Humboldt Foundation. Her book on "Identity and War in IVth century Phocian memory culture" is forthcoming.

Dr. Julie Laskaris, is an Associate Professor, in the Department of Classical Studies, University of Richmond (Virginia, USA). She received her doctorate from the University of California, Los Angeles, 1999. Her research interests centre on ancient medicine and pharmacology. Her publications include "The Eros of Achilles: Homoerotic Bonding Among Combat Soldiers," *Transnational Law & Contemporary Problems*, 10, 1 (2000), 139-190; *The Art is Long*: On the Sacred Disease *and the Scientific*

Tradition (Brill, 2002) and "Metals in Medicine: from Telephus to Galen" forthcoming in *Popular Medicine in Classical Antiquity.*

Konstantinos Lentakis was awarded a MA in Politics by the University of Glasgow in 2006, and a MSc in Classics by the University of Edinburgh in 2007. Currently, he is in the final stages of writing his PhD thesis at the University of Panteion in Athens, focusing on Athenian grand strategy in the fourth century BC. In 2014 he was appointed special advisor to two consecutive Greek ministers of Defence, and at present is pursuing a career in public administration, dealing with defence and foreign policy.

Dr. Matthew Lloyd received his DPhil in Archaeology at the University of Oxford. He is the author of "Warfare and the recovery from Palatial collapse in the 12th century BC: A case study of the Argolid and Achaea" in *Tough Times: The Archaeology of Crisis and Recovery* (ed. Van der Wilt and Martínez Jiménez, 2013) and "Weapons" in *A Companion to the Archaeology of Early Greece and the Mediterranea*n (ed. Lemos and Kotsonas, forthcoming).

Dr. Stephen O'Connor is an assistant professor of history at California State University, Fullerton. He received his PhD. in ancient history from Columbia University in 2011. His research focuses on the logistics of classical Greek warfare, and especially on what an analysis of the provisioning of Greek armies and navies can tell us about the structure and performance of economies in the classical Greek world. His article on the daily grain consumption of classical Greek sailors and soldiers appeared in Chiron in 2013 and a second article on the institutional infrastructure of markets in Greek military camps is forthcoming in Classical Quarterly.

Dr. Giorgia Proietti is a post-doc, at the University of Trento, where she received her PhD. Her thesis: "Stories before Herodotus' *Histories*. The pre-historiographical memory of the Persian Wars" is now under revision for publication.

Alberto Pérez-Rubio holds a M.A. in Ancient History by the Autónoma de Madrid (UAM), Spain, and the Universidad Complutense de Madrid. He is currently a PhD candidate in Ancient History. His thesis is focused on the coalitions and military alliances in Western Iron Age Europe. He is also the editor-in-chief of Desperta Ferro Antigua y Medieval, a bimonthly Spanish journal devoted to the Military History of Antiquity and the Middle Ages.

Dr. Aimee Schofield completed a PhD at the University of Manchester in August 2014. Her research focuses on the development of artillery in the Classical and Hellenistic periods, as well as ancient siege warfare and early Greek technical writing.

Professor Hélène Whittaker is Professor of Classical Archaeology and Ancient History at the University of Gothenburg. Her research is mainly concerned with the Greek Bronze Age but she has also published within various areas of Greek and Roman history, philosophy, religion, and literature. Her latest book is *Religion and Society in Middle Bronze Age Greece* (CUP 2014).

Dr. Graham Wrightson is Assistant Professor of History at South Dakota State University. His research focuses primarily on Macedonian military history. He gained his PhD at the University of Calgary, Canada. He has published a number of articles and papers on Macedonian warfare and is currently a co-editor of: *Greece, Macedon and Persia: Studies in the Social, Political and Military Consequences of Conquest Societies.* (Oxbow 2015); *The Many Faces of War in the Ancient World.* (CSP 2015). He is also working on a textbook for Western Civilization 1 tentatively entitled: *Becoming Civilized* (Cognella 2015).

Dr. Matteo Zaccarini received his PhD (Bologna and King's College London, 2013) in Ancient History. He is currently affiliated to the University of Bologna (Dip. Storia Culture Civiltà; Dip. Beni Culturali) and to Birkbeck, University of London (Dpt. History, Classics and Archaeology: Honorary Research Fellow).. He is a member of the Brill's New Jacoby project (Brill Academic Publishing, NL).

INDEX OF PLACES

Abai (Kalapodi), 20
Achaia, 16
Aegean, 1, 3, 5, 10, 11, 12, 14, 16, 17, 21, 30, 114-5, 115, 145, 191-209, 350
Aegospotami, 114
Afghanistan, 112
Africa, 168, 276, 328, 336, 345
Akrotiri, 198, 200
Alexandria, 34, 167, 171, 263
Amphipolis, 52-3, 59, 63
Anatolia, 133, 135, 189, 193, 197, 199, 208
Araxes River, 130, 136
Argos, 15, 17, 26-7, 51, 108, 112, 120, 350
Asia, 119, 186, 255, 349
Asia Minor, 119
Athens, 11-26, 30, 61, 68, 72, 74, 78-9, 97, 111-23, 146, 153, 165, 170, 205-251, 267, 269, 270-1, 302, 308, 349, 351
Athens-Agora, 23
Athens-Kerameikos, 23
Athribis, 194
Atlantic, 43, 187, 189
Attica, 14, 97, 114, 153, 233, 243, 251
Babylonia, 127, 136, 139-43
Baecula, 317-20, 326
Balkan Mountains, 301
Beth-Zacharia, 87-8
Bibracte, 315
Bithynia, 68, 165
Boeotia, 95-6, 110, 116-19, 187
Britain, 1, 177-8, 182, 188-90, 302, 307-8, 328-9
Byzantium, 32, 34, 68, 114, 134, 150, 271

Cairo, 194
Calgary, 86, 352
Canaan, 193
Cannae, 316, 346
Cappadocia, 68, 165
Carthage, 336
Caudine Forks, 346
Celaenae, 135
Central Greece, 119, 246
Chalus River, 136, 137
Charmande, 127-43
Cisalpine Gaul, 181
Claenae, 339
Colchester, 310, 328
Corbridge, 310, 326
Corcyra, 110-11, 114-15
Corinth, 110, 112, 115, 120, 214
Coronea, 108
Corsote, 127-33, 137-8, 140, 143
Crete, 1-16, 20, 26-7 30, 119, 203, 206-7
Culloden, 313, 325, 328
Cunaxa, 124-44
Cyclades, 193, 208
Cynoscephalae, 89, 315
Cyprus, 195, 197, 204-7
Dardas River, 137
Decelea, 215
Delphi, 26, 181, 185, 238-43, 250, 259, 261-2
Eastern Mediterranean, 173, 191, 195, 199, 200, 204, 206, 350
Egypt, 2, 6, 29, 76, 167, 193-4, 198-206, 209, 285, 288
Elis, 116, 120
Epirus, 16
Eretria, 21, 25-9
Essex, 310
Europe, 1, 3, 11, 12, 25, 28, 30, 172,

175-7, 181, 183-90, 255, 351
Eurotas River, 117
Flodden, 313
Gaugamela, 86, 91
Gaul, 177, 180, 182-3, 190, 344
Germany, 276, 295, 298, 308, 317
Gettysburg, 312, 328
Greece, 14, 16, 17, 20-22, 26, 28-31, 44, 53, 64, 92, 94, 104, 107, 111-12, 116, 119-22, 145-48, 172-3, 182, 187, 219, 226-31, 239, 246, 251, 263, 269, 272, 274, 303, 307, 329, 348-51
Halicarnassus, 81, 95, 99, 101-3
Harzhorn, 317-21, 325-30
Heliopolis, 194
Herculaneum, 75
Hyampolis, 238, 242-3, 250-1
Iraq, 112
Issos, 127, 133
Isthmia, 26
Italy, 28, 67, 188, 271, 276, 316, 348-9
Ithome, 110, 117-120
Juktas, 2, 4, 5, 7, 11, 13
Kalapodi, 243
Kalkriese, 316-330
Knossos, 7, 9, 13, 17, 19, 29, 204
Kos, 196-199
Kynos, 197, 202, 205
Lambaesis, 1578, 165
Lamia, 114, 228
Lasithi plateau, 4
Lefkandi-Toumba, 19, 20, 23
Leuctra, 116-7, 153
Levant, 139, 197, 209
Little Bighorn, 313, 325, 329
Lycaonia, 135, 137
Lyncus, 58
Macedonia, 16, 92, 96, 106, 248
Magnesia, 89
Malia, 7, 9
Malli, 80
Mantinea, 49, 50, 113, 117, 119, 153
Marathon, 64, 232, 244, 249, 251, 313, 327

Massalia, 177
Medinet Habu, 191-209
Mediterranean, 2, 5, 34, 130, 193, 195, 199-201, 206-209, 249, 270, 351
Megalopolis, 120
Mesopotamia, 136, 140, 275
Messene, 118
Mons Graupius, 177, 292, 301, 307-8
Mount Taygetus, 118
Mycenae, 176, 196, 199, 204, 206
Near East, 2, 6, 10, 11, 29, 130, 182, 204, 206
Nemea, 108, 120
Nichoria, 17
Nicomedia, 68, 92, 167, 170
Nicopolis, 68
North African coast, 194
Northern Africa, 157
Northumberland, 310
Numidia, 294
Numistro, 314
Oberesch, 317-330
Olympia, 6, 26, 250, 261-2
Orchomenos, 104
Orontes, 71
Osnabrück, 317
Pella, 101
Peloponnese, 16, 117, 119, 120
Perati, 16
Pergamon, 183, 188, 282
Persia, 47, 63, 101, 106, 352
Phaestos, 9
Phocis, 104, 119, 187, 229, 237, 245, 251
Plataea, 47, 48, 52, 54, 61, 64, 104, 232, 235
Po River, 302
Prinias, 20
Psyttalea, 213
Ptolemais, 295
Pydna, 71, 89
Pylae, 127, 130-144
Pylos, 57, 64, 192, 202-209
Pyrgos Livanaton, 203

Raphia, 89
Rhineland, 177
Rhodes, 16, 34, 72, 118, 122, 247, 248
Rome, 68, 71, 72, 75, 91, 145-6, 157, 163, 167-8, 186, 189, 228, 271, 303-349
Royal Road, 135, 141
Saguntum, 336
Salamis, 211- 215
Sardis, 132, 135, 143
Sicily, 113-14, 221
Slovenia, 310
Sounion, 26
Spain, 156, 172, 317, 339, 351
Sparta, 17, 61-64, 110-22, 225, 228, 350
Sphacteria, 56-7
Switzerland, 25

Sybotae, 216
Syracuse, 53, 113, 116, 214-15, 218, 220
Syrian Apamea, 71
Syro-Canaanite coast, 193
Tanis, 191, 201, 209
Tarsus, 134, 137
Thapsacus, 125, 127, 133, 136
Thebes, 56, 94-122, 153, 241
Thermopylae, 54, 57
Thessaly, 16, 18, 119
Thrace, 119, 177
Tigranocerta, 301
Tiryns, 17
Towton, 313, 327, 329
Troy, 6, 226, 252, 255-270
Vercellae, 315
Waterloo, 312, 328-29

Index of Units

antesignani, 292, 302-5
archers, 54, 55-61, 81, 97, 100, 150-51, 163-64, 184, 211-12, 217-20, 291, 294-95, 305
auxiliaries/*auxilia*, 162-3, 276, 291-308, 318, 320, 323
boatswains, 222
bodyguard, 54, 61, 101, 178
cavalry, 54-55, 60-61, 66-69, 80-88, 97-98, 103-4, 147, 148-54, 162-66, 172-77, 182-85, 226, 276, 295-302, 319-325
chariot, 86, 156, 176-190
crew, 57, 193, 200, 203, 210, 215-16, 220-21
doctors, 273-285
driver, 179-183
epibatai, 211-16, 221-4
fleet, 113-15, 191-2, 203, 210, 212, 221, 225, 302
footmen, 294
foreigners, 99, 105, 113
galleys, 192, 197, 200-203
gladiators, 282, 302, 305-6
guerrilla, 311
helmsmen, 215, 218, 221
hoplite, 43 – 68, 78, 102, 107-8, 114, 119, 182, 211 – 228, 303
horsemen, 148, 150, 153, 162, 167, 173-76, 182-85, 294
hypaspists., 101
infantry, 46-61, 65, 69, 80, 83-4, 87-8, 97-9, 108, 117, 162-67, 182, 202, 211, 217-18, 291-304, 349
insurgent, 109-112, 121
javelin thrower, 56, 214, 217-220, 305
knights, 220
legionaries, 292-306, 328

marauders, 191
marine, 211
mercenaries, 55, 95, 113, 125-129, 132-146, 173, 183, 191, 303
mob, 218, 220-21
naval force, 107, 213
navy, 212, 218-27
officers, 46-60, 81-2, 84, 162, 222, 298
orderlies, 274-75
pedites, 296
pentekontarchoi, 222
phalanx, 63-4, 92, 308
pike-bearer, 155, 163
pirates, 191
prisoner, 104, 297
rebel, 95, 311
recruits, 316
reinforcements, 53, 57, 60, 102-3
reserve, 60, 98-9, 135, 301
rowers, 192, 197, 200, 203, 212, 221
runner, 45, 182
Sacred Band, 62
sailors, 212, 219, 221, 351
scouts, 295-99
seamen, 221-22, 228
servants, 173
ships, 57, 191, 195-203, 210-224, 342
shipwrights, 222
slaves, 99, 104, 221, 275
slingers, 55, 282, 291, 294
spear-bearer, 178, 182, 184
spy, 297
steersman, 200, 222
trireme, 210-13, 216, 220, 227-8
veteran, 51, 99, 275
warrior, 11, 12, 14, 29-31, 190-1, 195-99, 207-08, 272
watchers, 192

INDEX OF ARMAMENTS

armour, 1, 6, 15, 24, 26-28, 30, 152, 160, 167, 178, 213, 295, 302-3, 306, 315-6, 318-19, 321, 323-326
arrow, 15, 21, 55, 155, 160, 202, 213-4, 274, 277-8, 281, 283-4, 313, 320
artillery, 32, 34, 41, 352
axe, 4, 5, 7, 8, 11, 320
blades, 4, 6, 7, 20, 26, 213
bolt, 35, 318
catapult, 32-41, 277, 318
cuirass, 213
engine, 33-38, 96, 107
grapnel, 201-2
grappling iron, 214
greaves, 196
helmets, 15, 28, 161, 196-99, 299-300, 319
javelin, 56, 60, 81, 100, 150, 152, 159, 167, 177, 182, 192, 211, 213-4, 217-20, 305
lance, 81, 318, 320
lead balls, 282
mail, 303, 318-19

miniature, 4, 198, 200
missiles, 35, 57, 81, 159, 178, 224, 276, 281-2, 291, 324
musket, 68
non-torsion, 35-7
panoply, 27, 183, 185, 213
pebbles, 282
pike, 65, 68, 81, 155, 163
projectiles, 182, 214, 313-26
ram, 202, 210
replicas, 4, 5, 32, 33, 86
sarissa, 65-6, 69, 80, 82, 86, 93
shield, 19, 178-180, 184, 213-4, 261, 262, 299, 304, 316, 319, 322
sling, 159, 202
socket, 20, 318
stones, 3, 4, 159, 213-4
sword, 11, 12, 14, 187
tools, 206
torsion, 32, 34
weapon, 15, 269, 270, 313, 328-9, 351
wooden shaft, 19, 319, 324

GENERAL INDEX

alliance, 47, 107, 110-16, 120, 241, 351
ally, 112, 115, 153
amphora, 261, 264
artefact, 5, 6, 8, 33, 309-326
assemblage, 309-26, 349
audacia, 301- 306
bandage, 275, 278-80, 287
barricade, 52, 98
battalion, 82-3, 88, 100-102, 275
battlefield, 20, 27, 28, 33, 47, 48, 50, 95, 182, 220, 232, 236, 254, 277, 309, 310-329, 349
bloodletting, 273, 278, 280
booty, 299, 314, 315
borders, 51, 111, 135, 153, 194, 310
brails, 200- 201
bread, 134
bronze, 4-9, 19, 25, 28-9, 34, 161, 178-82, 192, 198, 213, 246, 262, 280, 318, 320, 344
burial, 1,4, 8, 14-30, 176-7, 184-5, 235-6, 274, 309, 322, 341
Caduceator, 340, 341
caduceus, 331, 337-40, 343-47
camp, 70, 97, 100, 124-5, 142, 294, 296, 299, 314-5, 321-2, 341, 351
carnyx, 180
carts, 52, 176, 183, 193
casualties, 59, 114, 120, 220-1, 226, 275, 312, 325
cautery, 279-80
children, 24-5, 99, 103, 179, 193, 222, 238, 256, 258, 278, 312
circumvallation, 56
clash, 55, 99, 107, 266
coast, 192- 195
cohesion, 112, 120
cohort, 84, 88, 159, 162, 304
coins, 9, 157, 180, 201, 313, 320, 344
column, 293-7, 300, 306
commemoration, 201, 226, 230-245
confusion, 49, 101- 103
coordinate, 192
copper, 286-90
counter-plate, 32, 36-7
courage, 216-306
cremation, 17- 26
cult, 3-4, 157, 231-236, 244, 267
cupping, 280
curvature, 38
dead, 14, 27, 47, 55, 68, 117, 128, 221, 227, 229-237, 244-5, 312, 315
deck, 201-2, 210, 214-15, 302
defile, 88
democrats, 109-11, 115
denial, 263, 311, 323
deposit, 4, 5, 10, 14-15, 310 post-depositional, 18,26
dimension, 35-38, 335
divisions, 50, 67, 88-90, 110, 157, 163
draught, 52
drills, 85-66, 147, 160, 162, 166-167
elite, 2, 3, 6, 8-10, 53-4, 61, 100-119, 157, 182-5, 192, 228, 312
embassy, 72, 322, 336, 339, 341, 346
envoys, 331-33, 336-8, 341-44
epic, 22, 25, 153, 174, 231, 236-7, 244, 254, 350
era, 149, 155, 157, 167, 178
evacuation, 192, 324
famine, 128-9
feather, 196-7, 199
female, 8, 179, 181, 252-7, 265,

266-9, 285
fence, 98-101
festival, 151, 233, 237-8, 242-5
fetiales, 331-40, 344
fides, 332, 337, 342, 346
file, 48-9, 62, 84, 87, 205
flank, 59, 178, 292
flour, 124, 128-31, 136, 140-44
fodder, 127, 138
food, 9, 46, 127-45, 158
formation, 24, 43, 49-50, 55, 65, 69, 72-3, 84-7, 107-8, 116, 147-8, 152, 157, 162, 215-16, 223, 237, 278, 295, 299, 311
fortifications, 1, 100, 107, 300
fortress, 94-101, 328
frame, 35, 37- 41, 230, 237, 252, 315
freedom, 95, 143, 232-3
front, 4, 58, 81, 85-6, 96, 180, 184, 200, 232, 294-6
funeral, 18, 156, 232-6
games, 156, 232-6, 242
gangrene, 280
gangways, 214
gates, 59, 97, 101-103, 153, 235
gender, 252-58, 265, 267-8, 350
geography, 52
god, 5, 10, 27, 29, 99, 104-5, 151, 154, 260-61, 265-7, 331, 345
goddess, 11, 252, 257- 268
grain, 125, 128-9, 132, 135-8, 300, 314, 351
handbooks, 65-6, 78, 150, 226
hay, 134
headdresses, 195-7
hegemony, 94, 104-121
hemorrhage, 273, 277- 87
hemostasis, 273, 279-83, 288
herald, 204, 331, 337-38, 341, 343
heroes, 18, 23, 25, 184, 231, 232-8, 240, 242-5
hierarchy, 84-5, 88-90, 118, 178, 221, 224, 346
historiography, 73, 291, 293
history, 2, 6, 66-74, 88, 109, 118, 145-6, 157, 167, 187, 192, 195, 225, 227-8, 230, 243-5, 253, 268, 281, 286, 294, 307, 338, 344, 351-2
hoards, 1, 9, 310, 322, 328
hole-carrier, 37-9
honour, 43, 152, 232, 236, 264-5
honours, 232, 234-5
hoplomachia, 78
horse, 55, 145, 151-2, 156, 159-67, 173-184, 233, 266, 297, 299, 320
identity, 15-16, 75, 212, 224, 226, 229-31, 237-38, 244-5, 250, 254
impact, 44, 48, 55, 99, 224, 311, 313, 323, 349
inhumation, 17-18, 24
initiation, 237, 240-5
innovations, 8, 34, 77, 87, 147, 157
intelligence, 56, 154, 294-99, 307
invader, 46, 301
ladder, 96, 203
land, 51, 114, 116, 127, 129, 131, 153, 193, 195, 202, 213-33, 225, 232-3, 274, 313
legate, 68, 165, 331-46
legion, 87-9, 291-5, 300-02, 306
ligature, 280, 283
logistics, 144, 329, 351
loot, 315
male, 8, 25, 179, 254, 268
manual, 45, 65-91, 147-54, 166, 169, 349
mare, 174, 175
maritime, 114, 191-2, 195, 199, 201, 204, 211, 217, 225, 350
market, 128, 132-35, 139, 141, 312, 351
mass, 46, 103, 108, 117, 221, 309
massacre, 103, 238
memory, 61, 99, 105, 120, 226, 229, 230, 234, 244, 346, 350, 351
mercy, 103
metal, 19-21, 24-5, 27, 281, 286-7, 309-13, 316-18, 322-23, 325
millet, 134
monument, 105, 187, 232, 237, 241-

43, 245
morale, 58, 152, 294
motivation, 109, 187, 253
myth, 6, 227-8, 239, 245-6, 256, 259, 263
nail, 310, 319, 345
network, 177, 185, 230-1, 234, 237-8, 244
non-combatant, 95, 109
oath, 47, 48, 255, 256, 261, 263, 265
oil, 279
old, 15, 103, 112, 148, 180, 201, 217, 233, 237, 243-5, 245, 258, 275, 279
oligarchs, 109-11, 222
oratores, 335, 340-1
panic, 45-6, 51, 116, 203, 221
peace, 2, 51, 98, 109, 118, 166, 253, 331-347, 350
phase, 58, 100, 182, 240, 254, 324
plan, 46, 50, 62, 98, 139
plaster, 279, 287
plumes, 196, 198
post-partum, 284, 285
priests, 104, 267, 332-5
provisions, 112, 127, 129, 131-43, 213
rampart, 317, 320, 323
rank, 49-50, 58, 62, 70, 80-2, 86, 120, 161-2, 178, 184, 305
rations, 125, 196
republic, 118
research, 1, 14, 34, 36-7, 86, 111, 125, 147, 229, 253-4, 292, 309, 321, 349-52
resist, 51, 61, 99
retaliatory, 252, 254-6, 260-1, 264-8
rig, 200-202
rite, 16-17, 19, 22, 24, 237, 240, 243, 247, 251, 334-5
route, 3, 12, 46, 49, 57, 125, 130, 132, 135, 138, 141, 145, 318
sacrifice, 151, 232-5, 243, 249
sails, 200- 201
sanctuary, 2, 4-10, 20, 24, 26-8, 157, 239, 257-9, 263-68
scorched earth, 138, 142
sea, 2, 7, 11, 191-195, 198-204, 210, 213-226, 260
sex, 264-5
silver, 105, 180, 198, 286, 322, 324
site, 2, 4, 16-18, 96-7, 153, 246, 278-86, 309-26
skill, 19-20, 28, 78, 154, 178, 214-20, 273-6, 280-1, 284-5, 296, 299, 304, 306, 344
social, 1, 2, 5, 15, 21, 24, 27-8, 30, 62, 108-121, 164, 172, 184, 212, 220-30, 237, 244-5, 254, 305-6, 346
spectacle, 154, 166-7
spectators, 7, 151-2, 160-1
spoils, 28, 241, 262, 265
spolia, 184, 315
spring, 34-41, 153
stanchions, 36-41, 203
statue, 165, 238-41, 255-8, 262-8
strongpoints, 100
styptic, 278-9, 283, 286-7
subordinate, 45-62
suppliant, 257-9, 263, 266
supplicatio, 336
supply, 9, 41, 98, 124, 128-45, 220, 311-14, 322, 325
symbol, 15, 105, 154, 177, 183, 234, 337-, 344
syntagma, 83-4, 87
tactics, 61-99, 109, 155, 163, 166, 215, 291-302
teamwork, 49
temple, 99, 183, 192-3, 241, 258-9, 263, 346
tenon, 39, 41
terrain, 7, 44-5, 52, 58, 127, 183, 291, 297, 300-7, 319, 325
terror, 46, 107-09, 112, 114, 120
threat, 45, 51, 53, 55, 116-7, 153, 192, 194-5, 199, 294
tombs, 16, 23, 27, 96-7, 177, 221, 232-5

towers, 56, 96, 102
train, 70, 86, 129, 131, 141, 143-4, 166, 314-5, 317, 320, 322
trauma, 273, 280
trench, 18, 23, 98
truce, 133, 266, 332, 338, 341-2
trumpets, 59, 99, 315
turrets, 310
vase, 8, 19, 28, 196, 198-9, 233, 258, 261-2, 266
venesection, 273, 278-288
vinegar, 279, 287
virtus, 293, 301, 304-7
volunteers, 86
wagons, 124-45, 177, 320-1
wall, 2, 4, 45, 51-2, 56, 60-1, 80, 95-119, 151, 158, 198
water, 4, 9, 136, 213, 216, 218, 278-301, 306
wine, 46, 124, 128-144, 256, 279
wing, 60, 67, 85, 89, 163, 295, 339
women, 103, 193, 219, 252-61, 265-8, 278, 284-5
wounds, 273-283, 286-7
περίτρητον, 37
ὑπόθεμα, 32-3, 36-41